Public Sociology series

Series Editors: **John Brewer**, Queen's University, Belfast, North Ireland and **Neil McLaughlin**, McMaster University, Canada

The *Public Sociology* series addresses not only what sociologists do, but what sociology is for, and focuses on the commitment to materially improving people's lives through understanding of the social condition. It showcases the wide diversity of sociological research that addresses the many global challenges that threaten the future of humankind.

Out now in the series:

The Public Sociology of Waste
Myra J. Hird

The Public and Their Platforms
Public Sociology in an Era of Social Media
Mark Carrigan and **Fatsis Lambros**

Public Sociology As Educational Practice
Challenges, Dialogues and Counter-Publics
Edited by **Eurig Scandrett**

Find out more at
bristoluniversitypress.co.uk/public-sociology

Public Sociology series

Series Editors: **John Brewer**, Queen's University, Belfast, Northern Ireland and **Neil McLaughlin**, McMaster University, Canada

International editorial advisory board

Find out more at
bristoluniversitypress.co.uk/public-sociology

CRITICAL ENGAGEMENT WITH PUBLIC SOCIOLOGY

A Perspective from the Global South

Edited by
Andries Bezuidenhout, Sonwabile Mnwana
and Karl von Holdt

BRISTOL
UNIVERSITY
PRESS

First published in Great Britain in 2024 by

Bristol University Press
University of Bristol
1-9 Old Park Hill
Bristol
BS2 8BB
UK
t: +44 (0)117 374 6645
e: bup-info@bristol.ac.uk

Details of international sales and distribution partners are available at bristoluniversitypress.co.uk

© Bristol University Press 2024

British Library Cataloguing in Publication Data
A catalogue record for this book is available from the British Library

ISBN 978-1-5292-2114-5 hardcover
ISBN 978-1-5292-2115-2 paperback
ISBN 978-1-5292-2116-9 ePub
ISBN 978-1-5292-2117-6 ePdf

The right of Andries Bezuidenhout, Sonwabile Mnwana and Karl von Holdt to be identified as editors of this work has been asserted by them in accordance with the Copyright, Designs and Patents Act 1988.

Cover design: Andrew Corbett
Front cover image: Plasteed/Shutterstock

Contents

List of Figures and Table

Figures

Table

Notes on Contributors

Andries Bezuidenhout is Professor of Development Studies at the University of Fort Hare, South Africa.

Sakhela Buhlungu is Vice Chancellor of the University of Fort Hare, South Africa.

Michael Burawoy is Professor of Sociology at the University of California, Berkeley, US.

Ercüment Çelik is with the Institut für Soziologie, Albert-Ludwigs-Universität Freiburg (Institute for Sociology, Albert Ludwigs University, Freiburg), Germany.

Aninka Claassens founded the Land and Accountability Research Centre, University of Cape Town in South Africa and is now retired.

Jacklyn Cock is Professor Emerita in the Department of Sociology at the University of the Witwatersrand and an associate of the Society, Work and Politics Institute, South Africa.

Brittany Kesselman is Postdoctoral Research Fellow at the Society, Work and Politics Institute at the University of the Witwatersrand, Johannesburg, South Africa.

Sonwabile Mnwana is Professor of Development Studies in the Department of Sociology at Rhodes University, South Africa.

Nokwanda Sihlali is Researcher at the Land and Accountability Research Centre, University of Cape Town, South Africa.

Dasten Julián Vejar is with the Instituto de Historia y Ciencias Sociales, Universidad Austral de Chile (Institute of History and Social Sciences, Austral

University of Chile). He is also an associate of the Society, Work and Politics Institute at the University of the Witwatersrand, Johannesburg, South Africa.

Karl von Holdt is Professor and former Director of the Society, Work and Politics Institute at the University of the Witwatersrand, Johannesburg, South Africa.

Edward Webster is Professor Emeritus and the founder of the Society, Work and Politics Institute at the University of the Witwatersrand, Johannesburg, South Africa.

Ntokozo Yingwana is Researcher and PhD candidate with the African Centre for Migration and Society (ACMS) at the University of the Witwatersrand, Johannesburg, South Africa.

Acknowledgements

We would like to thank the Ford Foundation for funding a programme on Research and Social Justice, matched by the University of the Witwatersrand Research Office, that allowed a number of postdoctoral fellows to join the Society, Work and Politics Institute (SWOP). One of them was Alberto Arribas Lozano, who shook up our thinking on 'public sociology' and 'critical engagement' with his article 'Reframing the public sociology debate: Towards collaborative and decolonial praxis', quoted in many of the chapters of this book. Alberto started out with us on the project of producing this volume before his travels took him elsewhere. We would like to thank him for his critical engagement, his belief in the importance of producing this volume and his friendship. We would also like to thank the Friedrich-Ebert-Stiftung, South Africa, for funding the initial workshop in 2018, which led to the production of this book. Sonwabile Mnwana wants to thank the Stellenbosch Institute for Advanced Study (STIAS) for dedicated time to concentrate on writing. We would like to thank the editors of this series, John Brewer and Neil McLaughlin, as well as Shannon Kneis at Bristol University Press, who guided us through the review and revision process. We also thank the two anonymous reviewers for their recommendations. Then, we give our appreciation to Sakhela Buhlungu for agreeing to reproduce his article on South African labour studies in this volume. The book would have been incomplete without his voice. We would like to thank Eddie Webster for his contribution not just to this book but to shaping and theorizing the South African tradition of critically engaged research. We would like to acknowledge Michael Burawoy, a long-standing inspiration and partner in sociology as combat sport, and thank him for his contribution to this volume. Finally, we would like to thank Prishani Naidoo, the current director of SWOP, for her support for this project.

Series Editors' Preface

John D. Brewer (Belfast, Northern Ireland)
Neil McLaughlin (Toronto, Canada)

Sociology is a highly reflexive subject. All scholarly disciplines examine themselves reflexively in terms of theory and practice as they apply what sociologist of science Robert Merton once called 'organized scepticism'. Sociology adds to this constant internal academic debate also a vigorous, almost obsessive, concern about its very purpose and rationale. This attentiveness to founding principles shows itself in significant intellectual interest in the 'canon' of great thinkers and its history as a discipline, in vigorous debate about the boundaries of the discipline and in considerable inventiveness in developing new areas and subfields of sociology. This fascination with the purpose and social organization of the discipline is also reflected in the debate about sociology's civic engagements and commitments, its level of activism and its moral and political purposes.

This echoes the contemporary discussion about the idea of public sociology. 'Public sociology' is a new phrase for a long-standing debate about the purpose of sociology that began with the discipline's origins. It is therefore no coincidence that students in the 21st century, when being introduced to sociology for the first time, wrestle with ideas formulated centuries before, for while social change has rendered some of these ideas redundant, particularly the social Darwinism of the 19th century and functionalism in the 1950s, familiarity with these earlier debates and frameworks is the lens into understanding the purpose, value and prospect of sociology as key thinkers conceived it in the past. The ideas may have changed but the moral purpose has not.

A contentious discipline is destined to argue continually about its past. Some see the roots of sociology grounded in medieval scholasticism, in 18th-century Scotland with the Scottish Enlightenment's engagement with the social changes wrought by commercialism, in conservative reactions to the Enlightenment or in 19th-century encounters with the negative effects of industrialization and modernization. Contentious disciplines, however, are condemned to always live in their past if they do not also develop a vision for their future – a sense of purpose and a rationale that takes the discipline forward. Sociology has always been forward-looking, offering an analysis and diagnosis of what C. Wright Mills liked to call the 'human condition'. Interest in the social condition and in its improvement and betterment for the majority of ordinary men and women has always been sociology's ultimate objective.

At the end of the second millennium, when public sociology was named by Michael Burawoy, there was a strong feeling in the discipline that the professionalization of the subject during the 20th century had come at the cost of its public engagement, its commitment to social justice and its reputation for activism. The vitality and creativity of the public sociology debate was largely fuelled by what Aldon Morris called 'liberation capitalism', created in social movements of political engagement outside of the universities in the years after the social turmoil and changes of the 1960s.

The discipline has mostly reacted positively to Burawoy's call for public sociology, although there has been spirited dissent from those concerned with sociology's scientific status. Public sociology represents a practical realignment of the discipline by encouraging a focus on substantive and theoretical topics that are important to the many publics with whom the discipline engages. Public sociology, however, is also a normative realignment of the discipline through its commitment to enhance understanding of the social condition so that the lives of people are materially improved. Public sociology not only changes what sociologists do; it redefines what sociology is for.

Sociology's concern with founding principles is both a strength and a weakness of the discipline. Nothing seems settled in sociology; the discipline does not obliterate past ideas by their absorption into new ones, as Robert Merton once put it, as the natural sciences insist on doing. The past remains a learning tool in sociology, and the history of sociology is contemporaneous as we stand on the shoulders of giants to learn from earlier generations of sociologists. We therefore revisit debates about the boundaries between sociology and its cognate disciplines, or debates about the relationship between individuals and society, or about the analytical categories of individuals, groups, communities and societies, or of the primacy of material conditions over symbolic ones, or of the place of politics, identity, culture, economics and the everyday in structuring and determining social life. The boundaries of sociology are porous and as many sociologists have asserted, the discipline is a hybrid, drawing ideas eclectically from those subjects closely aligned to it.

This hybridity is also sociology's great strength. Sociology's openness facilitates interdisciplinarity, encourages innovation in the fields to which the sociological imagination is applied and opens up new topics about which sociological questions can be asked. Sociology thus exposes the hidden and the neglected to scrutiny. There is very little that cannot have sociological questions asked of it. The boundaries of sociology are thus ever expanding and widening; it is limitless in applying the sociological imagination. The tension between continuity and change – something evident in society generally – reflects thus also in the discipline itself. This gives sociology a frisson that is both fertile and fruitful as new ideas rub up against old ones and as the conceptual apparatus of sociology is simultaneously revisited and renewed. This tends to work against faddism in sociology, since nothing is entirely new and the latest fashions have their pasts.

Public sociology is thus not itself new, and it has its own history. Burawoy rightly emphasized the role of C. Wright Mills, and broader frameworks allow us to highlight the contribution of the radical W.E.B. Du Bois, the early feminist and peace campaigner Jane Addams and scores of feminist, socialist and anti-racist scholars from the Global South, such as Fernando Henrique Cardosa in Brazil and Fatima Meer in South Africa. Going back further into the history of public sociology, the Scots in the 18th century were public sociologists in their way, allowing us to see that Burawoy's refocusing of sociology's research agenda and its normative realignment is the latest expression of a long-standing concern. The signal achievement of Burawoy's injunction was to mobilize the profession to reflect again on its founding principles and to take the discipline forward to engage with the relevance of sociology to the social and human condition in the 21st century.

Despite the popularity of the idea of public sociology and the widespread use of such discourse, no book series is singularly dedicated to it. The purpose of this series is to draw together some of the best sociological research that carries the imprimatur of public sociology, done inside the academy by senior figures and early career researchers as well as outside it by practitioners, policy analysts and independent researchers seeking to apply sociological research in real-world settings.

The reflexivity of professional sociologists as they ponder the usefulness of sociology under neoliberalism and late modern cosmopolitanism will be addressed in this series, as the series publishes works that engage from a sociological perspective with the fundamental global challenges that threaten the very future of humankind. The relevance of sociology will be highlighted in works that address these challenges as they feature in global social changes but also as they are mediated in local and regional communities and settings. The series will feature titles that work at a global level of abstraction as well as studies that are micro ethnographic depictions of global processes as they affect local communities. The focus of the series is thus on what Michael Ignatieff refers to as 'the ordinary virtues' of everyday life, social justice, equality of opportunity, fairness, tolerance, trust and respect, and how the organization and structure of society – at a general level or in local neighbourhoods – inhibits or promotes these virtues and practices. The series will expose the dynamics of social suffering through detailed sociological analysis, and it will celebrate the hopes of social emancipation.

The discourse of public sociology has permeated outside the discipline of sociology as other subjects, such as public anthropology, public political science and public international relations, take up its challenge and reorientate themselves. In pioneering the engagement with its different publics, sociology has therefore once again led the way, and this series is designed to take the debate about public sociology and its practices in new directions. In being the first of its kind, this book series will showcase how the discipline of sociology has utilized the language and ideas of public sociology to change what it does and what it is for. This series will address not only what sociologists do, but also sociology's focus on the commitment to enhance understanding of the social condition so that the lives of ordinary people are materially improved. It will showcase the wide diversity of sociological research that addresses the many global challenges that threaten the future of humankind in the 21st century.

Most of these issues are on wonderful display in the latest addition to the series. The editors skilfully collect an experienced set of contributors to reflect on issues of social justice, equality and political change in the Global South. It stands to be an extremely significant contribution to its field, raising issues central to public sociology and to the discipline of sociology as a whole. As the discipline decolonizes its subject matter and approach, engages practically with emancipation from injustice, inequality and political oppression, and shifts towards honouring sociology in the Global South, Bezuidenhout, Mnwana and von Holdt's edited collection will be recognized as a major marker in the process.

Critical Engagement with Public Sociology: A Perspective from the Global South works on many levels. In one sense it celebrates the work of Eddie Webster's Society, Work and Politics Institute (SWOP) at the University of the Witwatersrand, Johannesburg, during its engagement with apartheid society and since. It is also, however, an account of sociology's ambiguous positioning within South Africa under apartheid, where some practitioners engaged with, supported and, indeed, contributed to state-sponsored apartheid, while others pursued liberal policies of distance and detachment from the apartheid state but with no real radical critique of sociological knowledge production under the constraints of apartheid. On the other hand, SWOP offered a subaltern and radical engagement with the unjust, unequal and oppressive nature of apartheid society, along, of course, with others in South African social science. South Africa, however, is used only to engage with a much broader sociological landscape. Alongside chapters on Chile and Turkey, the South African lens contributes to the formulation of what the editors call a 'Southern sociology': a sociology in and of the Global South.

This leads the editors and contributors into a fascinating argument that seeks to make two distinctions: between public sociology and what they call 'engaged sociology', and between the two sociologies in and of the Global North and the Global South. The volume is an exemplar of engaged sociology in the Global South.

The editors establish South Africa's credentials in having helped Michael Burawoy develop his ideas on public sociology, arising from his many visits to the country and his deep respect for the tradition of radical critique in some forms of South African sociology, and Webster's work in particular. This is merely the starting point to the contrast contributors are keen to make between public sociology and critically engaged sociology in systems of social injustice, economic inequality and political repression. They also challenge public sociology, including Burawoy himself, for the Global North bias of its focus and interests.

The volume ends with answers to the three questions posed in the introduction. Is there a distinctive Southern sociology? Is it comprehensive enough to constitute a thorough perspective in the discipline? And does it challenge the hegemony of sociology in the Global North? They give a resounding yes to each question. Let such a debate begin.

December, 2021

Typographical Note

Context matters when it comes to writing convention. On the use of terms that refer to race, the Bristol University Press style convention states the following: 'Black is a term that embraces people who experience structural and institutional discrimination because of their skin colour and is often used politically to refer to people of African, Caribbean and South Asian origin to imply solidarity against racism. In the past, Black has generally been written in lower case. In line with common usage, Bristol University Press now uses initial capitals for Black and White.' In the South African context, writing convention is influenced by the fact that the apartheid state capitalized racial descriptors and the non-racial movement (subscribing to the Freedom Charter) used the convention of not capitalizing the words 'black' and 'white' in response to this. The Black Consciousness movement took a different approach and capitalized the word 'Black'. Given this history and political context, and the ongoing contestation over terminology and the meaning of racial identity, we agreed with our publishers to allow for inconsistency across the manuscript and to retain the individual approach followed by chapter authors.

Introduction: Critical Engagement in South Africa and the Global South

Andries Bezuidenhout, Sonwabile Mnwana and Karl von Holdt

Public sociology's South African link

The idea of public sociology in its global form was inspired by sociological practice in South Africa. When the US sociologist Michael Burawoy visited South Africa in 1990, just as the negotiated transition to democracy was getting underway, he was struck by the social and political engagement of South African sociology and the vibrant quality of the debates at the annual conference of the South African Sociological Association. He subsequently paid several visits to what is now known as the Society, Work and Politics Institute (SWOP), a research unit at the University of the Witwatersrand, Johannesburg, invited by its then director, Edward (Eddie) Webster. In 2004 Burawoy addressed the South African sociological conference on his elaborated concept of 'public sociology',[1] which was, he stated, inspired by South African sociology in general and the work of SWOP in particular. Thus, it was Burawoy's association with the South African academy and social movements in the 1990s that inspired his campaign for public sociology in the United States and, subsequently, for popularizing the practice on a global scale. Yet, in South Africa, the practice he named 'public sociology' had been conceptualized as 'critically engaged sociology', or 'critical engagement' for short, and had significantly different emphases from those that characterize sociology as formulated by Burawoy (2004, 2005a, 2005b).

This volume returns to what we may call the birthplace of public sociology in order to explore the trajectory of critical engagement before and after Burawoy's visit, comparing this to the trajectory of public sociology which was forged in the very different context of US sociology and, from there, widely disseminated during Burawoy's tenure as president of the International Sociological Association. Burawoy has remained a colleague, collaborator and associate of SWOP ever since, and this provides a unique opportunity to reflect on three decades of dialogue and concept formation between a sociologist located in the epicentre of Northern sociology and a university research institute located in the Global South – Johannesburg, South Africa. This volume, then, presents a distinctive perspective on the tension-filled enterprise of sociological – or social scientific – engagement with struggles for social justice and change.

We provide a comparison of the connected but divergent trajectories of the two concepts across the dominant sociology of the North and the emergent sociology of the South over a 40-year period, using this to interrogate deeply the contradictions, challenges and profound contribution of social science research to popular struggle – and the equally profound contribution of popular struggles to the formation of new sociological knowledge.

While this volume presents an *exploration* of the concept of critical engagement, as a starting point we provide here a brief synopsis of the difference between the concepts of critical engagement and public sociology, drawing on the chapters by Ercüment Çelik and Karl von Holdt to present four key features of critical engagement:

1. Critical engagement arises in societies characterized by a 'permanent condition of radical social change' and hence 'unstable democracy', where the political choices confronting sociologists are stark and radical politics seems possible and necessary, in contrast to public sociology, which emerged primarily in the stable democracies of North America and Europe (see Çelik, this volume).
2. Critical engagement focuses on the formation of sociology at the 'intersection between the sociological field and the political field' and the tensions this entails, while public sociology focuses on the internal structure of the sociological field and the specific tensions this involves for the public sociologist (see von Holdt, this volume).
3. Critical engagement presents 'a critique of sociology as a field of domination in which the dominant sociology tends to be aligned broadly with the status quo in society', and hence it seeks to transform the sociological field. This is in contrast to public sociology, which understands 'the sociological endeavour as one characterized by pluralism … between different sociologies' (see von Holdt, this volume).
4. Critical engagement focuses on 'a distinctive process of knowledge production that is generated in the tension between the political field and the sociological field, carries symbolic power in both these fields

and is potentially conceptually innovative'. This contrasts with 'public sociology, which is silent about knowledge production and conceptual innovation and tacitly allocates them to professional' or critical 'sociology' (see von Holdt, this volume).

In writing these lines, we are mindful of the way US democracy, in particular, seems to have entered a new state of polarized confrontation and instability with deep roots in its history of colonialism, slavery and racial oppression, which may suggest that the distance between North and South is not so great and that Burawoy's (2021a, 2021b) turn to consider the sociology of W.E.B. Du Bois and its potential for the decolonization of sociology may impart a more radical thrust to public sociology.

Our focus is mainly on South Africa, and on one research institute, but we use this specific focus as a point of departure for a broader exploration of the nature of engaged research in the Global South. In addition to chapters dealing with South Africa's turbulent past and present, we include perspectives from Chile (Dasten Julián Vejar) and Turkey (Ercüment Çelik) as counterpoints of analysis. These chapters were written by colleagues associated with SWOP and the South African tradition of engaged scholarship.

SWOP was founded by Eddie Webster – one of South Africa's most influential sociologists – in 1983 as the Sociology of Work Project, a university-based research and teaching unit that supported the emerging trade union movement. It started out as an organization explicitly set up to research the world of work and support the emerging labour movement in the 1980s. The knowledge produced by staff and associates of SWOP was situated between the South African and global (mainly Northern) sociological fields. SWOP transmitted and mediated Northern approaches and theory in the South African context, but also spoke back with new concepts and approaches from the South African experience. SWOP's work within the field of labour studies flourished as the labour movement flourished, but entered a period of crisis that mirrored the decline of the South African labour movement (see Sakhela Buhlungu's chapter in this volume). In the post-apartheid era, it maintained its labour links and identity, but extended its approach to engage with social movements more broadly and became more international in outlook. Within the South African sociological field, SWOP made an important contribution to transforming the racial division of labour in knowledge production, but a major weakness of this project was the fact that the original theoretical contributions of an older generation of black South African sociologists were marginal to its sociology. Engagement with their work may have stimulated the adoption of a decolonial perspective at an earlier point.

The concept of critical engagement was forged within the tensions and pressures faced by politically committed sociologists in South Africa during a period of mass popular and trade union struggle against apartheid, and it was characterized by Webster as follows:

> Pressure exists on scholars to make a clear declaration that their research and teaching should be constructed as support for, and on behalf of, particular organizations. To prevent this subordination of intellectual work to the immediate interests of these organizations, I prefer the stance of critical engagement. Squaring the circle is never easy, as it involves a difficult combination of commitment to the goals of these movements while being faithful to evidence, data and your own judgment and conscience. (1995: 18; see also Webster's chapter, this volume)

The concept underwent further elaboration, in dialogue with Burawoy, over the two decades that followed (von Holdt, this volume).

Throughout the past four decades, SWOP has maintained a commitment to engaging publics, mostly from the vantage point of working with movements and communities. This process of critical engagement has taken the form of research interventions, some of which are collected as case studies in this volume. However, SWOP has also trained postgraduate students and had a structured internship programme designed to challenge what was described internally as 'the racial division of labour in knowledge production'. SWOP also has a public face in the form of monthly breakfast research seminars. These seminars have been running since the early 1990s and take place on the campus of the University of the Witwatersrand, typically early on Friday mornings. A member of SWOP's team presents a paper, and this is followed by lively debate and discussion. SWOP's breakfast seminars are typically attended by members of the academic staff at the University of the Witwatersrand, but the main audiences are trade unionists, community activists and people involved in government policymaking and implementation. SWOP researchers have also traditionally published their work in more popular and accessible publications, such as the *South African Labour Bulletin* – a journal co-founded in 1974 by Eddie Webster, which over time became a place where academics and labour activists debate research and ideas.

All the authors gathered in this volume are in some way associated with SWOP. Most of the chapters in this book question the applicability of the very notion of public sociology as a global concept. US sociology, within which the concept of public sociology arose, is very different from sociology in South Africa and much of the Global South. Whereas in the United States, public sociology arose as the focus of a campaign to legitimate public engagement within a highly professionalized, hierarchical and disengaged sociological field, in South Africa, critical engagement arose in the context of a radicalized social science responding to the re-emergence of black worker and student resistance in South Africa on the one hand and a positivist academic field orientated towards supporting and legitimising racial domination and white settler capitalism on the other, while also inspired by the emergence of a New Left social science in the North. Critical engagement attempted to specify the contradictory challenges of politically engaged scholarly work in this politically and intellectually challenging moment.

The South African sociological field

For the duration of the apartheid era, which came to an end in the early 1990s, South Africa's sociological community was highly fragmented, divided between three positions. First, there were those who uncritically supported the apartheid state. The discipline in South Africa was at the very heart of the apartheid project. Apartheid as an ideology was elaborated from within the discipline, and its social technocrats were trained by the discipline (Bozzoli, 1990; Ally et al, 2003). This could be described as a form of 'engaged complicity' – engaged because sociologists were committed to the elaboration of apartheid as an ideology and practice, and complicit because they participated in and legitimated the perpetration of a brutal project of white domincation.

Second, there was a liberal tradition that was critical of the apartheid project, but disengaged from popular struggle. In the 1970s, these sociologists often did quantitative studies of attitudes towards race relations (utilising the Bogardus Social Distance Scale, which reads somewhat awkwardly in hindsight). However, these acts of dissent remained largely academic and limited to the university circuit, a position that could be described as 'critical disengagement'. As Ally et al (2003: 78) argue: 'The liberalism of this strand of South African sociology was decidedly opposed to racialism, but the paternalism, which underpinned their attitude, is clearly evident in their writings and research postures.'

Third, there was a more radical critical tradition that openly supported the anti-apartheid movement. From the 1970s onwards, the rise of Black Consciousness (BC) among black students posed a challenge to the liberal tradition and white academics generally. In response to the rise of BC, a new generation of white sociologists found inspiration from the student movement and the rise of neo-Marxism in Europe and the United States. In this, they were responding as much to the rival tradition of sociology linked to the project of the apartheid state and the inadequacies of the liberal tradition of sociology as to the challenge posed by BC. Richard Turner was a leading figure in this and was an inspiration for someone like Eddie Webster.

The wave of strikes by black workers in 1973 reinforced the emergence of this critical tradition with its emphasis on Marxism, class analysis and the importance of labour studies. A lot of research and theoretical work happened at the interface between the university, the labour movement and the liberation movement, as well as in the movements themselves. This meant that sociological problems were defined by the needs of popular movements, but it also meant that there was a specific field of tension between university-based intellectuals and the needs and politics of political formations. A significant part of sociological knowledge was produced outside the scope of the university.

These tensions shaped the practice of critical engagement. Some argued that those critical of apartheid had to maintain an autonomous position within the space of the university. The fear was that an association with the resistance movements would produce 'bound intellectuals' intent on reproducing a political line rather than independent analysis. This position of academic autonomy held that a critical distance from the movement was important for impartial and rigorous analysis. On a practical level, openly associating with the liberation movement could lead to imprisonment, assassination or having to go into exile.[2] Others worked within the movement, often from exile, in both the African National Congress and the South African Communist Party, and were subjected to the movement's disciplinary (and other) internal processes. There were bound intellectuals also within the internal trade union and community movements. There were times when radical intellectuals in the movement were even expelled due to disagreements over ideology, strategy and tactics. Webster, SWOP and a number of other university-based intellectuals and organizations charted a third path, which Webster termed 'critical engagement' – a balancing act between the two positions of being immersed in the liberation movement or being completely detached from it (see chapters by Webster and von Holdt in this volume for more detail on this). It is this third path that inspired Burawoy to formulate his position on public sociology. Organizations such as SWOP also experienced hostility in the institutional contexts where they operated. SWOP, for example, had a particularly close relationship with the National Union of Mineworkers (NUM), but was located at a university with close historical ties with South African mining capital.

The South African sociological context shaped SWOP's tradition of critical engagement. It was a response to the engaged complicity of sociology in apartheid, but also the position of critical disengagement in more liberal circles and the 'unbound' current within the critical tradition, as well as the submission to organizational discipline of others in the resistance movements. From the 1970s onwards, sociological thinking tended to be quite interdisciplinary in nature. This is, in part, because of the dominance of Marxism and feminism (see Bozzoli, 1983; Jubber, 1983), but also because the challenges posed by apartheid could not be addressed from a narrow

sociological perspective only. We should mention again that SWOP was by
no means the only place where such experimentation was taking place – it
was part of a broader movement of scholars and activists brought together
by a commitment to end apartheid. Here we can mention the Surplus
People Project, which documented apartheid's forced removals; innovation
around art and theatre, such as the Culture and Working Life Project; the
engagement of feminist scholars with the national liberation movement
(Hassim and Walker, 1993); the History Workshop at the University of the
Witwatersrand; and Fatima Meer's Institute of Black Research (Hassim,
2019: 45–7).

A major blind spot, however, in much of this critical tradition was the
works of important black South African thinkers such as Archie Mafeje,
Bernard Magubane and Fatima Meer – three of the important intellectual
figures who were marginalized within the mainstream of the South African
academy, including those considered to be progressive (see Hendricks,
2008; for more recent reappraisals of the sociological significance of Mafeje
and Magubane, see Nyoka, 2020, 2022; on Meer, see Hassim, 2019). In
addition to marginalizing black South African voices, the South African
tradition was somewhat isolated from what was happening on the rest of the
continent. In the postcolonial African context, an attempt to move beyond
colonial disciplinary boundaries was expressed through a radical version
of development studies, with different responses to how university-based
intellectuals should structure their relationships with liberation movements
as the governments of newly independent states. Ali Mazrui, at Makerere
University in Uganda, took an approach that prized academic autonomy,
which also led to him having to leave his position, whereas Walter Rodney, at
the University of Dar es Salaam in Tanzania, argued for a closer relationship
with the postcolonial state (see Mamdani, 2016). At the time, there were
some links between exiled South Africans and these debates, but by the
1970s in the country itself a type of South African exceptionalism took
root – an assumption that South Africa was different from other African
countries due to its levels of industrialization and urbanization and the size
of its settler population – and critical sociologists often looked towards
Western Marxism for theoretical inspiration. Mamdani (1996) was critical of
this exceptionalism, and South Africans ignored his warnings, maybe at our
own peril, appreciating too late the continued importance of postcolonial
rural transformations involving traditional leaders being captured by urban
elite interests (of course, there were exceptions; see Ntsebeza, 2005). To
quote Jimi Adésínà:

> I have noticed how eagerly we adopt every new concept and author
> that reaches our shores from the global North; the rapid uptake on the
> idea of 'Public Sociology' being the most recent case. Yet we hardly

give ourselves, our scholarship, and local resources the same degree of scholarly attention. (2006: 257, also see Cooper, 2017)

Having laid out in summary form the origins of critical engagement and of SWOP in the 1970s and early 1980s, and having located these within the fragmented field of South African sociology at the time, we return here to the trajectory of the concept of public sociology.

Critically engaged public sociology

Michael Burawoy's project of popularising and institutionalizing public sociology has been remarkably successful. The 2000s saw the publication of a range of books that introduced the notion of public sociology to a reading audience, with some taking on critical positions. The majority of these texts were written by scholars from the Global North, the United States in particular, since Burawoy's campaign for public sociology was initially aimed at addressing the insularity of the discipline in the United States (see Clawson et al, 2007; Nichols, 2007; Jeffries, 2009). Towards the end of the 2000s, publishing on the topic became more global but was still, in our view, mainly driven by Northern concerns. There were a number of publications what focused on traditions from countries and places other than the United States, notably Australia, Canada, Germany, Ireland, and, most recently, Scotland. A number of these books have become standard references in the field and some have seen updated editions (Nyden et al, 2012; Brewer, 2013, 2014; Aulenbacher et al, 2017; Germov and Poole, 2019; Scandrett, 2020). The 2010s saw the publication of a range of books that applied the idea and practice of public sociology to specific fields, such as Nickel's (2013) use of the concept to study the state and the domain of social policy (also drawing on Foucault) as a way to reshape and challenge internships (see Tolich, 2018) and its use in understanding struggles around migrants and citizenship in the United States (Carty and Luévano, 2017). An innovative and much-needed contribution is the recently published analysis of the relationship between social media and public sociology (Carrigan and Fatsis, 2021). The inclusion of chapters on public sociology in introductory texts to sociology directed at undergraduate teaching (Jones, 2021) and the recent publication of an international handbook of public sociology are indicative of the extent to which Burawoy's campaign for public sociology has been institutionalized (Hossfeld et al, 2021). While mostly preoccupied with and located in the Global North, at least some contributors to this latter volume write on countries such as Colombia, India, the Philippines and South Africa.

Notwithstanding the many interesting contributions made in these texts, they tend to reproduce the conception of public sociology as a specialist practice involving the dissemination of sociological knowledge to non-academic audiences that is located within a highly institutionalized, professionalized and hierarchical sociological field. In contrast, with this book we attempt to recover and elaborate a political practice of sociology and its theorization as it has emerged in a distinct context of national liberation, democratization and radical social instability. In this context, critical engagement is conceived as a complete sociological practice involving distinctive processes of knowledge production in partnership with popular movements as well as the development of theory through the interaction between scholarly and political practices.

These qualities impart to critical engagement a radically critical stance in relation to mainstream sociology and to Northern perspectives and assumptions in general. In this regard, our contribution is also situated in the literature on theory in the Global South and in debates on decoloniality and knowledge production (Connell, 2007; Comaroff and Comaroff, 2012; Bhambra, 2014; Keim et al, 2014; Burawoy, 2021a, 2021b). This is not to say that public sociology is 'wrong', but rather that it is a concept elaborated in relation to a specific field of sociology in the North and that it fails to capture the theory and practice that emerged in South Africa and which resonates in a number of societies in the Global South. Nor is it to say that critical engagement is impossible in the North – indeed, it may be becoming increasingly possible and necessary in the context of escalating polarization and social crisis. At the same time, given its critique of mainstream sociology, particularly the domination of Northern perspectives and assumptions, we pose the question in this volume as to whether critical engagement makes a contribution to the formation of a counter-hegemonic sociology.

We are acutely aware that South Africa offers but one example of a sociological practice in the Global South and that it cannot stand in for a universal Southern position – to do so would replicate the misconceived universalization of the European and US experiences to the rest of the world. In order to address this, we include chapters on Chile and Turkey. Dasten Julián Vejar's chapter on Chile documents an attempt to set up a SWOP-like organization in the context of that country. In the course of writing this book and revising our chapters, Julián was dismissed by his university and the research unit where he was based moved its affiliation to another university, where it is able to operate more autonomously. Ercüment Çelik's chapter provides an equally riveting account of sociology, this time in Turkey. The clampdown on academic freedom in Turkey also meant that Çelik had to relocate to Germany. Both these contributors have links and shared histories with South Africa and SWOP. Again, we do not present these chapters as a full representation of the Global South, but merely as a point of departure for a more sustained Southern critique of public sociology as universal theory of the critical engagement of sociologists with popular movements and other publics. Nevertheless, while we do not want to universalize our experience, we do think that this perspective potentially contributes to counter-hegemonic possibilities in relation to the Northern approaches. This means theorizing our practice of critical engagement not only as engagement with social struggle but also as critique of the dominant powers within sociology, including the domination of the field by professionalized Northern sociology. Is it possible that in the field of sociology, or social science more broadly, critical engagement is transformed into an alignment between popular struggle and critical social science to challenge the alignment of dominant social science paradigms with the dominant forces in society? We return to this and other questions in our conclusion to the volume.

This collection presents a space to critically evaluate and potentially deepen our understanding of socially engaged research. In the context of shifting political and social orders globally, it is crucial to understand contemporary challenges, struggles and lessons that can be drawn from the interface of public engagement and social research, as an example of what might be possible in the context of the Global South. We hope that it represents a small step in displacing the centrality of Northern knowledge and concepts in making meaning of the experiences and practices of the 'other' knowledges and actors on the periphery of the global capitalist order.

Contributing chapters: an overview

We asked the contributors to this volume to focus their chapters on the question of knowledge production, particularly the tension between the production of scholarly knowledge and the production of political knowledge. Accordingly, this volume is organized in three broad groups of chapters. The first group of chapters use the history of SWOP as a point of departure to explore the context and significance of the South African *practice* of critical engagement. These four chapters illustrate some of the dilemmas associated with critical engagement and also map out how SWOP's focus shifted from a national focus on the anti-apartheid and labour movement to a more globally oriented research focus while maintaining a grounding in attempts to reconstruct South African society. They also highlight the political *and socio-economic* context in which knowledge is produced in a place like South Africa. These chapters have in common a historical dimension in that they attempt to situate the critically engaged tradition in continuities and breaks with the past. Because these chapters deal with one institute as a point of departure, though for different purposes, there is some overlap in terms of content. As editors, we decided against artificially imposing a more linear narrative, in part because we want the same story to be told by different voices and different perspectives.

The second group of chapters document current experiments with engaged research in the South African context. Whereas in the past SWOP focused almost exclusively on the labour movement, its current research moves beyond this to include issues of land and mineral rights, rural dispossession, environmental justice, food security and feminist activism. These five chapters introduce topics such as the dilemmas associated with combining activism with legal action, the opportunities presented by the participatory action tradition of research, and the inherent contradictions associated with combining environmental and labour activism.

With the third and final group of chapters, we shift our focus beyond South Africa. We start out with chapters on Chile and Turkey, written by comrades and colleagues who have been associated with SWOP and South Africa. These two chapters document similar challenges to those faced by South Africans, but explore the significance of different national sociological traditions and political contexts. In the case of Chile, universities emerge from an authoritarian dispensation to democracy under a neoliberal order. This context is quite similar to the South African dynamic. Turkey, on the other hand, operates in the context of political coups and the continued repression of academic freedom. The case raises the issue of personal risk involved in socially engaged research in a stark way. It also introduces the concept of 'sociology *across* the Global South' as opposed to theory 'of', 'from' or 'for' the South (see Burawoy, 2021b: 259). Also included in this section is a response by Michael Burawoy as the volume's main interlocutor.

The first set of chapters elaborate explicitly what critical engagement and public sociology would mean from the vantage point of SWOP in South Africa and explore this question historically.

In Chapter 2, Andries Bezuidenhout and Karl von Holdt survey SWOP's history by means of an overview of its main research themes and engagements with theory. This survey is used to trace how SWOP's engagement with Northern theory shifted over time. It started off from a position where the institute disseminated Northern approaches in the South African context, but also developed local concepts for understanding the realities they faced. Over time, this shifted towards a more conscious positioning of the institute as located in and engaged with the Global South, as a position from which to rethink Northern theory. The chapter also explores how the institute's research agenda shifted alongside a changing labour movement, up to the point where the relationship broke down. Over time, this opened up scope for new areas of research, much of which informs the chapters collected in the second group of chapters in this volume.

Bezuidenhout and von Holdt's chapter on the history of SWOP is followed by three chapters by former directors of the institute, thus covering three different eras. In Chapter 3, the founder and director of SWOP, Edward Webster, presents an account of the kind of research intervention that led him to develop the concept of critical engagement in an attempt to capture the challenging but productive tension between scholarly research and political engagement. He details two research interventions that he and fellow SWOP researchers undertook in the 1980s, during apartheid South Africa. These studies were conducted with the NUM – a union formed by black mineworkers who at that time were battling to obtain formal recognition from the mining companies while also facing state repression. For Webster, the strength of critical engagement was rooted in the ability of SWOP researchers, while retaining their academic autonomy, to choose to take sides for the purpose of empowering mineworkers and giving them a 'voice' during a very volatile period in South Africa's history.

After a career as a trade union educator and leader, Sakhela Buhlungu was for many years senior researcher and deputy director at SWOP. Drawing on the South African experience, Buhlungu's contribution (Chapter 4) traces the trajectory of politically and socially engaged scholarship in South Africa's sociology – labour studies, in particular – for almost four decades (from 1970 to the late 2000s). In his account, Buhlungu argues that for the most of the 1970s, South African sociology did not have proper engagement with marginalized classes and worker movements despite this being a significant moment in the country's history, including the labour unrest that began in Durban in 1973 and the youth protests of 1976. For Buhlungu, it was the formation of more assertive black worker unions in the late 1970s that marked an era in which South African sociology engaged directly with anti-apartheid movements and other agents ('publics') outside the academy. The escalation of the anti-apartheid struggle in the late 1970s and 1980s pushed public sociology off its earlier elitist position of privilege in the ivory tower and into engagement with social and political movements and worker unions. This engagement brought the 'sub-discipline' of labour studies and public sociology to the centre of South African sociological thinking and practice. Buhlungu also notes that shifting power relations and political landscape in the post-apartheid order led to a decline in the popularity of labour studies and ultimately a notable waning (or 'retreat') of public sociology. Buhlungu's chapter was previously published as an article in a special edition of *Work and Occupations* on public sociology, edited by Michael Burawoy. A collection of this nature would not be complete without this historical perspective on the shifting relations with the trade union movement.

Karl von Holdt had a long association with SWOP as a union-linked editor, PhD student and researcher before he joined the institute in 2007. He became director in 2011. His contribution in Chapter 5 provides a detailed analysis of the processes through which the concepts of public sociology and critical engagement evolved in the course of a 30-year dialogue between US sociologist Michael Burawoy and researchers at SWOP. Through this account, he is able to examine the elaboration of the concept of critical engagement in response to both Burawoy's work on public engagement and the pressures of SWOP's research, detailing the distinctive practices of knowledge production at its heart.

At this point, the volume shifts from its focus on the history of critical engagement to contemporary examples of activist and socially engaged research in South Africa. In Chapters 6 to 10, authors provide a variety of case studies of politically engaged research and knowledge production.

In Chapter 6, Sonwabile Mnwana details and explores the challenges of producing political and sociological knowledge in a complex and highly contested local context: the rural platinum mining frontier where he has conducted field research for more than a decade. Mnwana demonstrates how the rapid entry of mining into the impoverished rural areas dispossesses villagers while enriching local chiefs, producing a highly fractious political and social landscape. Mnwana draws on Webster's concept of critical engagement to demonstrate the tensions and challenges of conducting socially engaged research in such a landscape and how quality sociological knowledge can to lead to positive political outcomes for the marginalized classes. However, Mnwana argues, such positive outcomes are only possible after a long period in engagement with all social classes, and the researcher must be prepared to 'travel' extensively and engage with all the existing local 'social worlds'. At the same time, constant negotiation and engagement with various activist groups permits a co-production of knowledge to emerge over time. Hence, co-production and professional objectivity complement each other in the production of research that has sufficient depth and credibility to influence court decisions.

Jacklyn Cock is professor emerita in the Department of Sociology at the University of the Witwatersrand and a long-standing associate of SWOP. In Chapter 7, she describes two different social initiatives: first, a trade union project in which SWOP participated mainly in the form of public sociology, disseminating instrumental knowledge to a non-academic audience; and, second, a SWOP critically engaged sociological project which involved working with popular movements in the co-production of new knowledge, which had theoretical implications. This form of participatory action research is in tune with decolonial and feminist research practices that emphasize empowerment through reflexivity, dialogic learning, valuing lived experience, horizontal social relations and reciprocity. The focus of both initiatives was on the concept of a just transition from a carbon-based economy.

Ntokozo Yingwana is a researcher at the African Centre for Migration & Society, located just down the corridor from SWOP and a fellow research centre at the University of the Witswatersrand. Her contribution (Chapter 8) explores the co-production of knowledge, both empirical and conceptual, which emerges through employing feminist participatory action research to critically analyze three apparently incongruent identities: African, sex worker and feminist. Yingwana adopts an 'insider–outsider' approach and constantly negotiates and renegotiates this position.

Similarly, Brittany Kesselman's contribution (Chapter 9) on the opportunities and the challenges of doing research that aims to contribute to food justice critically analyzes the co-production of knowledge integral to participatory action research practice. Kesselman is a postdoctoral fellow at SWOP. Participatory action research provided Kesselman with methodological and analytical tools to conduct research with poor urban residents in Johannesburg, on urban agriculture, food consumption and food justice. Yingwana and Kesselman both critically engaged publics outside the university.

The last chapter in this second group, like Mnwana's chapter, analyzes research and activism in the arena of struggles over land and law. Aninka Claassens and Nokwanda Sihlali are based at the Land and Accountability Research Centre at the University of Cape Town, which has worked collaboratively with SWOP on rural research over the past decade. In Chapter 10, they produce a detailed account of the process of co-production of knowledge in close partnership with rural communities and the sophistication and conceptual innovation of the analysis that this produces. This knowledge has been deeply peer-reviewed and stress-tested through the contested legal and political forums in which they engage, and yet, despite its intellectual rigour and analytical depth, it cannot be recognized as 'academic' within the university. This mode of research is implicitly a critique of the narrowness, and distance from real-life, of the contestations of professional academic knowledge production.

The book then returns these debates to the international arena. Chapter 11 illustrates how ideas and practices travel across the Global South. Dasten Julián Vejar is a young sociologist from Chile who was inspired by his postgraduate studies at the Institute of Sociology in the Friedrich Schiller University Jena and by his encounters with Michael Burawoy and SWOP to establish the Work Studies Group from the South (GETSUR), a group that strongly resembles SWOP. His chapter offers a Latin American experience of striving to create locally relevant knowledge through a process that defies and seeks to avoid hegemonic and hierarchical approaches to knowledge production. Also adopting an action research design and methodology, the Chilean case highlights the challenges of working with trade unions to produce knowledge in the context of precariousness of work and life, and other methodological, institutional, social and economic obstacles. In spite of significant academic outputs, GETSUR was not formally recognized by the university and, as mentioned, Julián was eventually dismissed. He had to relocate to another university, but learned important lessons in the process. His newly constituted action research group is set up in the form of a non-governmental organization.

In Chapter 12, Ercüment Çelik charts the travel of critical engagement as a concept from South Africa to Turkey and advocates for an expanded engagement across the Global South. He provides a detailed historical analysis of critical engagement and knowledge production in Turkey since the 1950s. In this compelling account, Çelik argues for direct engagement between Southern scholars, first in the form of exchange of knowledge and ideas produced in the South – a process he terms 'learning across the South' or a 'sociology across the South'. Such analysis and sociological practice, argues Çelik, should be founded on mutual interest among Southern scholars in studying societies in the South and knowing each other's sociological work. For Çelik, this process should precede engagement with the currently dominant Northern sociologies and processes of knowledge production that shape global sociology.

As mentioned earlier in this introduction, Burawoy has been a critic, comrade and colleague of SWOP, and it was in this spirit and because of our primary engagement with his formulation of public sociology that we asked him to respond to the analyses contained in this volume. In Chapter 13, Burawoy presents an analysis of the chapters in this volume in order to clarify his own understanding of critical engagement as idea and practice. He questions a number of assumptions made in the volume, including assumptions about the distinctiveness of sociology practised in the Global South and how this relates to the critical sociological traditions of the Global North.

Karl von Holdt concludes the volume by returning to three central questions alluded to in this introduction: whether critical engagement represents a *Southern* sociology that is both scholarly and politically engaged; whether critical engagement constitutes a *whole* sociology, in that it engages in knowledge production and theoretical innovation, not only the dissemination of academic knowledge to non-academic publics; and whether the tradition of critical engagement constitutes a counter-hegemonic sociology in relation to the dominant sociology of the Global North.

Notes

[1] The idea of public sociology as sociological practice – taking the critical side of the discipline out of the domain of the academy and into the domain of the public – has become a global movement with associated institutions and publications. While the term was introduced in Ben Agger's (2000) *Public Sociology: From Social Facts to Literary Acts*, it was conceptually elaborated and popularized by Michael Burawoy as president of the American Sociological Association and, later, as president of the International Sociological Association. As such, the idea of public sociology is associated with Burawoy's personal and intellectual trajectory and his recently published autobiography is titled as such. Of course, the practice now described as public sociology precedes most of our lifetimes, and it could be argued that the likes of Karl Marx (through public activism and his having to live in exile), W. E. B. Du Bois (with his involvement in the anti-racist and anti-colonial

movements) and even Émile Durkheim (if only in the event of the Dreyfus affair) all practised what some today call public sociology (see Carrigan and Fatsis, 2021: Chapter 5).

[2]   Richard Turner was 'banned' in the 1970s, meaning that he was under house arrest and was not allowed to publish anything or meet more than one person at a time. Webster was arrested in 1975 and tried under the Suppression of Communism Act the following year. Turner was assassinated by agents of the apartheid state in 1978, although those responsible were never brought to book. Turner's (1972) book *The Eye of the Needle* remains a foundational text of South Africa's critically engaged tradition of research and activism. The politically engaged anthropologist, David Webster (no relation) was assassinated outside his Johannesburg home on 1 May 1989 by agents of the regime. Webster's killer was convicted of the murder in 1998.

References

Adésínà, J.O. (2006) 'Sociology beyond despair: Recovery of nerve, endogeneity, and epistemic intervention', *South African Review of Sociology*, 37(2): 241–59.

Agger, B. (2000) *Public Sociology: From Social Facts to Literary Acts*, Washington, DC: Rowman & Littlefield.

Ally, S., Mooney, K. and Stewart, P. (2003) 'The state-sponsored and centralised institutionalisation of an academic discipline: Sociology in South Africa, 1920–1970', *Society in Transition*, 34(1): 70–103.

Arribas Lozano, A. (2018) 'Reframing the public sociology debate: Towards collaborative and decolonial praxis', *Current Sociology*, 66(1): 92–109.

Aulenbacher, B., Burawoy, M., Dörre, K. and Sittel, J. (eds) (2017) *Öffentliche Soziologie. Wissenschaft im Dialog mit der Gesellschaft* (Public sociology. Science in dialogue with society), Frankfurt am Main: Campus Verlag.

Bhambra, G.K. (2014) *Connected Sociologies: Theory for a Global Age*, London: Bloomsbury Academic.

Bozzoli, B. (1983) 'Marxism, feminism and South African studies', *Journal of Southern African Studies*, 9(2): 139–71.

Bozzoli, B. (1990) 'From social engineering to bureaucratic sociology: State, authority and the alienation of the intelligentsia in South African social science', *South African Sociological Review*, 3(1): 69–76.

Brewer, J. (2013) *The Public Value of the Social Sciences: An Interpretive Essay*, London: Bloomsbury.

Brewer, J. (2014) 'Society as a vocation: Renewing social science for social renewal', *Irish Journal of Sociology*, 22(2): 127–37.

Burawoy, M. (2004) 'Public sociology: South African dilemmas in a global context', *Society in Transition*, 35(1): 11–26.

Burawoy, M. (2005a) 'For public sociology', *American Sociological Review*, 70(1): 4–28.

Burawoy, M. (2005b) 'Third-wave sociology and the end of pure science', *American Sociologist*, 36(3–4): 152–65.

Burawoy, M. (2021a) 'Decolonizing sociology: The significance of W.E.B. Du Bois', *Critical Sociology*, 47(4–5): 545–54.

Burawoy, M. (2021b) 'Why is classical theory classical? Theorizing the canon and canonizing Du Bois', *Journal of Classical Sociology*, 21(3–4), 245–59.

Carrigan, M. and Fatsis, L. (2021) *The Public and Their Platforms: Public Sociology in an Era of Social Media*, Bristol: Bristol University Press.

Carty, V. and Luévano, R. (eds) (2017) *Scholars, Activists, and Latin Migrants Converse on Common Ground*, Leiden: Brill.

Clawson, D., Zussman, R., Burawoy, M., Misra, J., Gerstel, N., Stokes, R. and Anderton, D.L. (eds) (2007) *Public Sociology: Fifteen Eminent Sociologists Debate Politics and the Profession in the Twenty-first Century*, Berkeley: University of California Press.

Comaroff, J. and Comaroff, J.L. (2012) *Theory from the South or, How Euro-America Is Evolving toward Africa*, New York: Routledge.

Connell, R. (2007) *Southern Theory: The Global Dynamics of Knowledge in Social Science*, Sydney: Allen & Unwin.

Cooper, D. (2017) 'Concepts of "Applied and Public Sociology": Arguments for a Bigger Theoretical Picture around the Idea of a "University Third Mission"', *Journal of Applied Social Science*, 11(2): 141–158.

Germov, J. and Poole, M. (eds) (2019) *Public Sociology: An introduction to Australian Society* (4th edn), London: Routledge.

Hassim, S. (2019) *Fatima Meer: A Free Mind*. Cape Town: HSRC Press.

Hassim, S. and Walker, C. (1993) 'Women's studies and the women's movement in South Africa: Defining a relationship', *Women's Studies International Forum*, 16(5): 523–34.

Hendricks, F. (2008) 'The Mafeje affair: The University of Cape Town and apartheid', *African Studies*, 67(3): 423–51.

Hossfeld, L., Kelly, E. Brooke and Hossfeld, C. (eds) (2021) *The Routledge International Handbook of Public Sociology*, London: Routledge.

Jeffries, V. (ed) (2009) *Handbook of Public Sociology*, Plymouth: Rowman & Littlefield.

Jones, P. (2021) 'Public sociology?', in K. Murji, S. Neal and J. Solomos (eds) *An Introduction to Sociology*, London: Sage, pp 443–56.

Jubber, K. (1983) 'Sociology and its social context: The case of the rise of Marxist sociology in South Africa', *Social Dynamics*, 9(2): 50–63.

Keim, W., Çelik, E., Ersche, C. and Wöhrer, V. (eds) (2014) *Global Knowledge Production in the Social Sciences: Made in Circulation* (Preface by Michael Burawoy), Farnham: Ashgate.

Mamdani, M. (1996) *Citizen and Subject: Contemporary Africa and the Legacy of Late Colonialism*, Princeton: Princeton University Press.

Mamdani, M. (2016) 'Between the public intellectual and the scholar: Decolonization and some post-independence initiatives in African higher education', *Inter-Asia Cultural Studies*, 17(1), 68–83.

Nichols, L.T. (2007) *Public Sociology: The Contemporary Debate*, New Brunswick, NJ: Transaction Publishers.

Nickel, P.M. (2013) *Public Sociology and Civil Society: Governance, Politics, and Power*, Boulder, CO: Paradigm Publishers.

Ntsebeza, L. (2005) *Democracy Compromised: Chiefs and the Politics of Land in South Africa*, Pretoria: HSRC Press.

Nyden, P., Hossfeld, L. and Nyden, G. (2012) *Public Sociology: Research, Action, and Change*, London: Sage.

Nyoka, B. (2020) *The Social and Political Thought of Archie Mafeje*, Johannesburg: Wits University Press.

Nyoka, B. (2022) 'Mafeje and Magubane: Two concepts of the "South African revolution"', in S.J. Ndlovu-Gatsheni and B. Ngcaweni (eds) *The Contested Idea of South Africa*, Oxford and New York: Routledge, pp 114–33.

Scandrett, E. (ed) (2020) *Public Sociology as Educational Practice Challenges, Dialogues and Counter-Publics*, Bristol: Bristol University Press.

Tolich, M. (2018) *Public Sociology Capstones: Non-neoliberal Alternatives to Internships*, London: Routledge.

Turner, R. (1972) *The Eye of the Needle: Towards Participatory Democracy in South Africa*, Durban: SRO-CAS.

Webster, E. (1995) 'Taking labour seriously: Sociology and labour in South Africa', in A. van der Merwe (ed) *Industrial Sociology: A South African Perspective*, Johannesburg: Lexicon Publishers, pp 1–27.

2

Critical Engagement and SWOP's Changing Research Tradition

Andries Bezuidenhout and Karl von Holdt

Introduction

In this chapter, we provide an overview of the research trajectory of the Society, Work and Politics Institute (SWOP) at the University of the Witwatersrand (colloquially referred to as Wits) and how this was shaped by its commitment to supporting the labour movement in particular as well as South Africa's liberation movement and social movements in general. Wiebke Keim (2011, 2017) argues that the international division of intellectual labour represents a centre–periphery relationship. Given the uneven playing field, she argues, scholars from the Global South can attempt to 'catch up' with the North, deconstruct (or provincialize) Northern theory or form counter-hegemonic strands. She defines counter-hegemonic strands of sociology as 'original, autonomous sociologies at the periphery' (Keim, 2011: 130) and cites South African labour studies as an example of this. In her analysis, SWOP's researchers, in the context of South African labour studies, constantly engaged Northern theory but adapted these theories to local contexts and succeeded in building up a significant and dense body of publications that constitutes a local tradition. The strength and richness of this local tradition later on enabled South African labour studies to make a global impact.

The aim of this chapter is to map out and describe the institute's research traditions as they evolved from the founding of SWOP in the early 1980s up to the contemporary era. We do this in order to highlight the tensions and contradictions involved in a critically engaged research tradition. Keim's analysis of South African labour studies happened at a moment of transition, a moment when the once-powerful labour movement entered a period of decline. We comment on how the post-apartheid fragmentation of the labour movement subsequently impacted on labour studies itself and how SWOP responded to tensions between researchers and trade unions in flux and under attack in the post-apartheid era. We do this to supplement Buhlungu's narrative (Chapter 4), originally published in 2009, as well as Keim's, published shortly thereafter, and to comment on how the breakdown in some of SWOP's relationships with trade unions impacted on the institute's trajectory. The chapter is also intended as an introduction to the South African context and some of its sociological debates, for readers not familiar with the country's history. It also provides contextual background for the three chapters that follow, which are written by former SWOP directors: Edward Webster, Sakhela Buhlungu and Karl von Holdt – additional elements of SWOP's history and its research traditions are revealed in these chapters.

In this chapter we discuss how, in response to changing relationships with its labour partners, SWOP researchers broadened their research foci to include topics well beyond the scope of labour studies. We show how SWOP's work was influenced mainly by critical sociological thought in the form of Marxism and feminism, as well as critiques of the racial division of labour in knowledge production in South Africa and much of the world. Over time, the institute became more aware of its location in the Global South and the need to re-evaluate the critical tradition of Northern theory that had shaped its research agenda.

The main focus here is SWOP's research programme, but mention should be made of its structured attempt to address the racial division of labour in knowledge production, as it was referred to in the 1990s and 2000s, primarily through a well-resourced research internship programme. Judging by the contribution this programme made to increasing the number of black sociologists, it could be deemed a success (Buhlungu and Metcalfe, 2001; Metcalfe and Cock, 2010). The programme initially focused on the training of master's students, but as this cohort grew, it became clear that there was also a need to provide support for doctoral candidates. A grant from the Ford Foundation made it possible, and SWOP went on to host a highly successful postdoctoral programme. Historically, full-time researchers have also been involved in undergraduate and postgraduate training programmes, primarily in the Department of Sociology. SWOP also participated in the establishment of The Global Labour University, a transnational programme aimed at training trade union intellectuals based in Germany, South Africa, India, Brazil and, later on, the United States.

SWOP's research programme: an overview
Early days, anti-apartheid commitments and supporting black trade unions
Eddie Webster, at the time a member of the Department of Sociology at Wits, established the Sociology of Work Programme in 1983 under the

acronym SWOP.[1] In the immediate sense, SWOP grew out of Webster's doctoral research, on the impact of the organization of work on the health and safety of foundry workers, as well as an approach to him by a group of science and engineering graduate students who were interested in health and safety issues and were organized in the Technical Advice Group. However, the programme built on a decade of involvement by Webster in supporting the emerging democratic trade union movement in South Africa. Webster was a part of a network of young intellectuals from Durban who formed a political grouping around political philosophy lecturer Richard (Rick) Turner (1972). With Turner and others, Webster had founded the *South African Labour Bulletin* (SALB) in 1974.

In addition to publishing research in support of the emerging labour movement, young (mostly white) intellectuals provided technical support to the emerging unions. Turner advocated participatory democracy – a peaceful but strategic approach to collective mobilization – as a way to counter the apartheid regime. Webster was recruited by Dunbar Moodie to build the industrial sociology programme at Wits, which was, typically at the time, in the mould of mainstream industrial relations. Moodie shared with Webster an association with the group around Rick Turner in Durban, and Moodie's own work had turned from an interest in Afrikaner nationalism to a focus on the migrant labour system in South Africa's mining industry, through which he pioneered the ethnographic approach that came to dominate South African labour studies. Wits was located in Johannesburg, part of the biggest conurbation in southern Africa and the hub of industry and the economy in the region – a good location for an academic project focused on researching the world of work and supporting trade unions. The renaissance in Marxist labour process theory was at the heart of this project, following Harry Braverman's (1974) publication of *Labor and Monopoly Capital* and subsequent debates in which Michael Burawoy (1979) also played an important part. At the very heart of the labour process debate was a critique of Braverman's thesis that new forms of mechanized production (Fordism) and managerial control (Taylorism, or scientific management) over the labour process would deskill the working class over time. This was criticized as being too structuralist and for not taking into consideration various forms of worker agency and resistance against deskilling and managerial control (Friedman, 1977; Burawoy, 1979; Edwards, 1979).

Webster's (1985, 1987) analysis revealed a twist to this debate. He showed how mechanized production in South Africa's foundries led to the deskilling of a segment of white workers, who dominated the labour market through their control of craft unions. Especially from the Second World War onwards, this process allowed for an emergent class of black industrial workers to build a strong shop floor movement in the form of industrial unions, described as social movement unionism. In Turner's idea of participatory democracy,

Webster found a compelling critique of dogmatic Marxist structuralism. The social agency implicit in the idea of participatory democracy found concrete expression in social movement unionism.

The 1980s saw the high point of insurgent mass struggle against apartheid, characterized by the exponential growth of the trade union movement and a proliferation of popular organization, centred for the most part on the United Democratic Front, as well as global solidarity and an increasingly effective international boycott and disinvestment campaign. The banned and exiled African National Congress (ANC) was also increasingly active inside the country. The state responded with reform initiatives and increasingly militarized repression. It was in this environment that SWOP refined its strategy of 'critical engagement' with the trade unions it supported through research and educational programmes (see the chapters by Webster and Buhlungu, this volume), building on Webster's work over the previous decade.

During this period, SWOP's researchers focused their intellectual work on workplace analysis and trade union resistance, with studies of health and safety in mining and metal industries, HIV/AIDS[2] and mineworkers. Significant theoretical contributions were made with the concept of 'social movement unionism' to explore the interpenetration of trade union and community movements (Webster, 1987) and with the concept of 'tacit knowledge' to denote the ability of mineworkers to interpret imminent dangers of rockfalls through the sounds ('talking rocks') made by stressed rock formations (Leger, 1985, 1992). This critique of the view that mineworkers possessed little skill addressed theories of industrial education as well as continued debates around the nature of skill, following Braverman's deskilling thesis. Again, the South African research highlighted the importance of workers' agency in the workplace. At the same time, Webster was plunging himself into building the discipline of sociology, and particularly the sub-discipline of industrial sociology, as President of the Association for Sociology in Southern Africa (1983–85) and as head of the Wits sociology department (1988–94).

In 1987, the university formally recognized the entity as a programme. The years 1989 and 1990 opened up a period of transition with the unbanning of the ANC, the release of political prisoners and the beginning of negotiations between the liberation movement and the apartheid regime. It was also a time of extraordinary violence as regime-funded 'third force' groups launched violent attacks and massacres on working-class commuters, migrant hostels and political meetings across the Witwatersrand conurbation as well as in Natal, while underground networks linked to the ANC established armed self-defence units in response, and violent youth movements became a law unto themselves. The context was the emergence from the 1970s onwards of a Zulu nationalist movement in the form of Inkatha and the establishment of the United Workers' Union of South Africa, set up as a rival to the unions linked to the freedom struggle. Inkatha collaborated with the apartheid system in creating ethnic 'homelands' (less politely called 'bantustans') for black South Africans as an alternative to democratic rights in the country as a whole. Up to a few days before the first democratic elections in 1994, Inkatha refused to participate in peace and transition negotiations.

The 1990s and 2000s: resistance, worker participation, disillusionment

While continuing to work with trade unions, the intellectual focus of SWOP shifted to grapple with the role of labour in transition and the challenges of reforming labour law and labour markets. At the time, SWOP had a strong focus on various forms of worker participation. SWOP researcher Judy Maller (1992) adapted Northern theories of worker participation to write an empirically informed monograph on the topic. Tanya Rosenthal, also a SWOP researcher during the 1990s, developed an interest in workplace restructuring. On this basis, she went on to work as a full-time official for the Chemical Workers' Industrial Union. She also served as editor of SALB and was employed by the Congress of South African Trade Unions (COSATU) as national coordinator for industrial policy. Rosenthal's trajectory shows the closeness of the relationship between SWOP and trade unions at the time. Sakhela Buhlungu, a former trade unionist and by now a staff associate of SWOP, was appointed to serve on the Labour Market Commission, a body set up by the new democratic government to consider labour law and labour market reforms.

The early 1990s also saw the transition of formerly state socialist countries to market-based economies. The leading theorist of these transitions, Adam Przeworski, argued that countries where there was a pact between old and new elites tended to be more successful but these pacts were essentially conservative in nature. Landmark work provided a conceptual challenge to this prevailing theory of democratic transition, with Eddie Webster and Glenn Adler (Adler and Webster, 1995; Webster and Adler, 1999) arguing that the strength of the labour movement in South Africa had the potential to push through a programme of radical reform, rather than an elite pact. This led to a fierce debate in South Africa and beyond, with SWOP being accused of turning from 'intellectual' to 'salesman'– the organization was losing its critical edge and was sailing too close to government power, some argued (see, for example, Desai and Bohmke, 1997). In 1996, SWOP was granted unit status by the national science body, the Centre for Science Development. Webster had successfully garnered additional resources, both within the university and through external funding, and he was able to employ one or two researchers and to finance graduate students whose research topics meshed with SWOP's research interests and who were attracted by its political engagement. At the same time, SWOP increasingly undertook research projects for government departments, primarily the Department of Labour, which was understood to be implementing a progressive agenda.

If the 1990s was a period of transition to democracy, the late 1990s and 2000s can be considered a period of democratic consolidation – but a consolidation undermined by the neoliberal orientation of the ANC government. A new labour dispensation, to which SWOP had contributed (including the idea of workplace forums, an attempt to introduce German-style co-determination in the workplace), ran up against a process of rapid trade liberalization and the decimation of jobs in the manufacturing sector. Much of SWOP's work responded to this 'triple transition' – a simultaneous process of political democratization, economic liberalization and need for racial redress (von Holdt, 2003). How did restructuring in the economy impact on attempts to reconstruct workplaces? The concept 'apartheid workplace regime' (von Holdt, 2003) was central to much of this work, with numerous detailed ethnographic case studies tracking attempts to create a new workplace order (Webster and von Holdt, 2005). The idea of an apartheid workplace regime drew on Marxist labour process theory, but attempted to localize the theory by taking into consideration South African history and conditions. In response to new labour laws and economic pressure, many South African firms had started to turn permanently employed positions into casualized jobs through subcontracting or short-term contracts. During this period, SWOP was breaking fresh intellectual ground with research into deindustrialization, outsourcing and informalization (Mosoetsa, 2011) as well as public sector unionism, and it began to conceptualize the emergence of new forms of work as well as incipient organizational innovations in attempting to challenge negative conditions.

The location in the university of a politically engaged entity like SWOP, with its collaboration with working-class and popular movements, is not an easy one. Universities generally are rather conservative and hierarchical institutions with strong stakes in the prevailing order of things. Webster and his colleagues' commitment to systemic change and their willingness to work with subaltern organizations made them many enemies in the university. At the same time, SWOP's strong credibility and the quality of its work were an asset to the university. In his chapter in this volume, Webster mentions a particularly bruising moment in SWOP's history, namely attempts in 2000 by SWOP staff and associates to reverse a decision by the University of the Witwatersrand Council to outsource the institution's cleaning, grounds, catering, transport and maintenance functions. Our studies had shown that the consequences of outsourcing and other forms of subcontracting were dire for attempts to reconstruct the labour market and efforts to dismantle the apartheid workplace regime. Often outsourcing was legitimated in the language of market efficiency, but in reality it meant reducing wages and dismantling the ability of trade unions to represent the most vulnerable segments of the labour market effectively (see Kenny and Webster, 1998; Kenny and Bezuidenhout, 1999a, 1999b).

A number of SWOP researchers (including Sakhela Buhlungu and Bridget Kenny), along with colleagues from the sociology and politics departments, informally constituted a group of academics (the 'concerned academics') to communicate these issues to the Wits community. Wits being an academic institution, and the concerned academics including some of the country's leading experts on labour, their intention was to use their profession to convince the University Council (the university's highest decision-making body) to apply their minds and consider a number of unintended consequences. They wrote a critique of the process that had been followed to arrive at the decision to outsource, arguing that this would 'lead to the intensification, rather than the transformation of the apartheid legacy at Wits' (Adler et al, 2000: 1). The campaign against outsourcing was framed in a language that connected the impact of outsourcing to intersections between race, class and gender and drew on von Holdt's notion of the apartheid workplace regime. The concerned academics also had informal discussions with the leadership of the National Education, Health and Allied Workers' Union (NEHAWU) as well as students who were critical of the strategy, mainly from the South African Students Congress and the Postgraduate Association. They were careful not to align themselves formally with the trade union, because this could, in the eyes of conservative colleagues, impact on their credibility.

NEHAWU members staged a number of protests, including blocking traffic in front of the university's main entrance. Students put up 610 crosses to signify the impact outsourcing would have on the workers who were about to be retrenched and re-engaged by contractors. They wrote opinion pieces in the media and briefed sympathetic journalists on the case, which led to a number of critical news reports on the events. They presented their critique to a special meeting of the Wits council, but in spite of this, the university management decided to proceed with the process. Eddie Webster was asked by the vice chancellor to discipline staff who had opposed the outsourcing of support staff. He refused, but SWOP was overlooked in the allocation of university resources. Those opposing the decision went on to document the consequences of outsourcing in academic journals (van der Walt et al, 2001; van der Walt et al, 2002; Bezuidenhout and Fakier, 2006). This chapter in SWOP's history reveals the risks associated with a critically engaged position that chooses sides – as Webster puts it, that challenges injustice in the researchers' home institution.

A particularly interesting series of surveys tells a revealing story of the changing relationship between SWOP (and other labour scholars) and the labour movement, COSATU in particular. In 1994, SWOP participated in the first of a series of longitudinal surveys of COSATU members – titled 'Taking Democracy Seriously' – which was to continue for five national parliamentary elections. The surveys were to explore empirically the relationship between participatory trade union democracy and parliamentary representative democracy. The expectation was that the tradition of participatory democracy in the labour movement would act as a check on parliamentary democracy and drive a progressive agenda of social transformation. The assumption of much of this work was that the trade union movement would remain a mobilized, militant, democratic and influential factor in the political landscape – an assumption which proved mistaken over the next decade, casting doubt on Adler and Webster's (1995) thesis regarding radical reform, mentioned earlier. The longitudinal surveys started out with close cooperation between the researchers and COSATU but ended with an acrimonious process where the labour movement was so divided and the survey had become so controversial that there was no longer any official support from union leaders.

The surveys culminated in a number of books that mapped the changes in the labour movement over time. The first volume represented a hopeful phase where unions would drive radical reform (Ginsburg et al, 1995). By the second survey, it was clear that COSATU was unable to assert a more progressive programme as part of an alliance with the ruling party. This led to attempts to understand why support for the ANC continued despite the ruling party's adoption of neoliberal policies (Buhlungu and Psoulis, 1999). This was followed by more cautious readings of a labour movement that was in the process of becoming compromised itself – while it still had institutional influence, it was losing organizational power (Buhlungu, 2006; Buhlungu and Tshoaedi, 2013). The publication of Sakhela Buhlungu's (2010) groundbreaking monograph on COSATU – where he analyzed what he called the 'paradox of victory', the problem of how institutionalized democracy had demobilized and compromised the labour movement – led to COSATU openly attacking him in the media.

At the time, in response to a feminist critique of labour studies more generally, Malehoko Tshoaedi took up the matter of lack of representation of women in leadership positions in trade unions, even in unions with majority-female membership. The surveys showed clearly that support for the ANC among union members was significantly lower among women in COSATU, especially after Jacob Zuma was elected as ANC president at the party's national conference in Polokwane in 2007. COSATU played an active role in backing Zuma, who was the subject of an accusation of rape that had gone to trial at the time. The final and last survey happened before the elections in 2014. By this time, it was impossible to get agreement from COSATU for their members to participate in the survey. The researchers used their links to individual unions in order to gain access to workplaces for interviews with union members. On conclusion of the survey, it had not been possible to present the findings to a meeting convened by COSATU before survey findings went public, as had been the tradition. Instead, in an attempt to remain impartial, the research team resorted to presentations on two separate occasions at the head offices of two of the major unions on opposing sides, as well as a follow-up presentation at the request of individual unions. However, despite efforts to mediate, COSATU's leadership at the time refused to meet in the same room. Shortly afterwards, COSATU split in two when its metal union was expelled and then formed a rival federation. The last volume to be published on the basis of the surveys presents an analysis of reasons for the fracturing of COSATU (Bezuidenhout and Tshoaedi, 2017).

Throughout, labour scholars attempted to maintain their link with the labour movement in the form of COSATU. As Buhlungu points out in his contribution to this volume, the relationship was less complicated and could be characterized as a form of close engagement when the movement was strong and internal democracy thrived. When scholars became more critical and pointed to fractures in democratic processes, the relationship became more strained, to the point where the research itself was so politicized and contested that the relationship with the federation broke down. This illustrates the level of difficulty when working with movements during a transition process. In addition to participating in the nationwide survey with a broader network of labour-linked scholars, SWOP did work for individual unions. This included supporting union members in formulating a response to an investigation into racial discrimination in a mining company (for the National Union of Mineworkers – NUM), an analysis of unions' internal job grading systems (for the Chemical, Energy, Paper, Printing, Wood and Allied Workers' Union), the formulation of industrial policy for specific industrial sectors (for example, for the National Union of Metalworkers of South Africa – NUMSA) and, most importantly, attempts to understand unions' servicing of their members (from the NUM and NUMSA). This kind of research gave SWOP researchers direct access to the internal dynamics of trade unions, but it also tested the limits of critical engagement.

A particularly interesting set of investigations involved research for NUM on the quality of the union's services to its members. This project turned out to be a repeat engagement involving large-scale surveys using semi-structured interviews with members in various regions followed by focus groups in branches selected on the basis of the survey findings (Bezuidenhout et al, 1998; Bezuidenhout et al, 2005; Bezuidenhout et al, 2010). There was formal agreement between SWOP and the NUM that academic articles could be published in the basis of the research, but these were to be run past the general secretary of the union for approval prior to publication (examples include Buhlungu and Bezuidenhout, 2007, 2008; Bezuidenhout and Buhlungu, 2011). There was never any attempt by the NUM to block publication, but with later investigations, the union became reluctant to include the clause in the contract on independent academic publications. The union only agreed after SWOP communicated that the clause would be a precondition for conducting the research.

The background and context of this tension between commissioned research and academic publication is explored in depth in Webster's chapter in this volume. The researchers were careful to not reinforce what was known (in the North American literature at the time) as the 'servicing model' of trade unionism as opposed to the 'organising model' of unionism. The reports underscored the fact that members rated services higher in branches with strong cultures of internal democracy, even in cases where technical servicing levels were relatively weak as compared to other branches. So servicing, in the SWOP reports, was also a matter of solidarity and democracy. The findings highlighted aspects that negatively impacted on the traditional basis of solidarity within the NUM. These aspects included the rise of subcontracting, illegal mining, the fact that workers were moving out of mine compounds (dormitory-style, single-sex accommodation) and into informal settlements, making it more difficult to organize them, and the fact that the union's internal culture often marginalized and excluded women members. It also pointed to the rise of a class of unaccountable officials who used their positions for corrupt means. An issue that became controversial after the Marikana massacre was the fact that reports consistently highlighted the Marikana region (Rustenburg) as being particularly weak (see Bezuidenhout et al, 1998; Bezuidenhout et al, 2005; Bezuidenhout et al, 2010).

As pointed out in von Holdt's chapter, the massacre was in response to a violent strike by workers in the platinum mines against their union, the NUM, and their employer. Rather than investigating and arresting striking workers who had committed murder (of an NUM office-bearer, police officers and fellow workers suspected of being management and police informants) during the strike, on 16 August 2012 the police opened fire on the workers indiscriminately, killing some who were fleeing, execution style. The shocking reality is that this crime was perpetrated by the police of a democratically elected government, not by the apartheid state. It also graphically illustrates the direct links that had been established between trade unions, the ANC as ruling party, corporate mining interests and the state. The person of Cyril Ramaphosa loomed large – he was a former general secretary of the NUM, a major shareholder in Lonmin (platinum mining corporation) the ANC's deputy president (Forrest, 2015). These contradictions and tensions directly contributed to the split in COSATU.

How does one classify this engagement with the NUM that stretched over many decades? It contained an element of 'public sociology', since the research was intended to contribute to a movement – a union that had played a key role in the demise of apartheid and breaking down barriers to the advancement of their members in the workplace. The research was discussed in the media after the tragic events at Marikana. But it was also, technically speaking, 'policy sociology', since the research was commissioned by the NUM. It contained elements of 'professional sociology', since the research was based on rigorous survey methods, triangulated with qualitative methods such as focus groups. The findings were published in quality academic journals. At the theoretical level, these findings were firmly located in the field of 'critical sociology' or even the critical tradition of geography. These distinctions drawn from Burawoy's conception of sociology do not really capture this type of research engagement between SWOP and what remains one of South Africa's most significant trade unions. As a process of critical engagement, it raises all the complexities associated with the practice. What are the implications when trade union members abandon their own union? As a political choice, where do we position ourselves as researchers? There was a commission of enquiry into the reasons for the massacre, and former SWOP researchers assisted the lawyers of both the NUM and the new rival union in preparation of their cases. Can one really talk about the co-production of knowledge when the community is so fraught with divisions and its own internal power struggles? Several of the chapters in this volume address this dilemma directly, also in the context and aftermath of Marikana.

The research for NUM highlighted the plight of women mineworkers. Due to an equity-driven commitment that mining companies made in order to meet targets set by a transformational mining charter they had agreed to, there was a process of employing more female mineworkers to do underground work alongside men. Inspired by feminist approaches to labour markets, SWOP intern Asanda Benya (2009, 2016) took this up as a research topic and did an ethnographic study of women working underground. In addition to highlighting company practices that did not support women, this work also exposed the union's own role in reinforcing a macho occupational culture. Benya went on to switch her focus to the construction of femininities by women who worked underground, qualifying as a mineworker herself in order to immerse herself in the working culture.

Benya's research echoed SWOP's critique of looking at industries dominated by men, mainly manufacturing and mining. Already in the 1990s, SWOP researcher Bridget Kenny had undertaken research on casualization in the retail industry and developed an approach inspired by feminist approaches to labour markets and social reproduction in order to link the domain of production to social reproduction (see Kenny, 1998; Kenny and Webster, 1998). The increase in unemployment following South Africa's 'shock treatment' liberalization of trade in the late 1990s as well as the rapid processes of subcontracting and casualizing work highlighted the need for an approach to trade unions, labour markets and the workplace that took household dynamics – the hidden domain of social reproduction – seriously.

In SWOP, the overall theme for this work became known as 'work and welfare', and there was a concerted attempt to understand the crisis of social reproduction in post-apartheid South Africa from the perspectives of households themselves and not only workers as seen from the vantage point of the workplace (see Fakier and Cock, 2009). Kenny's interest in labour geography and the work of Karl Polanyi became a central theoretical preoccupation in the organization. Along these lines, Sarah Mosoetsa (2011) investigated the impact on households of the demise of footwear and garment manufacturing in KwaZulu-Natal. For this, she developed a critique of sustainable livelihoods theory and presented households in former industrial areas as fragile sites of stability to which unemployed people returned. Here, people were dependent on reciprocal relationships and the sharing of welfare benefits by household members and the care work of an older generation of women. Khayaat Fakier (2009) took this topic further and investigated care work itself – how migrant women working in Johannesburg used mobile phones to keep in touch with children at home in rural KwaZulu-Natal.

Even before the events at Marikana illustrated the entanglements between the ruling party, the emerging black business elite and the labour movement, the ANC's adherence to neoliberal macroeconomic policies had brought it into conflict with COSATU as its trade union alliance partner. To better understand this, as well as potential options for the labour movement, SWOP turned its attention to relationships between other African labour formations and liberation movements that had become ruling parties. Here, SWOP partnerships with academics and trade unionists from across the continent produced an insightful collection of case studies, pointing to potential options for the labour movement (Beckmann et al, 2010). This was also part of a commitment within SWOP to try to move beyond South Africa's own exceptionalist and isolationist history – it was part of an internal critique of its own lack of engagement with the rest of the African continent. A number of SWOP studies at this time were regional in nature, comparing countries in southern Africa, but also exploring links between unions in the region as part of a broader interest in labour internationalism. In this vein, SWOP arranged field trips with postgraduate students to countries like Mozambique, Namibia and Zambia.

SWOP's relationship with the NUM also highlighted the need for an environmental focus on workers and their communities. Often, mining trade unions are at odds with the concerns and campaigns of environmental movements. In the late 1990s, for example, there was a global campaign led by a coalition of non-governmental organizations (NGOs) to drive down the cost of gold by convincing central banks to sell their gold reserves. This was aimed at opencast gold mines with grim environmental impacts as well as poor human rights records. The NUM took umbrage, because South

African gold-mining companies were laying off mineworkers. SWOP got caught up in the dispute between the NUM and this coalition at a meeting hosted by the Third World Network Africa in Ghana – the NUM did not attend, but there was a representative from SWOP, who had to bear the brunt of the disappointment with the union. This illustrates again the difficulties in a critically engaged position. Jacklyn Cock explores this tension between labour and environmental movements in more detail in her chapter in this volume. In the early 2000s, SWOP was commissioned by the United Nations Research Institute for Social Development to conduct an important large-scale investigation into corporate social and environmental responsibility. The project was led by David Fig, a SWOP staff associate and member of the sociology department at Wits. This study culminated in a series of research reports, public engagements on the topic and a book (see Fig, 2007). SWOP's increased focus on environmental concerns was also due to the presence and increased involvement of Jacklyn Cock. This entirely fresh field of investigation of the relations between society and nature was reinforced when Cock, a long-standing colleague of Webster in the sociology department, joined SWOP as an honorary research associate, focusing her work on the 'slow violence' of environmental pollution in the steel industry (Cock, 2013) and broader questions about the relationship between society and nature (Cock, 2007, 2019).

During the same period, SWOP members started participating systematically in the International Sociological Association, specifically the Research Committee on Labour Movements (RC44), with the goal of mobilizing and increasing participation from fellow countries of the Global South and reinvigorating and radicalizing what was a rather staid committee focused on European industrial relations. Webster was elected secretary in 1998 and President in 2002, during which time he led a process of broadening its scope and ultimately, together with Robert O'Brien (McMaster University, Canada), co-founded the online *Global Labour Journal*. The idea was to globalize the tradition of the *South African Labour Bulletin* and for the new journal to be a meeting place for labour-linked scholars and trade unions who were interested in how to globalize trade unionism as a response to ecological crisis and neoliberal globalization. In line with these concerns, as well as SWOP's participation in the Global Labour University programme – a transnational effort to explore, alongside trade unions, this global response – Webster's own work took on an increasingly international comparative perspective over this period. This culminated with *Grounding Globalisation: Labour in the Age of Insecurity* (2008), co-authored with SWOP associate Rob Lambert from the University of Western Australia and SWOP researcher Andries Bezuidenhout. The book was awarded the American Sociological Association's labour studies scholarly book award in 2009. It was described as taking a major step towards theorising the place of the South within a world order dominated by the North. ... Through historical and cross-national comparisons, it provides the basis of a sociology for the South. ... A sociology that can excite sociologists from Europe and North America as well as from Asia, Africa and Latin America, but a sociology that never forgets its political origins and its political context. (Burawoy, 2010: 22–3)

The *Global Labour Journal* and *Labor History* dedicated special editions to discussion of the book. We should mention here that *Grounding Globalisation's* main concern is the South as *political* terrain, rather than original *theory* from the Global South – its engagement is firmly with Marxist and Polanyian theory, although the concluding chapter explores Rick Turner's idea of utopian thinking; critics of the book, including Burawoy, found the latter least convincing.

For much of the 1990s and the 2000s, SWOP's research agenda could be characterized by four main themes:

- a continued focus on the labour movement in the form of organized labour;
- a focus on various forms of workplace restructuring, including attempts to reconstruct the apartheid workplace regime in a post-apartheid era, but also setbacks for this project, such as the rise of new forms of workplace authoritarianism and the use of subcontracting, casualization and informalized work practices;
- an interest in and focus on work and welfare, meaning various investigations into how the restructured economy impacted on households an communities, including an understanding of new forms of state welfare, such as child support grants, disability grants and public works programmes designed to alleviate poverty;
- an increased focus on ecological and environmental concerns, including tensions between the labour movement and the environmental movement, but also a political economy approach – that is, a critical approach – to corporate social and environmental responsibility programmes.

There were clearly theoretical and thematic overlaps between these themes, and at times individual SWOP staff members or associates were actively involved in all four via simultaneous projects. We should mention here that SWOP was but one example of a number of labour-linked research entities in the country at the time and formed part of a South African and international community of scholars. This is also the point at which Wiebke Keim published her analysis of South African labour studies as an example of a counter-hegemonic strand of sociology.

After Marikana: beyond labour

The massacre in 2012 of striking mineworkers at Lonmin's Marikana mine was a turning point in South African history. The chapters by Karl von Holdt and Sonwabile Mnwana in this volume provide more detail on this massacre and its historical context. In the aftermath, SWOP research on the NUM became controversial, because it showed that the NUM had been aware of many of the internal problems that led to their members abandoning them and joining a rival union. The union leadership was offended by the fact that it was not prominently pointed out that they had themselves commissioned the research. Moreover, two PhD students at SWOP, Crispen Chinguno and Asanda Benya – working, respectively, on autonomous workers strikes in the platinum mines that rejected the union and on women working underground – were presenting highly critical perspectives in public. The NUM called SWOP into a meeting of their National Executive Committee and expressed their frustration that we had not publicly defended them in the aftermath of the massacre. They felt our presentations at SWOP breakfasts and opinion pieces in the media were skewed against them. The relationship has never been repaired. The NUM approached another research organization for a subsequent project on servicing. Another interesting twist to the tale is that French researcher Raphaël Botiveau (2018) also blamed SWOP for the NUM's demise, arguing that the research on servicing was part of the NUM's drift towards communist-style democratic centralism – that union democracy had come to be driven by research rather than the needs of membership. He also argued that SWOP had a romantic view of unions during the 1980s and that many of the authoritarian and corrupt tendencies had precedents that went further back than the 1990s and 2000s. This critique points (whether it is true or not in this specific case) towards an occupational hazard of critical engagement – the danger that researchers are 'captured' by specific interests in the union or community, potentially blinding them to alternative analyses.

As Webster neared retirement, it became clear that there was resistance in the university to granting SWOP institute status, which would ensure its continuity. The context to this resistance was the critical position SWOP took on matters of internal university restructuring, including the controversial decision to outsource support staff. After contesting this internal resistance, SWOP was granted provisional institute status in 2007, dependent on raising funds for a full-time director. Then Sakhela Buhlungu, SWOP director and head of the sociology department, left the university after serious conflict with the hierarchy over racial discrimination. In 2008, Webster retired, and after an uncertain transition Karl von Holdt was appointed the first full-time director. SWOP was confirmed as an institute and renamed the Society, Work and Development Institute, joining the ranks of the pre-eminent academic research entities at the university. This meant that SWOP was no longer located in the sociology department, but reported directly to the dean of the Faculty of Humanities. In 2018, SWOP was renamed the Society, Work and Politics Institute, a closer match to its research programme and realigned with its four-decades-old acronym!

In the second decade of the 21st century, SWOP's focus underwent a series of significant shifts. The earlier optimism about democratization, transformation and trade unionism was replaced with a darker analysis of state corruption (von Holdt, 2019), violence (von Holdt, 2014b; Idrissa, 2018), ongoing accumulation by dispossession, rampant environmental degradation and the sclerosis of democratic trade unionism. Subaltern organizations were not exempt from these critiques, as research found that both shop stewards and the leadership of community protests were involved in corrupt patronage networks (von Holdt et al, 2011; Langa and von Holdt, 2012; Chinguno, 2015. There was a decrease in research on trade unions, partly because of the more fraught relations discussed in this chapter and in the chapters by Buhlungu and von Holdt, but also because they had lost their status as centres of social innovation and of the struggle for change. Instead, the focus changed to urban protest movements in South Africa (von Holdt et al, 2011; von Holdt and Naidoo, 2019) and across the BRICS[3] countries (Nilsen and von Holdt, 2019), environmental movements, rural communities and the new frontiers of mining in the former bantustans, which were still ruled by rural chiefs. In recognition of the broadening of SWOP's research horizons since 2008, as well as these more recent shifts, the newly established institute attempted to frame these multiple foci as a conceptual concern with 'the making and unmaking of social order' in a 'precarious society'. It was also during this period that SWOP formally committed itself to 'generating' and 'problematising' a 'Southern perspective' on 'society, work and precariousness' (SWOP, 2012), thereby signalling more explicit theoretical ambitions.

With regard to mining, two new research projects shifted the focus towards emerging forms of urbanization, rural struggles, land dispossessions and new forms of rural differentiation that emerged as mining capital expanded into the former 'homeland' areas, which increasingly became the new mining frontiers in the southern African region. Karl von Holdt and Dunbar Moodie led a series of studies on community formation, spatial reorganization, environmental degradation, retrenchments and workplace change (Moodie and von Holdt, 2015), funded by the National Research Foundation, while Gavin Capps and Sonwabile Mnwana led research teams investigating case studies of different communities on South Africa's platinum belt, where contestations over land, power and mining revenues intensified in the context of mining activities under the auspices of the Mining and Rural Transformation in Southern Africa project funded by the Ford

Foundation (Mnwana, 2014, 2015; Capps, 2015, 2016, 2018; Mnwana, 2014, 2015; Mnwana and Capps, 2015; Beinart et al, 2021). This work primarily explored the evolving patterns of the new rural struggles erupting across the platinum belt and hypothesized that the forms these were taking were profoundly shaped by the specific local and regional land, and social and political histories.

The chapters by von Holdt and Mnwana in this volume detail how the research on mining and rural struggles contributed to supporting litigation and advocacy work. This was an entirely new arena for critical engagement, structured by the intersection of multiple political fields – the legal field, the field of bantustan politics (which involved both the traditional chiefly authorities and the local and provincial states) and the field of corporate economic power – in contrast to the relatively simple arena of industrial relations in which critical engagement was forged. The socially engaged approach to research located SWOP within strong collaborative networks with other research institutes such as the Land and Accountability Research Centre (LARC; see the chapter by Claassens and Sihlali), NGOs and grassroots movements working on defending land rights of the rural poor against mining capital and unaccountable local chiefs on the platinum belt. Carefully researched local histories were published in working papers that documented and affirmed local 'truths', claims and struggles, and these papers were launched and widely distributed in rural villages. Some of this research played critically important roles in landmark legal cases. As discussed also in the chapter by Claassens and Sihlali, support for social justice and mobilization work receives very little affirmation and support from the university. The dominant liberal university approach to knowledge production perceives critically engaged research as a diversion from scientific scholarly accomplishment. SWOP and LARC, on the other hand, have always maintained that the interface between scholarly research and social activism is essential for generating quality sociological knowledge and conceptual innovation.

In line with the central role played by mining in South Africa's economic development and political economy, this emphasis on the transformations wrought by the rapid expansion of platinum mining in the bantustans was joined by fresh research on coal mining, the environmental degradation of farmland, water and rural livelihoods, and pathways to a 'just transition' from coal to a low-carbon future. This work was explored in an innovative series of discussions with communities dependent on livelihoods associated with coal mining, as discussed in the chapter in this volume by Jacklyn Cock (see also Forrest and Loate, 2017; Cock, 2019; Munnik, 2019; Skosana, 2019).

In a final twist to the expanding sites of experimentation with critical engagement, SWOP's offer to provide support to militant black students who emerged in the form of a new movement, #FeesMustFall, was treated with a great deal of scepticism and gave rise a critique of SWOP's position in the hierarchy of the university structured by coloniality and white male power. In the end, the support was accepted but students took full control of the project to produce a publication documenting their experiences, thus appropriating and recasting the production of knowledge to exclude the academic interlocutor. This turn in the experience of supporting the struggle against injustice in our own institution was doubly salutary in that the students won the reinstatement of outsourced workers through their mobilization and commitment, in stark contrast to the contestation of outsourcing by the 'concerned academics' two decades before.

As we have noted, there was within SWOP more concerted engagement with the notion of 'Southern theory' and a concomitant critique of what was argued to be 'Northern theory'. Emergent concepts included 'violent democracy' (von Holdt, 2013a, 2014a, 2018), 'informal political systems' of patronage, factionalism and violence (von Holdt, 2019), 'movement landscapes' (von Holdt and Naidoo, 2019) and the 'dual nature of protest' (Langa and von Holdt, 2012), exploring the contradictory combination of popular mobilization and elite class formation. Cock embarked on a reworking of the concept of a 'just transition' – which in its Northern origins took a narrow, reformist and technicist form – to give it a more radical focus on eco-socialist transformation while exploring the modalities of such a transition (Cock, 2018, 2019) in the face of complex union and community implication in (often minor) benefits from the expansion of coal mining (Cock, this volume; see also Munnik, 2019; Skosana, 2019). Innovative reconstructions of Marxist theory were undertaken in relation to landed property (Capps, 2016, 2018) and in relation to an intriguing staging of a series of 'conversations' with Bourdieusian concepts (Burawoy and von Holdt, 2012; von Holdt 2013b, 2018).

Conclusion

In the international division of intellectual labour, due to continued resource scarcity in much of the underdeveloped world, former colonies are often still studied from the Global North. South Africa, in contrast, has succeeded in establishing a certain density insofar as its sociological community is concerned. You cannot study South African society from elsewhere without engaging with South African scholarship. We started this chapter with a brief discussion of Wiebke Keim's argument that South African labour studies represents an example of counter-hegemonic sociology in that it built up, over time, a rich tradition and a measure of research density. This allowed the South African sociological community to impact beyond its borders. The aim of this chapter was to illustrate this through a historical survey of

SWOP's research engagement. Some of SWOP's research output has received international recognition and continues to be taken up in global scholarship.

But, as Keim also recognizes, the story is more complicated than one of Southern theory that challenges Northern understandings. In its early days, SWOP's research projects localized Northern theory and in some instances was able to speak back, and it was recognized for that. Over time, the institute's researchers became more critical of that endeavour. Dominant critical theories, Marxism in particular, were not always able to adequately deal with changing local realities around the racial and gendered contours of disadvantage and how these intersected with class. Feminist theories became more central to the programme. The institute had to radically rethink its position, also because its relationships with the labour movement as historical partner became increasingly strained. While attempting to maintain those links, the institute broadened its research focus in order to understand a rapidly changing South African social order. Northern theories could no longer just be localized, and the institute actively sought out partnerships with colleagues facing similar challenges in other parts of the Global South. Furthermore, South Africa's contours of power and disadvantage were (and still are) reflected in knowledge production, obviously in mainstream sociology but also in the critical and liberation tradition. We mentioned in the introduction to this volume how, due to the fragmented nature of the South African academy, important black South African intellectuals are not always taken up in debates, as reflected in institutionalized sociology. The fact that South Africa's elite universities developed to serve the needs of the settler colonial population still defines much of the discipline's current sensibilities, including those at Wits.

For scholarship in fractured societies like ours, the challenge of finding appropriate theoretical tools is not an academic game, but a matter of wanting to better understand and capture the traumatic transformations that South African society is undergoing. Often, hegemonic theories of the North, even from critical traditions, are not able to capture those realities. SWOP's positioning of itself as an institute committed to building theory from the South was not a moment, but a process. It moved from an early tradition inspired by Marxist thought and concepts to later attempts to take seriously white domination and black resistance to this in the workplace and society. There were constant feminist critiques in the context of patriarchal silencing. Also, the institute actively attempted to break South Africa's settler colonial structures of higher education, seeking to expand its research links and connections to the rest of the African continent. Our attempts at critically engaging colleagues, movements and publics remain works in progress. More importantly, we hope that we are able to find a more accurate conceptual language to express our reality and the world we inhabit, study and are committed to change. This includes how we understand our own attempts to move beyond the academic space into the terrain of the political. We hope that this volume contributes to this ongoing engagement with Northern perspectives from the vantage point of one place and its connections to both the North and elsewhere in the South.

Notes

[1]   Burawoy (2010) provides a vivid and insightful account of Webster's career as a politically engaged academic, and of SWOP's rich intellectual contribution (see also Webster's own contribution to this volume).

[2]   Human immunodeficiency virus/acquired immune deficiency syndrome.

[3]   Brazil, Russia, India, China and South Africa.

References

Adler, G. and Webster, E. (1995) 'Challenging transition theory: The labor movement, radical reform, and transition to democracy in South Africa', *Politics & Society*, 3(1): 75–106.

Adler, G., Bezuidenhout, A., Buhlungu, S., Kenny, B., Omar, R., Ruiters, G. and van der Walt, L. (2000) *The Wits University Support Services Review: A Critique*, https://lucienvanderwalt.files.wordpress.com/2013/03/adler-bezuidenhout-buhlungu-kenny-omar-ruiters-van-der-walt-the-wits-university-support-services-review-a-critique-doc.pdf

Beckman, B., Buhlungu, S. and Sachikonye, L. (eds) (2010) *Trade Unions & Party Politics: Labour Movements in Africa*, Cape Town: HSRC Press.

Beinart, W., Kingwill, R. and Capps, G. (eds) (2021) *Land, Law and Chiefs in Rural South Africa: Contested Histories and Current Struggles*, Johannesburg: Wits University Press.

Benya, A. (2009) *Women in Mining: A Challenge to Occupational Culture in Mines*, Master's dissertation, Department of Sociology, University of the Witwatersrand, Johannesburg, South Africa.

Benya, A. (2016) *Women in Mining: Occupational Culture and Gendered Identities in the Making*, PhD thesis, Department of Sociology, University of the Witwatersrand, Johannesburg, South Africa.

Bezuidenhout, A. and Fakier, K. (2006) 'Maria's burden: Contract cleaning and the crisis of social reproduction in post-apartheid South Africa', *Antipode*, 38(3): 463–86.

Bezuidenhout, A. and Buhlungu, S. (2011) 'From compounded to fragmented labour: Mineworkers and the demise of compounds in South Africa', *Antipode*, 43(2): 237–63.

Bezuidenhout, A. and Tshoaedi, M. (eds) (2017) *Labour beyond COSATU: Mapping the Rupture in South Africa's Labour Landscape*, Johannesburg: Wits University Press.

Bezuidenhout, A., Kenny, B., Masha, G. and Tshikalange, H. (1998) *A Strong Branch is a Strong Union: Servicing the National Union of Mineworkers*, research report commissioned by the National Union of Mineworkers, Johannesburg: Sociology of Work Unit, University of the Witwatersrand, and National Union of Mineworkers.

Bezuidenhout, A., Buhlungu, S., Hlela, H., Modisha, G. and Sikwebu, D. (2005) *Members First: A Research Report on the State of Servicing in the National Union of Mineworkers*, research report commissioned by the National Union of Mineworkers. Johannesburg: Sociology of Work Unit, University of the Witwatersrand.

Bezuidenhout, A., Bischoff, C. and Masondo, T. (2010) *Meeting Expectations? A Research Report on the State of Servicing in the National Union of Mineworkers*, Johannesburg: Society, Work and Development Institute, University of the Witwatersrand.

Botiveau, R. (2018) *Organise or Die? Democracy and Leadership in South Africa's National Union of Mineworkers*, Johannesburg: University of the Witwatersrand Press.

Braverman, H. (1974) *Labor and Monopoly Capital: The Degradation of Work in the Twentieth Century*, New York: Monthly Review Press.

Buhlungu, S. (2006) *Trade Unions and Democracy: COSATU Workers' Political Attitudes in South Africa*, Pretoria: HSRC Press.

Buhlungu, S. (2010) *A Paradox of Victory: COSATU and the Democratic Transformation in South Africa,* Durban: University of KwauZulu-Natal Press.

Buhlungu, S. and Psoulis, C. (1999) 'Enduring solidarities: Accounting for the continuity of support for the alliance amongst COSATU members', *Society in Transition*, 30(2): 120–30.

Buhlungu, S. and Metcalfe, A. (2001) 'Breaking the racial division of labour in knowledge production: Reflections on internship programmes', *Perspectives in Education*, 19(2): 67–84.

Buhlungu, S. and Bezuidenhout, A. (2007) 'Old victories, new struggles: The state of the National Union of Mineworkers', in Sakhela Buhlungu, John Daniel, Jessica Lutchman and Roger Southall (eds) *State of the Nation, South Africa 2007*, Pretoria: HSRC Press, pp 245–65.

Buhlungu, S. and Bezuidenhout, A. (2008) 'Union solidarity under stress: The case of the National Union of Mineworkers in South Africa', *Labor Studies Journal*, 33(3): 262–87.

Buhlungu, S. and Tshoaedi, M. (2013) *COSATU'S Contested Legacy: South African Trade Unions in the Second Decade of Democracy*, Johannesburg: Wits University Press.

Burawoy, M. (1979) *Manufacturing Consent: Changes in the Labor Process Under Monopoly Capitalism*, Chicago: University of Chicago Press.

Burawoy, M. (2010) 'Southern windmill: The life and work of Edward Webster', *Transformation: Critical Perspectives on Southern Africa*, 72: 1–25.

Burawoy, M. and von Holdt, K. (2012) *Conversations with Bourdieu: The Johannesburg Moment*, Johannesburg: Wits University Press.

Capps, G. (2015) 'Labour in the time of platinum', *Review of African Political Economy*, 42(146): 497–507.

Capps, G. (2016) 'Tribal-landed property: The value of the chieftaincy in contemporary Africa', *The Journal of Agrarian Change*, 16(3): 452–77.

Capps, G. (2018) 'Custom and exploitation: Rethinking the origins of the modern African chieftaincy in the political economy of colonialism', *The Journal of Peasant Studies*, 45(5–6): 969–93.

Chinguno, C. (2015) *The Shifting Dynamics of the Relations between Institutionalization and Strike Violence: A Case Study of Impala Platinum, Rustenburg, 1982–2012*, PhD thesis, University of the Witwatersrand, Johannesburg, South Africa.

Cock, J. (2007) *War Against Ourselves: Nature, Power and Justice*, Johannesburg: Wits University Press.

Cock, J. (2018) 'The climate crisis and a "just transition" in South Africa: An eco-feminist-socialist perspective', in Vishwas Satgar (ed) *The Climate Crisis: South African and Global Democratic Eco-socialist Alternatives*, Johannesburg: Wits University Press, pp 210–30.

Cock, J. (2019) *Resistance to Coal and the Possibilities of a Just Transition in South Africa*, Working Paper 13, Johannesburg: Society, Work and Politics Institute, University of the Witwatersrand.

Cock, J., Lambert, R. and Fitzgerald, S. (2013) 'Steel, nature and society', *Globalizations*, 10(6): 855–69.

Desai, A. and Bohmke, H. (1997) 'The death of the intellectual, the birth of the salesman: The South African intellectual during the democratic transition', *Debate*, 3: 10–34.

Edwards, R. (1979) *Contested Terrain: The Transformation of the Workplace in the Twentieth Century*, New York: Basic Books.

Fakier, K. (2009) *The Impact of Migration on Emnambithi Households: A Class and Gender Analysis*, PhD thesis, Department of Sociology, University of the Witwatersrand, Johannesburg, South Africa.

Fakier, K. and Cock, J. (2009) 'A gendered analysis of the crisis of social reproduction in contemporary South Africa', *International Feminist Journal of Politics*, 11(3): 353–71.

Fig, D. (2007) *Staking their Claims: Corporate Social and Environmental Responsibility in South Africa*, Durban: University of KwaZulu-Natal Press.

Forrest, K. (2015) *Marikana Commission: Unearthing the Truth, or Burying It?* Working Paper 5, Johannesburg: Society, Work and Development Institute, Wits University.

Forrest, K. and Loate, L. (2017) *Coal, Water and Mining Flowing Badly*, Working Paper 9, Johannesburg: Society, Work and Development Institute, University of the Witwatersrand.

Friedman, A. (1977) *Industry and Labour: Class Struggle at Work and Monopoly Capitalism*, London: Macmillan.

Ginsburg, D., Webster, E., Southall, R., Wood, G., Buhlungu, S., Maree, J., Cherry, J., Haines, R. and Klerck, G. (1995) *Taking Democracy Seriously: Worker Expectations and Parliamentary Democracy in South Africa*, Durban: Indicator Press.

Idrissa, R. (2017) *The Politics of Islam in the Sahel: Between Persuasion and Violence*, New York: Routledge.

Keim, W. (2011) 'Counterhegemonic currents and internationalization of sociology: Theoretical reflections and an empirical example', *International Sociology*, 26(1): 123–45.

Keim, W. (2017) *Universally Comprehensible, Arrogantly Local: South African Labour Studies from the Apartheid Era into the New Millennium* (translated form German by Margaret Hiley), Paris: Editions des Archives Comtemporaines.

Kenny, B. (1998) 'The casualisation of the retail sector in South Africa', *Indicator South Africa*, 15(4): 25–31.

Kenny, B. and Bezuidenhout, A. (1999a) 'Contracting, complexity and control: An overview of the changing nature of subcontracting in the South African mining industry', *Journal of the South African Institute of Mining and Metallurgy*, 99(4): 185–91.

Kenny, B. and Bezuidenhout, A. (1999b) 'Fighting subcontracting: Legal protections and negotiating strategies', *South African Labour Bulletin*, 23(3): 39–46.

Kenny, B. and Webster, E. (1998) 'Eroding the core: Flexibility and the re-segmentation of the South African labour market', *Critical Sociology*, 24(3): 216–43.

Langa, M. and von Holdt, K. (2012) 'Insurgent citizenship, class formation and the dual nature of a community protest: A case study of "kungcatsha"', in Marcelle Dawson and Luke Sinwel (eds) *Contesting Transformation: Popular Resistance in Twenty-first Century South Africa*, London: Pluto Press, pp 80–100.

Leger, J.-P. (1985) *Towards Safer Underground Gold Mining: An Investigation Commissioned by the National Union of Mineworkers*, Labour Studies Research Report 1, Johannesburg: Sociology of Work Programme, University of the Witwatersrand.

Leger, J.-P. (1992) *'Talking Rocks': An Investigation of the Pit Sense of Rockfall Accidents amongst Underground Gold Miners*, PhD dissertation, University of the Witwatersrand, Johannesburg, South Africa.

Maller, J. (1992) *Conflict and Co-operation: Case Studies in Worker Participation*, Johannesburg: Ravan Press.

Metcalfe, A. and Cock, J. (2010) 'Public sociology and the transformation of the university', *Transformation: Critical Perspectives on Southern Africa*, 72: 66–85.

Mnwana, S. (2014) 'Mining, accountability and the law in the Bakgatla-ba-Kgafela Traditional Authority Area', *South African Crime Quarterly*, 49(1): 21–9.

Mnwana, S. (2015) 'Mining and "community" struggles on the platinum belt: A case of Sefikile village in the North West Province, South Africa', *The Extractive Industries and Society*, 3: 500–8.

Mnwana, S. and Capps, G. (2015) *'No Chief Ever Bought a Piece of Land!' Struggles over Property, Community and Mining in the Bakgatla-ba-Kgafela Traditional Authority Area, North West Province*, Working Paper 3, Johannesburg: Society, Work and Development Institute, University of the Witwatersrand, South Africa.

Moodie, T.D. and von Holdt, K. (2015) 'Introduction to the special issue: New frontiers of mining in South Africa', *Labour Capital and Society*, 48(1&2): 2–9.

Mosoetsa, S. (2011) *Eating from One Pot: The Dynamics of Survival in Poor South African Households*, Johannesburg: Wits University Press.

Munnik, V. (2019) *Coal Kills: An Analytic Framework to Support a Move Away from Coal and Towards a Just Transition in South Africa*, Working Paper 12, Johannesburg: Society, Work and Politics Institute, University of the Witwatersrand.

Nilsen, A.G. and von Holdt, K. (2019) 'Rising powers, people rising: Neo-liberalization and its discontents in the BRICS countries', *Globalizations*, 16(2): 121–36.

Skosana, D. (2019) *Grave Matters: Dispossession and the Desecration of Ancestral Graves by Mining Corporations in Tweefontein (Ogies), South Africa*, Working Paper 11, Johannesburg: Society, Work and Politics Institute, University of the Witwatersrand.

SWOP (Society, Work and Politics Institute) (2012) 'Vision & goals' [policy document], Johannesburg: University of the Witwatersrand.

Turner, R. (1972) *The Eye of the Needle: Towards Participatory Democracy in South Africa*, Durban: SRO-CAS.

van der Walt, L., Mokoena, D. and Shange, S. (2001) 'Cleaned out: Outsourcing at Wits University', *South African Labour Bulletin*, 25(4): 54–8.

van der Walt, L., Bolsmann, C., Johnson, B. and Martin, L. (2002) *Globalisation and the Outsourced University in South Africa: The Restructuring of the Support Services in Public Sector Universities in South Africa, 1994–2001*, Pretoria: Centre for Higher Education Transformation.

von Holdt, K. (2003) *Transition from Below: Forging Trade Unionism and Workplace Change in South Africa*, Scottsville, South Africa: Natal University Press.

von Holdt, K. (2013a) 'South Africa: The transition to violent democracy', *Review of African Political Economy*, 40(138): 589–604.

von Holdt, K. (2013b) 'The violence of order, orders of violence: Between Bourdieu and Fanon', *Current Sociology*, 61(2): 112–31.

von Holdt, K. (2014a) 'Critical engagement in fields of power: Cycles of sociological activism in post-apartheid South Africa', *Current Sociology*, 62(2): 181–96.

von Holdt, K. (2014b) 'On violent democracy', *The Sociological Review*, 62(2): 129–51.

von Holdt, K. (2018) 'Reading Bourdieu in South Africa: Order meets disorder', in J. Sallaz and T. Medvetz (eds) *The Oxford Handbook of Pierre Bourdieu*, New York: Oxford University Press, pp 105–28.

von Holdt, K. (2019) *The Political Economy of Corruption: Elite-formation, factions and violence*, Working Paper 10, Johannesburg: Society, Work and Development Institute, University of the Witwatersrand.

von Holdt, K. and Naidoo, P. (2019) 'Mapping movement landscapes in South Africa', *Globalizations*, 16(2): 170–85.

von Holdt, K., Langa, M., Molapo, S., Mogapi, N., Ngubeni, K., Dlamini, J., and Kirsten, A. (2011) *The Smoke that Calls: Insurgent citizenship, collective violence and the struggle for a place in the new South Africa: Eight case studies of community protest and xenophobic violence*, Johannesburg: Society, Work and Development Institute and Centre for the Study of Violence and Reconciliation.

Webster, E. (1985) *Cast in a Racial Mould: Labour Process and Trade Unionism in the Foundries*, Johannesburg: Ravan Press.

Webster, E. (1987) 'The two faces of the black trade union movement in South Africa', *Review of African Political Economy*, 14(39): 33–41.

Webster, E. and Adler, G. (1999) 'Toward a class compromise in South Africa's "double transition": Bargained liberalization and the consolidation of democracy', *Politics & Society*, 27(3): 347–85.

Webster, E. and von Holdt, K. (eds) (2005) *Beyond the Apartheid Workplace: Studies in Transition*, Scottsville, South Africa: University of KwaZulu-Natal Press.

Webster, E., Lambert, R. and Bezuidenhout, A. (2008) *Grounding Globalisation: Labour in the Age of Insecurity*, Malden, MA: Blackwell.

3

Choosing Sides: The Promise and Pitfalls of a Critically Engaged Sociology in Apartheid South Africa

Edward Webster

In his presidential address to the American Sociological Association (ASA) in 2004, Michael Burawoy (2005) argued the need for sociologists to transcend the academy and engage with wider, extra-academic audiences. He called this approach 'public sociology' and contrasted it with professional sociology – a form of sociology that is concerned primarily with addressing other professional sociologists.[1] His address triggered a lively debate among sociologists in the United States (Clawson et al, 2007). The debate went global when Burawoy was elected deputy president of the International Sociological Association (ISA) in 2006, and president of the ISA in 2010.

When Burawoy first introduced his analytical framework with its four types of sociology – professional, policy, critical and public – I found it very helpful in developing an analytical history of sociology in South Africa (Webster, 2004). Importantly, by naming public sociology as one of four types of sociology, Burawoy was legitimating what practitioners were in fact doing.[2] As Patricia Hill Collins (2007: 102) remarked when she was first introduced to Burawoy's notion of public sociology: 'I had been doing public sociology without even knowing it.'

Alberto Arribas Lozano (2018: 100), in a critique of Burawoy's notion of public sociology, argues that implicit in Burawoy's four types of sociology is a 'strong hierarchical configuration in which professional sociology appears as the *sine qua non* of all sociologies'. He suggests the need to 'go beyond Burawoy's dissemination model of public sociology – the unidirectional diffusion of "expert knowledge" to extra-academic audiences – and towards a more collaborative understanding of knowledge production' (Arribas Lozano, 2018: 102).

Arribas Lozano makes a powerful argument for a more collaborative understanding of knowledge production. Instead of 'working on social movements', Arribas Lozano suggests a collaborative approach that involves 'working and thinking together with social movement' activists, advancing research that might be meaningful for both social sciences and the 'research subjects' (2018: 103). Such an approach, Arribas Lozano argues, requires that researchers 'negotiate and/or determine what knowledge should be produced, how and for what purposes, asserting a significant degree of control during the research project to ensure that it is a non-extractive process, that benefits the communities, that meets their ethical standards and protocols, and that does not reproduce epistemic violence' (2018: 107).

This chapter will detail a comparison of two examples of research undertaken in the 1980s, during the apartheid period in South Africa. The interventions were undertaken with the newly formed National Union of Mineworkers (NUM), a union of black mineworkers struggling for recognition from deeply hostile employers and a repressive state. The interventions were intended to empower the miners in their struggle for better working conditions and to provide them with an institutional voice through the research. The research led to sharply different responses from the NUM, as well as significantly different policy outcomes.

The first intervention, an investigation into underground safety in the gold mines, represented the promise of engaged research. The research not only strengthened the union, leading to important policy reform, but also led to scholarly publications that deepened our understanding of skill formation on the mines (Leger, 1985, 1992). Furthermore, it was collaboratively conceived and implemented. The second intervention, a study of the potential impact of migrant labour on the spread of AIDS,[3] represented the pitfalls of engaged research. It called for an end to a system that took men away from their partners and families for extended periods of time. The research report showed how the system of migrant labour created a market for sex and a potential AIDS epidemic. But the study had been conceived by an international non-governmental organization (NGO) – Oxfam Canada – with no formal cooperation with the NUM Head Office. Faced with the report's uncomfortable research findings, the NUM attempted to suppress publication. They accused the researchers of racism for focusing on the sex lives of black workers (Jockelson et al, 1991).

These two studies raise questions about the role of sociologists in situations of large-scale suffering and exploitation. Should they take sides, and if they do, on what grounds can such choices be justified (Becker, 1967; Gouldner, 1968)? Along with Gouldner, I argue that one takes sides on the basis of certain value commitments.[4] But when sociologists go beyond the relative comfort of the classroom and engage with organizations outside the university, they dirty their hands.[5] This is the dilemma that lies at the heart of an engaged sociology – how to square the circle between practical engagement with outside organizations and a commitment by the sociologist to scholarship. I conclude by suggesting a response to this dilemma and classify it as 'critical engagement'.

The chapter begins by setting the context whereby a generation of sociologists in apartheid South Africa in the 1970s and 1980s developed a relationship with the emerging workers' movement.

Setting the context

In January 1973, over 100,000 workers unexpectedly went on strike in the coastal city of Durban, South Africa, shattering a decade of industrial acquiescence. The coercive capacity of the apartheid state appeared so powerful that it has been widely held that industrial action was not possible (Adam, 1971: 2). These beliefs were decisively refuted when the 1973 strikes triggered a process of widening worker unrest and rapid union growth among black workers.

Social scientists were ill-prepared to explain this rapid rise of a militant labour movement in a developing country such as South Africa. Dependency theory, which focuses on the claim that imperialism blocks national economic development, was dominant. This conception of change relegated labour to a secondary position at best. At worst, workers were identified, with little in the way of evidence or argument, as a 'labour aristocracy' aligned to metropolitan capital.

To understand, and to contribute to the development of this emerging social movement, a new generation of sociologists stepped outside the classroom. This new generation took sides and identified with the unorganized black workers, who were seen as vulnerable and unfairly treated.[6] They began to interview workers and learn about their past. A research programme emerged that took labour seriously. New concepts and methods were developed. A relationship with this workers' movement emerged in the early 1970s in South Africa (Webster, 1995).

A research and teaching entity, the Institute for Industrial Education, was established inside this embryonic movement. A journal, the *South African Labour Bulletin* (SALB), was created to record, analyze and legitimize the new movement. In 1983, the Sociology of Work Programme (SWOP) was established as a research institute attached to the Department of Sociology at the University of the Witwatersrand (Wits).[7] It was decided to partner with the recently formed NUM and focus research on the critical issue of health and safety in South Africa's deep-level gold mines. As its charismatic general secretary, Cyril Ramaphosa, emphasized, 'in the mines health and safety is a top priority. … You've got to be alive and uninjured to earn the wages' (cited in Maller and Steinberg, 1984: 66–7).

The findings of both research projects were presented publicly at Wits in the presence of both employers and employees. The outcome of research on health and safety in the mining industry was largely hidden from the public at the time.[8] Discussion on these issues was reduced to technical problems for 'experts' and thoroughly 'depoliticised' (Habermas, 1984). By making the findings public, the team was challenging the mining elite and forcing the key stakeholders to engage in a democratic discussion that included the voices of the precarious mineworkers.

Researching underground safety on the South African gold mines

The high accident rate on the gold mines is linked to the exceptional depths at which extraction of gold takes place in South Africa. The average depth is more than 1,600 metres, with the deepest reaching 4,000 metres underground. A major cause of accidents involves rockbursts and rockfalls. In 1983, the year the research began, 371 miners were killed by rockfalls (Leger, 1985: 1). Between 1900 and 1985, 66,000 miners died underground and more than a million were seriously injured (Leger, 1985: 1).

Although there has been a long history of resistance by African mineworkers, leading to 74,000 workers embarking on strike action for four days in August 1946, attempts to successfully organize workers into a union only emerged 36 years later when the NUM held its inaugural congress in December 1982 (Thompson, 1984: 158–63). A key issue that emerged early in the history of the NUM was the refusal of rank-and-file mineworkers to work under conditions perceived to be dangerous. In September 1983, a dispute occurred at the West Driefontein mine when a group of workers were transferred to a new area of the mine shortly after several workers had been injured there in rockfalls. They refused to work under these conditions and were dismissed. This was the trigger for a request to SWOP to undertake research on ensuring safer underground mining.

The SWOP study was carried out in close collaboration with the NUM. It was based on extensive in-depth interviews with 90 mineworkers and was completed in 1985 (Leger, 1985: 13). A number of crucial findings demonstrated that black workers' lives were being put at risk in the search for the white supervisors' bonuses: 'They [white miners] do not really care whether the place is safe or not safe. All they do is press on that the place should be blasted so that they get their bonus. But they are not the ones that get injured. It is the blacks that get injured' (respondent, in Leger, 1985: 67).

Miners, the research reported, would often refuse to work in dangerous conditions, but their perception of danger was not accepted as sufficient reason for not working (respondent, in Leger, 1985: 67). More than half of the respondents who refused to work were charged with disciplinary offences as a result (Leger, 1985: 68). There was a strong feeling among respondents that the right to refuse dangerous work and the right to representation on safety issues should be recognized: 'It is my right because when those hangings fall they will kill me' (respondent, in Leger, 1985: 71).

When both management and workers were invited to the policy dialogue at the university on the findings of the report, they took the event quite seriously. Large numbers of senior managers arrived early for the presentation, some landing in helicopters on the university lawns. Crowds of mineworkers came later, waving their union banners; armed with sticks, they entered the lecture hall singing militant worker songs. The atmosphere was electric; it was the first time both sides of the industry had met each other face to face.

I was in the chair with Cyril Ramaphosa at my side. Members of management were visibly angry with the findings and felt that their managerial prerogative to decide the organization of work underground was being unfairly challenged by a biased research report. They also felt betrayed by the university.[9] Following the presentation, management challenged the scientific basis of the study and, in particular, the sampling technique of expert choice used in the study. A senior sociologist from the Department of Sociology vigorously defended the study, arguing that the margin of error was statistically insignificant.

The NUM was delighted with the event. They had forced management to engage publicly on a central issue in their recruitment campaign. The research was turned into a popular pamphlet and translated into isiXhosa and seSotho, two of the indigenous South African languages.[10] A campaign was launched around the slogan 'the right to refuse to work in dangerous conditions'. It was a great success and was used to recruit and empower members of the NUM. The union expanded rapidly and was described at the time as the largest union in the country (Thompson, 1984: 164). The research contributed, in post-apartheid South Africa, to an amendment to Section 23 of the Mine Health and Safety Act 29 of 1996 allowing for the right to refuse to work in dangerous conditions. It is now part of safety culture on the mines, although recent research points to the inadequate role of health and safety representatives (Stewart et al, 2013; Coulson et al, 2018).

A surprising finding of the research was that the respondents felt that the rocks 'talked'. In other words, the miners felt they could anticipate rockfalls: 'You hear sounds, fine stuff falls and the whole place becomes dusty' (Leger and Mothibeli, 1988: 230). We decided to deepen our research and embark on a longer-term research project. We called it 'talking rocks' and drew on the concept of 'tacit knowledge' to understand why our respondents said the rocks 'talked' (Kusterer, cited in Leger, 1992: 11–12).

Mine management dismissed as 'primitive superstitions' the workers' claims that the rocks talked. They argued: 'Novices [sic] are not in a position to recognize the portents of danger from rockfalls. ... The science of rock mechanics is an elaborate one and a great deal of experience has been built up by the mining industry in South Africa' (Leger and Mothibeli, 1988: 32). Many scientists tended to dismiss this knowledge as 'romantic'. We argued that it is tacit knowledge and drew on Kusterer's argument that this 'working knowledge is indispensable to the production process, yet it is informally learned and generally unrecognized by anyone outside the workplace' (Kusterer, cited in Leger, 1992: 38).

The second intervention focused on AIDS, and it is described next.

Researching AIDS

A key feature of South African mining under apartheid is the system of migrant labour for black workers. Men would come from all over the southern African region to work on a contract that would keep them away from their families and partners for long periods of time. Most men were housed in single-sex hostels. Consequently, a system of casual sex and prostitution developed in the townships and shack dwellings around the mines.

In the mid-1980s, we became aware of the emergence of AIDS in Central Africa. In South Africa there were only about a hundred cases of AIDS at that time, but we saw a potential danger as the disease could spread rapidly in the mining industry and beyond to the rural villages that the miners came from. We were encouraged by – and received funding from – an international NGO to research the topic. We decided to embark on research in a gold mine in the city of Welkom, then at the centre of the gold-mining industry. Unlike the underground safety research, AIDS was not identified by the NUM as a topic for study. It was our idea to undertake the research, and informal contact was established with the local NUM branch.

Assisted by a middle-aged retrenched black miner, Monyaola Mothibeli, and a graduate student, Karin Jockelson, our research team interviewed the women who operated on the outskirts of the mine and the men who visited them. Mothibeli and Jockelson frequented the neighbourhoods near working mines, drinking beer and talking to the men and women about their lives and loves. The local branch of the NUM had offered help, but when the researchers arrived, no one was keen to arrange interviews. Lesley Lawson (2008: 38) writes in her account of the research: 'Perhaps they found it strange, offensive even: having a white girl, young enough to be their daughter, asking about their sex lives.' The women who lived around the mines were more cooperative.

When officials at the NUM head office saw the first draft of the report, they were deeply disturbed (Jockelson et al, 1991). Recalling, 30 years later, her reactions to the report, May Hermanus, at the time the NUM's health and safety officer, observes: "The report came as a surprise to me. We were very angry. We were concerned about the image of the miners. I sympathized with them because they were being victimized by employers and were looked down upon, and the stories about AIDS were leading to further stigmatization" (interview, 26 October 2018).

In the report, the women interviewed compared their activities to that of spanning donkeys or oxen: it was their only way of surviving. 'I worked for six months and saw that it is better to "span". I could send home money for my children to get something to eat', said one of the women (respondent, cited in Jockelson et al, 1991: 168). Most men had sexual relationships with several different women.

The report suggested that the system of migrant labour had enabled the rapid spread of AIDS as the miners practised unprotected sex with multiple partners. As one miner observes: 'You produce the money, have sex and go away immediately. Then the next man follows' (respondent, cited in Jockelson et al, 1991: 166). The report predicted an AIDS pandemic in South Africa and the region. 'Once HIV enters the heterosexual mining community, it will spread to the immediate urban area, to surrounding urban areas, from urban to rural areas and across national boundaries' (respondent, cited in Jockelson et al, 1991: 169). The report recommended that the NUM introduce a systematic educational programme on safe sex, provide their members with condoms and campaign for the abolition of the migrant labour system so that the men could live with their partners and their families.

When Cyril Ramaphosa first saw the report, he was outraged. He phoned me as director of SWOP and said that we must not publish the report. It was objectionable, he said, because it was publicly exposing the private lives of his members. He accused the researchers and SWOP of racism, as the report, he said, was pathologizing the sexuality of black men. The researchers were taken aback but were determined to present the research in a similar format to the previous research on mine safety. Their argument was that it was not about black mineworkers being promiscuous, but about the fact that migrant labour takes men away from their partners and therefore creates conditions for them to develop multiple sexual relationships. It was commoditizing sex, we said, and the only solution was to allow men to settle with their families next to the mines. We insisted on grounds of academic freedom that the research be published.

Careful negotiations took place between the NUM and SWOP over the presentation and publication of the research. Finally, we reached a compromise in which we would moderate the language and the findings would be published in an academic journal abroad but not in South Africa.[11] By compromising, I had, in the words of Sartre, 'dirtied my hands'.

Reflecting on the response of NUM decades later, I am of the realization that I had not fully understood the cultural dynamics of sexuality in the context of apartheid and the history of colonialism. Interviewed later by Lawson, I said,

> A white man with NGO support driving this kind of agenda is a complete non-starter, because of the history of pathologising black sexuality in colonial discourse, where the black man is portrayed as diseased and promiscuous. While being aware of this in a more general way, I gained more clarity on the matter when I began to read and reflect on President Mbeki's response to AIDS. (Webster, cited in Lawson, 2008: 40)[12]

The response of the employers' organization Chamber of Mines to the SWOP report was puzzling; employers denied that migrant labour presented a problem and embarked on a counter-study. Surprisingly, their study concluded that there was no danger of AIDS spreading, as the men were in large part celibate and did not engage in commercial sex with multiple partners. The study resolved that '80 per cent of employees are not, as commonly believed, promiscuous and therefore not likely to spread the infection ... we believe that the industry and its employees plays a very minor role in the spread of HIV in South Africa' (cited in Lawson, 2008: 40).[13]

At the time, I called the Chamber of Mines study the 'celibate miner thesis', as the employers were cynically using bogus research to deny any links between migration, single-sex hostels and AIDS. The response from COMRO was understandable from a crude and narrow management point of view, but it brought to the fore the differences in values that underpinned the 'two sides' of the industrial divide. The NUM's response, on the other hand, was a more complex matter, a complexity that led me to revisit the debate between Becker and Gouldner in the 1960s as well as the pressures experienced by the research team as publicly engaged intellectuals in the apartheid period.[14]

***

Discussion

Reflecting on these two case studies, it is clear that the underground safety study was more successful in terms of its impact on both policy and empowering mineworkers to challenge despotic control in the workplace (Leger, 1986). Furthermore, the research strengthened the union and facilitated its rapid growth. The fact that the report drew on workers' knowledge and showed how it enabled miners to exercise some control over their work explains why SWOP was enthusiastically embraced by the NUM.

Importantly, the research had the support of the NUM from its inception, and it was defined as a cooperative inquiry by both the researchers and the researched. One of the first reforms of the new democratic government of Nelson Mandela was to amend the Mine Health and Safety Act to allow for miners to refuse to work under dangerous conditions.

The AIDS study, on the other hand, was conceived by an overseas NGO and was not commissioned by the NUM. It became a source of conflict between the researchers and the NUM because it touched on a deeply sensitive issue within the black community. We were not sufficiently sensitive to this at the time. The controversial nature of the issue of race and sexuality became clearer when, a decade later, President Mbeki denied the relationship between HIV and AIDS, leading to a period of denialism by the government (Gevisser, 2007: 727–65). Eventually, in 2001, the Treatment Action Campaign went to the Pretoria High Court and won its case to force the government to provide AIDS sufferers with anti-retroviral medication (Heywood, 2015).[15]

This points to a fundamental difference between the two studies. The first study focused on the mining labour process and the need for new rules to regulate the conditions required for safer underground work. These rules – eventually turned into law – gave miners greater autonomy to resist dangerous work conditions, but they did not challenge the institutional structure of the industry. The new rules in the workplace have effectively drawn miners' safety representatives into management's system of control (Stewart et al, 2013). On the other hand, the study on AIDS and migrant labour critiqued the social institutions that entrenched migrant labour and challenged the source of the reproduction of cheap labour on the mines. Indeed, the report went further by challenging the leaders of the NUM; it made visible the patriarchal system and the exploitation of vulnerable women by the mineworkers.

In defending 'taking sides', Gouldner (1968) emphasizes an engaged sociology's ability to discover information often hidden from mainstream sociology. 'A feelingful commitment to the underdog's plight', writes Gouldner, 'enables us to do a better job as sociologists'; 'it also', he continues, 'made the suffering of the underdog "naked and visible" to the public' (1968: 105). Indeed, it is precisely this objective, to make the suffering of black mineworkers public, that led the research team to present its findings in the form of a public dialogue. It also allowed the team to present black mineworkers not as abstract categories, but as men who daily risked their lives underground and, during their leisure hours, risked their lives in another way.

But there are also many pitfalls in the practice of critical engagement. It can lead to a lack of analytical distance from the research subjects (Rodriques-Garavito, 2014). It can also lead to 'dispersal', where the sociologist 'leaps from one task to another' (Rodriques-Garavito, 2014). This is captured best through the metaphor of the engaged sociologist as a windmill, continually in motion, leading to difficulty in 'finding time to consolidate insights, deepen partial theories into something of more general applicability. The winds blow eternally, and the blades turn relentlessly. Research is driven frenetically from topic to topic' (Burawoy, 2010: 23). In authoritarian societies, such as apartheid South Africa, the 'critically engaged sociologist' faces the added danger of state repression, making their undertaking a precarious one.[16] But the greatest pitfall is the threat to the autonomy of the academic.

After the attempted censorship of the SWOP AIDS research, I penned:

> Pressure exists on scholars to make a clear declaration that their research and teaching should be constructed as support for, and on behalf of, particular organizations. To prevent this subordination of intellectual work to the immediate interests of these organizations, I prefer the stance of critical engagement. Squaring the circle is never easy, as it involves a difficult combination of commitment to the goals of these movements while being faithful to evidence, data and your own judgment and conscience. (Webster, 1995: 18)

The concept of critical engagement emerged directly out of the concrete struggles of the editors of SALB, since its launch in 1974, to assert its editorial autonomy in the face of pressures not to publish articles critical of the trade union movement. These conflicts came to a head in 1979 when the apartheid state granted African unions the same rights as other workers to register and participate in the collective bargaining system. The Federation of South African Trade Unions, predecessor to South Africa's largest trade union federation, the Congress of South African Trade Unions, decided to register. This triggered a fierce debate between 1979 and 1982 that opened divisions within SALB's editorial board. Eventually, after considerable consultation and debate, the editors agreed a position in 1988. They declared that they ascribed 'to a position of critical engagement – critical in the sense of not being subordinate to any one group or tendency and engaged in the sense that we are committed to give support to the democratic labour movement' (cited in Maree, 2010: 62). The document ends by arguing the case for the autonomy of SALB's publication policy.

This background is only mentioned because it goes beyond the argument for a critical sociology presented by Gouldner (1968) in the 1960s in North America. The argument we were developing was for public intellectual engagement with progressive organizations in a very different context (Webster, 1982). Progressive intellectuals in South Africa at that time were in a contradictory position, 'caught between the demands of the profession and its need for autonomous spaces for critical reflection and theoretical development and attempts to make themselves accountable to organizations outside the university' (Webster, 1982: 2). Establishing links with organizations engaged in practical activity had been done at a cost historically. (Here, I refer to the constraints placed on intellectual work under state socialism.) 'This', I conclude, 'is the dilemma of the social scientist as they try to develop a social science of liberation' (Webster, 1982: 8).

Conclusion

This chapter has identified the strengths that sociology draws from engagement with the public, but it has also pointed to its pitfalls. SWOP chose to take sides by using its sociological concepts and tools of investigation to empower black mineworkers. This was not done because SWOP thought the miners were victims; it was done because of SWOP's commitment to the belief that it was through the strategic use of their collective power that mineworkers could improve their wages and working conditions, and that through a powerful mineworkers' union, they could shape the transition to democracy.

In trying to explain the different responses of the NUM to the two studies, I had to revisit the process whereby the research was conducted. I have suggested that the underground safety study was more successful because it drew on workers' knowledge and was useful to the mineworkers in their day-to-day struggles underground. Most importantly, it had the support of the NUM from its inception and was defined as a collaborative project by both the researchers and the researched. The AIDS study, however, was conceived and commissioned by an international NGO, and the formal structures of the NUM never endorsed the study. It came as a surprise to them, and its findings touched a raw nerve that struck at the heart of the migrant labour system and the patriarchal values that underpinned it.

But in revisiting the AIDS study, a tantalizing question remains: had the research team followed a similar collaborative approach to that taken in the underground safety project, could the AIDS project have led to a more constructive outcome? May Hermanus believes a different outcome was possible. "It is a pity", she observes,

> 'that the study was not discussed with our department, because we could have used the study in our educational classes about AIDS with NUM members. The sessions we had with them were very lively. It was an issue that involved gender and it touched a raw nerve. It involved secret and unspoken things about the unsavoury aspects of hostel and mining life. The SWOP report would have been useful in these classes.' (Interview, 26 October 2018)

These observations suggest that the SWOP researchers, had they had the courage to approach the NUM more openly, could have won the support of the union for a collaborative study on AIDS. Are these observations simply the wisdom of hindsight, or was a more collaborative approach really possible? In theory such an approach may have been possible but it would have required a much deeper level of trust between the NUM and SWOP than seemed possible at the time. After all, the study was conducted at the height of apartheid repression.

An alternative approach to the AIDS study in the 1980s seems unlikely since, over a decade later, in 1999, SWOP researchers openly opposed the outsourcing of support staff at Wits but failed to build an alliance between workers and students (Bezuidenhout and Fakier, 2006). It was only some years later, in the wake of the #FeesMustFall movement of 2015–17, that SWOP researchers succeeded in building a degree of trust between students and black workers on campus. Commenting on the 1999 outsourcing, SWOP researchers, in their 2017 student-driven book on #FeesMustFall, expressed that:

> the majority of the student body at the time did not relate to the struggle of outsourced workers. This has changed over the years as more working-class students have occupied that space and perceive the same workers in a paternalistic mode as their fathers and mothers. The struggles of students and workers cannot be extricated, and the alliance emerged from the history of how workers were treated in the 1990s marketization project. (Chinguno et al, 2017: 35)

Clearly 'decolonization' is a process that will take many years. While SWOP has been committed from its conception to breaking down the racial division of labour in knowledge production, progress during the apartheid years was slow.[17] The advent of democracy presented opportunities in SWOP for the introduction in 1996 of a more systematic programme of research capacity building for black students (Buhlungu and Metcalfe, 2001; Metcalfe and Cock, 2010). But decolonization also involves, in the words of Walter Mignolo (2010: 2), 'epistemic de-linking ... as well as de-colonializing and de-colonial knowledges, necessary steps for imagining and building democratic, just, and non-imperial/colonial societies'.

What is clear is that in following the difficult path of institutional transformation and critical engagement, SWOP has been faithful to the classical tradition of sociology. As Claus Offe (1979: 15) states:

> To distance oneself from social practices is to forget that all great social and political theorizing in the nineteenth and twentieth centuries received its problematic and inspiration from social movements and contested conditions. In the past, this existential rootedness of social and political theory has always been a source of analytical strength.

For SWOP, rooting the sociological endeavour in the struggles of working people was an essential source of analytical strength. It was also an expression of the research team's commitment, incomplete as it was, to a more egalitarian society.

Notes

[1] The term 'public sociology' was first introduced by Herbert Gans in his 1988 ASA presidential address, 'Sociology in America: The Discipline and the Public'.

[2] Burawoy (2005) sees these four different types – or practices – as 'antagonistic interdependence' with their own distinct specializations, their own forms of knowledge, their own truths, their own modes of legitimation, their own accountability, their own politics and their own pathologies.

[3] Acquired immune deficiency syndrome.

[4] Unlike Becker (1967), who sees sociologists' value commitments as an 'inescapable fact of nature', Gouldner sees values about society as a 'necessary condition' for 'objectivity'. He argues, 'it is to values, not factions, that sociologists must give their most basic commitment' (Gouldner, 1968: 116).

[5] The metaphor of 'dirty hands' is drawn from Jean Paul Sartre's play of the same name, first performed in Paris in 1948, where Hoederer, the party leader in a fictitious communist state, defends the need for a national front between liberals and communists in the national interest. He says to Hugo, the young idealist: 'How you cling to your purity, young man! How afraid you are to soil your hands. … Purity is an idea for a yogi or a monk. You intellectuals and bourgeois anarchists use it as a pretext to do nothing. … Well, I have dirty hands, right up to my elbows. … Do you think you can govern innocently?' (Sartre, 1949: 223).

[6] It was a generation influenced by the New Left in the Global North and by the radical sociology of the time that argued for a committed radicalism (Turner, 1972). We were predominantly white males of professional/middle-class backgrounds. None spoke any of the indigenous African languages (Webster, 1992).

[7] SWOP grew out of my doctoral research on the impact of the organization of work on the health and safety of foundry workers and with input from a group of science and engineering graduate students interested in health and safety issues, the Technical Advice Group. In 1987 the university formally recognized the entity as a programme, and in 1996 SWOP was granted unit status by the national science body, the Centre for Science Development. In 2007 the university granted SWOP institute status and it was renamed the Society, Work and Development Institute. In 2018 it was again renamed the Society, Work and Politics Institute. It has kept the acronym SWOP and is now known as the SWOP Institute.

[8] The employers' research entity, the Chamber of Mines Research Organisation (COMRO), refused to make available for the research project 42 unpublished research reports concerned with safety and health hazards (Leger, 1985: Appendix 3).

[9] The University of the Witwatersrand was established at the beginning of the 20th century to serve the mining industry, and it has done so diligently over the years (Webster, 1985: iv).

[10] The pamphlet was called *A Thousand Ways to Die: The Struggle for Safety in the Mines, 1986*. Interestingly, it was not reproduced in the mineworkers' creole language, Fanakalo, a form of communication that had emerged through daily interaction among workers and between workers and management. Middle-class Africans tend to look down on Fanakalo as a legacy of colonialism (Chinguno, 2015: 229).

[11] This research was presented at a recent seminar where I was asked why the research team did not proceed to publish the findings without NUM's blessing. I responded by

noting that it would have been a risky gamble because the narrative championed by the apartheid state at the time was that HIV/AIDS had been brought into South Africa by returning exiles. The report could be construed as not only casting aspersions on black people's sexuality but also portraying these liberation movements in a bad light.

[12] Mbeki fell under the influence of AIDS dissidents and, when he became president in 1999, he publicly questioned the 'racist medical discourse' that HIV causes AIDS and that it is sexually transmitted (Gevisser, 2007: 727–65).

[13] Recent findings from the University of Oxford confirm the SWOP AIDS research on the role of migrant labour in spreading the virus. Their research shows that the HIV pandemic started in Kinshasa in the early 1920s and first spread along railroad and water transportation through migrant networks in the Democratic Republic of Congo (Keim, 2014).

[14] I am grateful to Michael Burawoy for his reminder on the debate and his insight in identifying Gouldner's stress on values as central to my argument.

[15] The state appealed to the Constitutional Court, which upheld the High Court's decision in June 2002. Mbeki's campaign against anti-retrovirals – and his attendant questioning of orthodox science – had been lost.

[16] The assassination of Richard Turner, a radical political science lecturer, on 8 January 1978 and the assassination of David Webster, a progressive anthropologist, on 1 May 1989, both by the apartheid security police, are examples of the risks attached to activist academics in apartheid South Africa.

[17] Developing black academics was difficult during the apartheid period as entry to Wits by black students was restricted by law. However, with the support of the Ford Foundation, we were able to employ a limited number of black research interns. Some of these interns, such as Simon Mapadimeng and Darlene Miller, went on to become leading sociologists in post-apartheid South Africa. We also employed a black research assistant with funding from the Friedrich Ebert Stiftung.

References

Adam, H. (1971) *Modernizing Racial Domination: The Dynamics of South African Politics*, California: University of California Press.

Arribas Lozano, A. (2018) 'Reframing the public sociology debate: Towards collaborative and decolonial praxis', *Current Sociology*, 66(1): 92–109.

Becker, H. (1967) 'Which side are we on?', *Social Problems*, 14(3): 239–47.

Bezuidenhout, A. and Fakier, K. (2006) 'Maria's burden: Contract cleaning and the crisis of social reproduction in post-apartheid South Africa', *Antipode*, 38(3): 462–85.

Buhlungu, S. and Metcalfe, M. (2001) 'Breaking the racial division of labour in knowledge production: Reflections on internship programmes', *Perspectives in Education*, 19(27): 67–84.

Burawoy, M. (2005) 'For public sociology', *American Sociological Review*, 70(February): 4–28.

Burawoy, M. (2010) 'Southern windmill: The life and work of Edward Webster', *Transformation: Critical Perspectives on Southern Africa*, 72/73: 1–25.

Chinguno, C. (2015) *The Shifting Dynamics of the Relations between Institutionalization and Strike Violence: A Case Study of Impala Platinum, Rustenburg, 1982–2012*, PhD thesis, University of the Witwatersrand, Johannesburg, South Africa.

Chinguno, C., Kgoroba, M., Mashibini, S., Masilela, B., Maubane, B., Moyo, N., Mthombeni, A. and Ndlovu, H. (eds) (2017) *Rioting and Writing: Diaries of Wits Fallists*, Johannesburg: Society, Work and Development Institute, University of the Witwatersrand.

Clawson, D., Zussman, R., Misra, J., Gerstel, N., Stokes, R. and Anderton, D.L. (eds) (2007) *Public Sociology*, Berkeley: University of California Press.

Coulson, N., Stewart, P.F. and Saeed, S. (2018) *South African Mine Workers' Perspectives on the Right to Refuse Dangerous Work and the Constraints to Worker Self-regulation*, Johannesburg: Centre for Sustainability in Mining and Industry, University of the Witwatersrand.

Gans, H. (1998) 'Sociology in America: The discipline and the public', *American Sociological Review*, 54(1): 1–16.

Gevisser, M. (2007) *Thabo Mbeki: The Dream Deferred*, Johannesburg and Cape Town: Jonathan Ball.

Gouldner, A. (1968) 'The sociologist as partisan: Sociology and the welfare state', *American Sociologist*, 3(2): 103–16.

Habermas, J. (1984) *Reason and the Rationalization of Society, Volume 1 of the Theory of Communicative Action* (originally published in German in 1981; English translation by Thomas McCarthy), Boston, MA: Beacon Press.

Heywood, M. (2015) 'The Treatment Action Campaign's quest for equality in HIV and health: Learning from and lessons for the trade union movement', *Global Labour Journal*, 6(3): 314–35.

Hill Collins, P. (2007) 'Going public: Doing the sociology that had no name', in D. Clawson, R. Zussman, J. Misra, N. Gerstel, R. Stokes and D.L. Anderton (eds) *Public Sociology*, Berkeley: University of California Press, pp 101–13.

Jockelson, K., Mothibeli, M. and Leger, J. (1991) 'Human immunodeficiency virus and migrant labour in South Africa', *International Journal of Health Services*, 21(1): 157–73.

Keim, B. (2014) 'AIDS traced to Congo expanding transportation network', *National Geographic*, 2 October: 15–19.

Lawson, L. (2008) *Side Effects: The Story of AIDS in South Africa*, Cape Town: Double Story.

Leger, J. (1985) *Towards Safer Underground Gold Mining: An Investigation Commissioned by the National Union of Mineworkers*, Johannesburg: Department of Sociology, University of the Witwatersrand.

Leger, J. (1986) 'Safety and the organization of work in South African gold mines: A crisis of control', *International Labour Review*, 125(5): 591–603.

Leger, J. (1992) *Talking Rocks: An Investigation of the Pit Sense of Fall-of-ground Accidents amongst Underground Miners*, PhD thesis, University of the Witwatersrand, Johannesburg, South Africa.

Leger, J. and Mothibeli, M. (1988) 'South African gold miners' perceptions of safety – 1984–1987', in Chamber of Mines of South Africa (eds) *Proceedings of the Mine Safety and Health Congress, November 1987*, Johannesburg: Chamber of Mines, pp 31–42.

Leger, J. and Mothibeli, M. (1989) 'Talking rocks: Pit sense amongst South African miners', *Labour, Capital and Society*, 21(2): 222–37.

Maller, J. and Steinberg, M. (1984) 'Health and safety: An issue in industrial relations', *South African Labour Bulletin*, 9(7): 60–75.

Maree, J. (2010) 'Against the odds: The sustainability of the South African Labour Bulletin', *Transformation: Critical Perspectives on Southern Africa*, 72/73: 48–65.

Metcalfe, A. and Cock, J. (2010) 'Public sociology and the transformation of the university', *Transformation: Critical Perspectives on Southern Africa*, 72/73: 66–85.

Mignolo, W.D. (2010) 'Epistemic disobedience, independent thought and de-colonial freedom', *Theory, Culture and Society*, 26(7–8): 159–81.

Offe, C. (1979) *Disorganized Capitalism: Contemporary Transformation of Work and Politics*, Cambridge: Polity Press.

Rodriguez-Garavito, C. (2014) 'Amphibious sociology: Dilemmas and possibilities of public sociology in a multimedia world', *Current Sociology*, 62(2): 156–67.

Sartre, J.-P. (1949) *Dirty Hands, a Play in Seven Acts*, New York: Vintage Books.

Stewart, P.N., Coulson, N. and Bakker, D. (2013) *Right to Refuse Dangerous Work*, Johannesburg: The Centre for Sustainability in Mining and Industry, University of the Witwatersrand.

Thompson, C. (1984) 'Black trade unions on the mines', in South African Research Services (eds) *South African Review Two*, Johannesburg: Ravan Press, pp 156–64.

Turner, R. (1972) *Eye of the Needle: An Essay in Participatory Democracy*, Johannesburg: Ravan Press.

Webster, E. (1982) 'The state, crisis and the university: The social scientist's dilemma', *Perspectives in Education*, 6(1): 1–14.

Webster, E. (1985) 'Preface', in J. Leger (ed) *Towards Safer Underground Gold Mining: An Investigation Commissioned by the National Union of Mineworkers*, Johannesburg: Department of Sociology, University of the Witwatersrand, pp 1–4.

Webster, E. (1992) 'The impact of intellectuals on the labour movement', *Transformation*, 18/19: 88–92.

Webster, E. (1995) 'Taking labour seriously: Sociology and labour in South Africa', in A. van der Merwe (ed) *Industrial Sociology: A South African Perspective*, Johannesburg: Lexicon Publishers, pp 1–27.

Webster, E. (2004) 'Sociology in South Africa: Its past, present and future', *Society in Transition*, 35(1): 27–41.

4

The Decline of Labour Studies and the Democratic Transition

Sakhela Buhlungu

Introduction

An important aspect of sociology is the study of society and processes of social change. Only in a few cases has the discipline, or a section of it, gone beyond merely studying society and sought to influence processes of change by engaging with actors outside the discipline and the academy. South Africa is one such case where some members of the discipline were intimately involved in debates and struggles for change and social justice. Although there are numerous examples, the broad sub-discipline of labour studies provides probably the best illustration of this engagement, which Burawoy (2004) has termed 'public sociology'. However, sociology in South Africa has not always been engaged in this fashion. Indeed, the discipline emerged and developed within a context of a racially divided society and a segmented system of education. The education system gave rise to a division of labour between those who were educated to service the labour needs of the burgeoning economy, on the one hand, and those who provided for the professional and intellectual needs of the economic and political structures, on the other. Research shows that up until the early 1970s sociology was oriented toward servicing the existing structures of power (Webster, 1978; Jubber, 1983; Ally et al, 2003; Ally, 2005). In this chapter, I discuss the centrality of labour studies to the public sociology that emerged in the 1970s; how public sociology, in turn, constituted an important intellectual contribution to the democratic transition; and how the conditions under which public sociology and labour studies are conducted have changed in the post-apartheid period.

Labour studies, as discussed in this chapter, encompass contributions from a variety of academic disciplines such as history, political science and philosophy. But it was sociology that became associated most closely with labour studies, and the reasons for that association are discussed below. The main impetus for the growth of labour studies came from the historic 1973 strikes when thousands of African workers in the greater Durban/Pinetown area embarked on strikes demanding wage increases. In a context where forms of African labour organization had been snuffed out following the banning of nationalist movements and the arrest of their leaders in the 1950s and early 1960s, the strikes inspired hope and confidence among activists. Many of these activists were to constitute the core organizers that spearheaded the formation of unions in the wake of the strikes. But the strikes also inspired a generation of young university-based intellectuals, creating conditions for them to sharpen and apply the Marxist concepts they had imbibed in their studies in Europe or in their reading about the New Left political ferment in Western Europe and North America. It was this group that took the lead in the revival of labour studies. But most important, I should add that it was in the dialogue between both groups – the activists and the university-based intellectuals – that public sociology emerged. Both shared a commitment to equality and social justice and drew deeply from the concepts that animated revisionist Marxism at the time.

Before I proceed to discuss the significance of labour studies for public sociology, let me make a few propositions about South African public sociology itself. First, public sociology emerged in opposition to the dominant power block and in support of the struggle for social justice. In other words, it involved a commitment not only to scholarship but also to equality and social justice. The themes that the scholars tackled in their writing sought to focus attention on the pertinent issues of the times – poverty, exploitation, violence, forced removals, gender inequality and so on. Second, public sociology emerged when Africans did not have sufficient resources to represent themselves organizationally and intellectually. Labour studies and public sociology were a response to this problem by helping black workers in general to form their own movements and organizations and by providing them with ideas and concepts to make sense of their circumstances.

Third, public sociology, as defined by Burawoy (2004), operated at the intersection between intellectual engagement, on the one hand, and political commitment and activism, on the other. The dynamism and significance of labour studies compared with other areas of scholarship can be attributed to its visibility as an engaged form of scholarship. As Webster (1982) has shown, this places intellectuals in a contradictory position where they have to balance the imperatives of political struggle against the need to maintain autonomous spaces for critical intellectual reflection.

Fourth, public sociology was not a one-way street. At the same time as it sought to communicate and engage with members of different publics, it was also shaped by those with whom it engaged – particularly labour, women, youth and community organizations. Concepts that public sociology presented and debated were often appropriated by these groups and given new meanings that were more in tune with the lived experiences of members of the public.

Finally, public sociology was never fixed, both in terms of its modes of engagement as well as the objectives it sought to achieve. This has to do with changes within the dominant economic and political structures, the changing nature of the relationship between scholarship and political activism, and changes in the composition and interests of the different publics. The post-apartheid environment provides the most vivid portrait of these changes.

Labour studies and public sociology

Although many scholarly disciplines made immense contributions, it was the discipline of sociology that left the most indelible mark on how scholars engaged with members of the public and their collective organizations. In a similar way, although other disciplines made their contributions, the study of labour continues to bear an especially strong imprint from sociology. The reasons for this are multiple. First, the subject matter of labour studies is located firmly within the concerns of sociology, particularly in a context where the Marxist paradigm serves as an overarching framework. Theoretical concerns such as the labour theory of value, class, class struggle, collective organizations and social change were all standard fare in the sociology that was introduced in the English-medium universities in South Africa from the mid-1970s onwards. Second, sociology produced (and continues to produce) the largest number of graduates in the social sciences and so had a much wider reach and impact. Unlike other disciplines, which produce mainly undergraduates, sociology also produced many postgraduates up to and including the level of PhD. Third, a large number of these graduates found their way into the labour movement and other community organizations as activists and, as such, became important interlocutors and public sociologists in their own right. Fourth, labour was also prioritized by the student organization, the National Union of South African Students, which had dedicated Wages Commissions in all the white English-medium universities. These commissions did research, outreach and advocacy work and sought to build awareness among students on labour-related matters. Fifth, in the period 1971–99 there emerged a large number of support organizations dedicated to the study, research and support of the new labour movement. At least 57 support organizations were active in this period, with some providing specialized labour support, whereas others also worked with other community organizations (Buhlungu, 2001).

Finally, the period from the 1970s to the early 1990s saw a proliferation of writing on labour. Whereas some of the writing was clearly targeted at academic audiences, a fair amount was presented in a popular form accessible to members and activists in the labour movement. In this regard, the *South African Labour Bulletin* came to play a pivotal role to bridge the academic–activist divide and as a vital platform for public sociology. Established in 1974 to provide intellectual support to labour activists, the Bulletin is today one of very few surviving organizations and publications from the 1970s and 1980s.

To illustrate the centrality of labour studies to public sociology in South Africa, I have chosen to trace the relationship back to the early 1970s, and in doing so, I have identified four different periods.

Public sociology from the ivory tower, 1973–78

Two watershed events took place in South Africa in the 1970s. The first was the wave of strikes that hit Durban in 1973, setting in motion a phase of union mobilization that was to result in the emergence of one of the most militant and resilient union movements of the late 20th century. The second event was the explosion of youth anger and militancy in June 1976 following an attempt by the apartheid regime to impose Afrikaans as a medium of instruction in African schools. Although the student revolt was more dramatic and its consequences more dire given the brutal response of the government, neither did it attract as much academic interest nor did it generate as much focused scholarly attention as did the Durban strikes and the worker mobilization that followed it. To this day, youth studies have not taken off in South Africa. In contrast, the strikes gave rise to a groundswell of academic interest and support for the burgeoning labour movement. Although the support and interest are understandable given the sense of mission that workers and the working class enjoy within the Marxist paradigm, it does not explain the near total lack of interest in the youth movement that, after all, comprised children of the very working class that was generating so much intellectual excitement.

Part of the answer to this puzzle lies with a small group of university-based intellectuals who wanted to transplant political trends and intellectual fads from other parts of the world onto the South African social and political landscape. At the same time, their interventions were extremely important and successful in forging engagement with the new labour movement, which desperately needed intellectual legitimation and respectability at a time when all forms of African organizations faced demonization and repression by the state and employers. Engagement with the new movement often took the form of transferring information or knowledge drawn mainly from local and international networks of the engaged academics. In the early years, for example, the *South African Labour Bulletin* regularly published reviews of new books on unions and the shop stewards movement in England and Europe as well as essays on topics that animated revisionist Marxism of the time.

Significantly, during this period, public sociology was often a one-way process with little or no involvement of the workers themselves. Where there was engagement, it was usually between university-based academics and white activists working in the union movement who, according to Maree (1982), at that time, had undisputed power and control in the unions.

The dominant labour studies at the time drew heavily on history and other experiences on the African continent and abroad. Scholarly output was replete with texts that sought to excavate lessons and examples about unionization, leadership and strategies from history, particularly that of the early to mid-20th century (see Webster, 1978; Maree, 1982, 1987). Although the *South African Labour Bulletin* was an important platform by then, it also suffered from an academic condescension toward workers. A survey of the contributions in the Bulletin from that period would show them to be a very diverse group of academics and researchers but with very little engagement by African workers and activists. The vast majority of the contributors to the journal were academics and researchers from English-medium universities and white activists within the union movement.

At this point I need to add another tradition of public sociology that then existed outside of labour studies, namely that practised by the Black Consciousness movement. It was marked, however, by limited resources, a lack of a secure base in the academy and the continued harassment from the state. Unfortunately, this tradition suffered a major setback following the death of Steve Biko and the banning of several organizations allied to it in 1977. Its legacy did survive in the student movement, in some unions and within the national liberation movements.

In the early years, labour studies and public sociology did not face the dilemma identified by Erwin (1992), namely, whether to lead or to follow. Under apartheid there was a vast asymmetry of power and resources between those drawn from the ruling racial power block, on the one hand, and those from the oppressed and exploited majority, on the other. The majority of intellectuals who engaged in labour studies and public sociology were Whites, drawn into these kinds of intellectual engagement precisely because they desired to break away from the ruling block. Thus, like the white union officials and activists that I have discussed elsewhere (Buhlungu, 2006a), these intellectuals were rebels with a contradictory relationship to the majority of the country's population. Their most important contribution was their knowledge and skills.

However, in seeking to find common cause with the excluded sections of the population, they often engaged in a morality play in which the virtues of socialism and its historic agent, the industrial worker, were extolled while the evils of capitalism and apartheid were condemned. The category of worker became synonymous with righteousness, courage and resilience, and problems in the movement were blamed on 'leadership', the bosses and the apartheid regime. Many of the intellectuals went further and cautioned against the dangers of nationalism and populism. An example of this morality play in public sociology and labour studies is Friedman's (1987) account of unionism among African workers in the period from 1970 to 1984. The book does an excellent job describing and analyzing the courageous actions of African workers as they went about building the new unions. But it plays down contradictions and weaknesses within the ranks of the unions and workers, and where these are too glaring to ignore, they are blamed on leaders, the bosses and the state. In these narratives, the complexities of the existing social worlds inhabited by African workers as well as the realities of a divided society were downplayed or ignored. Liberation was presented as a panacea that would resolve these problems and level the playing fields for all.

Sociology and the emergence of new publics, 1979–84

The decade of the 1970s ended well for the new labour movement. Not only had it survived the backlash unleashed by employers and the state, but also it was beginning to consolidate its strength. The formation of the Federation of South African Trade Unions (FOSATU) in 1979 marked the beginning of a new assertiveness. But this period also marked a new challenge for public sociology and labour studies as new collectivities and organizations emerged. Several of the new formations fell outside the ambit of traditional labour studies, so that public sociology had to adjust its dialogue to be responsive to these organizations and developments (see von Holdt, 1987). For the purpose of this discussion, I will single out four organizations that presented such a challenge to public sociology and labour studies. First, the formation of the South African Allied Workers Union (SAAWU), a general union aligned to the African National Congress tradition of liberation politics, introduced a new diversity into its repertoire of alliances that took it beyond the 'FOSATU tradition', SAAWU made a strong case for building strong union–community links, a dimension that had been missing in union mobilization up to that point. Second, there was the formation of the United Democratic Front (UDF) in 1983, a development that changed the landscape of political contestation and also gave the community a powerful voice. The UDF was a national coalition of numerous community organizations that was formed to oppose the cosmetic reforms introduced by the apartheid government of President P.W. Botha. 'Community unions' such as SAAWU were affiliates of the front, whereas the 'shop floor unions' tried to distance themselves from it. Third, there was the upsurge of unrest in African townships from 1984 onwards, which put the spotlight on problems faced by workers in their residential areas. Many unionized workers, particularly in the Transvaal, supported the community struggles and brought pressure to bear on their union leaderships to follow suit. Finally, the trade union unity talks that began in 1981 created new conditions for the practice of public sociology. The credibility and authority of university-based academics and their colleagues, some of them inside the unions, was challenged from certain quarters of the labour movement. The evolution of unity talks saw a growing assertion of the need for a leadership that came from workers and was rooted in the workplace but had strong links to communities and their struggles. This growing assertiveness within the union movement set the tone for what was to happen after the formation of the Congress of South African Trade Unions (COSATU) in 1985.

During this period, the changing landscape of union organization posed new problems for labour studies and its university-based intellectuals, especially with regard to the ascendant national liberation politics. A growing number of unions and unionists began to reject the binaries that labour studies had been founded on, namely that the struggle was either about race or about class, that its locus was either the shop floor or the community, or that the goal was either national liberation or socialism.

The labour movement begins to speak for itself, 1985–93

The formation of the COSATU in December 1985 marked the beginning of a new era for labour studies and public sociology. For the first time the labour constituency was finding its own voice, thus changing the terms on which public sociology and labour studies were conducted. In his opening address at the inaugural congress of COSATU, convener Cyril Ramaphosa proclaimed boldly,

> We have seen in the past four years that organizations of the oppressed have grown stronger. And at the same time we have seen trade unions growing stronger as well. We have seen trade unions not only broaden their areas of struggle on the shop floor, we have also seen them contribute to community struggles. (Ramaphosa, 1986: 45)

Ramaphosa's and other leaders' speeches set the tone for what was to follow in subsequent years. In speaking for themselves, the new labour movement made it clear that the binaries that had been so central to the discourse of public sociology and labour studies were now without meaning. The growing assertiveness of the labour movement was also marked by the internal development of organizational capacities previously provided by academics, and services that had been provided by labour support organizations to the nascent labour movement. These organizations had first emerged in the 1970s in a context where the unions had limited resources. University-based intellectuals, university graduates and some church organizations stepped in and provided resources, infrastructure and personnel to provide services such as research, media, legal services and occupational health and safety training to the new unions. The South African Labour Bulletin, the Industrial Aid Society (providing general education and training in organizing) and the Institute for Industrial Education (also providing education and training) were among the earliest of these organizations. Others such as the Cape Town Trade Union Library, the Technical Assistance Group (support in health and safety) and the Labour Research Service were established in the 1980s. Virtually all these organizations operated outside the formal structures of trade unions, were dependent on (mainly foreign) donor funding and provided their services free of charge to the emerging black unions. But from the late 1980s, a growing number of unions established their own education, legal, media and research departments and approached funders to channel financial assistance directly to unions rather than through labour support organizations.

Speaking at the University of Natal in March 1986, Jay Naidoo, then general secretary of COSATU, addressed the subject of the relationship between intellectuals and the federation.

> On this platform I would like to address a few words to the intellectuals amongst us. We extend our hand to you. We ask you to put your learning skills and education at the service of the workers' movement. ... But we believe that the direction of the workers' movement will develop organically out of the struggle of workers on the factory floor and in the townships where they live. Accordingly the role of intellectuals will be purely a supportive one of assisting the greater generation of working class leadership. As COSATU we believe that we have generated a working class leadership that is competent enough to debate its position and to direct the movement itself. (Naidoo, 1986: 37)

The labour movement's discovery of its own voice had far-reaching ramifications for labour studies and public sociology. First, unions began to develop their intellectual capacity internally, thus reducing their dependence on university-based intellectuals and those in labour support organizations. Such was the confidence displayed by the unions that by the early 1990s COSATU was posing questions about the relevance of the research produced by academics for the labour movement (Erwin, 1992). Second, many labour-supporting organizations found themselves increasingly without a role to play, especially as the funding on which they relied was being channelled directly to unions. Although some of the activists in these bodies found specialist jobs within unions, many moved out of labour studies and activism entirely, a trend that accelerated further after COSATU's second national congress in 1987. Finally, many university-based intellectuals, who had been active in labour studies as practitioners of public sociology, either searched for new niches for intellectual engagement or moved on into areas such as policy research and consultancy outside the universities.

At this point I need to point out that from the late 1980s some in labour studies did come to acknowledge the errors of viewing labour struggles through a binary lens of class struggle versus nationalism. Theoretically, this recognition was captured by the concept of 'social movement unionism', which celebrated the virtues of alliances between unions and community organizations. However, the literature glosses over the fact that the concept was forced on labour studies by the dynamics of concrete struggles and by a labour movement that was finding its own voice. This highlights the dimension of power that always governs relations between labour studies and its subjects and between public sociology and its publics so that the more powerful party always sets the terms and pace of the interaction.

The retreat of labour studies and public sociology, 1994–2005

The irony of the South African case is that the collapse of apartheid and the inauguration of democracy resulted in the weakening of labour studies and public sociology. As I have suggested above, in part this was because workers and other formerly excluded social groups could now speak for themselves. The granting of formal citizenship and organizational rights also meant that workers and unionists had access to other avenues and resources to exercise their rights and enhance their collective power. As the country entered the post-apartheid era there was another important development, which was to fundamentally alter the relationship between public sociology, labour studies and the labour movement. The links that labour studies and public sociology had with the unions were based on individual contacts and personal networks. Often, these were mediated by a thin but influential layer of white union officials, and by even fewer black leaders, based inside the unions and in labour support organizations (Buhlungu, 2006b). With the departure of these officials and activists at the dawn of democracy, the few researchers and academics that retained an interest in labour studies gradually lost contact with the unions.

At this point I need to add that the above refers to unions, principally those affiliated to COSATU, which had links of one kind or another with intellectuals. In the case of unions affiliated to the Africanist and Black Consciousness-oriented federation, the National Council of Trade Unions, and the formerly white unions in the Federation of Unions of South Africa, these contacts never existed in any serious way. In the post-apartheid period, contact between intellectuals and these unions has diminished even further, with the result that most accounts of South African labour studies omit these unions and federations.

In the meantime, the new union leadership that emerged with the democratic transition began to look elsewhere for ideas, inspiration and support. In addition to the internal intellectual capacities that they had begun to develop, they made new contacts in technikons and other local and international academic institutions, none of which had any record of involvement in public sociology and labour studies (Buhlungu, 2001). Even more significantly, the new leadership looked to the structures of the alliance between COSATU, the African National Congress and the South African Communist Party for guidance and direction.

Thus, the close cooperation and high levels of trust that had previously characterized the relationship between academics, researchers and unions were replaced by a high level of distrust displayed by union leaders toward intellectuals. Nowhere is this better illustrated than in the proceedings or processes of COSATU's September Commission (1997), which the federation established in early 1996 to investigate and recommend on appropriate organizational renewal strategies. The only university people who participated in the commission by way of providing research material or making presentations were Ian Macun and Sakhela Buhlungu of the Sociology of Work Unit at the University of the Witwatersrand (research) and Richard Hyman from Warwick University in the United Kingdom (discussion or presentation). Other researchers from outside the unions included Vincent Maphai of the Human Sciences Research Council (discussion or presentation) and Owen Crankshaw of the Johannesburg-based Centre for Policy Studies (research). None of the generations of academics and researchers who had been part of the early stages of labour studies and public sociology were invited to present their ideas.

On the flip side of the coin many traditional intellectuals who had supported the labour movement in its early years and who had been at the cutting edge of labour studies and public sociology retreated into the academy, entered the world of policy and consultancy or took off into business and politics. Those who remained in the academy largely took up what Burawoy calls 'professional' sociology, which required them to maintain a narrow disciplinary focus in a context where they were coming under increasing pressure to produce unengaged research to meet the requirements for professional advancement and promotion in the academy.

Thus, the location of public sociology at the intersection between intellectual engagement, on the one hand, and political commitment and activism, on the other, gradually came to an end. With a few notable exceptions, most academics and labour studies researchers ceased to regard their scholarship as part of a political commitment or activism. The effect of this has been to widen the distance between labour studies and the very movement it seeks to understand. In addition, the bulk of labour studies research that has been carried out in recent years tends to focus more on workplace restructuring and broader labour market trends under globalization and how these affect the labour movement. Little research is being undertaken on the sociology of the labour movement and how it is responding to the contradictions thrown up by what Webster and Adler (1999) called the 'double transition',

Flowing from the above, I need to make an observation about two specific kinds of engagement between intellectuals and the unions, namely, commissioned research and the writing of union histories. Given the long history of association between some intellectuals and unions, one would imagine that most union requests for commissioned research would be directed to university-based academics and researchers. In the 1980s and early 1990s, labour support organizations handled large volumes of research and other support work commissioned by unions. These organizations did not charge for their services. As I have shown above, by the early 1990s most of these organizations had closed down and one would have thought the work would be channelled to academics and university researchers. Although there are notable cases of these bodies, such as the Sociology of Work Unit at the University of the Witwatersrand, getting requests to conduct research for unions, the bulk of union requests are often sent elsewhere. In the early 1990s, COSATU established the National Labour and Economic Development Institute, which has done a substantial amount of research for the federation and its affiliates. But the legacy of the morality play by labour support organizations and intellectuals remains strong as many unions are still reluctant to pay for the commissioned research that they used to receive for free.

Over the last 15 years, several unions have commissioned researchers to write their histories. The most notable are the Chemical Workers' Industrial Union (Rosenthal and CWIU, 1994), the National Health Education and Allied Workers' Union (Molete, 1997), the South African Railways and Harbours Workers' Union (Kiloh and Sibeko, 2000), the National Union of Mineworkers (NUM) (Allen, 2003) and the South African Commercial Catering and Allied Workers' Union (Forrest, 2005). At one level, the processes of researching and writing the books are an admirable example of democratic and collective involvement in the telling of the union's history. However, it is clear that that in each of these cases the researchers had to restrict themselves to concerns that were important to the union. The result is that critical examination of union practice, strategic choices and decisions is either weak or non-existent. The two books that stand out as exceptions to this are the NUM and South African Railway and Harbour Workers Union (SARHWU) histories. The SARHWU history in particular broaches extremely sensitive subjects, including racial tensions within the union and violence by union members against scabs during the 1987 railways strike and at a time when union members were being shot by the police.

Labour studies and public sociology today

The retreat of public sociology and the decline of labour studies continued through the 1990s into the first decade of the new century. In addition to the explanations offered above, there are other reasons for this retreat and decline. First, for many, labour has lost its glamour and intellectual attraction, and the focus has shifted to the state and business. The high turnover of union leadership makes it extremely hard to follow events in the unions or to build sustained contacts and relationships. In contrast, the centrality of the state and business in the current transition as the providers of jobs, investment, social services, policies and so on, means that many scholars now focus their energies on following trends set by them. For some, labour only becomes relevant insofar as it engages with or seeks to influence the state and business. The result of this is that little research is being undertaken on labour either as a movement or as individual organizations, or how they perform their representative functions in advancing the interests of their members.

Second, sociology and other social science disciplines have had a serious difficulty producing a generation of engaged public intellectuals in general and labour studies scholars in particular. Although the total number of social science graduates has increased tremendously over the years, the number of those who take labour studies and public sociology seriously has become negligible. At present, the production of engaged postgraduates in labour studies takes place in no more than 5 of the country's 23 universities. This problem is exacerbated by the shortage of funding for research projects that focus on labour-related topics. As an increasing number of older and more established scholars in the field reach retirement age the problem is likely to become more acute, and the decline may take place at a much faster pace.

Third, the field of labour studies has not been particularly successful in attracting and producing black scholars and public sociologists. As a result, labour studies have been conducted by a predominantly white group of scholars and researchers studying an overwhelmingly black labour movement. Although this is not necessarily a problem, South Africa's continuing racial divide renders the research process extremely complex – a complexity that is most likely to affect younger white researchers who do not have much insight into the social world of black workers.

Even in cases where some black graduate students have come through and specialized in labour studies, the majority of them soon move out of the area and ultimately out of the academy and research. A major disincentive for them is often the unwelcoming institutional culture in the universities with strong labour studies, labour programmes and research institutes. Of course, there is a variety of other issues that make labour studies unattractive to young black scholars, not least the appeal of politics over academic life.

Fourth, in a context where public sociology is no longer a morality play, relations between movements and intellectuals tend to be fraught because the former had become accustomed to unquestioning support from the latter, or if there was criticism, it was rather anodyne and comradely. When criticism and engagement moves beyond this, most union leaders take offense and often respond defensively, in the process vilifying researchers and intellectuals and questioning their bona fides. Let me cite a couple of instances to illustrate the point. In 1994, I wrote an article pointing to what I called 'the big brain drain' of leaders and officials from COSATU and its affiliates (Buhlungu, 1994). So incensed were COSATU leaders by the article that when a colleague and I went to interview COSATU's national office-bearers for an article in the next edition of the *South African Labour Bulletin* (Buhlungu and von Holdt, 1994), they demanded an apology before they would proceed with the interview. They objected to what they saw as an insinuation in my article that all the best brains and leaders had left, leaving behind only lightweights who were not up to the task of taking the federation into the future. They also accused the Bulletin of allowing itself to be used as an anti-COSATU platform. Since then I have written several publications that commended, probed and criticized the labour movement, and each one has infuriated some union activists and leaders and made my relations with them rather frosty. Many other colleagues have faced similar anger from the unions, particularly COSATU.

The potential for tensions is exacerbated by the extremely instrumental view that unions have about intellectuals in general. For many in the unions, intellectual input is desirable, but only if it confirms the received wisdom held within the movement. A related phenomenon is the use of gatekeepers within unions to 'screen' intellectuals so that harmless ones can be allowed access to conduct research on unions while 'problematic' ones are denied such access. The gatekeeping can also be used to ensure that uncomfortable ideas are not allowed into the public domain.

Finally, the decline of labour studies is manifested in the decline in intellectual output. Of course, I should preface this remark by stating that the labour studies intellectual community in the country has always been small, and it was never spectacularly prolific in terms of publications. But there was a time when there was a steady output in the form of books and academic and popular journal articles. In recent years, particularly after 2000, output has declined significantly. In terms of books, I can think of ten that have come out in the last nine years, excluding the genre of trade union histories I discussed above. This in itself is not too bad until we start asking questions about the authors and their institutional location. All these books were produced in one city, Johannesburg, and nine of them were published by scholars in one university (two of them jointly with international scholars). Indeed, seven of the books were produced by scholars in one research centre! In alphabetical order, the books are by Adler (2000, 2001), Adler and Webster (2000), Alexander (2000), Bramble and Barchiesi (2003), Buhlungu (2006b), Hyslop (2004), von Holdt (2003), Webster et al (2008) and Webster and von Holdt (2005).

A further worrying trend is the absence of younger scholars contributing to labour studies. Although there were young scholars involved in some of the edited volumes in the list cited above, many of them have since moved into other areas or out of scholarship altogether.

Conclusion

In concluding this discussion, I need to point out that my concern here was not about public sociology in general, but about public sociology in the area of labour studies. Still, labour studies are probably the exemplar of public sociology in South Africa. The existence of a well-organized and increasingly assertive labour movement makes public sociology in this area a fascinating subject for sociological analysis. The foregoing discussion is a first attempt to draw out the main themes and chart a path for further exploration. As one tries to track the trajectory of public sociology in the field of labour studies, one stumbles on familiar themes about South African society – race, gender, class, the colonial legacy and so forth. The lesson I take from that is that the practice of public sociology is never divorced from its social context.

In reflecting on the subject, I have also become increasingly aware of the fact that public sociologists often send out different messages to different audiences or publics. For example, they may be sending out a message of condemnation to the state and business, one of sympathy and solidarity to subordinate classes and one of critique and polemic to other intellectuals. The result is often that public sociologists and their publics influence one another to the extent that where a consensus finally emerges, it is a hybrid product of the dialogue among public sociologists and their interlocutors.

Over the period that concerns this chapter, the context of public sociology has changed dramatically. Whereas in the past the audiences of public sociology were local or national, the globalization of human affairs has entailed the globalization of these audiences or publics. Indeed, the introduction of electronic means of information management and communication means that debates seldom occur merely at the local or national level. They are now global. The birth of the 'new social movements' in South Africa provides the clearest example of this. Although the movements themselves are fragile and numerically insignificant, they have animated debates among activists and intellectual publics across the world. When considering the fate of public sociology and labour studies, we can no longer ignore this global dimension.

Acknowledgements

Originally published as: Sakhela Buhlungu, *Work and Occupations* (vol 36, no 2), pp 145–61, copyright © 2009 by SAGE Publications. Reprinted by permission of SAGE Publications.

References

Adler, G. (2000) *Engaging the State and Business: The Labour Movement and Co-determination in Contemporary South Africa*, Johannesburg: Witwatersrand University Press.

Adler, G. (2001) *Working Time: Towards a 40-hour Week in South Africa*, Johannesburg: National Labour and Economic Development Institute.

Adler, G., and Webster, E. (eds) (2000) *Trade Unions and Democratization in South Africa, 1985–1997*, London: Macmillan.

Alexander, P. (2000) *Workers, War and the Origins of Apartheid: Labour and Politics in South Africa, 1939–48*, Athens: Ohio University Press.

Allen, V.L. (2003) *The History of Black Mineworkers in South Africa: Vol. III: The Rise and Struggles of the National Union of Mineworkers, 1982–1994*, Keighley: Moor Press.

Ally, S. (2005) 'Oppositional intellectualism as reflection, not rejection of power: Wits sociology, 1975–1989', *Transformation*, 59: 66–97.

Ally, S., Moon, K. and Stewart, P. (2003) 'The state-sponsored and centralized institutionalization of an academic discipline: Sociology in South Africa, 1920–1970', *Society in Transition*, 34(1): 70–103.

Bramble, T. and Barchiesi, F. (2003) *Rethinking the Labour Movement in the 'New South Africa'*, Aldershot: Ashgate.

Buhlungu, S. (1994) 'The big brain drain: Union officials in the 1990s', *South African Labour Bulletin*, 18(3): 25–32.

Buhlungu, S. (2001) *Democracy and Modernisation in the Making of the South African Trade Union Movement: The Dilemma of Leadership, 1973–2000*, PhD dissertation, University of the Witwatersrand, Johannesburg.

Buhlungu, S. (2006a) 'Rebels without a cause of their own? The contradictory location of white officials in black unions in South Africa, 1973–1994', *Current Sociology*, 54(3): 427–51.

Buhlungu, S. (ed) (2006b) *Trade Unions and Democracy: COSATU Workers' Political Attitudes in South Africa*, Cape Town: HSRC Press.

Buhlungu, S. and von Holdt, K. (1994) 'Facing the future: COSATU defines its role', *South African Labour Bulletin*, 18(5): 48–56.

Burawoy, M. (2004) 'Public sociology: South African dilemmas in a global context', *Society in Transition*, 35(1): 11–26.

Erwin, A. (1992) 'The research dilemma: To lead or to follow', *Transformation*, 18: 4–11.

Forrest, K. (2005) *Asijiki: A History of the South African Commercial Catering and Allied Workers' Union (SACCAWU)*, Johannesburg: STE.

Friedman, S. (1987) *Building Tomorrow Today: African Workers in Trade Unions, 1970–1984*, Johannesburg: Ravan.

Hyslop, J. (2004) *The Notorious Syndicalist: J.T. Bain: A Scottish Rebel in Colonial South Africa*, Johannesburg: Jacana.

Jubber, K. (1983) 'Sociology and its social context: The case of the rise of Marxist sociology in South Africa', *Social Dynamics*, 9(2): 50–63.

Kiloh, M. and Sibeko, A. (2000) *A Fighting Union: An Oral History of the South African Railway and Harbour Workers' Union, 1936–1998*, Randburg: Ravan.

Maree, J. (1982) 'Democracy and oligarchy in trade unions: The independent trade unions in the Transvaal and the Western Province General Workers' Union in the 1970s', *Social Dynamics*, 8(1): 41–52.

Maree, J. (ed) (1987) *The Independent Trade Unions, 1974–1984: Ten Years of the* South African Labour Bulletin, Johannesburg: Ravan.

Molete, M. (1997) *NEHAWU – the Unfinished Story: The History of the National Health Education and Allied Workers' Union, 1987–1997*, Johannesburg: NEHAWU.

Naidoo, J. (1986) 'The significance of COSATU', *South African Labour Bulletin*, 11(5): 33–9.

Ramaphosa, C. (1986) 'Opening speech to the inaugural congress of COSATU, 29 November 1985', *South African Labour Bulletin*, 11(1): 44–6.

Rosenthal, T. and CWIU (1994) *Struggle for Workers' Rights: A History of the Chemical Workers Industrial Union*, Durban: Chemical Workers Industrial Union.

September Commission (1997) *Report of the September Commission on the Future of Trade Unions*, Johannesburg: COSATU.

von Holdt, K. (1987) 'The political significance of COSATU: A response to Plaut', *Transformation*, 5: 94–103.

von Holdt, K. (2003) *Transition from Below: Forging Trade Unionism and Workplace Change in South Africa*, Scottsville: University of KwaZulu Natal Press.

Webster, E. (ed) (1978) *Essays in Southern African Labour History*, Johannesburg: Ravan.

Webster, E. (1982) 'The state, crisis and the university: The social scientist's dilemma', *Perspectives in Education*, 6(1): 1–14.

Webster, E. and Adler, E. (1999) 'Towards a class compromise in South Africa's double transition: Bargained liberalization and the consolidation of democracy', *Politics and Society*, 27(3): 347–85.

Webster, E. and von Holdt, K. (2005) *Beyond the Apartheid Workplace: Studies in Transition*, Scottsville, South Africa: University of KwaZulu-Natal Press.
Webster, E., Lambert, R. and Bezuidenhout, A. (2008) *Grounding Globalization: Labour in the Age of Insecurity*, Oxford: Blackwell.

5

From 'Critical Engagement' to 'Public Sociology' and Back: A Critique from the South

Karl von Holdt[1]

Much of the literature on the political engagements of sociologists has been framed by Michael Burawoy's concept of 'public sociology'. The aim of this chapter is to develop a critique of this concept, drawing from the writings and practices of a group of sociologists at the Society, Work and Politics Institute (SWOP) in Johannesburg, South Africa, and replace it with the concept of 'critically engaged sociology' – 'critical engagement' for short – which emerges through interaction between sociologists and movements in the struggle for change and captures more clearly than public sociology the richness and complexity of this kind of engagement. Doing this entails the simultaneous critique of the North Atlantic domination of global sociology (Bhambra, 2007, 2014; Keim, 2011, 2017) and the production of a Southern theory that provides a better concept of our world – and this is done by retracing a four-decade process of concept formation and dialogue between Burawoy and, notably, SWOP founder Edward (Eddie) Webster, one of South Africa's most eminent sociologists, as well as others at SWOP.

Before proceeding, it is useful to provide a brief synopsis of the difference between the two concepts. Critically engaged sociology focuses attention on:

- the all-important intersection between the sociological field and the political field, which is the foundation for the specific form of sociology we are discussing, in contrast to the focus of public sociology on the relations between different sociologies within the field of sociology;
- a critique of sociology as a field of domination in which the dominant sociology tends to be aligned broadly with the status quo in society, in

contrast to public sociology which presents the sociological endeavour as one characterized by pluralism and a division of labour between different sociologies;

- a distinctive process of knowledge production that is generated in the tension between the political field and the sociological field, carries symbolic power in both these fields and is potentially conceptually innovative, in contrast to public sociology which is silent about knowledge production and conceptual innovation and tacitly allocates them to professional sociology.

In developing this argument, the work of others in the SWOP orbit is used and expanded, particularly that of Eddie Webster, who first developed the concept of critically engaged sociology, Sakhela Buhlungu, who was for many years deputy director of SWOP, Alberto Arribas Lozano, a Spanish anthropologist who joined SWOP as a postdoctoral fellow between 2015 and 2017, and Wiebke Keim, who conducted doctoral research on South African labour sociologists, of whom three were located at SWOP – and of course Michael Burawoy, long-standing colleague, research associate and, more recently, advisory board member at SWOP.

The chapter is divided into two parts. Part I lays out a critical account of the dialogue between Michael Burawoy and SWOP over some three decades, focusing specifically on the process of concept formation that has taken place on both sides: on the one hand, the elaboration of critically engaged sociology in SWOP and, on the other, the elaboration of public sociology by Burawoy. The second part turns to the concrete research practice of new SWOP researchers to ascertain what is distinctive about the process of knowledge production through research within the practice of critically engaged sociology.

Part 1: Forging the concepts

The late 1970s and early 1980s was a period of significant change in South Africa, with the growth of an increasingly assertive set of popular movements and the strategic attempts of the apartheid regime to reform the structures of domination. Responding to these developments, the young sociologist Eddie Webster described the dilemmas of South Africa's social scientists as follows: to engage with the broader crisis by providing policy support for the regime reformers, to retreat into professional academic social science or to adopt a social science of liberation, which meant working 'to link their theory and knowledge more clearly to the practical activity taking place among the majority of South Africans'. Here Webster is not just discussing career options; he is presenting a moral and political choice which is at the same time a *critique* of both political pragmatism and the retreat into professionalism. He then goes on to discuss the tensions within a 'social science of liberation': working with organizations in struggle raises dilemmas of accountability and autonomy and means negotiating the 'distinction between the tactics of political struggle and the methods of social science'. The solution, he suggests, 'is not to abandon social science but to transform it' (Webster, 1982: 7–11. The following year, he established SWOP in the Department of Sociology at the University of the Witwatersrand as a locus for research with and on the labour movement (see Webster, this volume).

The perspective articulated at this point was developed out of the 'practical activities' of the previous decade, when Webster worked with other students and young academics around charismatic Durban lecturer Richard Turner to support the emerging trade union structures with education programmes and a labour journal, the *South African Labour Bulletin*. But he was quite explicit that this was not an expedient project in which the university was simply a base for activism; he was completely committed to a form of activism that forged a new social science and a transformed university. Consistent with this commitment, Webster was elected president of the Association for Sociology in Southern Africa the following year. In his presidential address, he discussed the changing paradigms in South African sociology and identified the emergence of a new 'critical sociology', which incorporated but was not limited to Marxism as the most significant trend (Webster, 1985).

A decade later, Webster returned to the problem of accountability and autonomy at the intersection between the academic and political fields with their different tactics and methods, drawing on ten years of research with trade unions through SWOP:

> Pressure exists on scholars to make a clear declaration that their research and teaching should be constructed as support for, and on behalf of, particular organisations. To prevent this subordination of intellectual work to the immediate interests of these organizations, I prefer the stance of critical engagement. Squaring the circle is never easy, as it involves a difficult combination of commitment to the goals of these movements while being faithful to evidence, data and your own judgment and conscience. (Webster, 1995: 18)

While there is a growing nuance to Webster's articulation of critical engagement, the central concern remains the intersection between the scholarly field and the political field, and the creative tensions between them. This is where the first phase of SWOP's conception of its practice ends, with Webster's development of the ideas of a social science of liberation, critical sociology and critical engagement.

In 1990, the year that negotiations between the African National Congress (ANC) and the apartheid regime began, Michael Burawoy was invited to address the Association for Sociology in Southern Africa conference, where he

> was stunned and exhilarated by the involvement of sociologists in the trenches of civil society, the ardent debates that emanated from those trenches and the originality of their theories of race, state and society. How different they were from what I had become accustomed to in the United States – a hyper-professionalised sociology that fetishised its separation from society. (2009: 191)

He also spent some time at SWOP, where he had been invited to participate as an advisor on the Deep Level Mining research project that was being conducted for employers and unions in the mining sector. By the time of his return in 2003 to address the sociological association (in its new form as the South African Sociological Association – SASA) on the dilemmas facing South African sociology, he acknowledged that his paper would not have been possible without his ongoing dialogue with Eddie Webster 'both about the changing face of South African sociology and the peculiarities of American sociology' (Burawoy, 2004: 11, footnote 1). It was at this conference that he introduced the concept of public sociology to South African sociologists.

Inspired by his experiences in South Africa, Burawoy had developed the idea of public sociology as a counter to the staid and self-referential 'professional sociology' that predominated in the United States. This led him to develop a typology of sociologies arranged in four quadrants – professional sociology and critical sociology, both addressing academic audiences, and public sociology and policy sociology, addressing audiences beyond the academy. Through addressing the structure of US sociology and reflecting on the relationship between the different elements, Burawoy hoped to legitimate public sociology and foster a greater engagement with social issues by US sociologists. But in undertaking this project, the concept of public sociology lost the critical edge entailed in Webster's account of SWOP's practice. Burawoy argued that all four sociologies were necessary to the health of each and that they constituted a division of sociological labour through which the multiple commitments of sociology could be met.

Thus, public sociology needed the professionalism, autonomy and legitimacy of professional sociology in order to strengthen its own interventions in the public sphere, while professional sociology was enriched by the discovery of fresh research problems that surfaced through the activities of public sociology. Critical sociology, on the other hand, needed urgent engagement with current social problems provided by public sociology to avoid a self-referential narcissism. Professional sociology was assigned by Burawoy the role of guardian of the sanctified protocols and procedures of the sociological discipline, which is essential for the integrity of sociology as a whole, including the other three sociological practices. In the process of elaborating this template, though, public sociology loses its own professional, research and theory-making capabilities, or appears to outsource them to other quadrants of the template.

These tensions were evident in Burawoy's presentation to the SASA conference. His paper begins by drawing a strong contrast between the 'hyper-professionalised American sociology' and the 'engagement of sociology, much of it Marxist, with the issues of the day' in South Africa, a contrast that casts interesting light on the 'peculiarities of American sociology' which requires 'a strange idea' – public sociology – for something 'which in South Africa is taken for granted' (Burawoy, 2004: 11–14). In his discussion of South African sociology, he draws on Webster's concepts of the social science of liberation and critical engagement. By the middle of his paper, however, he reverts to his typology of four sociologies, which, he argues, constitutes an abstract template of universal categories, albeit drawn from an analysis of US sociology, which serve to 'illuminate the history of South African sociology' and its dilemmas and potential future trajectories (Burawoy, 2004: 20). Instead of building on its own indigenous traditions, South African sociologists should think in terms of the structure of US sociology, and critical engagement and the critical sociological practices it entails are absorbed into that 'strange idea' from the United States – public sociology! The tensions in this process of (mis)translation across vastly different social realities are captured in the final footnote, which notes that 'the work of SWOP at the University of the Witwatersrand is noteworthy for its attempt to bring all four sociologies into concertation in developing a new research program' (Burawoy, 2004: 25, footnote 1). Thus, SWOP appears to reassemble the four different sociologies into a new whole when, in fact, they were never separate to begin with.

This is not to say that the attempt to develop a comparative perspective on different traditions and schools of sociology globally, or abstract categories to facilitate this, is a priori misguided. But it does demonstrate the pitfalls in attempting to translate concepts between different social realities – let alone doing this in a power-laden context such as that constituted by the domination of US sociology globally, despite its parochialism. Burawoy's template has travelled mightily, sparking symposia and publications in the United States, in many countries in Europe and in Brazil, China and Russia, among others. Certainly, this would not have happened with concepts developed in South Africa: it was their translation into the United States and the position of Burawoy in US and global sociology (as president of the American Sociological Association, then president of the International Sociological Association (ISA)) that made this possible. Ultimately, the template becomes prescriptive: if a national sociology is not so structured, that is because it is underdeveloped and should be so structured. This is to a certain extent how Burawoy presented his template at the South African Sociological Congress in 2003. But from our point of view, it could be said that the heart of the concept went missing in translation.

The question, really, is why would we want South African sociology to resemble US sociology? From the point of view of our society, on the periphery of the global capitalist order, shaped by four centuries of domination by the West, racked by the contradictions of poverty, inequality, race, violence and coloniality, it is appropriate that our sociology be predominantly a critical, public and policy sociology, all of these grounded in professionalism, which seeks to change the way we see the prevailing order of things, rather than being a sanctified professional sociology preoccupied with the minutia of the prevailing order. From here, US professional sociology appears more as an enforcer of orthodoxy than an agent of critique and change. Viewed in this light, the structure of US sociology presents a distortion of the original thrust and heart of sociology – which is to *critically* know our world. Burawoy's initial impulse was right – to attempt to transform US sociology in the direction of what was being done in South Africa – not the opposite, which was to present the template of US sociology as a model for everyone else. Indeed, Burawoy, reporting to an Italian readership on its reception by his South African audience, commented that they 'looked at me whimsically: what is this public sociology – isn't all sociology public? Why do we need the qualifier "public"?' (Burawoy, 2007: 7).

I think it is fair to say that in SWOP there was always a degree of ambivalence towards this typology. On one hand, the conception of public sociology appeared to point towards our practice, but on the other, it seemed to reduce its complexity – which includes elements from all four sociologies – to something rather simplistic. Nor did it speak to the real frisson of our practice. The notion of public sociology seemed somehow lifeless and lacking in dynamism compared to a practice that combined knowledge production and innovation, social engagement out of which concrete policy proposals and organizational strategies emerged, and the deployment of political and professional judgement in a context of personal bonds and political hazards – a turbulent, productive space that Burawoy, in his wonderful evocation of the life and work of Eddie Webster, termed the 'Southern windmill' (Burawoy, 2010). Nonetheless, we started to use the term, as is pointed out by our postdoctoral fellow Arribas Lozano (2018b). It provided a shorthand that had become internationally comprehensible – and since, after the transition to democracy in the early 1990s, SWOP researchers were increasingly active internationally, this made sense. Perhaps we also felt 'recognized', since our practice was now being engaged with in many different countries, even if in a mediated fashion. And at the same time, we ceased theorizing our own practice.

Sakhela Buhlungu's (2009) article on the decline of labour studies in South Africa straddles a transitional moment in SWOP's theorizing. Like all of the SWOP sociologists at that point, he deploys Burawoy's term 'public sociology' to describe the practice of labour sociologists in South Africa, but at the same time critically inflects it with the distinctive features of the South African practice. Notably, he recapitulates Webster's insistence on the tensions at the intersection between scholarship and political engagement, and moreover he stresses the way sociology was shaped by those with whom it engaged, alluding as well to the way publics (particularly labour movements) appropriated ideas from the sociologists and imbued them with new meanings. The encounter between sociologists and publics is thus a moment of creative meaning-making on both sides. Exploring different phases in the relationship between public sociology and trade unionists, he surfaces explicitly the question of the whiteness of virtually all labour scholars and their privileged relationship with the small number of strategically positioned white intellectuals in the unions, with whom they tended to share many assumptions. Finally, he argues that as the labour movement became more powerful and self-sufficient, and engaged in alliance with the national liberation movement, it became more critical of labour sociologists from the universities and insisted on engaging on its own terms, particularly after the transition to democracy. This meant that critical perspectives arising from the scholarly autonomy of labour sociologists, including a black sociologist such as himself, led to their rejection by trade unionists. The stress in Buhlungu's analysis is on the contestation over and mutuality of knowledge production, and the provisional nature of the relationship between the public sociologist and the organic public they work with. In making these arguments, he anticipates those of Arribas Lozano a decade later.

It was Burawoy's enthusiasm for public sociology and for the SWOP project that reawakened us to some of the issues at stake. In 2013 Burawoy invited me, as the new director at SWOP, to participate with a global network of 'public sociologists' in addressing his students in a weekly sequence of virtual lectures at the University of California, Berkeley. This led me to grapple with these concerns afresh. Webster's concept of critical engagement was resurrected as an alternative to the concept of public sociology in an analysis of my own engagement with transformation at a public hospital (von Holdt, 2014). The concept of critical engagement should be expanded to include not only the critical engagement with popular organizations beyond the field of sociology, but also a critical engagement with sociology itself: a critical engagement *within* the field of sociology inspired by popular struggles *beyond* the field of sociology.

This critical engagement took place across all four quadrants of Burawoy's schema, providing a critique of professional sociology and critical sociology, and generating a critical policy sociology rather than the policy sociology beholden to the dominant forces in society, envisaged by Burawoy. This way of thinking reveals that 'the field of public sociology is necessarily a contested one because of its intersection with the public domain, itself a site of symbolic struggle over the meaning, hierarchies and directions of the social world' (von Holdt, 2014: 190). Moreover 'sociology is itself *a field of power*, characterized by domination and contestation' in which policy and public sociology constitute not separate quadrants, but a continuum with two poles, and likewise professional and critical sociology (von Holdt, 2014: 192). The continuity with some of the analysis presented by Webster in 1982 should be clear – namely the fact that critical engagement is driven by the intersection between sociological and political fields, and that it constitutes a critique of dominant forms of sociology and aims to contribute not only to the transformation of the social world but also to the transformation of sociology itself.

My article together with the other articles in the volume of *Current Sociology* derived from that teaching experience and co-edited by Burawoy, provoked Burawoy to a substantial revision of his theory of public sociology, presented in the same volume. In his preface, Burawoy recognized that his own theory of public sociology had been concerned with 'a critique of academic knowledge' rather than the political practice of social engagement, and he adopted the argument that public sociologists operated in the intersection between the academic field and the political field – 'precarious engagements' on a 'treacherous political terrain' (Burawoy, 2014a: 138). Moreover, he fundamentally revised his theorizing of US sociology, replacing the pluralist typology of four different sociologies, each playing a vital role in the division of sociological labour and overseen by the scientific protocols sanctified by professional sociology, with the concept of sociology as a field of domination with 'a continuum between dominant and subordinate interests, between professional and critical sociology, and between policy and public sociology' (Burawoy, 2014b: 148).

Nonetheless, Burawoy's revision still lacks the idea on which critical engagement insists – that is, that the engagement with subaltern movements transforms sociology itself through the production of new knowledge, and not only empirical knowledge but also new concepts through which to know the world. This is something which Burawoy recognizes in SWOP and discusses with great perceptiveness in his article on Webster (Burawoy, 2010). Given that this new knowledge emerges out of research with, and on, the subaltern world, it constitutes a *kind of critical sociology* – critical of the structures of power in the social world but also critical in relation to the sanctified canon of established sociology – which is very different from the US version of critical sociology enshrined in Burawoy's typology, where it has an attenuated relationship with the world of social struggle. The space of critical engagement, then, is not for conveying the hallowed truths of sociology to the masses, but a dynamic space shaped by the tensions and contradictions produced within political fields *as well as those internal to sociology*, which combines elements from all four of the quadrants in Burawoy's schema (von Holdt, 2014). The critically engaged sociologist is therefore engaged in contestation across several different fronts. Contrast this with the rather more anodyne concept of public sociology and it becomes clear why to us in SWOP the latter seemed to point towards but fail to reflect our own practice.

The next step in the engagement between SWOP and Burawoy was the intervention by Alberto Arribas Lozano, a strong advocate of the co-production of knowledge between researcher and researched. Drawing on his experience in the field of anthropology in Spain, in Europe more broadly and in Latin America, he presented a much stronger critique of the Burawoy template than had been produced before in SWOP (Arribas Lozano, 2018b). He argues that the concept of public sociology projects the peculiar structure of US sociology as a hegemonic universal, that it empties public sociology of the radical content that had been integral to critical engagement and liberation sociology, and privileges 'professional sociology' for no good reason other than that it is dominant in the field of US sociology. Finally, and perhaps most important for Arribas Lozano, the concept of public sociology fails to consider the distinctive processes of knowledge production entailed in critical engagement and, in particular, the possibilities for the co-production of knowledge. It will be clear how much my analysis in the preceding pages owes to Arribas Lozano's intervention. Inspired by his observations, this chapter endeavours to return to the practice of critical engagement as it has developed within SWOP, *without* pursuing the detour through US sociology entailed by naming it 'public sociology', in order to understand our practice afresh so as to develop and deepen our concept of it – and then, hopefully, reinsert this concept into the field of global sociology.

In addition, Arribas Lozano challenges us in SWOP to think more carefully about our own processes of knowledge production. In the second part of this chapter, I reflect critically on concrete research practices in two projects in order to: first, demonstrate the distinctive nature of critically engaged research; second, explore the tensions between the production of academic and political knowledge; and, third, reflect on the relationship between that research and theory formation.

This is to suggest not only that the space of critical engagement in the Global South is a space of knowledge production, but also that that knowledge production may constitute a *counter-hegemonic* sociology. Here the research of Wiebke Keim (2011, 2017) on critically engaged South African labour studies is valuable. She focused on four South African sociologists, of whom three were located at SWOP, and concluded that such sociology may constitute a counter-hegemonic current that provides fertile ground for theory building with the potential to 'make original contributions to the advancement of the discipline' internationally (Keim, 2017: 22). I would add that if such a sociology is to be counter-hegemonic, which is to say engaged in a contestation over hegemony with the dominant forces in the field – the dominant sociologies of the North Atlantic – it needs to entail a critique of precisely those dominant forces. But to engage in such a contestation requires sociologists in the Global South, such as ourselves, first, to make the time to work more consistently and rigorously on concept formation and, second, to be more assertive in inserting conceptual work and the concomitant critique of hegemonic sociology that it implies into global disciplinary forums. While it is important to work and publish locally since a counter-hegemonic sociology can only be as strong as its local base, this is insufficient: such a sociology has to find ways of engaging more systematically in global arenas.

Here, it is worth considering the question of South–South engagement. It is true that even if SWOP had been more assertive at a theoretical level in global forums,[2] it is unlikely that our concept of liberation sociology and critical engagement would have gained the kind of global traction that the concept of public sociology did, produced as it was by a prominent and globally active US sociologist such as Burawoy. Nonetheless, it might have gained a very significant traction of a different kind in other peripheral sociologies emerging in relation to very intensive cycles of popular struggle. For an account that describes exactly such a process, see Çelik's chapter in this volume. Here the 'coincidence' that an anthropologist, Shannon Speed, in her work with an indigenous Mexican community engaged in land struggles, invented the virtually identical concept of critical engagement in order to capture very similar tensions to those noted by Webster suggests a profound resonance across disciplines and national contexts on the global periphery. (Speed [2008] notes the importance of her own identity as a 'mixed race' Native American raised in Los Angeles for how she approached this project.) And, indeed, a counter-hegemonic sociology will tend to resonate more strongly in other peripheral sociologies – or social sciences – than in those of the sociological centre, although here, of course, the difficulties of translation become even more complex in the context of diverse languages, whether these are colonial languages, such as English and Spanish, or, even more difficult, indigenous languages.

The critique of public sociology laid out here should in no way be taken to mean that collaboration and mutual learning between critical sociologists of the South and the North must not take place. The series of engagements between Michael Burawoy and ourselves has been richly productive in both directions, and continues to be so, ranging across not only the practice of engaged sociology but also the work of Marx, Bourdieu (Burawoy and von Holdt, 2012) and Polanyi, in addition to the work of Burawoy and Webster themselves. In the case of the process of dialogue and concept formation discussed here, Burawoy has drawn on the practices of SWOP and others to develop the conceptual weaponry for contestations within US sociology, while his work has provoked us to engage with and against that weaponry, in the process deepening our own understanding of our own critical practice as well as the relationship between US and South African sociology and the necessity to challenge tacit hegemonic practices. The very same process then requires Burawoy to consider how his own conceptions contribute to challenging the domination of professional sociology in the field of US sociology while obscuring the nature of its domination and even in some sense reproducing its domination internationally. This dialogue begins to reveal the hazards of concept translation across social realities and the way translation itself is not innocent but shaped by the relative power of the concepts to be translated – power that is constituted by the field of domination in which they are embedded.

Thus, the dialogue between critical sociologists in the North and the South, the centre and the periphery, can be enormously productive and challenging while at the same time – given the structure of global sociology – reproducing or obscuring the workings of appropriation and domination in the global field.

There are of course material reasons for this. The resources for knowledge production – funding and time for research, large numbers of graduate students, academic associations and conferences, journals and publishers (Burawoy, 2004) – are limited in peripheral locations such as South Africa, and the practices of critical engagement in political fields tend to be all-consuming, with the result that we don't think of ourselves as producing high-level theory and fail to devote the necessary time and resources to this task. In other words, we collude in our own domination. Countering this requires that we commit ourselves to investing time and resources into the conceptual project. Concept development is a slow process, requiring a constant revisiting of the problem through the lens of new empirical research and new readings – a process I call 'slow sociology', which requires working against the immediacy of the pressures ratcheted up on academics by the neoliberalization of universities on one hand and the demands of critical engagement in political fields on the other.

Before turning to an empirical examination of the practice of critically engaged research, it is important to address one final question posed by Buhlungu's article – that of the racial identity of the South African sociologist – not to speak of gender identity. In other words, *who is the 'Southern sociologist'*? In the exchanges considered here, the dominant voices are those of two white men – Webster and myself – in dialogue with a white man from the United States. To what extent, then, is our concept of critical engagement and of knowledge production shaped by our social position as South Africans of settler descent – a social position which historically enabled access to the pinnacles of the best universities with international visibility and research resources, compared, for example, to a black man like Archie Mafeje, his offer of a post at the University of Cape Town withdrawn under pressure from the apartheid regime, or a black woman like Fatima Meer, marginalized and at best tolerated at the University of Natal (Hassim, 2019: 46–8).

The experience of working on a publication with militant black students during the #FeesMustFall protests of 2015 and 2016 illuminates the question. #FeesMustFall brought the issues of popular struggle right into the institution where SWOP is based, the University of the Witwatersrand. How should a progressive research institute such as SWOP respond? It was decided to support the students by providing the space and resources for them to produce a written account of their struggle. Given that the students are scholars in training and that one of their critiques of the university centred on the academic appropriation of black stories and lives, it was obvious that there should be a high degree of student control over the writing and production of the publication. Nonetheless, the proposal was met with considerable hostility and suspicion by students, and it took three months of negotiation to establish a clear mutual understanding. This process entailed a harsh critique of myself as a representative of the un-decolonized white professoriate, of SWOP as a colonial, masculine space, and of our compromising relationship with the Congress of South African Trade Unions (COSATU) and thereby the ANC. The control of funding, editing and content of the publication had to be negotiated in detail, and the students welcomed the opportunity to interrogate the funders on what their agenda was. I was forced to concede a much greater degree of control to the student collective than I had initially envisaged, in the end managing the funds in consultation with the students and exercising a degree of ethical oversight in relation to the possibility of inflammatory language (which in the event proved unnecessary).

Once the terms of the arrangement had been settled, I was welcome to participate in meetings, offer advice and support where it was useful, and defend the project in the university. The result was a significant publication (Chinguno et al, 2017) and a record of many aspects of the student struggles, which both the students and SWOP could be proud of. This moment clarifies the historical positionality of the 'Southern theorist' in SWOP as white and male, the bearer of an oppressive inheritance in the form of settler colonialism, and of a university saturated by coloniality and Northern theory; and it poses the stark necessity for decolonization – one of the core demands of the student movement. This confrontation not only suggests the co-production of knowledge, but the appropriation of knowledge production by the black subaltern in an encounter that silences the Southern theorist before reconstituting the relationship on a different basis. The implication is that the concept of critical engagement still needs to undergo further critique and development – or replacement – by critical black scholars.

Part 2: The practice of critical engagement – political knowledge and sociological knowledge

In this second part of the chapter, I delve into two case studies to explore the processes of knowledge production in the turbulent intersection between the academic field of sociology and the political fields in which sociologists engage. Possibly the most substantive difference between public sociology and critical engagement centres on whether the sociological practice involves a distinctive process of knowledge production or the public projection of knowledge that is produced and validated elsewhere through traditional research processes. And if such sociology is a site of knowledge production, does this knowledge have specific qualities that make it different from sociology produced in other ways, such as through 'professional sociology'?

The key point to bear in mind in this exploration of knowledge production is that critical engagement takes place at the intersection between two fields – the sociological field and the political field in which the engagement takes place. The knowledge that is produced must therefore work in both these fields – it has to constitute both *sociological knowledge* and *political knowledge* – knowledge that has the symbolic power to address a political problem, which is not the same as a sociological problem. There is a tension between sociological knowledge and political knowledge since they must accomplish different kinds of work, and it is precisely this tension that Webster's concept of critical engagement addresses. The sociologists navigating this tension have to temper their political 'commitment to the goals of these movements' with sociological rigour – that is, keeping faith with 'evidence, data and your own judgement and conscience' (Webster, 1995: 18).

From the point of view of knowledge production, the question is whether there is something distinctive about conducting research under these conditions – is there something distinctive about producing knowledge which must work in two different fields at the same time? Are there specific tensions that distinguish this kind of sociological practice from sociological research that is conducted solely within the sociological field for professional sociological purposes? And does the knowledge produced in this way have the potential not only to empower those who are dominated to challenge their domination in the political field, but also to generate insights that disturb the sociological field itself, providing the basis for a critical engagement with the dominant paradigms in *this* field – a counter-hegemonic sociology in Keim's words?

These questions are pursued through accounts of two different research projects undertaken by SWOP researchers in the period since the negotiation of democracy in South Africa. The first project studies violence during the platinum strikes, which culminated in the Marikana massacre and produced a rupture in the relationship between SWOP and the National Union of Mineworkers (NUM). The second project is a major SWOP project to understand processes of mining, rural stratification and dispossession in rural South Africa, and the intersection between scholarly work and a very different political field to that constituted by labour struggles, namely the field of tribal politics and constitutional litigation.

The rupture of Marikana

SWOP's origins lay in its research on the world of work and support for the struggles of the emerging black trade union movement. This work continued after the negotiation for democracy as the new ANC government enacted legislation and established institutions founded on the struggles, demands and institutions that had already been forged in the mass labour struggles of the 1980s, entrenching the union movement at the centre of a system of national collective bargaining, labour rights and tripartism. SWOP research ranged from workplace studies under the guidance of joint union–management committees to national surveys of union members for trade unions, as well as research for the government's Department of Labour and more strictly scholarly studies, often PhD research into the world of work and local trade unionism. By and large, this research was shaped by tacit assumptions that the new democratic labour regime was progressive and, in some cases, the research contributed to strengthening institutions and labour's role within them.

One study, undertaken in the platinum mines of Implats (one of the biggest platinum mining companies in the world), placed SWOP at the epicentre of the platinum strikes that erupted at this company in 2012. Crispen Chinguno was conducting his PhD research on strike violence in the mining sector under joint supervision by myself and another professor at SWOP. Chinguno had identified a platinum mine that had been racked by a series of extremely violent strikes, and he had chosen Implats as a contrasting case because the highly institutionalized relationship between the NUM and management, and the union's solid support among workers, seemed to contribute to a relatively non-violent climate in labour relations. There were numerous strikes across the entire mining industry in the years after the democratic settlement, but at Implats these had been largely without violence.

Chinguno found lodgings in an informal settlement near one of the Implats mines and began to establish relationships with the workers. Just two weeks later, the rock drillers launched a wildcat strike across Implats, demanding that their skills and centrality to production be recognized with an occupational wage increase. They rejected union representation or negotiation, elected their own workers committees and demanded direct negotiation with management. Management refused and insisted that the strikers had to follow the established procedures and negotiate through the trade union. The strike rapidly turned violent, with workers assaulting the union shop stewards, driving them out of the mine and establishing a 'violence committee' to punish strike breakers. The very institutionalization that we had hypothesized as the basis for stable industrial relations and peaceful strike action had been forcibly rejected by the workers and collapsed within a matter of days.

Despite mass dismissals and an intensive police presence, workers held to their strike for six weeks and only settled when a substantial wage increase was granted across the board. A few weeks later, workers at the Lonmin platinum mining company Lonmin downed tools in a very similar pattern, rejecting the NUM representation and demanding direct negotiations. Violence in this strike escalated even more rapidly, with ten deaths, including strikers, NUM representatives, company security guards and police officers, before the shocking massacre of 34 strikers by police paramilitary units. A similar pattern – though with much less violence – emerged in the Amplats strike that started soon after. Within months, the NUM had been rejected across the three biggest mining companies on the platinum belt, and a previously insignificant splinter union, the Association of Mineworkers and Construction Union (AMCU), had been invited by the strikers to come and recruit members. Within a year, this union had replaced the NUM as the dominant union in the platinum industry, reaching 100,000 members while a shattered NUM, previously the biggest affiliate in COSATU, sustained huge membership losses.

How does critically engaged sociology negotiate this situation, where the political field constituted by trade unionism and labour struggles was fundamentally disrupted, undergoing rapid transformations and shifts in power over the period of research and after? In order to pursue this question, it is necessary to reflect on Chinguno's shifting position and allegiances in relation to the union hierarchy, and the way knowledge was produced in his interaction with officials, shaft stewards and workers.

To begin with, Chinguno was introduced to the regional structures of the NUM on the platinum belt by the deputy president of the union, with whom he travelled from Johannesburg to a union funeral in Rustenberg (interview with Chinguno, November 2019). The deputy president and the regional unionists knew the work of SWOP well and welcomed Chinguno, sharing with him some of the problems they were experiencing with the local Implats branch – the largest in the union at the time. As a former worker and trade union activist himself, Chinguno found it easy to establish good relationships with the NUM unionists. They described tensions between the branch structures, made up of leading shaft stewards at Implats, and the region, as well as tensions within the branch structure and between the branch and its members. They stated that the local branch was highly unstable, with representatives being elected and recalled frequently, and that there was clear dissatisfaction and contestation among the workers. They hoped that Chinguno's research, with its focus on violence and non-violence, would help them to understand some of these tensions.

Chinguno thus entered the research context as a sociologist familiar with and committed to trade unionism, and he was seen as such by the union leadership. There was an understanding that his research would be meaningful to the trade unionists and would help them to gain a better understanding of the problems they were experiencing. The research was not initiated by the union, let alone characterized by the co-production of knowledge advocated by Arribas Lozano. Rather, information was shared and access facilitated on the understanding that the research results would be useful and would be shared, as was known to be standard practice by SWOP researchers. Chinguno himself viewed his work not just as an academic PhD project but as research that would be valuable to the union and help it to overcome some of its problems.

Chinguno was then introduced to the branch leadership by the union's vice president and began to explore relations between the union shaft stewards and the company, and their relations with workers. He was taken by the shaft stewards to a tavern where they socialized informally, and there Chinguno met many other workers. He noticed tensions between them and some of the shaft stewards. He began to establish close relations with the ordinary workers and became aware of their deep grievances with, and distrust of, the union structures. He felt that it was necessary to pay close attention to their views, but this required that he distance himself to some extent from the shaft stewards; this was necessary to earn the trust of the workers but also because the union representatives were operating as gatekeepers, attempting to control who he had access to and who he interviewed. This did not change his own understanding of his research – he still assumed that what he discovered by talking to the workers would be of value to the union in terms of overcoming the problems it was experiencing and closing the gap between its structures and its members. Even so, some shaft stewards began to cool towards him.

Thus, even before the strike started, Chinguno found himself negotiating multiple layers and complex power relations within the union. His mandate from the official structures and their endorsement of his research was increasingly irrelevant the further down the hierarchy he went. Some of the leading shaft stewards and experienced shop-floor union members knew of SWOP's research and surveys with the union, and they welcomed him.

But as he 'drifted away from the shaft stewards and towards the workers', he became known to them simply as a student who was interested in understanding the union, rather than as a representative of a research institute that supported trade unionism. Nonetheless, grassroots workers were hugely generous with their time and support, taking him along to meetings and discussions and sharing their grievances and hopes with him. When the strike started, therefore, Chinguno was already well placed to track the unfolding developments.

The knowledge that was emerging through these shifting engagements with trade union officials and structures and via ordinary members was subtly changing in its focus and meaning. Moving on from gaining knowledge of weaknesses in order to help strengthen the union, the study became more profoundly critical. Since the strike constituted in essence a fundamental critique of the union and the way shaft stewards and officials had become enmeshed in company institutions and procedures, transformed thereby into a power that dominated and contained workers, the knowledge that was produced through Chinguno's close involvement with the striking workers became a fundamental critique of the entire corporatist edifice through which the union had been incorporated into the company and de facto performed a managerial role in containing conflict. Thus, through the process of critical engagement with the union and its members, a new critical sociological knowledge was constructed that went beyond what was initially anticipated. The giant trade unions that had been tempered in revolutionary struggle through the 1970s and 1980s were revealed as compromised and weak, enmeshed in the current order of things and acting to incorporate workers into the system of domination rather than challenge it. The sophisticated and complex architecture of industrial relations that these trade unions had been so active in creating was revealed as oppressive and fragile. The result was a sociological knowledge that was potentially explosive – both in the political field and in the sociological field.

While Chinguno continued to see his research as valuable to the NUM, the union leadership increasingly saw him as a hostile agent. Once the dust had settled, he spent an afternoon reporting to the regional structure – by this time the old guard had been voted out of office and was replaced by new officials – and they seemed to find his analysis useful. But the union was collapsing right across the platinum belt, and many of the workers Chinguno was closest to had joined the rising new union, the AMCU.

In fact, the NUM leadership proved entirely incapable of absorbing what had happened. The national officials who attended various SWOP seminars and conferences attacked Chinguno and SWOP, claiming they had been betrayed. They variously ascribed their collapse across the platinum belt to a management plot to replace the NUM with the AMCU, or a 'third force' project to attack the ANC by driving the NUM out of the region. More than a year later, the NUM invited SWOP to address a leadership strategic workshop. There, they made it clear that they had expected SWOP, with which they had enjoyed a long-standing relationship of mutual trust, to rally to their defence in their hour of crisis rather than join with their attackers. They were still convinced that they had done nothing wrong, that they had delivered consistent and previously unimaginable benefits to workers, and that their collapse was therefore inexplicable, unless through the workings of a devious and malevolent force. The NUM and the Tripartite Alliance (of the ANC, the South African Communist Party and COSATU) in which it was a leading force, closed ranks, adopting a siege mentality. It became clear that the political field – and the position of the NUM in it – had shifted so dramatically that for the union, no intersection with the sociological field was possible. What they wanted was political propaganda, not critical sociological analysis. For the NUM, sociological knowledge had become impotent with no traction or symbolic power. In fact, research engagement with trade unions had always been characterized by tensions, negotiation and shifts, as argued by Buhlungu (2009) and as demonstrated in the case of the NUM in Webster's chapter in this volume.

This was not the end of engagement in the political field, though. Chinguno (2013) produced an accessible SWOP working paper, *Marikana and the Post-apartheid Workplace Order*, which was widely distributed among workers on the platinum belt. While the NUM shunned the paper, the National Union of Metalworkers of South Africa – which by then was the biggest COSATU affiliate and was engaged in critical internal discussions about the political significance of the Marikana massacre which would lead ultimately to its rejection of COSATU's alliance with the ANC and its expulsion by the union federation – ordered 2,000 copies for its 2013 Congress so as to ensure a deeper debate about the disaster that had befallen the NUM.

Turning to the sociological field, what was produced was a powerful critical knowledge regarding the character of the NUM, COSATU and the Tripartite Alliance, as well as the corporatist industrial relations regime that had been put in place after apartheid. In exploring the internal workings of this form of unionism, it was revealed as an important anchor of the current order of things, but a precarious one in the face of a determined insurgency by workers. This critical knowledge presented a new view of the order of things in post-apartheid South Africa and had the potential to contribute to a critique of dominant sociological narratives. This process reveals the critical stance at the heart of the practice of engaged sociology – a critical engagement not only with social partners in political fields, but also with theory in the sociological field, as already mentioned. Thus, what Burawoy calls 'public sociology' is revealed as a critical sociological practice in its own right, one that may generate new knowledge and theory.

Of course, this was not the only possible outcome. Chinguno was astute enough to gravitate towards the workers who represented the critique and to risk the disapproval of officials and shaft stewards. It need not have been like this. He could have chosen to continue working with the latter, on the grounds that SWOP had a historical allegiance to them and he was committed to a knowledge which would strengthen the union. But the critical spirit which animates engaged sociology made Chinguno sensitive to the tensions between union structures and members, and drove him to pursue a deeper understanding. While this produced critical sociological knowledge, the result in the political field was the production of knowledge that had lost its power and become unintelligible – at least in that part of the field occupied by the NUM.

Chinguno's account of his research journey illustrates the importance of the *autonomy* of the critically engaged sociologist – an autonomy that is integral to our understanding of critical engagement. However, it also demonstrates how complex, negotiated and nuanced this autonomy actually is, especially so with deep ethnography in the context of the power-laden structures and allegiances of the political field. In the end, the decisions on how to proceed depend on individual 'judgement and conscience', as Webster argues – on professional judgement, in other words. Professional sociology in this sense is integral to the practice of critical engagement, rather than occupying a separate quadrant as in Burawoy's template.

In fact, there was another sociologist, a French PhD student, Raphaël Botiveau, conducting research on the NUM at the same time as Chinguno. This student worked very closely with the NUM structures and shaft stewards, whereas Chinguno, observing the manner in which the shaft stewards attempted to manage his research and set up interviews for him, distanced himself from them. The result was a very different kind of sociological knowledge, one that focused on an analysis of the nature of the union organization and its internal bureaucracy (Botiveau, 2017). Botiveau's book presents an illuminating analysis of the internal dynamics of the union in historical perspective and argues that the 2012 collapse was the result of an internal leadership style that constrained democracy and reduced the interaction between leadership and membership. It is not that this study is wrong or weak, but that it is significantly circumscribed in its perspective. By contrast, Chinguno's profoundly *engaged* research strategy aligns his work with a more fundamental critique of the union and its place in the industrial relations system, requiring an interrogation of the prevailing sociological concepts in the field of South African industrial sociology.[3]

The changing historical conditions with the transition to democracy – the move from an insurgent trade union movement allied with a liberation movement to an incorporated trade union movement allied with a ruling party – may indeed have terminated the possibility of critical engagement as undertaken by SWOP in the 1980s. However, there are several other arenas in which oppressive conditions have given rise to popular challenges to domination, and in which a critically engaged sociology may thrive. One of these is the struggle by rural communities against dispossession of their land.

The sociology of land struggles and engagement in the field of law

The second case study used here to explore the dynamics of knowledge production at the intersection of the sociological field and the political field concerns SWOP's research on the impact of mining in rural communities in the North West Province. In fact, the sociological field in this case intersects with two politically relevant fields – the field of tribal politics and the field of law – rendering it even more complex than the trade union case previously discussed.

This research project emerged as an extension of SWOP's research on the platinum mining belt and was facilitated by a large-scale multi-year grant from the Ford Foundation, which, uncommonly for a social justice funder, believed that fundamental scholarly research could yield insights that could fruitfully inform social justice strategies. The project brief was to research the diverse patterns of mining penetration, land dispossession and chiefly authority in the different regions of the platinum belt with contrasting land histories. In addition to the deep scholarly insights which might help inform strategy, the study was to produce more immediate analyses that could inform constitutional litigation in support of the village communities who bore the brunt of dispossession, and other strategies adopted by NGOs and communities. Thus, the tension between the production of academic knowledge and the production of political knowledge that could be effective in the legal field was inscribed in the project from the beginning (the intersection with the field of tribal politics is dealt with in the chapter by Mnwana in this volume).

The broad context for this study was the penetration of mining, particularly the massive expansion of platinum mining, on the new mining frontier in the former tribal homelands in South Africa, which are characterized by communal land tenure – which in turn is conditioned by the complex interplay between customary practices and precedents and colonial and apartheid appropriation and codification in law. The net effect is that the chief acts as the custodian of the land, which is communally held and allocated to and used by households according to long-standing local precedents and practices. The strategy through which mining companies have gained access to platinum deposits has involved them striking deals with chiefs in their capacity as 'representatives of the community' (for which no legal basis exists): the 'tribe' is allocated a shareholding in the mining company in exchange for the right to mine the land. In practice, this has meant the enrichment of the chiefs and their allies but also the dispossession of the village communities and the loss of their traditional rights to use the land.

One of the cases researched by the SWOP team was the Bakgatla-ba-Kgafela Traditional Authority Area. Some of the village communities in this area had quite acrimonious relations with the Bakgatla chiefs and had engaged in various disputes with them. One reason for this was that these communities, having migrated from different areas and settled in the area, had not been part of the Bakgatla people historically but were forced to come under their sway because of the policies of the South African state to only recognize tribal communities. Deep research by the SWOP team revealed oral and documentary evidence for the claims by leading clans in these villages that their ancestors had in fact purchased farms from white farmers but had been forced by the colonial and apartheid legal regime to register the farms as part of the Bakgatla tribal trust. The research also showed that the communities were highly differentiated, with different groups joining at different times, and that despite the farms having been purchased by the ancestors of specific families, the land had actually been managed communally according to customary procedure without major distinction between original purchasers and other families. This knowledge had rich sociological implications and, simultaneously, quite explosive potential politically in both the legal and tribal fields.

The research experiences described by Mnwana (interview, November 2019), the main field researcher who led the student researchers in the field and the drafting of the SWOP working paper, resonate with those of Chinguno in the labour field. From the onset, it was understood that the research would produce both a rigorous sociological and historical study and potentially explosive political knowledge. This was how it was viewed by the members of the research team and the leaders and activists in the three villages selected for research[4] – though it was not clear exactly in what ways the political knowledge produced by the research would be useful. The research was not conducted for a specific purpose, such as a court case, but many in the villages felt it would help highlight the injustices they faced and make their struggles visible to the wider world.

Despite this shared political understanding, the autonomy of the critically engaged researcher was extremely important and had to be continuously negotiated in a field of complex relationships, allegiances and powers. According to Mnwana,

'the political implications and pressures required that our research be more rigorous even than normal academic research. In order for the results to be credible, we had to get accounts from all different sources and work hard to avoid manipulation by one or other group that attempted to capture our work and prevent us from talking to opponents or rivals. We made the case that for this research to be credible, we had to be objective and speak to everyone. For example, we insisted that we would speak to the chief even though the villagers were locked in opposition to him. We also insisted that we would speak to women in order to get their understanding of the history and the meaning of the land. We demonstrated in practice the meaning of powerful research and what it could do, so they came to understand and trust us and our stance.' (interview, 2019)

Accountability was established through reporting back to community meetings to validate research findings, and this was accompanied by lively debate in which new information emerged. The result, according to Mnwana, was research of a better quality than that produced by ordinary "professional" sociology, because "it had undergone a very rigorous process of criticism and scrutiny"; it constituted "a true slow sociology" (interview, 2019).

Mnwana's account suggests that critically engaged sociology is necessarily rooted in a distinctive process of knowledge production that is both autonomous and accountable to the community, rigorous in its methodology, and acutely attuned to complexity by virtue of the requirements of the political fields in which it constitutes an intervention. Indeed, Gavin Capps, the research leader of this project and co-author with Mnwana in drafting the working paper, was able to draw on his own experience as an expert witness in an earlier and very similar case to ensure that the working paper was carefully drafted to avoid the hazards of the legal terrain.

A year after the working paper was published, the encroachment of one of the mines partially owned by the Bakgatla chiefs on the land of one of the villages prompted the community to approach lawyers for help in drafting a legal challenge. The translation of sociological knowledge into legal knowledge is a complex one. In this case, the social justice lawyers involved decided that the historical evidence of private land purchase on the part of the original purchasers provided the best possible basis to challenge the power assumed by the chief over the land of the villagers. This meant constituting the client as an association of land purchasers whose land the Bakgatla chiefs had no right to alienate – a strategy which drove a deep wedge into the solidarity of the community. This decision was criticized by other land activists and social justice lawyers on two grounds: first, it would split the community into landowners who have much to gain and the rest of the community who had everything to lose; and, second, there was no case in law to contest the mines' access to the platinum resources on the basis of private land rights, since the relevant mining legislation had separated mineral rights from surface rights and explicitly provided that mineral rights trumped land rights.

Mnwana refused to support the case as an expert witness, objecting to the splitting of the community through this legal strategy, but the lawyers included the SWOP working paper in the documents supporting their case. The case went to the High Court and was duly lost. The lawyers appealed to the Supreme Court, but this was unsuccessful. The next, and final, step was to take the appeal to the Constitutional Court. At this point, Aninka Claassens, one of the most experienced land activists in South Africa and the director of the Land and Accountability Research Centre, submitted an expert affidavit on behalf of the Xolobeni community, who had applied to join the case as amicus to the court. Xolobeni as the amicus put forward a somewhat different argument against the land grab by the chiefs and the mining company. This was based on the fact that the *informal* land tenure rights of communities on communal land (as distinct from private ownership) are explicitly protected by the Constitution and, indeed, by a law enacted by parliament as directed by the Constitution (the Interim Protection of Informal Land Rights Act of 1996 – IPILRA). The reason for this constitutional and legal protection is that informal land rights are particularly vulnerable to further erosion, given their lack of formal definition and the historical context of colonial and apartheid dispossession. Therefore, Claassens argued, the Bakgatla village communities – all of them, not just the private landowners – are protected both by the Constitution and the law from expropriation without consultation. She was able to use the SWOP working paper, which was already before the court, to support her explanation of the complex history of the land, including the land purchase.

The Constitutional Court's judgement ultimately upheld IPILRA, requiring the consent of all those whose land rights were affected before the termination of rights and the eviction of rights holders. The judgment struck a potentially deadly blow against the unholy alliance of government departments, mining companies and chiefly authorities, which have colluded to dispossess so many rural communities of their land, homes and livelihoods. Claassens maintains that the SWOP working paper drafted by Mnwana and Capps (2015), and the research that underpinned it, was crucial to this victory and makes a point about the power that specifically *academic* research has in the legal system because of the authority and prestige of academic professionalism (interview, January 2019). This comment adds a further twist to how the intersection of the sociological and political fields is understood, in the sense that the sociological field itself has the status to confer on research a significant symbolic power in at least some political fields – precisely because of the *professional* autonomy and rigour of the scholarly researcher.

This case demonstrates the complexity of the translation of sociological research into the legal field. The researcher needs to be vigilant to ensure that the research is not mistranslated and that the researched community is not prejudiced as a consequence. In the sociological field, however, the research has produced an innovative sociological analysis of powerful interests that combine to dispossess poor villagers and how this is accomplished. The substantive contribution will only be apparent over the next few years as various publications, including three or four books, are finally completed.

Together, these two cases demonstrate the distinctive features of research as the foundation of knowledge production[5] in the practice of critical engagement. Most importantly, researchers are located at the intersection between two very different fields, the sociological field and the political field, in the simultaneous endeavour to produce political and sociological knowledge. There is thus a political relationship between the researchers and the community or trade union; the high stakes of the political knowledge mean that there is a struggle on the part of different interests to appropriate the researcher and the research, while the researcher is simultaneously broadly partisan *and* critical, accountable *and* autonomous. This imparts dynamic tensions and a potential for depth of analysis. Specifically:

1. The research sites present a differentiated and power-laden field in which individuals and networks are embedded in hierarchies, structures of domination and processes of contestation over a range of political and social stakes. This makes the negotiation of commitment and autonomy a complex process. The Marikana case presents the limits of the combination of commitment and autonomy: the explosive nature of the sociological knowledge ruptures the relationship with the NUM, commitment is trumped by autonomy, and the two fields become unintelligible to each other. On the other hand, it can be argued that the more radical commitment was to the insurgent workers who drove the union out of the mines, as the political commitment to the overall goals of a democratic workers' movement overrode the specific commitment to the union.

2. It is the very intersection between sociological and political fields, with all its attendant tensions, that accounts for the power of both the sociological knowledge and the political knowledge that is produced from this turbulent space. While there may be tensions and difficulties with the translation of research findings from one field to another, these two forms of knowledge are not totally divorced. On one hand, political knowledge gains significantly from the data and rigour of the sociological research in terms of the richness of its findings and its status as academic research, which in turn rests on the autonomy of the researcher. On the other hand, sociological knowledge gains immeasurably from the nuance and complexity that is attained precisely because of its high political stakes to the community or movement being studied, and because of the scrutiny

with which it is interrogated not only by those being researched but also by critical outsiders and opponents, such as lawyers, judges and companies.

3. The complexities of the practice of critically engaged research demonstrate a combination of sociological practices that are, in the public sociology model, split off into separate quadrants – public, critical, professional and policy. Here they are integrated in a complex blend that makes for a particularly rich sociological practice.

4. Finally, these two cases suggest limits to the kind of co-production advocated by Arribas Lozano. In complex and power-laden political fields whose dynamics are not fully understood by the researcher prior to undertaking research, selecting a specific stratum of participants with whom to collaborate in defining the purpose of the study may lead to the alignment of results with the interests of that particular group – with the leadership of a union branch or with a particular clan of landowners, for example – to the detriment of social justice outcomes. Hence, in contrast, critical engagement suggests a significant degree of autonomy.

Conclusion

In this chapter, an examination of a process of sociological concept formation was conducted focusing on the practice of politically engaged research over four decades of interaction between a sociologist located in the centre of sociological production, in the United States, and a group of sociologists located in a South African research institute on the periphery of sociological production. The lifelong collaboration and friendship between Michael Burawoy and Eddie Webster along with the institutional durability of the research institute, which meant that concept formation could be extended over two or three generations of sociologists, presents an opportunity for reflection that is perhaps unique in its reach, since it allows an analysis across both temporal and spatial dimensions.

In contrasting the concept of critically engaged sociology, forged in engagement with movements in the struggle against apartheid, with the concept of public sociology, elaborated from the example of South African sociology used by Michael Burawoy in his attempt to revitalize US sociology, I have shown how dialogue and mutual learning entailed processes of translation, appropriation, domination and contestation. The emergence of the concept of public sociology subordinated and silenced the concept of critical engagement, and the latter had to be resuscitated in order to contribute to the emergence of a decolonized Southern sociology with counter-hegemonic potential.

The second half of the paper investigates empirically the process of knowledge formation through critically engaged research in order to deepen our understanding of this kind of sociological practice. This is done through an analysis of two SWOP research projects which demonstrate how engaged sociology is committed to the production of political knowledge and sociological knowledge in a complex interaction between autonomy and accountability, partisanship and critical distance, in which each form of knowledge influences and strengthens the other. The terms 'critical', which rests on autonomy, and 'engaged', which points towards partnership are both essential, and it is out of the tension between them that new knowledge and, potentially, theoretical innovation may emerge.

Notes

[1] I would like to thank my colleagues at SWOP, Jackie Cock, Hannah Dawson, Tasneem Essop, Prishani Naidoo, Mbuso Nkosi, Dineo Skosana and Eddie Webster, as well as participants at the Wits Interdisciplinary Seminar in the Humanities, particularly Shireen Hassim, for commenting on earlier drafts of this chapter, as well as my co-editors, Sonwabile Mnwana and Andries Bezuidenhout, and Michael Burawoy, colleague and friend, for ongoing conversations about SWOP and sociology. Without a generous grant from the Ford Foundation, this chapter would never have been written.

[2] Here I am referring specifically to critical engagement; SWOP sociologists have in fact been active and influential globally in many ways – in the ISA and in establishing the *Global Labour Journal*, to take two examples.

[3] A contrast to Botiveau's book is that by Alexander et al (2013), which appeared very soon after the momentous events of 2012. Like Chinguno's research, Alexander et al embedded themselves with the striking workers at Lonmin, but unlike Chinguno, they committed themselves to a political intervention in support of the strikers in the immediate aftermath of the massacre. While Alexander et al's book collates important information and a vivid account, it does not seek to make a critical intervention in the sociological field (of course this does not exhaust the authors' contribution to the sociology of the strikes and massacre – see Alexander, 2013, and the powerful book by Sinwel and Mbatha, 2016). Thus, neither Botiveau nor Alexander et al exhibit the full range of critical engagement in both the sociological and the political fields.

[4] Mnwana was known to them as he had conducted some of his PhD research in the very same villages.

[5] I distinguish between research as an element within knowledge production and the totality of activities involved in knowledge production as a whole. To fully grapple with the production of knowledge through the practices of critical engagement would require investigating the full trajectory from research in the field to, on one hand, the drafting of political texts and, on the other, scholarly outputs, in order to discern the framings, pressures and compromises involved in each through, for example, interactions with peer reviewers, editors and publishers as well as academic reviews. To date, most of the evidence in the literature on critical engagement and public sociology is *reflexive* – that is to say, it is the self-reporting of practitioners. What we need is an analysis by sociologists who are *outside* the research process and would be able to bring a different perspective to bear.

References

Alexander, P. (2013) 'Marikana, turning point in South African history', *Review of African Political Economy*, 40(138): 605–19.

Alexander, P., Sinwel, L., Lekgowa, T., Mmope, B. and Xezwi, B. (2013) *Marikana: A View from the Mountain and a Case to Answer*, London: Bookmarks.

Arribas Lozano, A. (2018a) 'Knowledge co-production with social movement networks: Redefining grassroots politics, rethinking research', *Social Movement Studies*, 17(4), 451–63.

Arribas Lozano, A. (2018b) 'Reframing the public sociology debate: Towards a collaborative and decolonial praxis', *Current Sociology*, 66(1): 92–109.

Bhambra, G.K. (2007) *Rethinking Modernity: Postcolonialism and the Sociological Imagination*, London: Palgrave Macmillan.

Bhambra, G.K. (2014) *Connected Sociologies*, London: Bloomsbury.

Botiveau, R. (2017) *Organise or Die? Democracy and Leadership in South Africa's National Union of Mineworkers*, Johannesburg: Wits University Press.

Buhlungu, S. (2009) 'South Africa: The decline of labour studies and the democratic transition', *Work and Occupations*, 36(2), 145–61.

Burawoy, M. (2004) 'Public sociology: South African dilemmas in a global context', *Society in Transition*, 35(1), 11–26.

Burawoy, M. (2007) 'Public sociology: Mills vs. Gramsci: Introduction to the Italian translation of "For public sociology"', *Sociologicala*, 1: 7–13.

Burawoy, M. (2009) 'Public sociology in the age of Obama', *Innovation – The European Journal of Social Science Research*, 22(2): 189–99.

Burawoy, M. (2010) 'Southern Windmill: The life and work of Edward Webster', *Transformation*, 72/73: 1–25.

Burawoy, M. (2014a) 'Preface', *Current Sociology*, 62(2): 135–9.

Burawoy, M. (2014b) 'Introduction: Sociology as a combat sport', *Current Sociology*, 62(2): 140–55.

Burawoy, M. and von Holdt, K. (2012) *Conversations with Bourdieu: The Johannesburg Moment*, Johannesburg: Wits University Press.

Chinguno, C. (2013) *Marikana and the Post-apartheid Workplace Order*, Working Paper 1, Johannesburg: Sociology, Work and Development Institute, University of the Witwatersrand.

Chinguno, C., Kgoroba, M., Mashibini, S., Masilela, B.N., Maubane, B., Moyo, N., Mthombeni, A. and Ndlovu, H. (eds) (2017). *Rioting and Writing: Diaries of Wits Fallists*, Johannesburg: Society, Work and Development Institute, University of the Witwatersrand. Available: https://www.swop.org.za/_files/ugd/de7bea_8ff05c74ed634e1fbf3d179284f74cd6.pdf

Hassim, S. (2019) *Voices of liberation: Fatima Meer*, Cape Town: HSRC Press

Keim, W. (2011) 'Counterhegemonic currents and internationalisation of sociology: Theoretical reflections and an empirical example', *International Sociology*, 26(1): 123–45.

Keim, W. (2017) *Universally Comprehensible, Arrogantly Local: South African Labour Studies from the Apartheid Era into the New Millennium*, Paris: Editions des archives contemporaines.

Mnwana, S. and Capps, G. (2015) *'No Chief ever Bought a Piece of Land!' Struggles over Property, Community and Mining in the Bakgatla-ba-Kgafela Traditional Authority Area*, Working Paper 3, Johannesburg: Society, Work and Development Institute, University of the Witwatersrand, South Africa.

Sinwel, L. and Mbatha, S. (2016) *The Spirit of Marikana: The Rise of Insurgent Trade Unionism in South Africa*, Johannesburg: Wits University Press.

Speed, S. (2008) 'Forged in dialogue: Towards a critically engaged activist research', in C.R. Hale (ed) *Engaging Contradictions: Theory, Politics, and Methods of Activist Scholarship*, Berkely and Los Angeles: University of California Press, pp 213–36.

von Holdt, K. (2014) 'Critical engagement in fields of power: Cycles of sociological activism in post-apartheid South Africa', *Current Sociology*, 62(2): 181–96.

Webster, E. (1982) 'The state, crisis and the university: The social scientist's dilemma', *Perspectives in Education*, 6(1): 1–14.

Webster, E. (1985) 'Competing paradigms – towards a critical sociology in Southern Africa', *Social Dynamics*, 11(1): 44–8.

Webster, E. (1995) 'Taking labour seriously: Sociology and labour in South Africa', in A. Van der Merwe (ed) *Industrial Sociology: A South African Perspective*, Johannesburg: Lexicon Publishers, pp 1–27.

6

The Antinomies and Opportunities of Critical Engagement in South Africa's Rural Mining Frontier

Sonwabile Mnwana

Introduction

Epistemological ambiguities about the process and practice of critically engaged social research abound. This chapter details challenges and opportunities for the publicly engaged sociology on the platinum belt – South Africa's rapidly expanding rural mining frontier. It details complex paradoxes associated with producing knowledge in a fractured rural landscape characterized by power asymmetries and intense local conflict. Such a local context imposes challenges for the process of knowledge production and the 'autonomy' of a researcher.

'How will your research help us?' This question was asked frequently by villagers who faced mining-led dispossession and exclusion from mining benefits, as local elites – mainly chiefs and their close associates – held strong control over mining revenues that accrued to local communities. Confronted with a similar question a few decades ago while conducting research on local gender relations in South Africa's former Ciskei homeland, Anne Mager (1999: 13) observed: 'Some elderly people who had struggled from their homes on this hot, windy day were upset to hear that I had not brought solutions to their problems. I hope their grandchildren will find some value in this book.' Mager's response to participants' expectations was apt. No sensible scholar of social science can possibly make a bold claim and promise their research will bringing solutions to people's problems. I demonstrate in this contribution that quality sociological knowledge produced over a long period in engagement with all social classes in a highly fractured rural local social landscape (like the platinum belt) has great potential to lead to positive political outcomes for the marginalized classes. However, I argue that production of such sociological knowledge can also pose serious dilemmas. Primarily, I employ Edward Webster's (1991) concept of 'critical engagement' as a conceptual schema to explain the challenges and possible triumphs of socially engaged research in a complex rural landscape where ordinary villagers continue to demonstrate amazing resilience and agency in their struggle to defend their land and livelihoods against mining capital and powerful local chiefs.

I reflect on the dilemmas encountered while conducting ethnographic research among the rural communities that host large platinum mining operations in South Africa. The expansion of mineral extractive operations into rural areas has produced intense struggles at the local level. This account draws on the case of platinum mining in the rural areas located in South Africa's North West and Limpopo provinces. It details how the law, as a tool for social justice, can be instrumental in defending the land rights of the poor and powerless against mining capital and powerful local actors, particularly when backed by rigorous and detailed research. The legal 'triumph' and successful knowledge production are, however, subject to significant challenges in a context where power and wealth asymmetries and conflict and tensions pervade the local landscape.

I outline the complexities of navigating the challenging terrain between the potential subornation of knowledge to the demands of local powerful interests and the maintenance of 'researcher autonomy', while also supporting the struggles of the marginalized and dispossessed villagers. Such a challenge underscores the costs and dilemmas of striving towards prioritizing knowledge production as a crucial 'moral exercise and political force' (Burawoy, 2005: 6), aiming for research integrity while at the same time being sensitive to local social justice issues.

Researching a polarized rural landscape

The rural local contexts in South Africa are fraught with complexities. Not only are these spaces characterized by extreme socio-economic inequalities, but they are also defined by strong power asymmetries and struggles. In this highly congested rural landscape, poverty resides alongside extreme wealth. Local chiefs – the assumed custodians of communal land and natural resources – are also directors of multiple corporations and control complex business portfolios that run to billions of rands on behalf of their largely impoverished 'subjects'. They have entered into complex business contracts with mining companies, often without proper consultation with the members of their communities (Mnwana et al, 2016). This control over vast community revenues significantly elevates the power of chiefs and their close associates. As a result, ordinary villagers feel excluded and even exploited by the rapidly expanding mining operation in rural areas.

On one cloudy Sunday afternoon in May 2008, I arrived, for the first time, in Rustenburg in the North West Province to conduct fieldwork for my PhD study. Except for the information that I had obtained from media sources and a few academic journals, I had very limited knowledge about this rapidly emerging platinum mining frontier. Little did I know that my arrival that afternoon marked the beginning of an extensive research endeavour that has kept me working on the platinum belt for almost 14 years. I have since taken numerous research trips and spent varying periods of time in impoverished villages that fall under various traditional authority areas in the North West and Limpopo provinces. These villages host the some of the largest global platinum mining companies. Almost nothing has changed in the impoverished villages that are scattered on the dry bushveld that covers the largest known platinum reserves in South Africa. My PhD study in 2008 sought mainly to understand the character of local struggles over mining royalties and community participation in platinum wealth utilization as well as the conditions under which community participation promoted or hindered local community development. I joined the University of the Witwatersrand as a researcher in the Society, Work and Politics Institute (SWOP) in 2013, and here the study focus grew considerably to investigate various issues including emerging struggles over land and mining revenues, inequality, community participation, customary land rights and new forms of dispossession. A large segment of this work was conducted between 2013 and 2016 together with research teams (of which I was a part) under the Mining and Rural Transformation in Southern Africa (MARTISA) project based at SWOP. This study took place in two traditional authority areas that host large-scale platinum mining activities in the North West Province: the Bafokeng and Bakgatla-ba-Kgafela traditional authority areas. For this contribution, detailed fieldwork notes from participant and non-participant observations and in-depth interviews that were conducted since 2008 are used. I conducted most of the interviews together with other members of the research team (mainly research assistants[1]). We wrote field notes after every day of observation and interviewing, and from these a careful selection was made of empirical material documented over the years.

The Bafokeng traditional authority is one of the most powerful modern chiefdoms in South Africa – thanks to the substantial reserves of platinum group metals beneath the land that the chief of Bafokeng controls. In 2008, during my initial visit to Phokeng, the main village in the Bafokeng area, I was received by a local businessman who gave me a tour of the area, including the Civic Centre, where I was warmly received by some *dikgosana* (headmen) and shared a brief informal conversation. A day later, I conducted an in-depth interview with one of them. The Civic Centre is a modern structure in which the administrate offices of the Bafokeng traditional are located. It is also a quasi-parliament where the Bafokeng

Supreme Council and Traditional Council hold their meetings. The Civic Centre is located on top of a hill, right above the village of Phokeng. It does not need the most perceptive observer to deduce that such geographical positioning could enhance surveillance over the entire village. During this pilot visit, accompanied by an informant friend, I visited Legato (the King's Palace) and had a brief exchange of greetings with the Queen Mother (the mother of Kgosi [chief] Leruo) – Mmemogolo as she is affectionately called by her 'subjects'.

It was not until the latter half of 2009 (during my subsequent stay) that I came to know and experience the tight bureaucracy and gatekeeping measures of the Royal Bafokeng Administration (RBA). On my arrival at the RBA offices, the front-desk staff referred me to a white female American anthropologist who was the head of Research and Planning Department (RPD) of the RBA. Although she was unavailable for at least a week, her male colleague, who welcomed me, informed me that before proceeding with the study I had to go through a gatekeeping procedure. The office of the RPD had authority to decide whether or not I could continue with the study. I was then supplied with a lengthy research application document. This document was meant to be a vetting tool for independent researchers wanting to conduct research in the villages that fall under Bafokeng area. I was informed that I had to wait at least a month before commencing with the study, since the application had to be sent to at least 11 RBA offices, including the Office of Kgosi, the Office of Mmemogolo and the Office of the Head of the Traditional Council. This was an unexpected and intimidating procedure to me as a PhD student.

Without creating any additional delays, I populated the documents with the required information and returned with my application the following day. In addition, I pleaded with the research office for special consideration regarding the long waiting period, as I had limited financial resources (as a PhD student at the time) to sustain myself beyond the initial duration of the study. A week later, the plea was heeded and I was called to a meeting (called 'an interview') with the head of the RPD. This meeting was not long. After answering several questions on various aspects of the study, including the selection of respondents and the methods, the head of the RPD commented that the study was in most respects "a bit too political" and needed to be refocused. The interviewer sarcastically commented: "We are not telling you to go and redo your entire proposal – but we are." She then went on to volunteer to assist me with refocusing the study if I was willing. I asked to be given a day or two to think carefully about these 'suggestions'. I was alarmed and slightly angered by what appeared to be an attempt by the Bafokeng elite to control my research.

I sent a polite email within a day, thanking the RPD representative for her suggestions but also politely stating that the focus of the study and the methods of data collection would not change. Fortunately, this letter triggered a slightly positive response, and permission was granted, albeit not without conditions. The following is an excerpt of the response granting permission:

> We are very happy to grant you permission to conduct research in your selected villages, along the lines you articulated in the research statements you provided to us. We are looking forward to interact with you, and be of any assistance possible from our end. *We are interested in the data you are gathering and, of course, your research results. It is* [sic] *possible that you can periodically spare some brief moments to share some of your experiences with us during your stay here?* (Emphasis added)

I thanked the RPD representative but did not give a direct response to her request. Acceding to sharing my data with the local traditional authority would potentially compromise the data and the trust established with the respondents, potentially exposing them to potential danger. The RBA had its own paramilitary police who patrolled the streets of Phokeng and other villages on a daily basis. Several villagers cautioned me to be wary of them. They cited their own experiences of being harassed by the Bafokeng police. I did not return to the RPD office in the Bafokeng Civic Centre until I left Phokeng.

Were the tight bureaucratic gatekeeping procedures exercised by the RBA warranted? Lengthy vetting procedures may be a standard practice in many organizations and institutions the world over. Gatekeeping procedures are common in ethnographic research sites where participants could be classified as vulnerable, such as healthcare institutions and primary care settings, refugee camps, correctional institutions where sex offenders are held, and even business corporations. But it remains a puzzle why an ordinary traditional community like the Bafokeng would exercise almost similar gatekeeping procedures to protect ordinary villagers from potential harm when participating in a research project. Another important question is whether it is even the role of a chief (a traditional leader) to decide whether villagers should take part in an independent study and to put in place elaborate bureaucratic procedures to screen researchers. Be that as it may, vetting procedures can lead to surveillance of fieldwork by those in power. I viewed this as an attempt by the dominant class to control or even oppose the research.

Chiefs and the law

SWOP's focus in the second decade of the 21st century extended to investigating the making and unmaking of social and political orders in the rapidly expanding rural mining frontiers of South Africa. The research studies shifted the focus towards emerging rural struggles, land dispossessions and new forms of rural differentiation that emerged as mining capital expanded into the former 'homeland' areas, increasingly becoming the new mineral commodity frontiers in the southern African region. At this time, I was part of a SWOP research team conducting detailed local field research in the North West and Limpopo provinces to investigate the multiple impacts of platinum mining activity on rural communities in these former homeland areas. This work was part of the larger MARTISA research project funded by the Ford Foundation in South Africa. Later (in 2016) I established a new research project, titled Mineral Wealth and Politics of Distribution on the Platinum Belt, which was funded by the Open Society Foundation for South Africa, to continue this work.

This research on mining and rural struggles supported litigation and advocacy work. The socially engaged approach allowed SWOP to establish strong collaborative networks with NGOs and grassroots movements working on defending land rights of the rural poor against mining capital and unaccountable local chiefs on the platinum belt. As discussed in other contributions in this volume (see Claassens and Sihlali, for instance), support for social mobilization and advocacy work receives very little support to from the university. The dominant liberal university approach to knowledge production perceives critically engaged research as a diversion from scientific scholarly accomplishment. SWOP, on the other hand, has always maintained that the interface between scholarly research and social activism is essential for generating quality sociological knowledge and conceptual innovation.

Common in many communities on platinum-rich land is the intensified conflict and protracted legal battles between powerful local chiefs (colluding with mining companies) and ordinary villagers who are fighting against land dispossession and other negative impacts of mining. The Bakgatla community in the North West Province epitomized this phenomenon. For many years, groups of villagers in 32 villages under the Bakgatla traditional authority have been resisting land dispossession by mining companies and sought to dethrone the local chief, Kgosi Nyalala Pilane, from control over mineral revenues. He failed to engage with the community over mining agreements in the Bakgatla area, and village activists have levelled serious allegations of corruption and mismanagement of finances against him (Mnwana and Capps, 2015). These struggles were mainly fought in the law courts. In fact, the chief effectively used the law to suppress resistance and silence villagers. Kgosi Pilane has repeatedly used the vast financial resources at his disposal to suppress and punish those who opposed him. Because the chief had access to some of the most powerful legal resources in the land, he managed to intimidate his opponents with court interdicts, arrests and legal charges (Mnwana, 2014). On several occasions the chief used these processes against villagers who attempted to convene meetings to call him to account for the mining deals he signed on their farming land and the mining revenues he had accumulated ostensibly on behalf of the community (Mnwana, 2014).

One of the most heighted land disputes in the Bakgatla area was a case involving a farm called Wilgespruit 2 JQ, near the village of Lesetlheng, one of the impoverished villages along the north-eastern foothills of the Pilanesberg. For generations, this farm was used for pastoral and grazing land. However, escalating mining activities on Wilgespruit have significantly affected the agrarian lifestyle of Lesetlheng's residents. In 2008, the state[2] granted mining rights to a company owned by the Bakgatla chief (ostensibly on behalf of the community), called Itereleng Bakgatla Mineral Resources (Pty) Limited (IBMR). In 2012, IBMR ceded a significant portion of this right to the Pilanesberg Platinum Mines (Pty) Limited (PPM) – a mining company that had operated massive open-pit operations in the Bakgatla area since 2008. In 2015, when PPM expanded their operations into Wilgespruit, they filed for an order at the North West High Court to evict the Lesetlheng farmers. The company rapidly fenced off significant portions of the farm, but the farmers resisted this eviction by simply refusing to remove their livestock and ploughing equipment from the farm. A protracted legal battle ensued. This order was granted in February 2017.[3] Among the key findings of the High Court in granting the eviction order were that the farmers of Lesetlheng were not the owners of the Wilgespruit farm and neither did they reside on the farm. As such, the court deemed their rights to the farm invalid in the face of an existing mining right held by IBMR and PPM. The court also imposed an interdict restraining the villagers from entering or using the farm in any way, including erecting structures. This judgement was a major blow to the villagers. PPM continued to erect fences on the farm, prohibiting entry by farmers, even though many of them still had their cattle on the farm.

With the help of human rights lawyers,[4] a group of Lesetlheng farmers made an appeal to the Constitutional Court. The farmers claimed ownership of the farm based on their forebearers having purchased the farm between 1916 and 1919 as a land-buying syndicate of African farmers, constituted by members of 13 clans of Bakgatla ethnic origins who resided in Lesetlheng. Due to the oppressive colonial laws that denied Africans private property rights at that time, the white colonial state had prohibited the buyers from registering the farm in their names. Instead, the title deed to the farm was registered in 1919 under the name of the Bakgatla chief (as an assumed trustee for the 'tribe') and then transferred to the Minister of Native Affairs (a 'state trustee') of behalf of the 'tribe'.[5]

In October 2018, the Constitutional Court issued its judgement in favour of the Lesetlheng villagers who represented the families of the 13 clans that comprised the land claimants. The Court's judgement[6] found that existing customary land rights are protected even if a mining right has been granted on a piece of land. Customary land rights are protected under the Interim Protection of Informal Land Rights Act of 1996.

It is crucial to understand the law itself as a field of power. It took significant years of research, dedicated public interest lawyers and the extraordinary tenacity of village activists to secure the Constitutional Court victory. Detailed and quality socially engaged research was central to this court victory. The knowledge that we produced, as university researchers based at SWOP together with the local villagers on the platinum belt, played an important role in the legal field. The law, as a tool for achieving social justice, can prove skewed and slippery for the poor and powerless. This significantly skewed terrain of power – in favour of local chiefs and mining capital – made it difficult for villagers to access courts and even defend their rights through the existing laws. In the Bakgatla area, for instance, when faced with arrests, interdicts and forceful eviction from their land, the impoverished villagers had limited options. To access legal relief, they needed financial resources, which they did not have. This is where socially engaged research became useful.

Throughout the lengthy court battle, villagers displayed increasing confidence in the research. The research reports we produced were packaged as easily accessible, yet detailed, SWOP working papers. The working papers proved useful for the community's fight against mining-led dispossession. In March 2015, we produced a detailed working paper titled '*No Chief ever Bought a Piece of Land!' Struggles over Property, Community and Mining in the Bakgatla-ba-Kgafela Traditional Authority Area* (Mnwana and Capps, 2015). It not only drew media attention, but also proved worthwhile in local struggles against dispossession. The working paper was a product of a detailed investigation into the social impacts of mining and research on land histories in the Bakgatla area. It detailed the emerging local struggles and connected them to regional histories of land dispossession and group land buying by Africans during the colonial and apartheid eras. More than 150 people were in attendance at the launch of the research report in Johannesburg. Villagers from the North West, including the Lesetlheng land claimants, arrived at the crack of dawn in five minibuses. The report was well received.

In May 2016, the public interest lawyers representing the Lesetlheng land claimants approached me to submit an expert affidavit and provide a detailed expert account on the history of farm Wilgespruit 2 JQ. I was conflicted by this request: the respondents in Lesetlheng and other villagers on the platinum belt would have been very encouraged if I had produced such an affidavit. However, I decided against this. Two main reasons shaped this decision. First, there was insufficient time, as the lawyers gave me less than a day to produce the affidavit, which was an impossible call. Second, and more importantly, there were divisions and tensions on the ground that

I felt might be inadvertently aggravated by the legal strategy pursued by the lawyers. I expand on these in the section below.

Local tensions

The positive response to the research was the result of years of production of socially engaged knowledge with the local community members. Socially engaged research needs time. It took several years to build trust with the local participants, including land-claiming groups in different villages in the North West Province. While working as a researcher at SWOP on the MARTISA project, I and my colleagues had extensively researched several mineral-rich farms in the Bakgatla area where the chief had signed deals with mining companies and where local villagers were contesting such deals and reclaiming their land. Wilgespruit was one such farm. Over several months between 2013 and 2016, we collected detailed oral histories in several villages on the platinum belt. We also gathered archival materials from the national and provincial archives repositories.

The land dispute was already at an advanced stage in 2013. The Lesetlheng land claimants mobilized against land dispossession through a movement at village level: the Lesetlheng Land Committee (LLC). This had been formed in 2007 as the Bakgatla Land Committee, but by 2013, when I returned, it had been renamed the LLC. This was an indication that the forum was now specifically focusing on land dispossession in Lesetlheng village. Other villages (though not all) in the Bakgatla area had similar village-based forums.

In 2009, while still a PhD student, I had attended some of the Bakgatla Land Committee meetings. During the first meeting, despite being invited and introduced by the local activists, tensions quickly escalated, as some community members (especially those unfamiliar with me) grew suspicious of me and were uncomfortable continuing the meeting in my presence. It was finally agreed that I should be 'excused' from the meeting (as the chairperson put it in English) 'so that he can carry on with his interviews in the village [Lesetlheng] ... we do not want to delay him, he has a lot of work to do'. This was a polite way to send the researcher away from the gathering. My expulsion (although quite gentle) angered some research participants in Lesetlheng who felt that the research could help the community's struggle for land. However, this incident did not have a lasting negative impact. Over the years, my relationship with the Lesetlheng community and the research participants continued to grow. Gradually, villagers who participated in the research showed commitment to making sure the research process was respected and undertaken without undue influence. This was a result of a constant open engagement between all social agents involved about the social value of knowledge and how social science knowledge can make a meaningful contribution to the social justice struggles of marginalized classes.

The LLC had always enjoyed a popular following in Lesetlheng. In 2012 the LLC made an application for a change to the title deed of Wilgespruit – to reflect their names as the direct descendants of the original buyers. This application was made through the Department of Rural Development and Land Reform.[7] A commissioner was appointed to investigate the application in relation to the Land Titles Adjustment Act 111 of 1993. Before the application, the LLC was perceived as representing the village of Lesetlheng as a whole. However, things took an unexpected shift in 2012 when the Land Title Adjustment Commission began its process of verifying the claimants. The commissioner appointed to investigate the claim requested the claimants' family trees. Thus, claimants were required to demonstrate who the original buyer was in each family and how the claimants are related to members of the original land-buying syndicate. Sensitive issues started to surface. Some of the elders had always known that not every family that was ploughing on Wilgespruit was descended from the original buyers. The requirement for land claimants to produce family trees raised two contentious issues. First, those who were not descendants of buyers were not going to submit family trees. As such, they were excluded from the process, and some became discouraged. Subsequently, support for the LLC dwindled with many people deciding not to attend land meetings because they felt left out of the land title adjustment application. This application had, therefore, exposed divisions between the descendants of buyers and other claimants.

As previously mentioned, my refusal to write an expert affidavit in the land case was mainly due to the legal strategy failing to take account of the complex tensions on the ground. The lawyers representing the community had overlooked the rights of those not descended from buyers of Wilgerspruit, and risked marginalizing those villagers and escalating the local divisions. The narrow legal terms used by the lawyers had potential to empower certain groups while excluding other parts of the community. However, the lawyers were directed to the SWOP research report that was produced in 2015, and in their presentations at North West High Court and at the Constitutional Court, they drew significantly from the report to articulate the history of the farm.

Victory in Constitutional Court has led to some new promises and tensions in Lesetlheng. As this chapter is being written, new developments are taking place in the village of Lesetlheng. After protracted negotiations between the village farmers and the PPM, the LLC signed an agreement – a settlement offer – with the mine in June 2020 on behalf of the Lesetlheng villagers. The mine, now renamed the Sedibelo Platinum Mines, granted the Lesetlheng farmers compensation of more than R60 million and given them alternative land to farm. In return, the settlement contract grants the mine full access to the mineral-rich land on Wilgespruit. Although this settlement has been lauded as a 'significant monetary compensation' (Arnoldi, 2020), the full details of the actual contract are still not known publicly. However, there are already emerging tensions in Lesetlheng over the new agreement with PPM. Some families among the dispossessed farmers dispute the legitimacy of the LLC to represent them and sign the agreement on their behalf. They argue that individual families should enter into agreement directly with the mine. There is also a major debate as to whether, or how, Lesethleng community members who have never enjoyed customary land rights on Wilgespruit can be included in and benefit from the new agreement. Thus, the signing of the settlement agreement with the mine is still contested and could potentially intensify divisions and local conflict. The true effects of the PPM's settlement agreement are yet to unfold.

Distrust

Responding to participants' needs and addressing some of their expectations does not amount to acceding to manipulation by them. It is important to clarify that no promise was made to any participants other than that the findings of the research would be available to them and the communities in which the research was conducted. As indicated earlier, this was not enough for some potential respondents, who thought the research could and should do more to fight for their cause. It was repeatedly explained that quality social research takes time and must be sufficiently rigorous. We resisted pressures from holders of power (from above and below) who insisted on *their* side of the story being heard. In this way, we gained space and credibility as researchers, not activists. Once the study was complete, some of the research funds were used to organize community workshops where the findings were presented to the research participants. As already noted, working papers were produced (see Mnwana and Capps, 2015; Mnwana et al, 2016) and research reports written in accessible language were distributed to community members during the workshops. The workshops were co-convened with the Land and Accountability Research Centre (LARC), based at the University of Cape Town, and the Land Access Movement of Southern Africa (LAMOSA) in order to make them more effective. These organizations work with rural grassroots movements across South Africa, advocating for land rights and fighting against human rights violations by the state and mining capital. The workshops provided an opportunity for a broader public platform to engage with the research reports and offered an effective model of critically engaged social research. Ordinary villagers took great interest in the research findings, even criticizing them at times. Most important to them was the fact that their struggles had been documented in a detailed way and they had copies of the research reports and working papers. Facilitators of the workshops from LARC and LAMOSA communicated in Setswana, Sepedi (both local languages spoken in the communities researched) and English, and interpreters were used when presenting the findings.

Community workshops provided good opportunities for the local 'publics' to engage with the research and see how it could be used to defend their rights. The working papers attracted a great deal of attention from a diverse array of publics. They were launched twice: in the communities where the study took place and at SWOP. People came in large numbers to the launches, and the reports gained good media coverage. But, most importantly, some of the working papers have been used as part of the evidence presented in court by public interest lawyers representing communities defending their land rights against mining companies and corrupt chiefs. Some of the work has been used extensively in parliamentary reports on mining impacts and lack of accountability by some local chiefs. Also, I was invited to make a contribution based on the research to the Land Working Group of the High Level Panel on the Assessment of Key Legislation and the Acceleration of Fundamental Change, chaired by former president Kgalema Motlanthe in 2016–17. These were great opportunities for effective 'public sociology' interventions. Of course, this was a product of prolonged open dialogue about research expectations between the researchers and the participants. Without compromising the validity and reliability of the findings (focusing on professional sociology), it is possible to produce rigorous research that can be used by marginalized classes to defend their rights. While this did not meet the expectations of all concerned, including some among the subaltern classes, as they later understood, social research practice must remain accountable to standards of quality scientific knowledge and its focus and must not bend to pressures of narrow interests from above or below.

The instances highlighted here of distrust from below and opposition from above are rooted in the complexity of the rural sociopolitical milieu. These cases challenge the traditional epistemological foundations and orientations of social research. How does a researcher navigate mistrust and 'opposition'? These instances are indicators of multiple layers in the local order of society that are shaped by the new mining-led capitalist transformations. As described, in this study, the constant engagement with participants helped establish good rapport and trust. For this to be realized, I had to navigate the social 'worlds' of the participants. Breman (1985) drawing from in-depth research experience in rural India, identifies two social 'worlds' that existed in rural India: those of the dominant and the subaltern classes. He argues that rural social contexts experiencing rapid social transformations can be extremely complex, and he highlights two main obstacles that posed a 'formidable' challenge to his research in the very socially and economically skewed rural India: 'the mistrust of the poor and the opposition of the dominant classes' (Breman, 1985: 6). To deal with this challenge, Breman explains how he explored both 'social worlds' – the 'world' 'of the landowners on the one side and the landless on the other' (Breman, 1985: 30) – and he paid 'attention to the other side of the coin' (Breman, 1985: 30). However, the rural social milieu can be even more complex than Breman's 'worlds', as was evident in South Africa's platinum belt. Not only were the elite are better off than other villagers due to significantly skewed benefits from mining, but ordinary villagers were excluded from decision-making and suffered loss of farming land due to massive mine relocations.

From this, it is clear that there exist several 'social worlds'. Quite often, the 'world' of the poor has its own gatekeepers – for instance, the local youth groups that focus on unemployment, the environmental forums, the groups claiming land and those organizing against abuse of power and alleged corruption by local chiefs. Within the communities around the platinum belt, it was the amount of power, not wealth, that these local activists/leaders held in village-based movements that gave them status and influence. They raised very important questions about research and even challenged us on the role of research in social justice issues. Most of the community leaders were unemployed and lived in poverty. They were vulnerable to co-option by mining companies, and many reported several instances where powerful local chiefs and mining companies would entice them with well-paid jobs and business opportunities. Some eventually fell into that trap and shifted their allegiances, but many did not. Community group leaders who attempted to call the chiefs to account were often interdicted from meetings and even faced serious penalties through cost orders granted to the chiefs by the courts. This raised fears among marginalized rural residents about challenging their chiefs and promoted a general lack of faith in the country's justice system (Mnwana, 2014). In such a polarized and complex environment, distrust and attempts to control or influence the researcher came as no surprise. But such challenges also brought opportunities for critical engagement.

On critical engagement and analytical rootedness

The complex balance between striving for quality knowledge and scientific integrity while contributing to the political cause of marginalized groups amplifies the dialectic at the core of critical engagement. Webster (1991: 64) attests that critical engagement 'involves a difficult combination of commitment to the goals of … [local] movements while being faithful to evidence, data, and your own judgement and conscience'. Critical engagement constitutes a researcher's positionality – a stance which the researcher adopts to strike a balance between fulfilling a moral commitment to social justice (the political goals of the marginalized groups) and maintaining scientific rigor. As demonstrated in this chapter, this does not come without risks and challenges. The risk of subornation of knowledge, or even the process of producing knowledge, to the will of local interests is always present (Webster, 1991:64). However, the strength of critical engagement lies in its 'existential rootedness' (Webster, 1998: 128) in the social and political conceptual worlds. This analysis demonstrates how my own rootedness also becomes 'a source of analytical strength' (Webster, 1998: 128) in the complex social and political context of the rural mining frontier in South Africa.

This contribution also demonstrates that analytical rootedness is a slow process. Critical engagement emerges out of a shared commitment to the value of social science knowledge in addressing the political goals of the oppressed. In our experience, this was realized through commitment to a slow negotiated process of knowledge production. It took several years of field research, which involved negotiation on how socially engaged science can be relevant to the needs and struggles of the rural poor. Such a process is much closer to Speed's (2008) account of 'critically engaged activist research'. For Speed, this refers to 'the overt commitment to an engagement with our research subjects that is directed toward some form of shared political goals' (2008: 215). As demonstrated in the case of the research on the platinum belt, reaching the point of shared commitment and political goals happened over time as the respondents became more aware of the long-term benefits of quality sociological knowledge and its relevance to their political struggles. It was this constant negotiation and mutual co-production of knowledge that ultimately produced quality social science that withstood political and even legal scrutiny. Eventually, the research was able to contribute to some of the most notable legal victories by South African villagers fighting to defend their land, without exacerbating the marginalization of some social groups. Thus, critical engagement is a reflexive process. Without such reflexivity, it is not possible to grasp the complex power dynamics on the ground.

Conclusion

Sociology is itself a field of power with its own internal contested relations of subordination and domination (Arribas Lozano, 2018). As such, von Holdt (2014) identifies the inadequacy of Burawoy's four-quadrant model of public sociology and argues that each of the four quadrants is a contested field of power characterized 'by dominant sociologies and subordinate sociologies' (von Holdt, 2014: 182). He goes on to argue that 'public sociology should be thought of not merely as a kind of "outreach" through which sociological wisdom is made accessible to the public but also as a practice of knowledge formation that may have far-reaching implications for the discipline of sociology itself' (von Holdt, 2014: 183).

The discussion in this chapter adopts critical engagement precisely to demonstrate the strength of publicly engaged sociology when applied beyond Burawoy's compartmentalized model, which culminates in a highly professionalized 'ivory tower' approach to public sociology –an 'outreach' kind of model delivered largely by university intellectuals to the 'external publics'. The analysis has highlighted that tensions and challenges provide a firm ground for open dialogue between researchers and research participants, and opportunities for a mutually rewarding engaged sociology. It is crucial to note that when people are exposed to rapid social shifts, heightened inequality and threats to their land, livelihoods, culture and natural resources, they are likely to expect research to address their suffering directly. When the purpose of research was explained, the participants realized that it might not alleviate their pain in the short term, or at all. Nonetheless, they understood that quality social research on their situation would be useful in exposing their pain (to the public audience) and could be used effectively to defend their rights legally. We were not the first and will not be the last researchers to encounter this challenge of balancing the expectations of research participants for immediate benefits with the fact that knowledge production in the social sciences requires time, academic rigor and the scrutiny of professional peers. This is the phenomenon that Burawoy (citing Ryan) describes as 'the contradictory demands between the immediacy of public sociology and the career rhythms of professional sociology' (Burawoy, 2005: 12). Quality socially engaged knowledge with an effective political contribution was the main goal in this endeavour.

Notes

[1] I am grateful to the following colleagues who worked as researchers and research assistants during different phases of field research: Popopo Mohlala, Katlego Ramantsima, Farai Mtero, Stanely Malindi and Gregory Maxaulane.

[2] The Department of Mineral Resources, in line with the regulations of the Mineral and Petroleum Resources Development Act 28 of 2002.

[3] See *Itireleng Bakgatla Mineral Resources (Pty) Ltd and Another v Maledu and Others* (495/2015) [2017] ZANWHC 86 (16 February 2017).

[4] Lawyers for Human Rights (mainly) and the Legal Resources Centre.

[5] Wilgespruit is still registered as 'tribal land' in the name of the Minister of Rural Development and Land Reform, who apparently 'owns it' (as stated in the title deed) 'in trust for the Bakgatla-Ba-Kgafela community'.

[6] See *Maledu and Others v Itereleng Bakgatla Mineral Resources (Pty) Limited and Another* [2018] ZACC 41.

[7] Now the Department of Agriculture, Land Reform and Rural Development/

References

Arnoldi, M. (2020) 'Pilanesberg reaches agreement with community around Wilgespruit', *Mining Weekly*, 11 June. https://www.miningweekly.com/print-version/pilanesberg-reaches-agreement-with-community-around-wilgespruit-2020-06-11

Arribas Lozano, A. (2018) 'Reframing the public sociology debate: Towards collaborative and decolonial praxis', *Current Sociology*, 66(1): 92–109.

Breman, J. (1985) 'Between accumulation and immiseration: The partiality of fieldwork in rural India', *The Journal of Peasant Studies*, 13(1): 5–36.

Burawoy, M. (2005) '2004 American Sociological Association presidential address: for public sociology', *The British journal of sociology*, 56(2): 259–294.

Burawoy, M. (2005) 'For public sociology', *American Sociological Review*, 70(1): 4–28.

Burawoy, M. (2014) 'Introduction: Sociology as a combat sport', *Current Sociology*, 62(2): 140–55.

Mager, A.K. (1999) *Gender and the Making of a South African Bantustan: A Social History of the Ciskei, 1945–1959*, Cape Town: David Philip.

Mnwana, S. (2014) 'Mining, accountability and the law in the Bakgatla-ba-Kgafela Traditional Authority Area', *South African Crime Quarterly*, 49(1): 21–9.

Mnwana, S. (2015) 'Mining and "community" struggles on the platinum belt: A case of Sefikile village in the North West Province, South Africa', *The Extractive Industries and Society*, 3: 500–8.

Mnwana, S. and Capps, G. (2015) *'No Chief ever Bought a Piece of Land!' Struggles over Property, Community and Mining in the Bakgatla-ba-Kgafela Traditional Authority Area, North West Province*, Working Paper 3, Johannesburg: Society, Work and Development Institute, University of the Witwatersrand.

Mnwana, S., Mtero, F. and Hay, M. (2016) *Dispossessing the Dispossessed: Mining and Rural Struggles in Mokopane, Limpopo*, Working Paper 7, Johannesburg: Society, Work and Development Institute, University of Witwatersrand.

Speed, S. (2008) 'Forged in dialogue: Toward a critically engaged activist research', in C.R. Hale (ed) *Engaging Contradictions: Theory, Politics, and Methods of Activist Scholarship*, Berkeley: University of California Press, pp 213–36.

Sprague, J. and Laube, H. (2009) 'Institutional barriers to doing public sociology: Experiences of feminists in the academy', *The American Sociologist*, 40(4): 249–71.

Statistics South Africa (2014) *Poverty Trends in South Africa: An Examination of Absolute Poverty between 2006 and 2011*, Government Printers: Pretoria.

von Holdt, K. (2014) 'Critical engagement in fields of power: Cycles of sociological activism in post-apartheid South Africa', *Current Sociology*, 62(2): 181–96.

Webster, E. (1982) 'The state, crisis and the university: The social scientist's dilemma', *Perspectives in Education*, 6(1): 1–14.

Webster, E. (1991a) 'Taking labour seriously: sociology and labour in South Africa', *South African Sociological Review*, 50–72.

Webster, E. (1991b) 'The search for a critical sociology in South Africa', in J. Jansen (ed) *Knowledge and Power in South Africa: Critical Perspectives across the Disciplines*, Johannesburg: Skotaville, pp 69–78.

Webster, E. (1998) 'The sociology of transformation and the transformation of sociology', *Social Dynamics*, 24(2): 117–129.

Webster, E. (2017) 'Choosing sides: The promise and pitfalls of public sociology in apartheid South Africa', in B. Aulenbacher et al (eds) *Public Sociology: Science in Dialogue with Society*, Frankfurt am Main: Campus, pp 273–87.

7

Sociological Engagement with the Struggle for a Just Transition in South Africa

Jacklyn Cock

This chapter describes two different sociological initiatives. The first was the Congress of South African Trade Unions (COSATU) project (2011–17) in which the Society, Work and Politics Institute (SWOP) participated. This took the form of 'public sociology', focused on disseminating instrumental knowledge to a non-academic audience. The second initiative was the SWOP Transition Project (2018–21), a critically engaged project that involved working with popular movements in the co-production of new knowledge, which had theoretical implications. This participatory action research was congruent with decolonial and feminist research practices that emphasize empowerment through reflexivity, mutual learning, valuing lived experience, horizontal social relations and reciprocity.[1] Both approaches maintain that 'the role of objective outsider with its resultant professional exploitation of subject matter can be viewed as an academic manifestation of colonialism' (Lewis, 1973: 581).

The normative aim of both projects was the same: to empower the excluded to become stronger and more active agents of transformative change. But the difference between the two approaches may be summarized as follows: the methodology of the 'critical engagement' process (horizontal and dialogic) created spaces for dialogue and exchange that was intrinsically empowering, while the public sociology approach (vertical and didactic) was more limited in the sense of only containing that potential.

The struggle for a just transition in the South African context

The definition of a 'just transition' is intensely contested. While there is some agreement that we need to change our dependence on fossil fuels, there is no consensus about the depth or direction of such change. The contestation is between powerful interests upholding the existing order and challenges to the current distribution of power and resources which makes South Africa one of the most unequal societies in the world.

At present, three broad approaches to the goal of a 'just transition' may be identified:

- The 'extreme' version of a green economy emphasizes providing capital with incentives to change. This formulation includes the 'financialization of nature' in the form of costing 'ecosystem services', reducing emissions from deforestation and degradation in developing countries, biodiversity and carbon offsets, all of which reduce nature to 'natural capital' and represent an attempt by capital to effect the last enclosure of the commons – that of 'nature' itself. This extreme version is being actively promoted by the powerful forces Susan George calls 'the Davos class', an alliance of government leaders, philanthropists and corporate executives who form the 'nomadic, powerful and interchangeable' elite created by capitalist globalization' (2010: 7).
- A more moderate version favours a low-carbon, resource-efficient and socially inclusive economy, sometimes framed as 'a new Green Deal'. Reformist change focuses narrowly on constructing a new energy regime with new technology, 'green' jobs, consultation and protection of the interests of the most vulnerable.
- An alternative notion views the climate crisis as a catalysing force for massive transformative change, an alternative development path and new ways of producing, consuming and relating to nature to create a more just and equal society.

These differences involve disparate strategic agendas that have been described as 'social dialogue' and 'social power' approaches (Sweeney and Treat, 2018). Social dialogue is today the dominant discourse for a just transition globally. This means that the concept 'has been defined in such a way that poses little or no challenge to the mainstream, pro-growth, business-dominated narrative, a narrative that was largely created by the liberal wing of the global corporate elite' (Sweeney and Treat, 2018: 27). It is framed in a benign and non-confrontational approach that marginalizes labour, allocating it a relatively passive role. 'The actual transition will be primarily the responsibility of others – mainly governments, corporations and investors'

(Sweeney and Treat, 2018: 19). By contrast, the social power vision of a just transition is radically democratic and inclusive, calling for the redistribution of power and resources. It holds at its centre a recognition that nothing short of a deep socio-economic and ecological transition will be sufficient for the challenges our planet currently faces. The social dialogue approach is simply not up to the task, but we have 'an obsession with dialogue' as a 'kind of panacea'. It promotes a hope that 'as long as we are having dialogues … all will be well'; 'somehow dialogues will somehow bring about change' (Swilling, 2020: 9). The social dialogue approach could be treated as stages rather than as alternatives. That would involve building 'counter power' in order to engage effectively in social dialogue.[2]

Overall, the South African state uses the social dialogue approach to a just transition, as is evident in the National Development Plan (National Planning Commission, 2012), the series of 'dialogues' with 'relevant stakeholders' all around the country and the cabinet's National Economic Recovery Plan. There is widespread official denialism of the depth and extent of the climate crisis, denialism similar to that of the AIDS[3] pandemic previously. 'Government cannot face up to what it sees coming because it remains wedded to the dominant interests of the mineral-energy complex. It remains locked in a view of the world in which economic growth constitutes the central organizing principle of development' (Hallowes, 2011: 18).

The coal-dominated electricity sector is an important component of the Minerals–Energy Complex, the system of accumulation that continues to dominate the economy and which has historically relied on cheap coal and cheap labour. It 'encompasses critical links and networks of power between the financial sector, government, the private sector and parastatals such as the Industrial Development Corporation and Eskom' (Baker et al, 2015: 8). The electricity utility Eskom, which has always been committed to coal, is in deep debt and disarray. Billions were stolen from it via state capture (Swilling and Chipkin, 2018). In addition, mismanagement cost overruns in building two of the largest coal power stations in the world, Kusile and Medupi, have pushed Eskom to the point of collapse.

At the same time, mining corporations are well organized in the Mining Council, which promotes the notion of coal mining and burning as the essential road to economic growth and stability and is seldom challenged. Coal provides 90 per cent of electricity and is a major source of employment and foreign exchange. The Integrated Resource Plan announced by the Minister of Mineral Resources and Energy in 2019 refers to the need for a just transition, but speaks only to the partial decommissioning of Eskom's 16 coal-fired power plants and of reducing reliance on coal to less than 20 per cent by 2050. The document appears oblivious to the urgency of responding to accelerating climate change.

Some trade unions, such as the South African Federation of Trade Unions (SAFTU), do recognize this urgency and advocate the social power approach that involves militant, class-based activism. It is willing to challenge existing power relations and call for public ownership and democratic control of key resources. However, the labour movement is marked by increasing fragmentation and ideological divisions, while their power is eroding as unemployment rises and more workers are in precarious, outsourced jobs.

South Africa's transition from coal is now underway slowly and unevenly, and is not the outcome of an inclusive and democratic process. It has been described as 'chaotic, unplanned and deeply unjust' (Hallowes, personal communication, 11 November 2020). Furthermore, a failure to contextualize the notion in an African context has led to some dismissals on the grounds that 'it is a northern notion that comes from highly developed countries and is not fair to us' (interview with National Union of Mineworkers (NUM) official, Johannesburg, 16 May 2019).

There is a general neglect of 'the social' in terms of impacts, interactions, relational ties, collective practices and institutions. This is not unique to South Africa. In the Global South generally, the social aspects of energy transitions are neglected. In these locations, 'energy transitions are still largely perceived as (and expected to be) top-down, government-led, private actor-driven, and/or donor-initiated interventions that highlight the technical – rather than the sociotechnical – potential of renewables and demonstrate their economic feasibility' (Marquardt and Delina, 2019: 91). It follows that there is also general neglect of power. 'A just energy transition is intensely political ... but a narrow focus on policy management (often focused on energy technologies ...) characterizes much of the literature' (Healy and Barry, 2017: 452).

Overall, the people most affected and least responsible for the climate crisis are neglected: the voices and lived experience of the 90,000 coal workers and the communities living near coal-fired power stations and mines are not heard. The fundamental cause of the climate crisis is not acknowledged, and the concept of a just transition has largely been appropriated by powerful elites, stripped of its visionary potential and shrunk to mean a shift to a new energy regime in a perverted form of 'green capitalism' dependent on expanding markets and new technology. As one analyst warns, 'there is a distinct danger that one direction of a transition is towards a decarbonised ecologically unsustainable future that leaves existing inequalities intact' (Swilling, 2020: 131).

This neglect of deepening inequalities is part of the inattention given to justice. Justice is not simply about the distribution of goods, but rather, as Nussbaum (2000) and Sen (1999) argue, their purpose: enabling people to develop the capabilities to create a good life. At present, 'a good life' is a remote possibility for coal workers, especially those working underground and exposed to serious lung (and other) diseases from inhaling coal dust, and communities living near coal mines and coal-fired power stations, who face serious injustices such as dispossession of their land and livelihoods as well as exposure to air and water pollution that bring many health hazards. This neglect may be traced to the 2015 Paris Agreement on climate change, where the word 'justice' appears only once and 'amounts to an explicit disavowal of the concept' (Ghosh, 2016: 158). Furthermore, discussions of energy rarely incorporate justice dimensions (Healey and Barry, 2017: 451). This neglect is evident in how the transition is unfolding at the local level.

In 2019, Eskom admitted that it had no detailed plans or budgets in place for the decommissioning of five older coal power plants – Grootvlei, Camden, Arnot, Kriel and Hendrina – which were said to be closing shortly with a loss of about 30,000 direct and indirect jobs. Two units at Hendrina have already been closed and the remaining eight will be 'parked' this year. The bulk of the workforce consists of 2,300 contract workers, hired by labour brokers, for whom Eskom is taking no responsibility (interview with Hendrina official, Pullenhope, 8 January 2018). No provision has been made for retraining and reskilling to address these job losses. This reflects the precarious nature of the overall labour force, as half of the coal workers are migrants employed on short-term contracts (Burton et al, 2018).

A public sociology approach: Working with organized labour (2011–17)

Sociological participation in this project with organized labour drew on SWOP's long-standing tradition of engagement with social movements. Based on his experience with SWOP, Michael Burawoy developed the notion of 'organic public sociology in which the sociologist works in close connection with a visible, thick, active and often counter-public' (Burawoy 2005: 269) – in this case, organized labour. For academics, this experience was inspired by SWOP's commitment to scholarly social engagement with a wider world outside the confines of the university and the rejection of what the French sociologist and activist Pierre Bourdieu calls 'scholastic enclosure', or a remote and detached academic elitism.[4]

Beginning in 2010, the labour movement in South Africa played a key role in introducing and promoting a transformative understanding of a 'just transition' from fossil fuels. One strategy was the establishment in 2011 by the research arm of COSATU of a reference group in which all 22 affiliate unions were represented along with activists from key environmental justice organizations. Drawing on 'coalition power', this potentially formed the embryo of a red–green coalition to drive a deep and transformative just transition.

The immediate sociological challenge was one of translation: the concept of a just transition was imported by the South African labour movement from the Global North. A document launched at the 2018 United Nations Climate Change Conference in Poland pointed out that while the idea of a just transition 'has gained traction in the international policy space and the global North, apart from a few notable exceptions – including South Africa – it is rarely referred to in the global South' (United Nations Research Institute for Social Development, 2018: 10). Thus, we defined the sociological task in this reference group as participating in translating this Northern notion to the Global South, specifically with reference to South African issues of working-class relevance such as rising unemployment, food insecurity and energy poverty. The commitment of sociology to 'making the invisible visible', in Burawoy's phrase, was especially relevant to providing workers with information about the climate crisis and specifically the relation between coal production, carbon emissions and the impacts of climate change.

Over a six-year period, this very active grouping engaged in various activities.

- Workshops were organized with all COSATU-affiliated unions to discuss popular education on climate change and the necessity of a just transition, and there were public seminars on concrete issues affecting the everyday experience of the working class, such as food, water and energy.
- Drawing from the British trade union experience, members of the group contributed to the initiation of a climate jobs campaign which engaged in extensive research and listed over a million new alternative 'climate jobs', meaning those that help to reduce the emissions of greenhouse gases and built the resilience of communities to withstand the impact of climate change (Ashley, 2016: 27). Examples include jobs in developing renewable energy plants, public transport and small-scale organic agriculture.
- Research was conducted on developing responses to climate change, such as energy alternatives and reducing water usage in a range of industries (including poultry and mining).
- This work contributed to a climate change policy framework which was endorsed by COSATU's Central Committee. A pioneering policy document claimed that a just transition meant 'putting the needs of working and poor people first in the social and economic changes ahead of us' (COSATU, 2011: 1). Furthermore it 'provides the opportunity for deeper transformation that includes the redistribution of power and resources towards a more just and equitable social order' (COSATU, 2011: 4). The document formulated 15 climate change policy principles linking sustainability and justice. It included recognition that the fundamental cause of the climate crisis is the expansionist logic of the capitalist system and argued that a new low-carbon development path

is needed which addresses the need for decent jobs and the elimination of unemployment.

However, 'while this framework has not been abolished, it did not feed into any specific union policies' (Rathzel et al, 2018: 507). In hindsight, there was too much focus within this group on principled rather than strategic questions. This red–green collaboration was grounded on promoting understanding the cause and effects of climate change rather than on the content and the modalities of a just transition. Furthermore, there were differences between the NUM and the National Union of Metalworkers of South Africa (NUMSA), which should have been addressed more directly. The NUM was increasingly defensive of the interests of coal miners, due to threats of job losses from mine closures, falling coal prices, mechanization, absolutist demands from environmental activists and the divestment movement. Then (and now) the NUM objected to the slogan 'keep the coal in the hole', and it continues to argue for 'clean coal' from expensive and untested technological innovation such as carbon capture and storage.

Since the time of the COSATU reference group, the notion of a red–green coalition to drive a just transition has faded. The environmental movement is increasingly adamant about the immediate closure of coal mines and coal-fired power stations, and a shift to renewable energy (in whatever form) is essential to a just transition. At the same time, growing unemployment means that the labour movement has largely (with the exception of SAFTU) retreated into the defence of jobs and is adamant that the state's privatized renewable energy policy is a threat as it will involve job losses and higher energy prices. Today, COSATU demonstrates the limitations of a social dialogue approach which fails to develop a strong counter power.

The difficulties involved in popular forces driving a just transition come not only from 'above' in terms of the marketized interests of the powerful; there are also challenges from 'below' in areas where the poor and the powerless have a material dependence on coal.

The research approach: Empowering through 'exchange workshops'

Following an approach of mutual learning, besides a review of primary and secondary sources, interviews and a scoping exercise conducted by three trained community researchers who interviewed informal traders and coal workers, the research relied on 'exchange workshops'. These involved an exchange of two types of knowledge: direct, experiential knowledge of the problems of living in a mining-affected community; and formal knowledge, such as information about other environmental justice struggles, new policy developments and contested understandings of a just transition.

From the outset, SWOP researchers were anxious to avoid what Mazibuko Jara calls 'an extractivist research methodology' which simply takes information from key informants, often using such knowledge as an instrument of oppression (interview, Johannesburg 2019). Instead, we had to 'create an alternative knowledge ... that is radical, gendered, empirically sound and politically enabling' (Mukherjee et al, 2011: 168). We understood 'politically enabling' to mean empowering community members with the information and confidence to formulate demands and participate, or deepening the effectiveness of those already active in the struggle, to ensure that the transition from coal is just and transformative. The exchange workshops were also empowering in the sense of providing (and provoking) collective reflection on people's everyday lives, including experiences often defined initially as individual troubles but, through discussion, redefined as shared social issues which require collective solutions (in other words, C. Wright Mill's definition of 'the sociological imagination').

We learned a great deal but were aware of 'the inherently paradoxical positionality of the researcher, at once reinforcing hierarchies of power at the same time as actively involved in transforming these relationships' (Motta and Nilsen, 2011: 22). Each member of the SWOP team spent some time introducing themselves, explaining that we wanted to learn from the lived experience of the participants and stressing that we aimed to work 'with' not 'on' the emerging anti-coal movement. Workshops included an average of 50–60 local people, invited by key local activists.

Each meeting lasted one day and was divided into two sessions. The morning sessions focused on the lived experience and understandings of participants. Researchers posed the questions: What is it like to live in a mining-affected community? What would a world without coal look like? After a substantial lunch, the afternoon sessions were spent answering questions on broader issues, such as the meaning of environmental justice, a just transition, changing legislation and policy regarding coal, and so on. Leaflets on climate change and a just transition were written, translated into different African languages and distributed at the end of the meetings.

Research sites

All the research sites are spaces of displacement deprivation and exclusion. Many of the communities have experienced dispossession by coal mining corporations, involving loss of their land and livelihoods, desecration of ancestral graves, damage to homes from blasting, the death of animals during forced removals, and illness from air and water pollution (Hallowes and Munnik, 2017). However, the sites are not homogenous, and there are striking differences between Somkhele, marked by powerful traditional authorities who control land and practise close surveillance over villagers, and the Mpumalanga sites, where people have different attitudes to nature, mining and sources of violence and intimidation.

Mainly women participated in exchange workshops in the different areas. In Somkhele, a group of some 4,000 residents of ten villages in KwaZulu-Natal between Hluhluwe–iMfolozi Park and Mtubatuba came together. They began a battle with Tendele Coal when it started mining in the area in 2004. Over the years, the mine has expanded and currently operates over a vast area affecting thousands of people. The residents, who had lived there for generations, lost the land on which they depended for grazing livestock and growing food. This involved massive social and ecological disruption. One of the residents is typical of those who were left destitute when her land was expropriated without compensation, she lost 52 head of cattle and two hectares of land, on which she had planted beans, cabbages, mealies, sweet potatoes and cabbages. On site visits, we were told that "everyone here is sick" from air pollution, and we witnessed the damage to remaining homes due to blasting as well as the fence that was blocking access to the stream that had been a major source of water.

In Mpumalanga, many communities are overcrowded, neglected townships or informal settlements. Most of the inhabitants are migrants from other parts of the country, who, unlike those in Somkhele, lack deep attachments to the land and are often excluded from municipal services such as housing, electricity, water and roads. The three Mpumalanga research sites – Phola, Vosman and Arbor – are situated near Emalahleni (literally, 'the place of coal'), which has been described as one of the most polluted places in the world. The Mpumalanga Highveld contains almost all of Eskom's 16 coal-fired power stations and accounts for 83 per cent of the country's coal production (Hallows and Munnik, 2017).

Vosman, outside Emalahleni, is surrounded by coal-fired power stations and mines, such as the Khutala Colliery, one of the largest underground coal mines in the world. An opencast mine is located close to people's houses. One resident, Promise Mabilo, maintained:

> 'we are living in hell here … it is not a happy place, with infrequent refuse removal, irregular supplies of water so people rely on streams which are already contaminated with sewage, and the air is dirty. … This is a very poor place. There are no jobs. People rely on the government grants and borrow money a lot. The miners are all from outside. Local people fail the induction tests.' (interview, Vosman, 8 June 2018)

By contrast, an informant from Arbor, which is surrounded by coal plants, described it as a "good place" despite a lack of basic services. We first interviewed her, together with five other women, in an airless container as they worked on sewing machines donated by the mine for production of worker uniforms. She said:

> 'People here don't want the mine to close. They put money into the community, but the local community is suffering, they only have enough to buy food. ... The mine sends in a truck roughly every two weeks to bring water to the community. ... Arbor is a good place. We look after each other like a family.' (interview, Arbor, 9 November 2018)

Our third research site, Phola township, is eight kilometres from the town of Ogies, next to more than three opencast coal operations across the N12 highway: Zibulo, Anglo American, Klipspruit (South32), Khanyisa and Kendal Power Station. Entering Phola, with its bustling streets lined with a variety of spaza shops, one is struck by the sight of vacant space next to big piles of rubble. This is all that remains of the municipal offices. On 14 August 2018, 7,000 residents took to the streets to deliver a memo to Mayor Linah Malatjie. When no meeting took place, the protest turned violent. Late that evening, the municipal building was burned to the ground, and all the offices inside were completely destroyed. According to Yvonne Vosman from the Greater Phola Ogies Women Forum, Phola township is a highly politicized place, known for community protests. These are often about the failure of the mines to employ local people, but also issues such as the relocation of over 1,000 graves by Glencore for their opencast mine.

Using an empowering research approach that emphasizes collaboration, sharing and co-production of knowledge, this chapter asserts the importance of the voices and lived experience of people in these coal-affected communities, which are largely absent from the present elite capture of the idea of a just transition. What emerged was new knowledge, including a complex pattern of contradictory, ambiguous resistance based largely on a material dependence on coal, especially in Mpumalanga.

Material dependence on coal

In many mining-affected communities, dependence on coal creates socially complex, ambiguous patterns of resistance, which sometimes undermine the possibilities of a just transition. Coal provides at least the possibility of employment, and coal workers provide a market for extensive informal sector activities. These forms of livelihood are crucial in the Global South (Mosoetsa, 2016). Activities identified in a scoping exercise on this dependence include selling fruit and vegetables, 'russians' (sausages), alcohol and cigarettes, or herbal medicine, carrying out shoe repairs, hairdressing, providing food, servicing taverns, running driving schools, repairing cars, and panel beating and spraying. Others rent backyard rooms to migrant coal miners, wash clothes and cars, drive the coal trucks and do cleaning work. In Arbor, one woman described how renting a backyard room to a coal miner brought in an income of R 800, which provided "food for the household". The food items consumed were "tea, sugar and mealie meal" (interview, Arbor, 12 November 2018).

Several informants expressed ambivalence about coal because of this dependence, though some stressed that there were no alternative forms of employment or income generation. One informant, a member of a local organization that describes itself as 'anti-coal mining', has a contract as a cleaner at a local mine. Some communities regularly receive wheelbarrows of inferior-quality coal from the mine, and many depend on coal as a source of energy because either they are not connected to the electricity grid or because "there are no trees here to warm our houses". There was no expression of alternatives to coal as a source of energy. "Coal is good because it gives us electricity. With coal you can cook and keep warm."

While local people do not think about coal in a single way, SWOP research found limited understanding of the relation between the 'shocks' of climate change – such as rising temperatures and droughts, carbon emissions, mine closures – and the need for a just transition. Participants in exchange workshops and the vast majority of the 120 informal traders and coal workers interviewed in the three different Mpumalanga communities were opposed to the closure of coal mines for a range of reasons. In Arnot, one woman said, "people here don't want the mine to close; there is mining everywhere in South Africa, we have nowhere to run to" (interview, 9 November 18). Another woman asked, "if the mine closes, how will I get compensation for the damage to my house from blasting?" The most common reason cited for opposing mine closures was that it would lead to higher unemployment. Instead of understanding a just transition as a space for positive change, it was even claimed in a workshop that "this just transition will kill us".

According to an environmental justice activist, "most people in Somkhele in KwaZulu-Natal want the mines to close, which differs from the situation in numerous Mpumalanga communities, where many residents' lives are marked by this material dependence on coal". Residents of Somkhele live on communal land and their livelihoods are not tied to coal. As one informant said: "Money will always be finished, but the land will never be finished." Many have deep roots in the area. All the executive committee members of the Mfolozi Community Environmental Justice Organisation (MCEJO) were born in the area, with one exception who arrived 50 years ago, "drawn by the fertility of the soil". However, in two separate workshops, closure of the mine was not advocated; most of the demands raised related to remedial action around consultation, compensation for relocation of homes and graves, damage to homes from blasting, water pollution and the problems of dust, and respectful treatment – as one person said: "The mine authorities treat us like we don't exist." It was frequently asserted that mine closure would not answer the needs of those demanding compensation. Also, because some people benefit from the mine, it was said: "if the mine closed, people will fight. There will be blood all over the place." However, in response to this speaker, another said: "We could not have attained our freedom if blood was not spilt, so if blood must be spilt to close the mine, so be it." At the same meetings, pride was expressed that the community had prevented the establishment of a new mine at Mfuleni. This success is attributed to the community being united and to support given by a range of non-governmental organizations (NGOs) working on environmental justice. However, Somkhele villagers were also subject to threats and intimidation, especially from "*indunas* [councillors] who disrupt our meetings … people are angry but afraid of them".

Frozen imaginaries

All these forms of dependence create a 'captive imaginary' that makes it difficult to conceptualize a just transition to a world without coal. In answer to the direct question "what would a world without coal look like?", most answered in catastrophic terms. For example: "A world without coal would be dark and bad with no electricity, fewer jobs and more crime"; "it will be the death of my business. It will mean going back to living like our forefathers, no electricity, no petrol, no development." In many of the exchange workshops and interviews, the notion of a just transition was found to be largely declarative, lacking substantive content, unrelated to everyday lived experience.

However, there were some alternative views. For example, one person commented that a world without coal would "be healthier, because there will be no dust, our streams will be clean, our trees will be safe, no one will cut them down for mining operations. It will be a greener world without coal." Another said "a world without coal would be a beautiful world, no sinkholes, no dust, no pollution, no dangers from all the coal trucks." Another coal worker said: "A world without coal will be better, less sickness, clean water and available land. Also we will be healthy … our generation is a sick generation." Illness from exposure to air and water pollution is common in all these communities living near coal-fired power stations and coal mines and is a key element in the ambivalence about coal.

For some, the notion of a just transition contains revolutionary possibilities for a better life, but for others, it is a threat to their jobs as the older coal mines and coal-fired power stations close or come under threat of closure. For a few critics, it is an empty notion, devoid of substantive content, which does not speak to their lived experience or daily needs and fails to provide any evidence of a world beyond coal. Many of these critics see the closure of the coal mines as extremely unjust.

Most of the respondents' ideas of a 'good life' were focused on having enough income: "money opens every door of what you need". However, there were also expressions of nostalgia for a more self-sufficient rural life. Having access to land was frequently cited: "having land is the key because you can do a lot of things yourself". On the whole, residents' aspirations were extremely low, but they noted the importance of respectful treatment and delivery of basic services. As one person said: "Being treated equal, having the same basic needs like water. Also having enough land to do farming so that you don't have to rely on other people for jobs." One very surprising statement, from a contract coal worker at Anglo American's Zizwe Mine, was that a good life meant that "the government can close the mines and people get land to farm and education on how to use that land. ... When we dig coal we are destroying nature, coal must stay under the ground as it was meant to be. ... Coal is destroying nature and people's lives."

A key question is how to break this 'frozen' or 'captive' imaginary? An alternative vision is necessary because, as James Ferguson suggests, we should 'link our critical analysis to the world of grounded political struggle'; we should move beyond 'denunciatory analyses' to ask 'what do we want? This is a quite different question (and a far more difficult question) than: what are we against?' (Ferguson, 2010: 181, 167). Many of us lack the political imagination required to do this. This inability is being further eroded by commentaries on the deepening ecological crisis that promote 'catastrophism', an apocalyptic vision of a future in which human existence is uncertain.

The problem is what David Harvey calls a 'double blockage'. As he says:

> While openings exist towards some alternative social order, no one really knows where or what it is ... a global anti-capitalist movement is unlikely to emerge without some animating vision of what is to be done and why. A double blockage exists: the lack of an alternative vision prevents the formation of an oppositional movement, while the absence of such a movement precludes the articulation of an alternative. (Harvey, 2011: 227)

Rethinking resistance: ambiguity and ambivalence

This research provoked a rethinking of 'resistance' as an ambiguous category. It is multilayered and multidimensional, containing different and sometimes contradictory meanings, forming a continuum of opposition rather than a clear binary between acquiescence and confrontation, or between resistance and collaboration. It operates on different scales, ranging from localized contestations which are scattered and small-scale to transnational advocacy involving widely different paths to agency. Whether ambivalent or direct, the question of asymmetrical power relations is central to understanding resistance. 'In a relationship of power, the dominant often has something to offer. ... The subordinate thus has many grounds for ambivalence about resisting the relationship' (Ortner, 1995: 175).

Collective action involving marches, 'strike' picketing and roadblocks are not the only forms of resistance. It is ever-changing and sometimes informal, and hidden. Scott (1985) warns that by focusing on visible historical 'events' such as organized rebellions or collective action, we can easily miss subtle but powerful forms of 'everyday resistance'. This chapter places small acts of defiance – such as damaging a fence erected by a mining company that blocked access to a stream which was an important source of water for villagers, or demands from individual households for compensation for homes damaged during mine blasting, or demands for the funding of social ceremonies at the reburial of ancestral graves – on a continuum of resistance.

The four research sites reveal a complicated and untidy picture in relation to coal, with various kinds of oppositional agency expressed in different forms of protest, defiance and empowerment. Overall, collective action is inchoate; there are diverse localized claims, grievances, demands and protests expressing resistance to the material conditions in many mining-affected communities and the power structures which maintain these conditions. Some collective actions are informal, but others are organized by an increasing number of the new grassroots organizations that are emerging and taking the form of horizontal networks. Coal is often one issue in mass protest actions about poverty, unemployment, lack of service delivery and corruption or in actions against specific *indunas*. In one case, the issue of coal triggered the mass burning of municipal offices in protest against the allocation of land adjacent to Phola township for two new coal mines.

For some, participating in protest actions provides a sense of power, while for others, this is not the case. "When Gwede Mantashe came to speak here (Phola), people were eating him." "We speak and speak, but we are just making noise." Little agency is gained by disruptive actions which, in immediate terms, leave extractivism intact. While there is extensive collective action in coal-affected communities, it is not generally against coal per se as a form of extractivism. Especially in Mpumalanga, in the exchange workshops, there was frequent rejection of the central issue implied in the notion of a just transition, namely the closure of the coal mines and coal-fired power stations. Most collective action, such as protest marches and roadblocks, are protests about how mining corporations, or provincial structures or Eskom, operate. These generate claims and demands regarding issues such as employment practices (particularly the neglect of local labour), compensation for the relocation of ancestral graves, damage to homes from blasting, loss of land

and land-based livelihoods, water pollution and lack of consultation about how mining and water licences are allocated. At the grassroots level, there is little generic critique of coal as a means of accumulation, although its health impacts are well known. Many people show a contradictory ecological location, both challenging coal and experiencing a dependence on it.

The reasons for participation in protest actions are often obscure and contradictory. The possibility of employment in coal mines and power stations operates to spur rather than smother resistance to coal. For example, X is active in the grassroots organization Mining Affected Communities United in Action (MACUA) and participated in the mass march of 5,000 people organized by MACUA at the giant coal power station Kusile, but her household depends on her income from selling *vetkoek* (doughnuts) outside the mine. According to one informant, many participants in the Kusile march took part to demand jobs.

Nationally, the majority of coal miners are migrants and younger, more skilled and better paid than in the past (Burton et al, 2018). For example, the Zibulo Colliery adjoining Phola employs 728 permanent workers and about 300 contract and subcontract workers. A survey found that 41 per cent of respondents were migrants, and only 1.4 per cent of those classified themselves as unskilled (Mashyamombe, 2018: 131). Formally employed coal workers clearly benefit from their wages, but they also experience impacts on their health. One miner commented that "there is nothing nice about a coal mine. When you go into the mine you are going to die. You are digging your death."

Sometimes a strange disassociation surfaces: as one coal miner commented: 'I know the more we mine next to people's houses, the more trouble we cause. Coal mining is affecting people in a very bad way. But this does not affect me because I have a job there now and money comes before everything else' (cited in Riven, 2018: 33). After losing her job with a coal company, a woman said: 'I only saw coal mining as a beautiful thing at the time. I did not realise all the negative impacts it caused because I was making money' (cited in Riven, 2018: 33). Riven concluded that 'community members are connecting coal mining with growth and job creation rather than with destruction and injustice' (2018: 34).

Besides these complex connections to coal, both formal and informal, there is often a normalization of toxic pollution as natural and inevitable. The causal connection between the more extreme weather events and accelerating climate change and carbon emissions are not directly obvious, and the relationship is not always put forward in the popular media. In several community workshops in Mpumalanga, it was evident that climate change – the bedrock of the argument for a transition from coal – was not understood and seemed remote and abstract to desperately poor communities concerned with immediate survival.

Material dependence on coal is not the only factor complicating resistance. There is also increasing repression, violence and intimidation of anti-coal activists. Fikile Ntshangase, deputy chairperson of the MCEJO and a strong opponent of the expansion of the Tendele mine in Somkhele, was recently assassinated in her home. To date there have been no arrests, and fear has spread and deepened. One woman has experienced threats to burn her house "because she wants the coal mines to close". There is rising collusion between mining corporations, various levels of government and traditional authorities, particularly in KwaZulu-Natal.

Several informants emphasized how mining corporations damage social cohesion in the community and frequently issue false promises. According to one respondent:

'They look for fault lines in the community and then fill them with money and shatter the unity of the community ... promises were made to the locals for jobs and contracts, promises which created tension and conflicts. ... They said mining would drive development, many people would pour into the area and there would be building jobs and taxis.' (interview, Pietermaritzburg, 8 June 2018)

In Somkhele, mine management instigated violence indirectly by linking resistance to job losses and reduced bonus payments.

In areas where the chiefs control natural resources, threats and intimidation of anti-coal activists are increasing. One informant said: "Organizing in Somkhele and Fulani is difficult because people are afraid of the chiefs. They fear for their lives. Even pickets and marches are becoming dangerous." A young Zulu woman at a workshop stressed the power of the chief and his *indunas* to allocate land and impose fines. Another Zulu informant commented: "With their powerful traditional authority, the chiefs rely on fear and intimidation to maintain power and control." The social dynamics in Somkhele are such that the traditional authorities control land and exercise close surveillance of villagers.

To date, the labour movement has largely failed to engage with these mining communities. Overall, there is a serious disconnect regarding the role of labour at national and local levels. One environmental justice activist committed to working with mining-affected communities recently met with NUMSA in Middleburg, but said: "I felt they were trying to intimidate me. They said the job losses from the closure of coal mines was because we insist on environmental compliance ... and at present, the debates on a just transition are not connected to our experience and our struggle" (interview, Middleburg, 13 February 2019). According to Matthews Hlabane, founder of MACUA: "COSATU affiliates understand about the just transition but they also have reservations because it has not been demonstrated. If we just theorize, we are bound to fail" (interview, Witbank, 21 June 2018). Several informants complained that the "NUM is not helping us."

In many communities, environmental justice activists act as 'catalysts of resistance'. Writing of the struggle against the Narmada dam in India, Nilsen suggests the process of informing and recognizing builds 'an infrastructure of contention' (Nilsen 2010: 76). This involves building knowledge, confidence and skills, which in South Africa involves gaining knowledge of constitutional protections such as the right to live in an environment that is not harmful to one's health and wellbeing. Furthermore, NGOs such as Groundwork and WoMin are promoting exchange visits and supporting grassroots alliances such as the Highveld Environmental Justice Network and the Greater Phola Ogies Women Forum, which describes itself as 'a feminist, anti-mining group'. Consisting of about 40 members, it meets weekly and focuses on energy and food 'because these are women's issues'.

Conclusion

The modalities of the sociological engagement in the two projects described above were very different (see Table 7.1). The empirical research conducted with organized labour as part of the trade union project illustrates the connections between policy and public sociology, in terms of Burawoy's quadrant. The process of critical engagement with mining-affected communities was itself empowering. It allowed for co-produced knowledge with both theoretical and strategic implications. It revealed a variety of complex and even contradictory patterns regarding coal mining and burning,

Table 7.1: Summary of the differences between the two approaches

	Public sociology	Critical engagement
Different methodologies	Didactic, conveying existing knowledge to union members	Creates spaces for dialogue to produce new knowledge
Depth of knowledge shared	Issues of principles and practices	Experiential, introspective, encouraging reflective thinking More concerned with modalities of a just transition than an assertion of foundational principles
Nature of social relations	Formal and vertical	Informal and horizontal
Boundaries of political affiliation	Strict, aimed specifically at supporting COSATU	Scattered initiatives of various environmental justice groupings, creating a challenge to build an anti-coal movement

ranging from confrontation to dependence, which raises difficult questions on how to theorize resistance as a continuum.

Whether we achieve a deep, transformative just transition will depend on political struggles between a wide range of social forces that represent divergent class interests. Otto and Terhorst (2011) discuss the dilemmas of the duality between the subaltern – those struggling for voice and mobility within the existing order – and activist researchers. While some researchers may struggle against subordination to the discipline of a movement, in the communities described in this chapter, there is no cohesive anti-coal movement with a coherent centre and tidy margins driving a just transition; resistance to coal is an inchoate sum of multiple, diverse struggles and organizations. However, there is another dimension if the activist researcher is part of a university, because 'we are encouraged to prioritise rapid academic publications over other types of slow and engaged forms of scholarship … and make it challenging to maintain enduring, meaningful connections with communities outside the university' (Legun et al, 2020: 3).

It is difficult to make any claims about the political outcomes of these two initiatives. Today, COSATU has retreated to a reformist understanding of a just transition and illustrates the limits of engaging in social dialogue. The challenge for SWOP's critical engagement initiative is how to draw the elements of grassroots resistance described in this chapter into a deeper critique of coal in order to build a social movement that has the capacity to link short-term and immediate demands to a broader movement for a deep and transformative just transition.

Notes

[1] This project was a modest attempt to contribute to the debate on what it means to democratize the concept of a 'just transition' and to give voice to those most affected: coal workers and communities living close to coal mines and coal-fired power stations.

[2] Using this stagist approach, Webster (2019) demonstrates the four dimensions of workers' power – structural, associational, institutional and societal – that were crucial to the transition from apartheid and which could be mobilized now in a just transition from carbon capitalism.

[3] Acquired immune deficiency syndrome.

[4] While this could be seen as 'the North' appropriating the ideas and practices of 'the Global South', Burawoy has frequently acknowledged SWOP's influence on his theorizing of a commitment to academia engaging with the real world in the form of public sociology. This is further developed in *The Extended Case Method* (Burawoy, 2009), which emphasizes the university as a site of contestation. Burawoy writes: 'This formulation (of Public Sociology) was, in part, a reaction to how public universities in the USA have responded to mounting attacks from the "right"' with 'market solutions – joint ventures with private corporations, advertising campaigns to attract students, fawning over private donors, commodifying education through distance learning and employing cheap, temporary professional labour' (2007: 27). Universities in South Africa face similar challenges.

References

Ashley, B. (2016) *One Million Climate Jobs. Moving South Africa Forward on a Low-carbon Wage-led, and Sustainable Path*, Cape Town: Alternative Information and Development Centre.

Baker, L., Burton, J., Godinho, C. and Trollip, H. (2015) *The Political Economy of Recognizing*, Cape Town: Energy Research Centre, University of Cape Town.

Burawoy, M. (2005) 'For public sociology', *The British Journal of Sociology*, 56(2): 259–94.

Burawoy, M. (2007) 'For public sociology', in M. Burawoy, D. Clawson, R. Zussman, J. Misra, R. Stokes, N. Gerstel and D.L. Anderton (eds) *Public Sociology: Fifteen Eminent Sociologists Debate Politics and the Profession in the Twenty-first Century*, Berkeley: University of California Press.

Burawoy, M. (2009) *The Extended Case Method*, Berkeley: University of California Press.

Burton, J., Caetano, T. and McCall, B. (2018) *Coal Transitions in South Africa*, Cape Town: University of Cape Town.

COSATU (2011) *A Just Transition to a Low Carbon and Climate Resilient Economy*, Johannesburg: COSATU

Department of Mineral Resources and Energy (2019) *Integrated Resource Plan (IRP2019)*. http://www.energy.gov.za/IRP/2019/IRP-2019.pdf

Ferguson, J. (2010) 'The uses of neoliberalism', in N. Castree, P. Chatterton, N. Heynen, W. Larner and M.W. Wright (eds) *The Point Is to Change It: Geographies of Hope and Survival in an Age of Crisis*, Chichester: Wiley-Blackwell, pp 166–84.

George, S. (2010) *Whose Crisis, Whose Future?* London: Polity Press.

Ghosh, A. (2016) *The Great Derangement: Climate Change and the Unthinkable*, Chicago: University of Chicago Press.

Hallowes, D. (2011) *Toxic Futures: South Africa in the Crises of Energy, Environment and Capital*, Pietermaritzburg: UKZN Press.

Hallowes, D. and Munnik, V. (2016) *The Destruction of the Highveld. Part 1: Digging Coal*, Groundwork: Pietermaritzburg.

Hallowes, D. and Munnik, V. (2017) *The Destruction of the Highveld. Part 2: Burning Coal*, Groundwork: Pietermaritzburg.

Harvey, D. (2011) *The Enigma of Capital and the Crises of Capitalism*, Oxford: Oxford University Press.

Healy, N. and Barry, J. (2017) 'Politicizing energy justice and energy system transitions: Fossil fuel divestment and a "just transition"', *Energy Policy*, 108: 451–59.

Legun, K., Keller, J., Bell, M. and Carolan, M. (2020) *The Cambridge Handbook of Environmental Sociology*, Cambridge: Cambridge University Press.

Lewis, D. (1973) 'Anthropology and colonialism', *Current Anthropology*, 14(5): 581–602.

Marquardt, J. and Delina, L.L. (2019) 'Reimagining energy futures: Contributions from community sustainable energy transitions in Thailand and the Philippines', *Energy Research & Social Science*, 49: 91–102.

Mashayamombe, J. (2018) *Sanitised Spaces: The Spatial Orders of Post-apartheid Mines in South Africa*, PhD thesis, University of Pretoria, South Africa.

Mosoetsa, S. (2016) *Eating from One Pot*, Johannesburg: Wits University Press.

Motta, S.A. and Nilsen, A.G. (2011) 'Social movements and/in the postcolonial: Dispossession, development and resistance in the Global South', in S. Motta and A. Nilsen (eds) *Social Movements in the Global South: Dispossession, Development and Resistance*, London: Palgrave-Macmillan, pp 1–34.

Mukherjee, S., Scandrett, E., Sen, T. and Shah, D. (2011) 'Generating theory in the Bhopal survivors' movement', in *Social Movements in the Global South*, London: Palgrave Macmillan, pp 150–77.

National Planning Commission (2012) *National Development Plan*. Pretoria: Office of the Presidency, Government Printers.

Nilsen, A. (2010) *Dispossession and Resistance in India: The River and the Rage*, London: Routledge.

Nussbaum, M. (2000) *Women and Human Development: A Study in Human Capabilities*, Cambridge: Cambridge University Press.

Ortner, S. (1995) 'Resistance and the problem of ethnographic refusal', *Comparative Studies in Society and History*, 37(1): 173–92.

Otto, B. and Terhorst, P. (2011) 'Beyond differences? Exploring methodological dilemmas of activist research in the Global South', in S. Motta and A. Nilsen (eds) *Social Movements in the Global South: Dispossession, Development and Resistance*, London: Palgrave-Macmillan, pp 200–26.

Rathzel, N., Cock, J. and Uzzel, D. (2018) 'Beyond the nature–labour divide: Trade union responses to climate change in South Africa', *Globalizations*, 15(4): 504–19.

Riven, D. (2018) *Resistance to Coal: The Challenge of Achieving Environmental Justice in South Africa*, MSc thesis, University of Lund, Sweden.

Sen, A. (1999) 'The possibility of social choice', *American Economic Review*, 89(3): 349–78.

Swilling, M. (2020) *The Age of Sustainability: Just Transitions in a Complex World*, London: Routledge.

Scott, C.J. (1985) *Weapons of the Weak*, New Haven, CT: Yale University Press.

Sweeney, S. and Treat, J. (2018) *Trade Unions and Just Transition: The Search for a Transformative Politics*, Working Paper 11, New York: Trade Unions for Energy Democracy.

Swilling, M. and Chipkin, I. (2018) *Shadow State: The Politics of State Capture*, Johannesburg: Wits University Press.

United Nations Research Institute for Social Development (2018) *Mapping Just Transition(s) to a Low-carbon World*, Geneva: UNRISD.

Webster, E. (2019) 'Building counter-power in the workplace', in D. Francis, I. Valodia and E. Webser (eds) *Inequality Studies from the Global South*, Johannesburg: Routledge, pp 220–39.

8

Feminist Participatory Action Research in African Sex Work Studies

Ntokozo Yingwana

Introduction

What does it mean to be an African sex worker feminist? In answering this question, two qualitative studies were conducted with African sex worker groups in 2014 and 2015; the South African movement of sex workers, known as Sisonke,[1] and the African Sex Workers Alliance (ASWA). Based on their embodied lived experiences, each participant described what it meant to be an *African*, a *sex worker* and a *feminist*, and then collectively discussed these in relation to each other and the social dimensions they occupy.

Both studies concur that even though these three identities may appear incongruent, in certain embodiments, they actually inform each other. The purpose of the studies was to allow African sex workers to conceptualize for themselves what feminism means, as it relates to their continental identity. The main objective of this work was to encourage so-called 'mainstream feminists' and sex worker rights feminists to start recognizing each other as comrades in the struggle for gender and sexual liberation, thus strengthening solidarity for sex worker rights activism across social justice movements; especially as some feminists still find it difficult to recognize selling sex as a legitimate form of labour.

To this end, a Feminist Participatory Action Research (FPAR) methodology was employed. Colleen Reid and Claudia Gillberg describe FPAR as a 'participatory and action-oriented approach to research that centres gender and women's experiences both theoretically and practically' (2014: 343). FPAR draws from feminist principles of knowledge production. It also prioritizes the research participants' active engagement in the meaning-making process and requires that the study output be used to advance a social justice agenda or some form of 'good change' (Chambers, 1997).

Generally, I understand FPAR to be a methodology that can be employed in any academic discipline. The distinguishing factor that makes it most appealing when working with stigmatized communities is that while other methodologies may indirectly contribute towards some positive change, in the FPAR approach, by its very design, social justice is explicitly the intended output (or action) of the study. Therefore, methodologically, FPAR is intrinsically a social justice inquiry, no matter what the discipline. Like Kathy Charmaz (2011: 359), '[w]hen I speak of social justice inquiry, I mean studies that attend to inequalities and equality, barriers and access, poverty and privilege, individual rights and the collective good, and their implications for suffering'. Hence, a social justice inquiry also entails critically engaging with structures of power and how those systems shape human lives (Charmaz, 2011).

While reflecting on both studies, this chapter focuses largely on the FPAR methods employed in the second study with the ASWA feminists in order to illustrate how this methodology can be used to unpack the embodied lived experiences of African sex worker feminists and help support sex worker rights activism in the continent.

Background and positionality

I strongly self-identify as an African feminist who practises as a sex worker rights scholar activist. As such, I am guided by African feminist principles and ideologies. In addition, the sex work scholarship I produce is directly informed by my activism, which in turn is strengthened by that scholarship. According to Mary Brydon-Miller, Davydd Greenwood and Patricia Maguire (2003: 20), this is not necessarily a limitation, because a participatory action researcher is essentially 'a hybrid of scholar/activist in which neither role takes precedence. Our academic work takes place within and is made possible by our political commitments and we draw on our experiences as community activists and organizers to inform our scholarship.'

I began working for the Sex Workers Education and Advocacy Taskforce (SWEAT) as a part-time (media) advocacy officer in 2008 and have, since then, been a sex worker rights activist. SWEAT is a non-profit organization (NPO) in South Africa that fights for the human rights of adult consenting sex workers. I was introduced to the organization through my online media consultancy work when I was initially employed on a freelance basis to update SWEAT's website with news content sourced through online media monitoring systems. I now serve on its board.

It was during my time as a consultant at SWEAT that I noticed how the media monitoring systems were only feeding the NPO clichéd narratives and representations of sex workers. Indeed, mainstream media tends to essentialize the sex worker as a poor, uneducated Black woman who sells sex in dark dingy street corners while wearing scanty outfits. She is also often portrayed as an HIV-positive alcoholic or drug addict who spends her earnings on her habits. Such media representations 'fail to portray the multiplicity and complexity of sex worker lives and reinforce negative stereotypes' (Sonke Gender Justice, 2014: 21). In addition, these representations differ greatly from the sex workers I was meeting at SWEAT.

The director of SWEAT was then approached with these concerns over misrepresentation, wherein I offered to facilitate digital storytelling workshops with the organization's beneficiaries on weekends. These workshops aimed to help sex workers tell unmediated stories of their own lives as a counter-narrative to the essentialist trite that still tends to populate the media, in the hope of humanizing the African sex worker image. The digital stories were uploaded to the SWEAT website, featured on the NPO's electronic newsletter and shared on its social media. I later became a full-time staff member as a (media) advocacy officer, which entailed training, mentoring and supporting SWEAT's provincial media liaisons. At times this involved doing media interviews, and, in solidarity, I would often use the plural 'we' when referring to sex workers. During interviews, when asked whether I was (or have been) a sex worker, my standard response was always 'I would rather not say'. With that said, even though I gained trust and rapport throughout the years of working with SWEAT and its birth child Sisonke – which made it easier to approach their beneficiaries and members to participate in later studies – I have always been apprehensive about misappropriating sex workers' struggles. As such, it is best to heed Kim England's caution that as feminist researchers we need to (repeatedly) ask ourselves: 'In our rush to be more inclusive and conceptualize difference and diversity, might we be guilty of appropriating the voices of "others"?' (1994: 81).

A peculiar incident took place during a lobbying meeting with a Cape Town-based local government official. During my time as the advocacy officer at SWEAT, I would sometimes accompany the lobbying teams to such meetings. At this specific meeting, the official enquired as to whether he could become a member of Sisonke. He was informed that unfortunately he could not join the movement as it is only for former and current sex workers. I went on to explain that I also could not join, even though I was working for SWEAT. It was later revealed that one of the lobbyists on the team expressed annoyance at me for clarifying that I was not a sex worker. This was read as a form of betrayal. Therefore, in my scholarship, I have had to carefully straddle the role of insider–outsider whereby I engage in feminist solidarity without misappropriating sex workers' voices.

It was through working for SWEAT/Sisonke – and conducting research and advocacy consultancy work for other sex worker rights groups and organizations, such as ASWA and the Global Network of Sex Work Projects (NSWP)[2] – that it became evident to me how ineffective it is to just passionately state the cause. I realized that research evidence is needed to help convince parliamentarians of the relevance and urgency of protecting sex workers' human rights. More so, it was frustrating that external researchers would frequently approach SWEAT to harvest us for data but rarely returned to share their findings. Beneficiaries and staff were seldom afforded the opportunity to set the research agenda or engage as co-creators in the knowledge production process. The research outputs were also often unhelpful in informing the organization's programming or advocacy work. Consequently, I left SWEAT in 2014 to pursue postgraduate studies that could help improve my activism.

Entering this study as a scholar activist meant having to straddle the blurry role of an insider-outsider, which demands being constantly aware of the tension between the activist and researcher roles (Olesen, 2000). This is not an easy task, as it is often assumed in certain academic disciplines that one cannot produce methodologically rigorous, ethically sound and conceptually innovative scholarship if driven by a social justice agenda. This is utter nonsense; if anything, scholar activists are expected to go the proverbial 'extra mile' in living up to academic knowledge production ideals. On the other hand, some activists consider scholar activism questionable – if not outright dismissible – as they strongly believe that being produced out of the so-called 'ivory towers' of academia renders such knowledge removed from the daily realities and struggles of the 'people on the ground'. Therefore, while straddling the insider–outsider role can offer nuanced perspectives, it can also leave the scholar activist, at least half the time, unpopular no matter where, or to whom, they present their work – be it an academic or extra-academic audience.

Scholar activists also tend to encounter far more institutional barriers from their universities when applying for research ethics clearance certificates. While sociologists doing critically engaged scholarship with stigmatized or vulnerable communities generally must show that they can mitigate all possibilities of harm, those of us working with criminalized communities have the added burden of convincing university ethics committees that we would not be breaking the law merely by conducting research with criminalized persons such as sex workers.

I open with these reflections because this chapter intends not only to illustrate how FPAR can be used to tap into sex workers' embodied lived experiences (using methods such as body mapping), but also to demonstrate how the methodology offers an opportunity to critically engage with debates pertaining to sociology as a discipline. Michael Burawoy's (2005) model of four distinct sociological practices clearly delineates between instrumental and reflexive knowledge production; critical sociology and public sociology are seen as reflexive practices, while professional sociology and policy sociology are considered instrumental. However, sex worker rights scholar activism that employs FPAR has proven otherwise by combining both instrumental and reflexive practices.

I argue that the co-production of knowledge together with sex workers, the commitment of this form of research to social justice and scholarly goals, and the complex and contradictory location of the scholar activist as both insider and outsider are more consistent with the conception of 'critical engagement' than that of public sociology. Therefore, you will notice in the upcoming case study that the body maps produced by the ASWA participants during the FPAR workshop served not only as prompts for the focus group discussion and follow-up interviews, but also as advocacy tools to encourage engagement between sex worker activists and feminists.

Methods and participants

The first research project was undertaken in 2014, though my engagement with the participants, a group of 12 Cape Town-based sex worker feminists, had begun the previous year as part of my advocacy work at SWEAT. During that time, I joined the group AWAKE! Women of Africa in its journey of collective self-discovery into what it means to be an African sex worker feminist (Yingwana, 2018). The participants were members of Sisonke.

Sisonke was established in 2003 at a meeting of about 70 sex worker members from across the country. The movement has since established offices in six provinces: Western Cape, Eastern Cape, KwaZulu-Natal, Gauteng, Limpopo and North West. Sisonke's vision is to see sex work fully decriminalized and recognized as a legitimate form of labour in South Africa, with sex workers' human rights protected (Sisonke, n.d.).

Since AWAKE! Women of Africa is fiscally hosted by SWEAT, the group held its fortnightly meetings at the NPO's head office in Observatory (Cape Town) to discuss literature on various strands of feminism and their social implications, specifically in relation to African sex workers' lives. There were robust discussions on contemporary feminist debates, such as the omission of Maya Angelou's sex work past in her obituary and bell hooks' reference to Beyoncé Knowles as an 'anti-feminist … that is a terrorist' to young Black women's minds (Diaz, 2014). Group members also received diaries to reflect on these ideas. As AWAKE! grew confident in its self-identification as a feminist group, members started to attend public lectures and were meeting privately with visiting postcolonial feminist scholars such as Nivedita Menon and Chandra Talpade Mohanty. Through this collective learning, the group members came to the realization that being an African and a sex worker did not exclude them from feminism and that actually, in certain embodiments, these identities intersect to inform each other.

In 2015 these findings were affirmed when the same question was asked to 17 members of ASWA – a pan-African network of 85 sex worker-led organizations/groups based in 23 countries across the continent. ASWA came about initially through learning exchange visits between eastern and southern African sex worker rights activists. It was officially launched at the first-ever African Sex Worker Conference, which took place in Johannesburg on 3–5 February 2009. Its founders cited Africa's political liberation movements as sources of inspiration (NSWP, n.d.-a).

The ASWA members who participated in the study self-identified as feminists and represented sex worker movements and organizations from seven countries across Africa. The FPAR approach followed for this study entailed an arts-based workshop that involved body mapping and continuum/positionality exercises, followed by a focus group discussion and semi-structured interviews. Participant observation and daily audio dairies also provided insights, which guided the analysis of the body maps and transcripts.

African feminism, scholarship and activism

Exploring the various strands of feminisms would go beyond the scope of this chapter. However, the two salient features of any form of feminism are subverting patriarchy and expanding women's agency (Richter, 2012: 65). For both studies, I drew on Desiree Lewis' (2001: 4) understanding of African feminism(s) to guide the analysis. According to Lewis, African feminists have 'a shared intellectual commitment to critiquing gender and imperialism coupled with a collective focus on a continental identity shaped by particular relations of subordination in the world economy and global social and cultural practices'.

As decolonial political projects, both inquiries sought to bring African sex workers' lived experiences into the global feminist discourse. Indeed, an 'ongoing process of self-definition and re-definition' characterizes the evolution of African feminist movements (Akin-Aina, 2011: 66). Therefore, by amplifying the voices of African sex worker feminists, such studies contribute towards the project of constantly *self-redefining* (African) feminisms. In both studies, the participants argued that feminism is not so much a foreign concept, but merely a foreign term, and that feminism is not just an identity, but rather something one does and lives by. Hence, advocating and lobbying for sex workers' rights was highlighted as a demonstration of one's activism and, by extension, evidence of one's feminism. As ASWA member Anita explained:

'I consider myself as a feminist. ... Yeah, because I fight for the rights of others. And I myself, I'm an activist in the women's movement. So I consider myself as a feminist.'

Engaging with African Sex Workers Alliance feminists

The 17 ASWA research participants represented sex worker movements and organizations from Ethiopia (Nikat), Kenya (the Kenya Sex Worker Alliance and the Bar Hostess Empowerment and Support Programme), Mozambique (Tiyane Vavasate), Nigeria (Precious Jewels), South Africa (Sisonke), Tanzania (Warembo Forum) and Uganda (the Women's Network for Human Rights Advocacy and the Lady Mermaid Empowerment Centre). All presented as Black Africans and self-identified as cisgender, transgender and gender-nonconforming. Their ages ranged from 25 to 41 years. The main research question explored was: 'What does it mean to be an African sex worker feminist?' The following sub-questions also guided the participants in our exploration:

- How do you as an African sex worker identify with feminism?
- What in your lived experience makes you believe you are a feminist?
- How does your self-identification as a sex worker feminist affect your lived experience?
- Does feminism have an impact on your sex work and vice versa?

These questions were largely derived from my initial honours[3] research project with AWAKE! Women of Africa. For my master's[4] study with the self-identifying ASWA feminists, the questions were updated to address sex work and feminism within the broader African context, in order to further probe insights gained from the first study. Instead of delving straight into the findings, this chapter aims to reflect on the FPAR methodology employed and its effectiveness in answering the main research question.

Feminist-oriented participatory action research

As already noted, these research questions were explored with the ASWA participants through an arts-based feminist-orientated Participatory Action Research – also referred to as Feminist Participatory Action Research (FPAR) – workshop that took place at the Changing Faces, Changing Spaces (CFCS) Conference in Kenya in 2015. The CFCS is a biennial conference organized by the East African Sexual Health and Rights Initiative (see UHAI EASHRI, n.d.) that brings together LGBTQI[5] and sex worker rights activists from across Africa and the diaspora. I was invited to the conference to present findings from my honour's study, and I took the opportunity to conduct my master's research fieldwork there. Before embarking on the field trip, the participant information sheet was circulated via the ASWA mailing list, inviting members who self-identify as feminists and who were already attending CFCS to be part of the research workshop.

The FPAR workshop was followed by 11 semi-structured interviews.[6] Unfortunately, since the conference only lasted four days, it was difficult to secure in-depth interviews during the short meal breaks. Notwithstanding, eight interviews (lasting 15 to 30 minutes) were conducted during the conference, and the remaining three interviews were done afterwards via Skype (lasting about 45 minutes each). Participant observation and daily audio dairies during the CFCS conference also provided insights, which guided my analysis of the workshop and the interview data.

Brydon-Miller, Maguire and McIntyre (2004: ix–x) define Participatory Action Research (PAR) as 'a counter-hegemonic approach to knowledge creation that challeng[es] established approaches to research by emphasizing collaborative processes of inquiry, education, and action'. Therefore, PAR is an approach that emphasizes collective participation with the aim of transforming societies (Reason and Bradbury, 2008). It stresses collective inquiry and experimentation grounded in experience and social history. Within a PAR process, 'communities of inquiry and action evolve and address questions and issues that are significant for those who participate as co-researchers' (Reason and Bradbury, 2008: 1). All forms of PAR (including FPAR) have in common the idea that research and action must be done *with* people and not *on* or *for* people. Therefore, the people involved are not just sources of data, but instead they are key partners in the inquiry process. Hence both research projects encouraged participants to engage as collaborators in the knowledge creation process. Indeed, Amina Mama (2007: 152) cautions against the global inequalities played out in the knowledge production arena in which she includes feminist knowledge creation processes, giving credence to the necessity of such an inclusive approach. In addition, Emily van der Meulen (2011: 370) asserts that PAR can be employed to 'build bridges, dismantle barriers, and establish new relationships of trust and support between feminists and sex workers'.

With that said, the decision to conduct a FPAR creative arts workshop was informed not only by the feminist qualitative nature of the study, but also by the fact that the research partners originated from various African countries with diverse linguistic backgrounds. An arts-based FPAR workshop was the most inclusive research method to employ as it allowed the participants to express their embodied experiences of being African sex worker feminists beyond linguistic barriers (Desyllas, 2013). According to Moshoula Capous Desyllas (2013: 772), arts-based research methods offer 'the opportunity for sex workers to (re)present their own needs and aspirations'. Nonetheless, translators of Amharic and Portugese also helped to facilitate conversations with the participants from Ethiopia and Mozambique (respectively) during both the FPAR arts-based workshop and the interviews. Fortunately, the UHAI EASHRI offers translators to its delegates at the CFCS conference in order to ensure diversity and inclusivity.

Data collection

The FPAR creative workshop with the ASWA members was held during the lunch break on Wednesday 17 June 2015, for approximately an hour. The workshop was split into three activities which supported the research participants through explorations of what it means to be an *African*, a *sex worker* and a *feminist*, and how these identities intersect and are simultaneously embodied. These activities involved a group discussion, body mapping and a continuum exercise. The workshop exercises were designed to encourage collective self-reflection and resulted in robust discussions, as detailed in the analysis.

The arts-based FPAR workshop began with an open discussion on the participants' understanding of feminism or what being a feminist means. This provided them with the opportunity to narrate their own understandings of feminism. *Testimonio*, a tool used commonly in FPAR, inspired this narrative approach. According to George Yúdice, *testimonio* is 'an *authentic* narrative, told by a *witness* who is *moved* to *narrate* by the *urgency* of a situation (e.g. war, oppression, revolution, etc.). Emphasizing *popular oral discourse*, the witness portrays his or her own *experience* as a *representative* of a *collective memory* or *identity*' (cited in Brydon-Miller et al, 2004: 42; italics in original). This was followed by a body mapping exercise. In a bid to save time, blank A4 copies of gender-neutral body outlines were provided, as opposed to having participants outline each other's bodies on large charts of paper as is the traditional approach in a body mapping workshop. The participants were asked to illustrate in layers on their body maps what it means for them to be an *African*, a *sex worker* and a *feminist*. This exercise was meant to aid the participants in exploring their embodied intersectionality of the three identities. Those who were comfortable sharing discussed their body maps with the rest of the group. This research technique was adopted because '[b]ody maps can be used for gaining access to people's perceptions of their bodies' and offer insights into how they live their lives through them (Cornwall, 1992: 1). According to Charlotte Morris et al employing participatory arts-based research methods such as body mapping is especially valuable for studies investigating sex and sexuality (Morris et al, 2018).

For the final exercise of the workshop, participants were presented with the statement 'feminism impacts on my sex work' and asked to physically position themselves along a continuum: 'strongly agree', 'neutral' or 'strongly disagree'. While standing, the participants discussed their reasons for positioning themselves at particular points on the continuum. Unfortunately, because of time constraints, this exercise could not be repeated with the statement phrased inversely: 'sex work impacts on my feminism'.

Nevertheless, the discussions ignited by these exercises began to illuminate some of the nuances that come with self-identifying as an African sex worker feminist. These were further explored in the one-to-one interviews, with reflections from the workshop and the body maps serving as prompts or starting points for discussion. The interviews not only substantiated initial findings from the FPAR workshop, but also enabled the participants to expand on their own understandings of sex work and feminism without necessarily being influenced by the presence of their fellow ASWA members.

Analytical tools

Thematic networks analysis was employed to unearth salient themes hidden within the data (Attride-Stirling, 2001). Thematic analysis is concerned with identifying themes and examining their patterns for meaning-making. The conversation analysis technique was also used. David Silverman (2006: 123) refers to conversation analysis as the 'narrative' approach, which involves treating the creative art (the body maps) and interview data (the focus groups and individual interviews) as stories or narratives through which people describe their worlds. This technique was employed as the studies were concerned with how the participants' daily experiences influence the meaning they ascribe to being African sex worker feminists.

Finally, the body maps were analysed through visual analysis. According to the Duke University Writing Studio (n.d.), 'the purpose of a visual analysis is to recognize and understand the visual choices the artist made in creating the artwork'. In observing and thinking about separate parts of the art object, one arrives at a better understanding of the art object as a whole and the meaning behind it.

Ethical considerations

Since the study with the ASWA feminists was conducted as part of a master's research project, the Research Ethics Committee at the University of Sussex had to approve the research ethics, and all research protocols were accordingly observed. Before signing consent forms, the participants were taken through the nature of the study, potential risks of being involved, how the research would be conducted and how the findings would be presented. Although the participants were encouraged to provide pseudonyms in order to protect their identities, a few insisted that their real names be used in the final thesis, probably because as sex worker rights activists, they were already used to their real identities appearing in the media and research reports.

During the research process, I endeavoured to maintain a rigorous stance with regards to ethics and remain vigilant to any biases that might taint the findings. Suspected biases during the study were acknowledged and reflected on in the final report. These included the fact that while still employed at SWEAT as an advocacy officer, I had helped establish the sex worker feminist group which later became AWAKE! Also, I continued to be involved in the group's meetings and activism with 'other'[7] feminists during the research. Therefore, I was always aware of the tension between my activist role and my researcher role (Olesen, 2000: 233). Furthermore, following years of advocating for sex workers' rights and the decriminalization of sex work in South Africa, I could not be the so-called 'objective researcher'. However, as a standpoint feminist researcher, I am not (entirely) apologetic for this lack of objectivity. Objectivity was never paramount in these studies; African sex worker feminists' lived experiences were. And besides, no research theory or set of guidelines can act as prophylactics against being emotionally invested in one's own research (Stanley and Wise, 2002: 160).

Nonetheless, Maria Mies' 'conscious partiality' approach, whereby constant reflection is key, was employed in a concerted effort to counter concerns about subjectivity; thus 'creat[ing] a critical conceptual distance between the researcher and participants' (Olesen, 2000: 234). My co-supervisors[8] – themselves sex worker rights scholar activists – served as sobering sounding boards, often playing 'devil's advocate' by challenging me to consider critiques they often also had to field when publishing/presenting their own research on sex work.

The shifting power dynamics that existed between participants and researcher were noted with sensitivity (England, 1994: 87). Although the respondents acknowledged my privilege as an academic, they never appeared intimidated, as they would constantly assert themselves as experts of their own lives. For instance, one of the ASWA participants teased me for studying African feminism at a university based in the United Kingdom. The irony of it all amused her. This seemingly insignificant jest further demonstrates the participants' claim to the power of their embodied wisdom of being African sex worker feminists. While this confidence was partly the result of the participants being conscientized sex worker rights leaders of their respective national movements, the initial framing of the FPAR arts-based workshop also contributed towards the participants' confidence in their embodied knowledge. At the start of the workshop, I put out a disclaimer that I did not know what it might mean to be an African sex worker feminist, but hoped for a collective deciphering of its meaning. Such an opening statement allowed the participants to recognize the knowledge and power that they bring to the research project.

To this effect, Alberto Arribas Lozano (2018: 102) argues that 'a narrow notion of public sociology, taken primarily as the unidirectional flow of knowledge from the academic expert to extra-academic audiences, is based on a weak understanding of dialogue and intersubjectivity'. He argues that Burawoy's concept of public sociology see publics as simple audiences that passively receive disseminated knowledge rather than as collaborators in knowledge production itself (Arribas Lozano, 2018). It is from this premise that the ASWA feminists were engaged as co-creators in the research project.

Explorations of being an African sex worker feminist

The participants often began by admitting that clearly defining feminism or what it means to be a feminist, let alone an African sex worker feminist, is rather difficult considering that current understandings of feminism are largely informed by scholarship from the West/Global North. Hence, many objected to a single scholarly definition of feminism, which they felt was removed from their daily realities as African sex worker feminists:

'[T]he definition of feminism, because already in the larger African context, the larger discussion about feminism is that it has been largely guided by how we have a white model of feminism; an American-European, that kind of feminism. ... Do we even have a word for "feminism" in any African language?' (Daniel)[9]

Daniel – a Kenyan male sex worker – posed this question to his fellow ASWA feminists during the discussion about sex work and feminism in Africa in the FPAR arts-based workshop. With that said, he does not believe that the essence of feminism did not exist in Africa prior to colonization. Many of the participants attested to having been feminists long before reading any book or attending any workshop about feminism. For them, feminism is not so much a foreign concept, but just a foreign term. In addition, the respondents felt they should be allowed to think for themselves and embrace a form of feminism that resonates the most with their lived realities. Hence, they vehemently rejected the notion of a universal textbook form of feminism:

'We should not all have the same definition of feminism. No, no, no, no, no. The way they understand feminism, it is their own. Let them change or let them not change, we don't care. But let them *allow us to think*, you know, and understand feminism the way we want. Or the way we know it should be. It's not about the definition that is in the books, because I never went to school to study feminism, but I understand what feminism is.' (Jolly)

Indeed, the purpose of both studies was to allow African sex workers to conceptualize for themselves what feminism means in relation to their continental context and identity. This is the premise on which most of the participants based their understandings of feminism:

'[I]t's important to sort of understand and bring sex work to the context, or bring feminism to the context of our conditions in sex work, our realities as sex workers and what we live in. Because the reality of the matter is not. … Feminism – yeah, you know like, a middle-aged, well-employed, white woman, or a middle-aged, educated, Black woman will be totally different to the feminism and the context … you'll get as a sex worker in Africa – right?' (Onko)

The following are some responses to being asked to define what feminism or being a feminist means for them:

'I think feminis[m] is like [when a] group of people came together to fight for … the political rights, social right[s] and other right[s] of female[s] in society.' (Zelda)

'It's a group of people coming together to fight certain beliefs that are around … religio[n], cultur[e] and challenging our values within our settings.' (Nyasha)

'Okay, so in my own understanding, feminism it's, ahhh, women that, uhm, fight against patriarchy, and very independent women that … made their own choices without being told.' (Kholeka)

Almost immediately, some participants began to draw correlations between sex work and feminism, with one even arguing that being a sex worker intrinsically makes her a feminist:

'For me, I'd say feminism is sex work. … If a person knows who a sex worker is, a sex worker is a best definition of feminism. Because … like [another participant] was saying, our society tells you what a woman should do, what a woman should wear. You're supposed to get married and have one husband, you know, have children. A sex worker is the opposite of that. We fit in the society by force.' (Rose)

Embodiments of being an African sex worker feminist

As stated, during the arts-based workshop, participants were asked to illustrate, using body maps, how being *an African*, *a sex worker* and *a feminist* manifested on their bodies. This exercise enabled them to articulate the complexities of embodying these three identities in relation to the social and political dimensions they occupy. The following analysis takes in four thematic areas: gender and sexuality, sociocultural norms and religious beliefs, sex and money, and activism as feminism in action, before attempting to answer the main research question: What does it mean to be an African sex worker feminist?

Gender and sexuality

The respondents agreed that anyone can be a feminist, cisgender men and transgender people included. They expressed that being a feminist is not just about the empowerment of women, but also about fighting hegemonic masculine, heteronormative ideals of being a man. Some of the male-bodied participants took issue with how certain African masculine ideals clashed with their self-identification as sex worker feminists:

'The fact that as an "African man" – quote, unquote – the definition of an African man is a strong, muscled, dark [man]. ... So you have to be tall, dark, handsome, and a provider; hence the big muscles, the fish and the machete thing. So that's the image of what an African man [is] – that you should be that.' (Daniel)

'But also sexuality – coming in on the whole aspect of hiding my sex, hiding my sexual orientation, and you know feeling so ashamed, to the point where I can now be public about it ... to me that [is a] feminist journey.' (Daniel)

Daniel went on to explain that as a male sex worker there is an assumption that he should be effeminate, have long hair, wear miniskirts and lipstick:

'Uhm – that I'm drag or trans or I'm feminine. ... That a male sex worker is like that – like a woman taking dick up their ass.' (Daniel)

This assumption about male sex workers being either gay or transgender was challenged by some of the participants' body maps, which had biceps to depict their masculinity and captions such as 'maintain pressure of my penis' (see Figure 8.1). Some of the participants also coloured their body maps black to illustrate being a Black African, while a few female-bodied participants also exaggerated their buttocks to accentuate the voluptuous figure often associated with an African woman's body (see Figure 8.2):

'So ahh, number one question is "how does being an African feminist affect your body?" Uhm, this is breasts. This is big ass. I don't know if you [can see but] ... I tried to push it out.' (Anika)

Figure 8.1: Daniel's body map

Note: Pencil notes read – line pointing to the mouth: 'lipstick'. Boxed arrow around the head: 'assumption that I'm feminine "Oh my God!" queen'. First line pointing to the coffin: 'lets kill old Western Feminism & birth "Ubuntu" African'. Second line from the coffin: 'Feminism is death/funeral'. Line from the feet - 'Black skin'.
Source: FPAR Workshop, used with Daniel's (pseudonym) permission

In relation to the emphasis on the buttocks, steatopygia is often perceived as the 'physical manifestation of [B]lack women's hypersexuality; thus they were defined as prostitutes' (Oyewùmi, 2003: 37). Oyèrónkẹ́ Oyewùmi (2003) also recalls that during the 19th century, European sex workers were often also visually portrayed with large buttocks as if they were Black. Perhaps it is this perceived hypersexuality that the participants are hinting at with these exaggerated illustrations of their buttocks.

Figure 8.2: Anika's body map

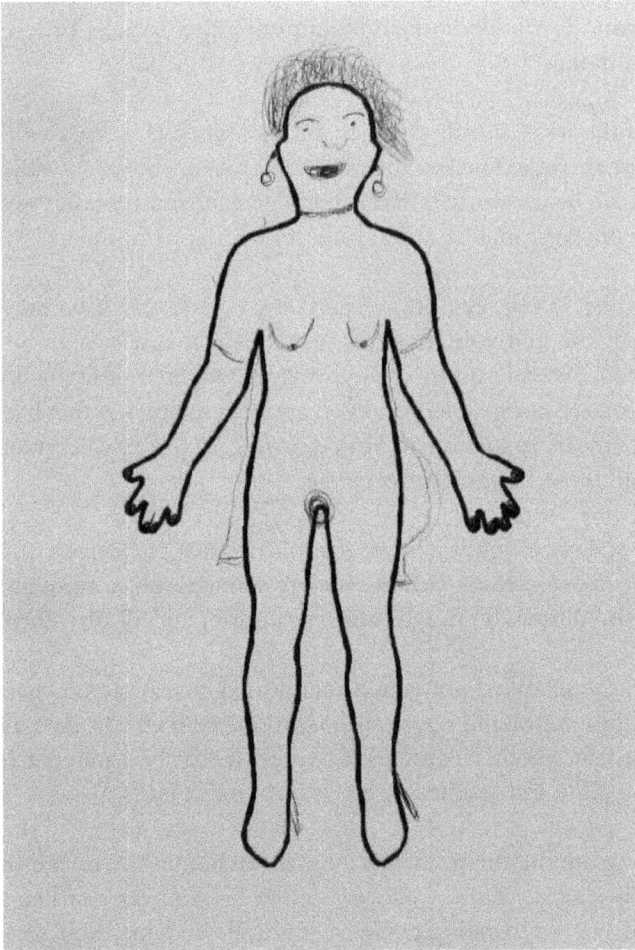

Source: FPAR Workshop, used with Anika's (pseudonym) permission

Many body maps attested to the need to spend money to beautify oneself to attract clients. Participants drew earrings, long hair and prominent nails to illustrate this. With that said, one participant drew her hair as being short, explaining that this represents both her African beauty and feminism: "I don't want to be told that a woman needs to have long hair."

Sociocultural norms and religious beliefs

It should be noted that this chapter sees African culture not in the sense that all cultures in the continent are homogenous, but rather aims to 'highlight those aspects of cultural ideology that are widely shared among Africans';

such as the ethos of *ubuntu*[10] and the legacies of imperialism and colonialism (Tamale, 2008: 49). All the participants agreed that most African cultures and religions deem sex work and feminism either socially unacceptable or wholly immoral:

> 'So, to me it's – already the fact that sex workers are sex working is feminist enough. The fact that they have taken, you know – they have decided to be sex workers in sex work, given that the whole "sex work, oh, it's un-African, blah, blah, blah, it's wrong, it's immoral."' (Daniel)

> 'Yeah, like, in my religion, we perfectly believe that if when you are not married, and you are sleeping with men, that you are a wasted person. ... So for you to even go where you are not living with the man, you are not married, and you are even selling it – that is a taboo. You are meant to be stoned. Yeah ... and I am [a] sex worker and I get to do all those things.' (Anika)

> '[T]he society is fighting to see that our vaginas or *vuginas*[11] ... for sex workers it's something that the society wants to *protect* through, uhm, religious cultures. Through, uhm, [tradition] and all that.' (Empress)

However, the so-called protection mentioned here is often experienced in the form of control and oppression over sex workers' (in fact, all) bodies. With that said, another participant expressed that being taught how to sit as a young Zulu girl instilled in her respect for herself:

> 'So those are the things in culture that teaches us of who we are. You see? They say in Zulu: "*hlala nge-ntombi*".[12] You can't sit like a man. Even if you are wearing trousers, it is still the same. You have to sit with your legs crossed like a girl so your private parts are respected. ... It grooms you as a woman to respect yourself, so you don't sit like you're soliciting.' (Penelope)

It is interesting to note how, even as a feminist, Penelope perceives sociocultural control over the visibility of women's vaginas as something that positively informs her cultural self-identity. This again points to the complexity endued in being an African sex worker feminist. Indeed, Sylvia Tamale (2008: 54) warns that in order to avoid cultural backlashes 'African feminists [need to] work within the specificities of culture' to discard its oppressive aspects, while embracing its emancipatory ones.

Some of the ASWA participants added that being a feminist was also considered by certain African religions as a sin in itself, in the same way that being a sex worker is a sin:

'And also, when it comes to religio[n]. I come from a Muslim family. When it comes to religio[n], it's a sin to be a sex worker, and again it is something very bad – like a sin – to be a feminist, because if I'm a woman, I'm supposed to be married to a man. As a Muslim, as someone coming from a Muslim family.' (Sanyu)

Many of the respondents expressed a sense of empowerment for having gone against sociocultural norms and religious beliefs in being sex workers and feminists. They pointed to societal expectations that as feminists they refused to adhere to, such as being submissive to their husbands. One participant questioned why, if wives are meant to be equal partners in a marriage, they must kneel in front of their husbands and beg for things they need:

'I looked at the women who did what the society wanted and they were not in good condition. Being beaten up by their husbands. In our culture here [in Kenya] you have to kneel down when asking [for] money to make your hair. You have to kneel down when you don't have money for soap. You know, you want salt you all have to crawl down in front of a man to get just a few shillings to buy salt. I was like, no, no, no, no – it can't be like this. Why do I have to kneel down to beg? Yeah, when you are married to someone you have to be equals. You have to respect each other. The fact that he is the one who works and brings food on the table doesn't give him the powers, you know, that you have to kneel down and crawl over him, you know, for him to provide something.' (Jolly)

As per her culture, at 17 years old, Jolly had been asked by her family to marry the man who had raped and impregnated her. When she refused, she was kicked out of her home by her sister. She worked as a bar hostess, but later turned to sex work because it generated a better income. Jolly asserted that defying the cultural expectation of marrying her rapist and selling sex to support her baby was quite empowering and liberating.

Sex and money

For all the participants, sex work is a "source of livelihood" (Nyasha). It gives them the opportunity to be self-employed. To illustrate this on their body maps, many circled and labelled their genitals as banks (see Figure 8.3).

'It [my vagina] is a bank; an ATM [automated teller machine]. You see? So when I do business, that's my bank. Because all the men that got to be attracted, it's because they wanted to have sex. So I charge for them. I don't do it for free. I always tell my fellow sex workers that I get paid to come. I don't just come for free. I'm very expensive [laughs].' (Penelope)

Penelope's response also suggests her own sexual pleasure derived from selling sex. Indeed, choosing to sell sex has become a 'contested symbol of female sexual agency within a male-dominated culture' (Ditmore et al, 2010: 29). Pro-sex work feminists such as Dorothy Aken'Ova and Andrea Cornwall argue that promoting women's sexual agency builds on the feminist principle of erotic justice (Cornwall et al, 2013: 21). '[S]exual pleasure as a feminist choice can be part of reclaiming women's agency' (Cornwall et al, 2013: 3). Conversely for anti-sex work feminists, sex workers have come to symbolize

Figure 8.3: Sanyu's body map

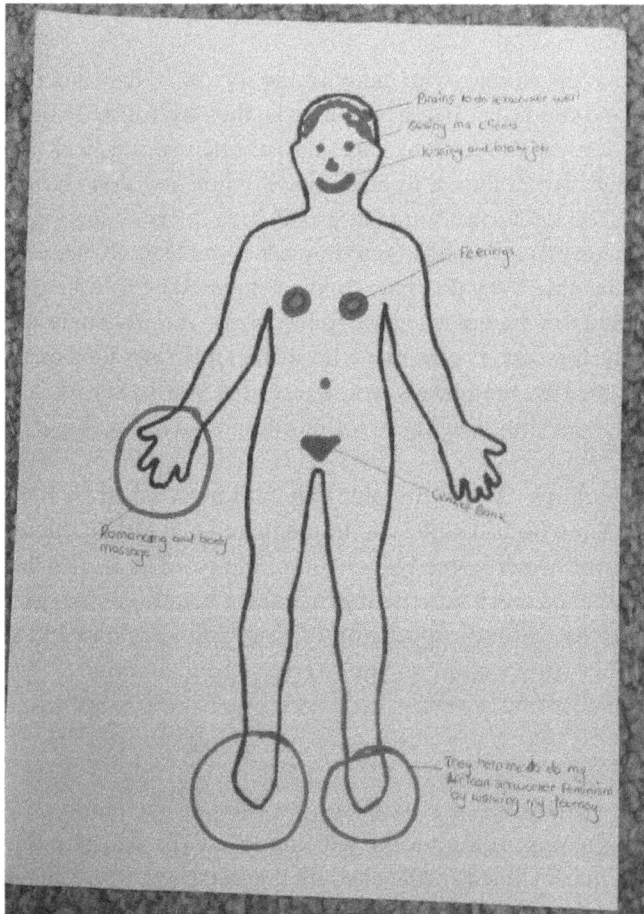

Note: Pen notes read: line pointing to the head: 'Brains to do [sex work] well'. Line pointing to the eye: 'Seeing [my] clients'. Line pointing to the mouth: 'Kissing and blow job'. Line pointing to the breasts: 'Feelings'. Line pointing to the genitals 'Central Bank'. Line pointing to the circle around the hand: 'Romancing and body massage'. Line pointing to the circle around the foot: 'They help me to do my African sex worker feminism by walking my journey'.
Source: FPAR Workshop, used with Sanyu's permission

the 'problem' of women's sexual agency (Ditmore et al, 2010: 36). However, most of the respondents described feelings of empowerment derived from selling sex.

'Because if I negotiate with a man, I tell a man I want a hundred dollars, and he gives me my money. And I decided what style of sex, how, the time, I decide the place. How do you tell me that that kind of work is not empowering?' (Jolly)

Indeed, it does appear that some degree of courage needs to be mastered when having to ask a client to pay for sexual services. Lisa Glazer (1997) recalls that in 1970s Lusaka (Zambia), there was not much in the way of Western-style, impersonal forms of sex work. Shantytown beer brewers sometimes had sex workers in their premises in order to attract male customers; '[h]owever, some of these "prostitutes" who wanted money in exchange for sex were sometimes too shy to demand it' (Glazer, 1997: 151).

Jolly explained that contrary to popular belief, the type of sex that the sex workers are having is no different to the sex everyone else engages in: 'it's not that for them [the client] their penis goes into the ear, or into the nose [laughs]'. Nivedita Menon (2012: 180) affirms this observation and argues that 'we need to demystify "sex" – it is only the mystification of sex by both patriarchal discourses and feminists that makes sex work appear to be "a fate worse than death"'. With that said, one of the workshop participants indicated on her body map that having multiple sexual partners had some negative health implications:

'And around the genital area she is, it is bringing [a] negative health impact, as she is engaging with different clients.' (Liya)[13]

There is evidence that sexually transmitted infections and HIV/AIDS[14] are prevalent among sex workers, and even more so among sex workers in Africa. According to a Joint United Nations Programme on HIV/AIDS (UNAIDS) study of 16 countries in sub-Saharan Africa in 2012, more than 37 per cent of the surveyed sex workers (across genders) were HIV positive (UNAIDS, 2014). Therefore, in as much as selling sex can be economically viable, sexually liberating and empowering, it can also have negative effects on one's sexual health. These are the nuances that need to be considered in the conceptualization of what it means to be an African sex worker feminist.

Activism as feminism in action

'[F]eminism is like a kind of a tool that really helps me to walk my journey as a single mother, as a sex worker, because I can make choices, and also know how I can deal with many things. Yes, as a human rights defender.' (Sanyu)

The participants all agreed that feminism was not merely an identity, but something one does and lives by. Therefore, advocating and lobbying for sex workers' rights was often cited as a demonstration of one's activism and, by extension, evidence of one's feminism. According to Mama (2007), initial[15] forms of African feminism(s) were informed by activism; political action was essentially combined with intellectual work. She explains, however, that the connections between feminist activism and feminist scholarship in African contexts has been compromised by the development of 'Western-style separation between thought and action' (Mama, 2007: 154). In addition, this is perhaps even more the case given Burawoy's (2005) conceptualization of public sociology, which sees a clear distinction between 'instrumental' and 'reflexive' knowledge, and the 'academic' and 'extra-academic' audiences. For the ASWA participants, Mama and other African feminist scholar activists like myself, such demarcations do not exist; scholarship (feminism) is intrinsically linked to praxis (activism). In addition, the empowerment gained by self-identifying as a feminist comes with the responsibility of empowering others as well:

'You see when somebody identifies to be a feminist, ahhh, has to be empowered to know herself and her right and so on, and the right of others as well. Yeah. So one has, she has – that feminist has to empower herself. To have empowerment, ahhh, to disseminate the information about the feminism.' (Yuran)[16]

Sanyu explained how feminism also influences her style of leadership as the executive director of the Lady Mermaid Empowerment Centre, a sex worker rights organization in Uganda:

'So, as a feminist that helps me in my leadership. So that I can treat people equally as an executive director. I can listen to them because I know they also have choices in life they want to make. Or maybe they are trying to tell me something I have to listen [to]. ... If I don't listen to them as a leader, then I don't know about my feminism, because I believe [in] equal rights for all women and persons.' (Sanyu)

During the continuum/positionality exercise many of the workshop participants stood on the 'strongly agree' end in relation to the statement 'feminism impacts on my sex work'. When asked to explain their position, one of the participants shared how being a feminist makes her assertive in her sex work when clients try to demand services she is not willing to offer.

'Why I strongly agree is because as a sex worker in Africa I will be able to tell a man, "although you are paying me, I don't want this" or "because you are paying me it shouldn't make me do whatever you want". I do what I want. If you know you cannot cope with it, you can go.' (Anika)

Even though "most of them [her clients] get very, very angry" when she refuses certain services, Anika claims to be unrelenting. That is how feminism informs her sex work; she would rather lose those clients and their money than compromise herself. However, even though most of the participants expressed that feminism informs their sex work, some felt the two could at times be at odds. As one participant who positioned themselves in the 'neutral' part of the continuum explained:

'Uhmm … because … uhmm, sometimes because of circumstances and different situations and yeah – at work *neh* [right]? You're a sex worker and you're at work, and for some reasons your feminism standards, your feminism understanding at that particular time will not work for you. I'm not saying it's right – right? But I'm saying you've been here at a hotspot for the whole night, it's a winter cold, very winter[y] cold. And you know, you've not seen one client, and then one client comes, but you're – you know? That situation is – I must pay rent, I must do this-this, so you end up doing something … yeah.' (Onko)

Onko acknowledges the challenges of realistically living up to feminist ideals while doing sex work. This demonstrates the constant negotiation and (re)negotiation with both patriarchy and feminism that African sex worker feminists often have to engage in. However, no one stood on the 'strongly disagree' end of the continuum.

So what does it mean to be an African sex worker feminist?

The participants in this research project were asked to help conceptualize who/what an African sex worker feminist is. Many were initially reluctant to give a concise definition, but pointed to elements that would constitute an African sex worker feminist. Drawing from their embodied experiences, they attempted to describe what being an *African*, a *sex worker* and a *feminist* means for them.

For most of the participants, being an African means embodying a particular physique, most likely having a dark complexion denoting being of Black race or, if you are a woman, a curvaceous figure. It means sharing a colonial history of white oppression and struggle for liberation while grappling with its present-day legacies of discrimination and inequality. It's sometimes having to adhere to, or negotiate, certain sociocultural norms and religious beliefs, while most certainly defying those that dehumanize.

For a sex worker, selling sex is a viable livelihood. It provides some degree of economic security and independence. It comes with the need to beautify oneself in order to be able to attract clients. It is about having the courage to ask for money in exchange for sex. It is even about being paid to get sexually aroused to the point of orgasm.

A feminist is empowered with knowledge and has agency to make informed choices. They fight against patriarchy and other forms of social injustice. They engage in activism and movement building. Their leadership embodies feminist principles of solidarity and equality. Therefore, a feminist can be of any gender identity or sexual orientation.

So, what does it mean to be an African sex worker feminist? It means embodying a political identity that intersects with multiple social dimensions. It is about negotiating and (re)negotiating with both patriarchy and feminism. It is struggling to provide for your family, because your work is not considered legitimate. It is having to manage the tensions of pro- and anti-sex work feminists who claim to know what's best for you. And it is about finding a language of feminism that speaks most honestly to the nuances and complexities of selling sex in Africa.

Conclusion

When asked at the end of her interview if she had any questions or anything to add, Sanyu replied with the following plea:

> 'What I should add on – as sex workers, if, if maybe, I don't know about the research and everything, but we are requesting, at least as sex workers in Africa, so that we can have those platforms where we can learn more about [being] feminist and feminism. Yeah – in the communities, in the workplace, in our families ... I know there is a lot of the information we don't know, but ... we are also discriminated [against] by our fellow feminists. Now my appeal goes to you, if we can get those platforms where we can discuss about our issues as African sex worker feminists.'

Indeed, one of the main principles of FPAR is an actionable outcome that contributes towards a social justice end. As mentioned at the start of this chapter, the main objective with both studies was to encourage so-called 'mainstream feminists' and sex worker rights feminists to start recognizing each other as comrades in the struggle for gender and sexual liberation, thus strengthening solidarity for sex worker rights activism across social justice movements. To this end, the combined findings have been presented in feminist, academic and activism spaces, such as the Black Feminisms Forum at the Association of Women in Development Forum in Brazil in 2016, with some of the ASWA members who were part of the second study. I have shared numerous panels with one of the former AWAKE! Women of Africa members, including at the University of the Witwatersrand Centre for Diversity Studies 'Decolonising Feminism' conference in 2016. It is important that the participants remain engaged well into the knowledge dissemination phase.[17] Therefore, I am also in the process of co-authoring a book chapter with this former member of AWAKE! Even in the dissemination phase, the participant still needs to be engaged as a collaborator in the knowledge production process. Over and above dissemination, the participants now have an explicit self-identification as African sex worker feminists and the confidence to engage in those spaces once considered antagonistic. This is how FPAR can be used to not only unpack the embodied lived experiences of African sex worker feminists, but also help support sex worker rights activism in the continent.

This chapter demonstrates how the co-production of knowledge was integral to the design of this project as a social justice one, and how that co-production empowered the participants in deepening their self-conception as sex worker feminists with the confidence to engage with mainstream feminists as well as other constituencies, such as academics and the media. At the same time, this research produced new knowledge which contributes to expanding sociological understandings of feminism and women's rights into challenging, uncomfortable and stigmatized domains of women's lives. This, I would argue, demonstrates a complete sociology – reflexive and instrumental, with political, policy and scholarly goals.

Notes

1   This means 'we are together' in isiZulu.
2   The NSWP is a membership-based NPO that advocates for sex workers' human rights globally. Its members are local, national or regional sex-worker-led organizations and networks across five regions: Africa, Asia and the Pacific, Europe, Latin America, and North America and the Caribbean. See NSWP (n.d.-b).
3   In South Africa an honours degree is a postgraduate specialization qualification which entails preparing students for research-based postgraduate study.
4   This was carried out at the Institute of Development Studies, University of Sussex, UK.
5   Lesbian, gay, bisexual, transgender, queer/questioning and intersexed.
6   Eight of the interviews were with participants who had been part of the workshop.
7   This chapter uses the term 'other' (with single inverted commas) to refer to so-called 'traditional/mainstream' feminists. This is adopted from Jill Nagle's collection titled *Whores and Other Feminists* in order to subvert the alienation and discrimination sex worker feminists experience when engaging with them.
8   Andrea Cornwall and Cheryl Overs.
9   In this chapter, I use participants' first names or pseudonyms to protect their identities.
10 *Ubuntu* is an Nguni term, which loosely translates to 'humanity'.

[11]   This is a term used by the workshop participants to refer to the anus, in relation to anal sex.
[12]   This Zulu saying loosely translates to 'sit on your womanhood' or 'sit like a girl'.
[13]   Interview was facilitated by an Amharic translator who was also present during the workshop.
[14]   Human immunodeficiency virus/acquired immune deficiency syndrome.
[15]   In the 18th and 19th centuries (perhaps even earlier).
[16]   Interviewed with the help of a Portuguese translator who was also present during the workshop.
[17]   This research has also been published in the *Feminist Africa* journal in 2017 and the *Meridians – Feminism, Race, Transnationalism* journal in 2018.

References

Akin-Aina, S. (2011) 'Beyond an epistemology of bread, butter, culture and power: Mapping the African feminist movement', *Nokoko*, 2: 65–89. Accessed 3 February 2020. https://carleton.ca/africanstudies/wp-content/uploads/Nokoko-Fall-2011-3-Sinmi.pdf

Arribas Lozano, A. (2018) 'Reframing the public sociology debate: Towards collaborative and decolonial praxis', *Current Sociology*, 66(1): 92–109.

Attride-Stirling, J. (2001) 'Thematic networks: An analytic tool for qualitative research', *Qualitative Research*, 1(3): 385–405.

Brydon-Miller, M., Greenwood, D. and Maguire, P. (2003) 'Why action research?', *Action Research*, 1(1): 9–28.

Brydon-Miller, M., Maguire, P. and McIntyre, A. (eds) (2004) *Traveling Companions: Feminism, Teaching, and Action Research*, Westport, CT: Praeger.

Burawoy, M. (2005) 'For public sociology', *American Sociological Review*, 70(1): 4–28.

Chambers, R. (1997). 'Editorial: Responsible well-being – a personal agenda for development', *World Development*, 25(11): 1744.

Charmaz, K. (2011) 'Grounded theory methods in social justice research', in N.K. Denzin and Y.S. Lincoln (eds) in *The SAGE Handbook of Qualitative Research*, Thousand Oaks, CA: Sage, pp 359–80.

Cornwall, A. (1992) Body mapping in health RRA/PRA. *RRA Notes*, 16: 1. https://pubs.iied.org/sites/default/files/pdfs/migrate/G01449.pdf

Cornwall, A., Hawkins, K. and Jolly, S. (eds) (2013) *Women, Sexuality, and the Political Power of Pleasure*, London: Zed Books.

Desyllas, M.C. (2013) 'Representations of sex workers' needs and aspirations: A case for arts-based research', *Sexualities* 16(7): 772–87.

Diaz, E. (2014) 'Bell Hooks calls Beyoncé a "terrorist"' [video], BET.com, 7 May: Accessed 30 January 2015 https://www.bet.com/news/celebrities/2014/05/07/bell-hooks-calls-beyonc-a-terrorist.html

Ditmore, M., Levy, A. and Willman, A. (2010) *Sex Work Matters: Exploring Money, Power and Intimacy in the Sex Industry*, London: Zed Books.

England, K.V.L. (1994) 'Getting personal: Reflexivity, positionality, and feminist research', *The Professional Geographer*, 46(1): 80–9.

Glazer, I.M. (1997) 'Alcohol and politics in urban Zambia: The intersection of gender and class', in G. Mikell (ed) *African Feminism: The Politics of Survival in Sub-Saharan Africa*, Philadelphia: University of Pennsylvania Press, pp 142–58.

Lewis, D. (2001) 'African feminisms', *Agenda*, 16(50): 4–10.

Mama, A. (2007) 'Critical connections: Feminist studies in African contexts', in A. Cornwall, E. Harrison and A. Whitehead (eds) *Feminisms in Development: Contradictions, Contestations and Challenges*, London: Zed Books, 150–60.

Menon, N. (2012) *Seeing Like a Feminist*, New Delhi: Penguin Books.

Morris, C., Boyce, P., Cornwall, A., Frith, H., Harvey, L. and Huang, Y. (eds) (2018) *Researching Sex and Sexualities*, London: Zed Books.

Nagel, J. (1997) *Whores and Other Feminists*, New York: Routledge.

NSWP (Global Network of Sex Work Projects) (n.d.-a) 'History of the NSWP and the sex worker rights movement: Event', https://www.nswp. org/timeline/event/african-sex-worker-conference-and-formation-aswa

NSWP (Global Network of Sex Work Projects) (n.d.-b) 'Who we are', https://www.nswp.org/who-we-are

Olesen, V.L. (2000) 'Feminisms and qualitative research at and into the millennium', in N.K. Denzin and Y.S. Lincoln (eds) *Handbook of Qualitative Research* (2nd edn), Thousand Oaks, CA: Sage, 215–55.

Oyewùmi, O. (2003) 'The white woman's burden: African women in Western feminist discourse', in O. Oyewùmi (ed), *African Women and Feminism: Reflecting on the Politics of Sisterhood*, Trenton: Africa World Press, 25–43.

Reason, P. and Bradbury, H. (2008) *Handbook of Action Research: Participate Inquiry and Practice* (2nd edn), London: Sage.

Reid, C. and Gillberg, C. (2014) 'Feminist participatory action research', in D. Coghlan and M. Brydon-Miller (eds), *The SAGE Encyclopedia of Action Research*, Thousand Oaks, CA: Sage, pp 343–7.

Richter, M. (2012) 'Sex work as a test case for African feminism', *BUWA!* 2(1): 62–9, https://www.academia.edu/2977113/Sex_Work_as_a_test_case_for_African_feminism

Silverman, D. (2006) *Interpreting Qualitative Data: Methods for Analysing Talk, Text and Interaction* (3rd edn), London: Sage.

Sisonke (n.d.) 'Who we are', http://www.sweat.org.za/who-we-are/

Sonke Gender Justice (2014) *Sex Workers and Sex Work in South Africa: A Guide for Journalists and Writers*, Cape Town: Sonke Gender Justice, Sisonke Sex Workers Movement, Sex Worker Education and Advocacy Taskforce, and Women's Legal Resource Centre, https://genderjustice.org.za/publication/sex-workers-and-sex-work-in-south-africa

Stanley, L. and Wise, S. (2002) *Breaking Out Again: Feminist Ontology and Epistemology* (2nd edn), Taylor & Francis e-Library, http://cdn.preterhuman. net/texts/thought_and_writing/philosophy/breaking%20out%20again.pdf

Tamale, S. (2008) 'The right to culture and the culture of rights: A critical perspective on women's sexual rights in Africa', *Feminist Legal Studies*, 16(1): 47–69.

UHAI EASHRI (East African Sexual Health and Rights Initiative) (n.d.) 'Home page'. https://www.uhai-eashri.org

UNAIDS (Joint United Nations Programme on HIV/AIDS) (2014) *The Gap Report 2014*, Geneva: UNAIDS. http://www.unaids.org/en/resources/ documents/2014/20140716_UNAIDS_gap_report

Van der Meulen, E. (2011) 'Action research with sex workers: Dismantling barriers and building bridges', *Action Research*, 9(4): 370–84.

Writing Studio (n.d.) 'Visual analysis', Duke University, https://twp.duke. edu/sites/twp.duke.edu/files/file-attachments/visual-analysis.original.pdf

Yingwana, N. (2017) '"I'm not a feisty bitch, I'm a feminist!": Feminism in AWAKE! Women of Africa', *Feminist Africa*, 22: 186–96, http://www.agi. ac.za/sites/default/files/image_tool/images/429/feminist_africa_journals/ archive/22/fa22_profiles_3.pdf

Yingwana, N. (2018) 'We fit in the society by force', *Meridians*, 17(2): 279–95.

9

Participatory Action Research for Food Justice in Johannesburg: Seeking a More Immediate Impact for Engaged Research

Brittany Kesselman

Introduction

The high levels of hunger, malnutrition and diet-related diseases in Johannesburg suggest a situation of severe food injustice. While the concept of food security is concerned with people having access to enough food, food justice goes further by addressing issues of equity, fairness and control in the food system. As an analytical lens, food justice recognizes the structural racism and economic injustice of the food system, while as a movement, it seeks to ensure that marginalized communities have equal access to healthy food and control over decision-making regarding their food systems (Alkon and Agyeman, 2011). Although the concept of food justice was developed in the United States, it is equally relevant in South Africa, where centuries of settler colonialism and decades of apartheid have created one of the most unequal societies in the world. Almost three decades into democracy, the unjust structure of South Africa's highly concentrated, industrial food system continues to deny most of the population access to healthy food, while generating billions of rands in profits for a few large national and multinational corporations.

In a situation of such severe food injustice, research on food cannot be detached or 'neutral'. It must, if it is to be relevant and ethical, actually contribute towards social change. This chapter argues that participatory action research (PAR), as both a normative commitment and an approach to inquiry, is a means by which research can contribute to food justice. Going beyond both 'public sociology' and 'critically engaged sociology' in its attempts to empower research participants and respond to their needs, PAR seeks to effect change not only through policy influence, but also through the very process of the research.

Drawing from my experiences doing research on urban agriculture (UA), food consumption and food justice in Johannesburg, this chapter highlights the importance of ensuring that research contributes to social justice, and discusses some of the challenges in doing so. My doctoral research on UA and food sovereignty in Johannesburg indicated that participation in community gardens was by no means a guaranteed path to improved nutrition, environmental sustainability or empowerment. It also indicated that many UA support programmes were designed and implemented in a top-down, disempowering fashion, ignoring structural constraints in favour of market-based solutions to poverty and hunger. The lessons learned through that research led me to search for a way to address some of the challenges facing urban farmers and their surrounding communities that would be empowering and have a more immediate, direct impact on their lives.

Thus, this chapter reflects on the need to conceive and do research differently, to steer research away from its tainted colonial past into a present in which it prioritizes the needs, knowledge(s) and solutions of local communities. It proposes PAR as the means to ensure that food research contributes to food justice, while also raising some contextual and institutional challenges that a researcher working on food justice may need to confront. The next section paints a stark picture of food injustice in Johannesburg, and then some of the historical factors that contributed to the current food crisis are described. This is followed by an overview of the values that inform PAR and the way it seeks to connect research to social change. Two examples are given of PAR for food justice from other parts of the world, along with lessons about the conditions that contribute to success. The chapter then turns to the Johannesburg context to assess its suitability for PAR. An overview of my own attempts at PAR for food justice provides concrete examples of the challenges. Finally, the chapter considers possible avenues by which PAR might raise awareness and contribute to food justice, and the chapter concludes with reflections on how PAR, as a tool of engaged scholarship, represents a different approach to not only knowledge production, but also the real-world impact of academic research.

Context: food injustice

In South Africa, less than half of the population is food secure: 28.3 per cent of the population is at risk of hunger and 26 per cent experience hunger (Shisana et al, 2013: 145). Despite being the economic engine of the country, the city of Johannesburg also suffers high levels of food insecurity. This varies dramatically between neighbourhoods, with estimates of food insecurity ranging from 42 per cent citywide (City of Johannesburg, n.d.: 68) to up to 90 per cent in the poorest wards (de Wet et al, 2008). Because almost all food in Johannesburg is accessed via purchase, high levels of poverty and unemployment translate into high levels of food insecurity (Rudolph et al, 2012).

Studies show that most South Africans cannot afford to sustain healthy diets – this is particularly true of fruits, which are not affordable in rand per calorie terms (Temple and Steyn, 2011). Because many subsist on a diet of highly processed foods, including refined maize meal, sugary beverages, bread and tea with sugar (Wenhold et al, 2012), the population shows signs of various nutrient deficiencies (Mchiza et al, 2015).

Due to a 'nutrition transition', wherein urban populations shift from more traditional rural diets to more convenient processed foods that fit into an urban lifestyle (Pereira, 2014), Johannesburg has seen increasing levels of obesity and associated non-communicable diseases (NCDs) such as hypertension, cardiovascular disease and diabetes (Department of Health, 2013). Paradoxically, nutrient deficiencies and NCDs are often found in the same people, especially the poor, who cannot afford healthy diets and instead subsist on cheap energy-dense foods that are high in fat and added sugar but low in essential nutrients (Temple and Steyn, 2011). This phenomenon is known as 'hidden hunger' (Wenhold et al, 2012).

In a postcolonial, post-apartheid South Africa, race-based marginalization remains a reality. Stark racial inequality in employment and income translates into highly unequal access to food. While food insecurity is almost non-existent among white South Africans (1.35 per cent food insecure and 9.4 per cent at risk of hunger), much of the black population is hungry or at risk of hunger (30.3 per cent food insecure and 30.3 per cent at risk of hunger) (Shisana et al, 2013: 146). At the same time, problems of food access are compounded by the legacy of apartheid spatial planning, which located many poor black households far from the city centre in areas not served by major supermarkets (City of Johannesburg, 2011). Food retail outlets in marginalized areas (whether street vendors, informal shops or small grocery stores) tend to have a more limited range of products and less fresh produce available than those in wealthier suburbs.

While many Johannesburg residents struggle to meet their nutritional requirements, the food industry in South Africa is highly concentrated and reaps enormous profits. Along the entire value chain, from agricultural inputs through commercial farming, processing, manufacturing and retail, the South African food system is dominated by a few large (usually corporate) players at each node (Greenberg, 2016). The control of the food industry by white (and often transnational) capital to the exclusion of the black majority is a stark reminder of the continuing need for economic transformation. A glaring example of food system injustice is the salary differential between the chief executive officer (CEO) of the country's largest supermarket chain and its workers: in 2017 the CEO earned 1,332 times more than the average employee, at R 100 million (plus incentives) versus R 75,150. Most of the lower-paid supermarket jobs, such as cashier and cleaner, are outsourced via labour brokers, so the real salary differential is even greater – in 2016, workers in these jobs received R 13 to R 23 per hour, or R 29,744 to R 52,624 per year, if they worked full time (eNCA, 2016).

Historical roots of today's food injustice

When Johannesburg was founded after the discovery of gold in 1886, the feeding of mineworkers to facilitate maximum extraction of labour power at the lowest cost was a constant concern of mining companies. Studies such as Wylie's (2001) *Starving on a Full Stomach* shed light on how mining companies and the government embraced the nascent field of nutrition science in order to address such concerns. The migrant labour system brought black men to the mines and placed them in all-male hostels, where they received rations from mines but also sometimes had to cook their own meals (or chose to supplement rations with additional foods). There were frequent complaints about the poor rations, while the foods men could access and prepare for themselves were quite limited (Wylie, 2001). At the same time, this system left black women and children in the rural areas to farm and fend for themselves on plots of land that were becoming more crowded and degraded. Rural development officers, missionaries and others sought to 'modernize' what they viewed as 'backwards' rural methods, but this was done in ways that demonstrated their biases towards European practices, crops and diets (Wylie, 2001).

These biases towards 'European' foods were translated into agricultural policies that favoured white farmers and the crops they grew (for example, wheat) over indigenous farmers and crops. For example, bread subsidies increased the market for white farmers' wheat crops by shifting dietary practices – in this case, increasing bread consumption. These agricultural policies were combined with a pervasive racist discourse identifying 'European' foods as superior while disparaging indigenous African ones, as seen in the promotion of bread and wine (European imports) over porridge or sorghum beer (Wylie, 2001). Black children educated in missionary schools were taught to look down on traditional foods and food practices, to see them as backwards compared to 'modern' white foods (Raschke and Cheema, 2008).

With increasing urbanization and the industrialization of the food system, a shift towards more processed foods has occurred, commonly referred to as the 'nutrition transition' (Popkin, 2008). Urban residents frequently value the convenience of processed foods, since they have less time for cooking due to long working hours and long commutes. In addition, in urban areas virtually all food must be purchased, as there is little time or space to grow one's own produce and keeping livestock is generally prohibited. Beyond convenience, industrialized foods tend to contain high levels of fat, sugar and salt to make them taste more appealing. In addition, fast foods are viewed as modern and associated with higher status, while traditional foods are perceived as 'poverty foods' (Ledger, 2016; Kroll, 2017). Industrialization and concentration of the food system have also led to a narrowing of choices, as large-scale production of standardized commodities is favoured by large-scale processors and retailers (Greenberg, 2015).

Participatory action research for social transformation

In the context of such clear and extreme food injustice in Johannesburg, the idea that research on food could be done in a detached manner, purely for the sake of increasing knowledge, seems ludicrous. Research on food can and must contribute to social justice. Whether it is called engaged scholarship, emancipatory research or scholar activism, research on hunger – a fundamental denial of basic human rights – must be explicitly committed to reducing human suffering. PAR is an ideal methodology for achieving this impact.

PAR (some now prefer the term 'community-led action research') represents not only a research method, but a normative commitment and an 'orientation to inquiry' (Reason and Bradbury, 2008: 1). PAR is a collaborative process of research, education and action, explicitly oriented towards social transformation. In its ideal form, community participants are involved in identifying an issue that requires research, developing a research question, designing and conducting the research, analysing the data and disseminating the results in a way that benefits them and their community (Kindon et al, 2007). Participants maintain ownership over all aspects of the research, while the role of the university researcher is to support and facilitate the community-led process (Pain, 2004). The fact that community participants lead the research and that the knowledge of university researchers and community members is equally valued, distinguishes PAR from more traditional 'extractive' research approaches. There are differences of opinion with regard to the degree to which a researcher may influence community processes; this ranges from a pedagogical or catalytic role (Rahman, 1993) to one that simply assists the community to frame their concerns as researchable questions (Genat, 2009).

PAR can involve various research methods, or instruments, as appropriate. Regardless of the specific research tools used, the PAR process is democratic and participatory in a way that not only generates new knowledge but also contributes to new norms of engagement among participants. Such practices can transform people's ways of imagining community life and their role in it. The action component of PAR refers to its explicit commitment to social change. The kind of knowledge that will be produced, in response to questions generated by community members and through research processes they control, is likely to be different from that resulting from more traditional research models. Likewise, who holds that knowledge, and how it is disseminated, may also differ.

Thus, the process of research itself is empowering, and participation has an immediate impact on participants in terms of skills and knowledge gained as well as actions taken towards social change. Through PAR, a people's praxis develops, in line with Paulo Freire's concept of conscientization in *Pedagogy of the Oppressed* (1970) and Orlando Fals-Borda's (1979) research for social change. This direct and immediate impact differs from the more traditional paths by which research seeks to bring about change. Models such as public sociology aim to influence policy, with the hope that policy changes will eventually improve the lives of those affected. Other research, such as critically engaged sociology, is often conducted for social movements or progressive non-governmental organizations (NGOs) so that they can use it in their advocacy and programmes. With PAR, influencing policy may be one of the intended paths of transformation, but *in addition* to that, the research itself is part of the impact, as the very process of participation can empower participants and alter their lives.

Examples of participatory action research for food justice

Researchers and activists have utilized PAR to advance the cause of food justice. For example, the Soils, Food and Healthy Communities (SFHC) project, started in northern Malawi in 2000 as a collaboration between researchers from a Canadian university and staff at the Ekwendeni Hospital, sought to address issues of food security, nutrition and health (Nyantakyi-Frimpong et al, 2017). The SFHC project worked with farmers to improve soil fertility, diversify crop production and implement agroecological production methods. The four main areas of focus included: farmer-led experimentation and innovation; improved access to a diverse range of seeds (including creation of community seed banks); community recipe and demonstration days and farmer exchange visits; and gender equity. The research involved democratic, participatory processes, such as the election by local farmers of their own representatives to be mentors and provide peer support as well as becoming community nutrition researchers. A key innovation of the project is the community recipe and demonstration days, in which farmers participate in preparing and tasting a wide range of foods produced on their own farms. Men are especially encouraged to participate in food preparation, in order to promote a more equitable gendered division of labour in the household.

More traditional agricultural research might have seen experiments with different planting methods undertaken by professional researchers on test plots at an agricultural research centre, with the most successful method then rolled out to local farmers via extension officers, without regard for local context. This research, by contrast, was undertaken by the farmers themselves, who tested out different methods of planting and different combinations of plants and then shared their results among themselves. In this way, farmer innovation leads to significant advances, which are more easily accepted by other local farmers in the face of visible evidence from peers that they work. Similarly, more traditional research on child malnutrition might have been undertaken by public health or medical professionals at the hospital without engaging community members in discussions, training, recipe days and other peer-to-peer learning activities. These participatory activities yielded useful information about the causes of child malnutrition, which went beyond narrow issues of food access to include women's excessive workload. More importantly, they yielded actions that led to social change, shifts in the gendered division of labour and ultimately improvements in child nutrition.

Because of these participatory processes, the project has contributed to improvements in soil health, resilience, food security, dietary diversity, child health and gender equity. These successes have contributed to the expansion of the project from 130 to over 10,000 farming households. The project had to overcome suspicion and scepticism on the part of local farmers as well as resistance to shifts in gender roles (Msachi et al, 2009). It has also grappled with some of the common challenges of PAR, such as power differentials between academic researchers and farmers, or competition between the need to produce publications and the desire to make progress in development work. However, through long-term engagement, flexibility, open communication and a strong commitment to building capacity and empowering participants, the project has achieved remarkable results.

Another example of PAR for food justice is the Sustaining Local Food Systems, Biodiversity and Livelihoods initiative in India, Iran and Peru (Pimbert et al, 2017). This is a long-term PAR project, undertaken in collaboration with peasant farmers and indigenous communities, which seeks to analyze how – and under what conditions – decentralized governance, peasant and citizen participation, and capacity building can help sustain local food systems, biodiversity and livelihoods. The project seeks to 'make sense of the world through efforts to transform it' (Pimbert et al, 2017: 102). As with many PAR projects, it has utilized several different research tools, such as participatory learning and action methods, community radio, peasant-led audits of national policies, peasant exchanges for mutual learning, citizens' juries, policy dialogues and many more. Methods, activities and time frames were selected by local participants, not by the academic researchers. The project has sought to incorporate, validate and protect local and traditional knowledge systems.

Through community video work, women peasant collectives in the Deccan plateau in India documented their situation and then created an alternative grain distribution system, which they supply and control. The women subsequently shared their experiences, and their video-making skills, with indigenous farmers in Peru. In Iran, nomadic tribes, using their traditional knowledge, were able to organize to influence government policy on rangeland management. In Peru, indigenous groups developed biocultural protocols for the protection of indigenous food knowledge rights. In each case, academic researchers facilitated participatory processes in which peasant communities determined what issues to research, conducted the research, implemented relevant actions and decided how to disseminate the outcomes. Some key enabling factors included: jointly developed rules of engagement, formation of safe spaces for intercultural dialogue, a shift in power dynamics and traditional roles, cognitive justice, extended peer review, open communication and flexible long-term funding. These enabled the project to evolve and develop in response to local conditions and needs, rather than sticking to a fixed plan.

These projects highlight the potential of PAR to make a real contribution to food justice struggles. Helpfully, they highlight the extensive range of research instruments in the PAR toolbox and some of the conditions that facilitate the success of PAR. In particular, a long-term commitment is required in order to build trust, test different strategies and capacitate the community participants to guide the process. In addition, flexibility is critical in order to respond to issues as they arise or to shift focus in response to community priorities. A willingness to shift power and control from university researchers to community members, and to embrace traditional and local knowledge, is also necessary.

Keeping in mind these critical success factors, we consider the potential of PAR to contribute to food justice in the unique context of Johannesburg.

Johannesburg: a challenging context for PAR on food justice

Returning to the situation of extreme food injustice in Johannesburg, it would seem an ideal context in which to use PAR to empower communities to address their own food-related challenges. Another aspect of the research context, however, raises challenging questions about the potential of PAR.

This is the low level of recognition of food injustice and the concomitant low levels of political mobilization around food justice issues.

South Africa is known for having the highest level of protests, per capita, in the world (Bond, 2010), with regular protests over access to water, electricity, education and other basic rights, yet there has been very little political mobilization around access to food (Greenberg, 2006). This may be because people do not recognize food as a right to be claimed from the state, in the same way as education or water, even though it is guaranteed as a right in Section 27 of the South African Constitution (South African Human Rights Commission, n.d.). For example, when I asked a community gardener in Johannesburg about the meaning of the right to food, she remarked: "A right to eat, but where will we get the food to eat? You'll go to Spar [supermarket] and say, 'I want to eat', yet you don't have money to buy food" (Grace, personal communication, 25 February 2015). It was inconceivable to her that food might be available by means other than purchasing it at a retail outlet.

As discussed, the impact of colonialism and apartheid on food access, practices, knowledge and norms cannot be overstated. A more recent development that has dealt a blow to the potential for mobilization around food injustice is the prevalence of neoliberal world views. Neoliberal mentalities, or subjectivities, refer to the ways 'market logic increasingly pervades individuals' and communities' everyday thoughts and practices as we embrace such ideals as individualism, efficiency and self-help' (Alkon and Mares, 2012: 348). One of the disempowering elements of neoliberalism, highlighted by Brown (2006), is its transformation of political and social problems into individual problems with market solutions. Thus, poverty and hunger are not viewed as challenges for political and economic policy, but as failures of individual entrepreneurship – food is viewed as a commodity, an item to be purchased through the market, and inability to do so is blamed on the individual's failure to develop his or her 'human capital' rather than on the economic system. In addition, neoliberal thinking privileges market solutions (for example, urban farming to sell produce) without recognizing the role of the market in causing hunger in the first place. It makes non-market solutions, such as socialized community kitchens, unthinkable.

In conducting research in Johannesburg's community gardens, it became apparent that the market logic of neoliberalism had been adopted by garden participants as well as the government, corporate and NGO personnel assisting them. Among the garden participants and support personnel, there was a tendency to blame the hungry and to see them as lazy, rather than recognizing historical and structural factors of exclusion and marginalization. One food garden participant said: "I think they [supermarkets] must help [the hungry], but if they've got money. Because also they must get something, and then they can manage to help people" (Margaret, personal communication,

26 February 2015). This view was expressed by a woman struggling to feed her family, regarding food retail giants, such as Pick n Pay, which made over R 860 million in 2015.

It is worth mentioning that while there is no broad-based food justice movement in Johannesburg, there have been attempts to increase the visibility of food injustice in recent years through the nascent South African Food Sovereignty Campaign, a national campaign spearheaded by the Cooperative and Policy Alternative Centre. In addition, there are various kinds of hunger- and health-related initiatives working at various scales (from community level to international level) and run by various actors (such as churches, NGOs, government departments and the private sector). These interventions tend to be framed as either charitable, as in the case of a soup kitchen helping the hungry, or as neoliberal self-help, as in the case of support for small-scale urban farmers to sell their produce to existing markets. These interventions are not grounded in an acknowledgement of the right to food, nor do they challenge the macro-level structural factors that inhibit people's enjoyment of that right.

A key tenet of PAR is that the community identifies an issue of concern and then develops the research and action to address it. One of the ways to support a community in such an endeavour is through a partnership with community-based organizations (CBOs) or social movements that have formed to address identified issues. In the absence of like-minded CBOs or a local food justice movement, can PAR be used to raise awareness of the right to food and the injustices of the food system? Can PAR have an impact on these challenges? If a community has not identified food injustice as a priority, can it be the focus of a PAR project? Can a researcher bring a concern for food injustice to a community, discuss it, find partners who share her vision and undertake PAR with them? The next section engages with these questions, drawing from my own experiences of food justice research in Johannesburg.

Attempts at participatory action research: the search for partners for a community food centre

My PhD research looked at the contribution of community gardens to food sovereignty in Johannesburg. More specifically, it assessed whether community gardens contributed to food security, sustainable livelihoods for farmers, environmental sustainability, food system localization and democratization, empowerment and gender equity. I used several research techniques, including participant observation in two case study gardens, interviews with government and NGO personnel who provided support to the gardens, and food diaries, food/life histories and other interviews with gardeners and their customers. Based on the UA literature, I approached the project with the expectation that food gardeners would be interested in food system issues and that their participation in the gardens would contribute to various aspects of food sovereignty. While the latter was true to a limited degree, it was found that food gardeners had a wide range of reasons for participating in garden projects, many of which had nothing to do with food. Further, I found that simply participating in a garden did not lead to any kind of increased consciousness of food system injustice. I also found that much of the support provided to gardens was in fact disempowering and that, as a result, it did not meaningfully contribute to food system transformation (see also Ledger, 2015).

The challenges faced by urban food gardeners often relate to macro-level socio-economic factors beyond the garden gate. Yet those providing support to the food gardens studied (government, NGOs and corporate social responsibility projects) failed to consider or address such structural constraints. As is the case with the general South African population, the food gardeners consumed relatively poor diets, including very low levels of vegetables, despite having free and unlimited access. This was due to lack of time, fatigue, poor cooking knowledge and skills, as well as dietary norms resulting from macro-level historical and economic forces, environmental factors and cultural preferences.

The research highlighted the importance of approaching food-related questions without any assumptions. It also demonstrated the need for a more empowering approach to UA support programmes. I began exploring ways to pursue other research that would contribute more directly to the improvement of conditions for urban farmers and their surrounding communities and which might help to raise consciousness around the injustice of the food system. Research on international food sovereignty and food justice struggles led to the concept of a community food centre (CFC).

The CFC idea is inspired by successful initiatives from other parts of the world. For example, Canada's CFCs are not-for-profit organizations that provide emergency food assistance, education and training, and community-building activities while also undertaking advocacy on food system issues (Levkoe and Wakefield, 2011; Saul and Curtis, 2013). Brazil's people's restaurants are a government intervention to ensure that all Brazilians enjoy the right to food, regardless of their ability to pay (Rocha and Lessa, 2009). Peru's community kitchens were started by indigenous women who migrated to cities and struggled to feed their families (Garrett, 2001; Schroeder, 2006). The not-for-profit, pay-what-you-want restaurant concept in the United States and elsewhere asks people to contribute what they can for a meal, rather than having fixed prices. My idea of a CFC drew from these and other examples to respond to Johannesburg's food-related challenges by providing free and/or affordable healthy meals, offering training on food and agriculture-related skills and issues (nutrition, food preparation, agroecological food gardening), raising awareness and conducting advocacy about the right to food and the injustice of the current food system – all while demonstrating alternatives.

While a CFC would address many of the challenges identified in my previous research, I was of the view that it would only be empowering if it resulted from a community-based PAR project. Such a process would ensure community buy-in while also empowering community members with new knowledge and skills, and creating new norms of democratic decision-making among participants. In addition, the process would demonstrate that alternative, non-capitalist models for food consumption are possible. Such a process would also, of necessity, involve a long period of building relationships and trust, even before the slow process of community-led research could commence. Significant funding would be required for the establishment of the CFC as well. Unfortunately, I was completing this work as part of a postdoctoral fellowship and had just 18 months and extremely limited funds for research activities. In spite of this, I proceeded to seek out community partners for the project with the knowledge that the initial phase would not result in the establishment of the CFC; rather, it would lay the groundwork by creating interest in the project, establishing partnerships and gaining additional knowledge about the community's needs and priorities.

An environmental organization based in Joubert Park in Johannesburg which had previously expressed interest in food-related issues was approached. While they were keen to partner on the project, they had limited resources and were unable to participate fully. In addition, their network of environmental organizations and entrepreneurs was scattered throughout the city, making meeting attendance and regular contributions to project development challenging.

I then approached another NGO, located in Hillbrow, not far from the environmental NGO. This one focused on skills development and livelihoods. There, NGO personnel agreed to collaborate, due to their personal interest in food, and permitted me to engage with participants in their handicraft training programme. What followed was a six-month programme of weekly visits to the craft group in order to discuss food-related issues, learn more about people's food knowledge and practices, and attempt to build support for the CFC concept. Participants were free to opt out of participation in the food programme, given that they were there for handicraft training. During the first meeting, I introduced myself, explained that the sessions were voluntary and described the project to the participants.

Most participants lived in the surrounding area, though some travelled from further afield. Almost all participants were from outside of Johannesburg – some were born in other provinces, while others came from other African countries. A majority of the participants were women, with an age range of 20–70 years old. Some were staying in homeless shelters and others stayed in flats. Household sizes ranged from two to six people. There were varying levels of literacy, and some participants had physical or mental disabilities. The diversity of the group provided a rich and interesting variety of relationships to food, though in general most participants struggled to afford a nutritious diet.

Given the diversity of ages, languages, literacy and abilities among participants, I opted to use creative arts methods to engage on food topics whenever possible. To facilitate the sharing of experiences, group work – whether small groups or the entire group – was preferred. Instruments used included the following:

- Food diaries: Drawn from nutrition research, food diaries (written or photographic) were kept over a five-day period, with participants noting down all foods and drinks consumed. These were then discussed in small groups, highlighting the most commonly consumed foods, the healthiest foods consumed, where foods were procured and who prepared them. Groups also discussed the obstacles to healthy eating.
- Food mapping: Using area maps as a background, participants marked places where they bought or received food, indicating the type of place (for example, spaza shop, supermarket, street vendor and so on), what they procured and why, the time it took to get there and the mode of transport used. As a group, participants discussed the positive and negative aspects of food resources in their areas.
- Historical/childhood food mapping: Participants used the previous week's mapping as a basis for drawing images of their childhood food environment. This included the places they purchased or acquired food (including domestic food gardens), which items they got (or produced) and the time and mode of transport. The group then compared current and childhood food environments, including different types of foods, different ways of getting and preparing them and different modes of travel. The notion of sharing food, and how that differed between childhood rural homes and current Johannesburg residences, was also discussed.
- Household food tasks: This entailed a discussion of the different food-related tasks in the household and who carries them out, together with a comparison of current and childhood households. In addition to highlighting age and gender in the division of food tasks, this activity also picked up on changes over time and space as well as leading to a discussion on the kinds of special occasion foods consumed in childhood versus now.
- Films: The group watched films on the innovative food interventions in Belo Horizonte, Brazil, and the CFCs in Canada. Then, in small groups,

participants discussed what they liked about the films, what aspects of those food programmes might work in Johannesburg and how the food environment could be more conducive to healthy eating.

- Urban farm visit: The group visited an organic farm in order to learn about growing food in the city and healthy eating. The group discussed how different ways of growing food affect its nutritional value and taste.
- Food with a story: Participants drew pictures that conveyed foods that held meaning for them (either a favourite dish or something linked to special memories) and then shared the stories around these foods with the group. The discussion also included different cultural meanings of food, such as how some foods are supposed to bring luck.
- Food budgets: In small groups, participants wrote down their most frequently consumed foods, along with the prices and sizes purchased. There was a discussion of monthly food budgets and why certain foods were frequently consumed instead of others.
- Body mapping: Participants drew bodies and indicated places where they, or people close to them, had illnesses or problems. They then drew or pasted on pictures of foods that contribute to those problems and foods that can prevent or alleviate those problems. This led to a discussion of nutrition and why eating behaviour is not always aligned to nutrition knowledge.
- Food history interviews: These one-on-one interviews covered individuals' historical relationships with food, including growing food, shopping, cooking, typical meals and special occasion foods. The interviews explored changes over time and the changes participants would like to make. They also provided space for feedback on what individuals had learned, and would like to learn, in the group sessions.
- Hands-on food preparation: In line with my commitment to reciprocity, I taught participants to make sushi. This was in response to their specific request to learn. People enjoyed making and eating their own rolls.
- Nutrition and health: This entailed small groups making lists of fruits and vegetables, indicating which they ate frequently or infrequently, and then discussing recommended daily intake, nutrients in different foods, the obstacles to eating more fruit and vegetables and how those could be addressed.
- Food as medicine: In this session, participants shared home remedies involving foods and, especially, indigenous herbal medicine. There was also a discussion on when and why people choose home remedies as opposed to pharmaceuticals.
- Traditional Ethiopian lunch: To introduce a healthy traditional African meal to participants, we went for lunch at an Ethiopian restaurant. The group discussed different kinds of traditional foods and their nutritional value.

In addition to these activities, which sought to learn from participants' experiences while also sharing knowledge in a reciprocal exchange, I brought a healthy meal every week to share, including printouts of the recipe to distribute to participants. The meal sharing became an important part of the group discussion in terms of familiarity with the ingredients, preparation methods, healthfulness and so on. The meal served as a token of appreciation in addition to being a demonstration of the kind of healthy food a CFC would serve. It was also the basis for interesting conversations and helped highlight people's embodied knowledge around food. Thus eating together became a part of the research methods.

The diverse array of methods used, ranging from traditional individual interviews to creative arts methods in groups, as well as experiential learning through hands-on food preparation and a farm visit, served several purposes. First, by creating multiple channels for data collection and analysis, they contributed to a more participatory form of knowledge co-production which produced knowledge that was useful to participants in addition to contributing to policy issues and academic debates. Second, they facilitated empowerment of participants through validation of their embodied knowledge and lived experience. Third, they contributed to the realization among participants that food struggles were shared, social problems rather than individual failures. These aspects of PAR suggest that both the means and depth of impact it can have surpass both public sociology and critically engaged sociology.

The weekly sessions provided an interesting picture of the complexity of people's relationship with food. While participants had very limited formal knowledge of nutrition, they demonstrated embodied knowledge of which foods felt "right" in their bodies and which did not. Older participants generally demonstrated greater knowledge of traditional foods than younger participants, while recent migrants from other African countries often made greater efforts to maintain access to their traditional foods than South African migrants from rural areas. Almost all participants had experienced significant changes in where and how they got their foods – with significant production of food (produce and even livestock) in their rural childhood homes replaced by purchases and consumption of prepared and processed foods in Johannesburg.

In line with my previous research, participants demonstrated a low level of interest in food justice issues, despite struggling to afford nutritious food and suffering health challenges as a result. They also were unfamiliar with the right to food or how it might work. The notion of food as a commodity was pervasive, but participants liked the idea of making good food available to everyone and saw the benefits of government food programmes when discussing Brazil's Fome Zero (Zero Hunger) policies and programmes after watching the film about Belo Horizonte. Despite liking the idea of a

CFC, no participants seemed particularly interested in becoming involved in such a project.

The factors that contribute to successful PAR projects – long-term engagement, flexibility, privileging of community needs – are often at odds with the rules and requirements of university research and funding (Manzo and Brightbill, 2007; Cuádraz, 2012; Stanton, 2014; Kepkiewicz et al, 2017). The short time frame of the postdoctoral fellowship made it impossible to establish a CFC, thus leading me to focus instead on laying the groundwork. In addition, the postdoc application process involved submitting a fully formed project proposal, not an idea that still needed to go through a process of co-development with community members. Just building trust with participants takes a significant amount of time, of which a short postdoc does not provide a great deal.

Likewise, the limited research funds were insufficient for a major CFC project; nevertheless, they served well to provide food and art materials for my engagement. However, university procurement regulations are not well suited to the more unusual project expenditures (for the action component), nor to purchasing goods or services from community members (who may not have the formal documentation required by university procurement regulations). Thus, payment to an urban farmer for a lunch she prepared as part of a farm visit proved rather complicated, though not impossible. The kind of longer-term, flexible funding that is required for deep, community-led engagement in true PAR projects is not generally available to early career or junior academics. Further, the kind of outputs valued by community members – such as cookbooks, art exhibits or shared meals – may be very different from the academic publications required for academic advancement.

Given the low level of interest in food justice issues among both community gardeners and the more recent research participants, I started exploring the possibility of partnering with movements or organizations that are engaged in struggles around social justice and transformation not related to food. Furthermore, I am investigating whether and how questions of food justice could connect and help strengthen their existing struggles.

What is the role of participatory action research in the absence of food justice mobilization?

In the absence of like-minded CBOs, a broad-based local food justice movement or even grassroots mobilization regarding food injustices, can PAR be used to transform the unjust food system?

Colonial- and apartheid-era racist policies and discourse, processes of urbanization and food system industrialization, and the more recent spread of neoliberal thinking, taken together, created a vicious cycle with regard to the food system. Loss of interest in, and access to, traditional foods has led to a loss of taste for such foods and of the knowledge required to prepare them. As a result, a narrowing of traditional food knowledge and preferences, along with a taste for convenience foods and a desire to demonstrate socio-economic status through such foods, has created a situation in which urban black South Africans frequently have neither knowledge of nor interest in indigenous foods. At the same time, the limited (and nutrient-deficient) diet that is available and affordable for most South Africans has become normalized to such a degree that people do not see it as unhealthy, while the concentrated and industrialized food system that produces this diet is not seen as unjust. On top of this, the government's responsibility to respect, protect, promote and fulfil the right to food is obscured by the dominance of neoliberal discourses around personal responsibility and market solutions. In such a context, it is unsurprising that people protest over jobs but not about access to food.

By adopting this macro-level view to understand the historical, political and economic processes that have contributed to the low levels of consciousness and mobilization around food injustice in Johannesburg, we can also begin to see some possible avenues for PAR. Engaging with existing organizations and movements (for example, labour, environment, human rights) is one such possibility. Another is to adopt a more Freirean approach to PAR in which university-based researchers can help to raise consciousness by helping those affected by food injustice to see: the macro-level or structural factors that have contributed to their suffering; that their suffering is shared by many others; and that there are alternatives to the current system that created their suffering. By facilitating awareness of the structural forces influencing food injustice and highlighting some of the possible ways to combat food injustice, researchers can help provide tools to affected communities to combat the influence of colonialism, apartheid and neoliberalism. My engagement with community members who are clearly affected by food injustice yet not directly engaged in struggles related to this or any other social justice issue suggests that the impact of PAR would be greater working with activists or movements.

Conclusion: participatory action research and the impact of engaged research

Many of the chapters in this volume focus on how critically engaged research is a different form of knowledge production, leading to the production of different forms of knowledge. That is certainly true of PAR as well, but the intention of this chapter was to highlight the way in which PAR as a form of engaged research conceives of its path to having an impact and contributing to social change. Traditionally, public sociology involves a professional researcher undertaking (often extractive) research and then disseminating the findings

– through academic publications and perhaps also policy briefs or media articles – in the hope that the findings will influence thinking among other academics and policymakers or practitioners and then lead to changes in the policies and programmes relevant to their field of study. Even critically engaged research undertaken for organizations or movements often follows this model, with movement leaders in the position of 'clients' receiving the research to use – or not – as they see fit.

In the case of PAR, however, engagement with policy is only one aspect of achieving transformation. Beyond that, the very process of doing the research is part of the impact. In other words, the participation of the affected community members in designing, undertaking and disseminating research based on their own assessment of their needs is empowering in itself. PAR shifts the power dynamics in terms of knowledge production from an individual researcher (in the case of public sociology) to co-production by participants. Further, the 'action' component of PAR is specifically designed to address community-identified challenges, thus incorporating transformative change into the research process. This transformative change is conceived as coming from below rather than being imposed from above, as in the case of often-remote policymakers. While my own research was unable to live up to the 'ideal type' of PAR, the feedback from participants indicates that their participation has indeed resulted in increased knowledge and awareness of food, nutrition and health issues. In some cases, it has also resulted in behavioural changes. While this impact may be small in scale, it is far more immediate than the more traditional model of research publication, policy/programme change and impact. With more time and financial resources, I am confident that the contribution of this kind of PAR to food justice in Johannesburg could be significant.

References

Alkon, A. and Agyeman, J. (2011) 'The food movement as polyculture', in A. Alkon and J. Agyeman (eds) *Cultivating Food Justice: Race, Class, and Sustainability*, Cambridge, MA: MIT Press, pp 1–20.

Alkon, A. and Mares, T. (2012) 'Food sovereignty in US food movements: Radical visions and neoliberal constraints', *Agriculture and Human Values*, 29: 347–59.

Bond, P. (2010) 'South Africa's bubble meets boiling urban social protest', *Monthly Review*, June, pp 17–28.

Brown, W. (2006) 'American nightmare: Neoliberalism, neoconservatism, and de-democratization', *Political Theory*, 34(6): 690–714.

City of Johannesburg (2011) *Joburg 2040: Growth and Development Strategy*, Johannesburg: City of Johannesburg.

City of Johannesburg (n.d.) *Summarised Version of the 2013/16 Integrated Development Plan (IDP)*, Johannesburg: City of Johannesburg.

Cuádraz, G. (2012) 'Ethico-political dilemmas of a community oral history project: navigating the culture of the corporate university', *Social Justice*, 38(3): 17–32.

De Wet, T., Patel, L., Korth, M. and Forrester, C. (2008) *Johannesburg Poverty and Livelihoods Study*, Johannesburg: University of Johannesburg.

Department of Health (2013) *Roadmap for Nutrition in South Africa*, Pretoria: Department of Health.

eNCA (2016) 'Outsourced Shoprite workers call for an end to outsourcing', 14 April. https://www.enca.com/south-africa/outsourced-shoprite-workers-call-end-outsorcing

Fals-Borda, O. (1979) 'Investigating reality in order to transform it: The Colombian experience', *Dialectical Anthropology*, 4(1): 33–55.

Freire, P. (1970) *Pedagogy of the Oppressed*, New York: The Seabury Press.

Garrett, J. (2001) *Comedores Populares: Lessons for Urban Programming from Peruvian Community Kitchens*, Washington, DC: International Food Policy Research Institute.

Genat, B. (2009) 'Building emergent situated knowledges in participatory action research', *Action Research*, 7(1): 101–15.

Greenberg, S. (2006) *Urban Food Politics, Welfare and Resistance: A Case Study of the Southern Johannesburg Metro*, Unpublished research report for the Centre for Civil Society, University of KwaZulu Natal.

Greenberg, S. (2015) *Corporate Concentration and Food Security in South Africa: Is the Commercial Agro-food System Delivering?* Cape Town: Institute for Poverty, Land and Agrarian Studies, University of the Western Cape.

Greenberg, S. (2016) *Corporate Power in the Agro-food System and South Africa's Consumer Food Environment*, Cape Town: Institute for Poverty, Land and Agrarian Studies, University of the Western Cape.

Kepkiewicz, L., Srivastava, R., Levkoe, C.Z., Brynne, A. and Kneen, C. (2017) 'Community engaged action research and food sovereignty in Canada', in The People's Knowledge Editorial Collective (ed) *Everyday Experts: How People's Knowledge Can Transform the Food System*, Coventry: Coventry University, pp 293–307.

Kindon, S., Pain, R. and Kesby, M. (2007) 'Introduction: Connecting people, participation and place', in S. Kindon, R. Pain and M. Kesby (eds) *Participatory Action Research Approaches and Methods: Connecting People, Participation and Place*, London: Routledge, pp 1–5.

Kroll, F. (2017) *Foodways of the Poor in South Africa: How Poor People Get Food, What They Eat, and How This Shapes Our Food System*, Cape Town: Institute for Poverty, Land and Agrarian Studies, University of the Western Cape.

Ledger, T. (2015) *Growing a Person: Poverty, Power and Freedom in Post-apartheid South Africa*, PhD thesis, University of the Witwatersrand, Johannesburg, South Africa.

Ledger, T. (2016) *An Empty Plate*, Auckland Park: Jacana.

Levkoe, C. and Wakefield, S. (2011) 'The community food centre: Creating space for a just, sustainable, and healthy food system', *Journal of Agriculture Food Systems and Community Development*, 2(1): 249–68.

Manzo, L. and Brightbill, N. (2007) 'Toward a participatory ethics', in S. Kindon, R. Pain and M. Kesby (eds) *Participatory Action Research Approaches and Methods: Connecting People, Participation and Place*, London: Routledge, pp 33–40.

Mchiza, Z., Steyn, N.P., Hill, J., Kruger, A., Schönfeldt, H., Nel, J. and Wentzel-Viljoen, E. (2015) 'A review of dietary surveys in the adult South African population from 2000 to 2015', *Nutrients*, 7(9): 8227–50.

Msachi, R., Dakishoni, L. and Bezner Kerr, R. (2009) 'Soils, Food and Healthy Communities: Working towards food sovereignty in Malawi', *Journal of Peasant Studies*, 36(3): 700–6.

Nyantakyi-Frimpong, H., Hickey, C., Lupafya, E., Dakishoni, L., Bezner Kerr, R., Luginaah, I. and Katundu, M. (2017) 'A farmer-to-farmer agroecological approach to addressing food security in Malawi', in The People's Knowledge Editorial Collective (ed) *Everyday Experts: How People's Knowledge Can Transform the Food System*, Coventry: Coventry University, pp 121–36.

Pain, R. (2004) 'Social geography: Participatory research', *Progress in Human Geography*, 28(5): 652–63.

Pereira, L. (2014) *The Future of South Africa's Food System: What is Research Telling Us?* Southern African Food Lab.

Pimbert, M., Satheesh, P.V., Argumedo, A. and Farvar, T.M. (2017) 'Participatory action research transforming local food systems in India, Iran and Peru', in The People's Knowledge Editorial Collective (ed) *Everyday Experts: How People's Knowledge Can Transform the Food System*, Coventry: Coventry University, pp 99–118.

Popkin, B. (2008) 'The nutrition transition and its health implications in lower-income countries', in J. Pretty (ed) *Sustainable Agriculture and Food* (vol 3), London: Earthscan, pp 240–69.

Rahman, M. (1993) *People's Self-Development: Perspectives on Participatory Action Research*, London: Zed Books.

Raschke, V. and Cheema, B. (2008) 'Colonisation, the new world order, and the eradication of traditional food habits in East Africa: Historical perspective on the nutrition transition', *Public Health Nutrition*, 11(7): 662–74.

Reason, P. and Bradbury, H. (2008) 'Introduction', in Reason, P. and Bradbury, H. (eds) *The SAGE Handbook of Action Research* (2nd edn), Los Angeles: Sage, pp 1–10.

Rocha, C. and Lessa, I. (2009) 'Urban governance for food security: The alternative food system in Belo Horizonte, Brazil', *International Planning Studies*, 14(4): 389–400.

Rudolph, M., Kroll, F., Ruysenaar, S. and Dlamini, T. (2012) *The State of Food Insecurity in Johannesburg*, Kingston and Cape Town: Queen's University and AFSUN.

Saul, N. and Curtis, A. (2013) *The Stop: How the Fight for Good Food Transformed a Community and Inspired a Movement*, New York: Melville House.

Schroeder, K. (2006) 'A feminist examination of community kitchens in Peru and Bolivia', *Gender, Place and Culture: A Journal of Feminist Geography*, 13(6): 663–8.

Shisana, O., Labadarios, D., Rehle, T., Simbayi, L., Zuma, K., Dhansay, A., Reddy, P., Parker, W., Hoosain, E., Naidoo, P., Hongoro, C., Mchiza, Z., Steyn, N.P., Dwane, N., Makoae, M., Maluleke, T., Ramlagan, S., Zungu, N., Evans, M.G., Jacobs, L. and Faber, M. (2013) *The South African National Health and Nutrition Examination Survey (SANHANES-1)*, Cape Town: HSRC Press.

South African Human Rights Commission (n.d.) *Report on Economic and Social rights 2012–2013. S184(3)*, Johannesburg: South African Human Rights Commission.

Stanton, C.R. (2014) 'Crossing methodological borders: Decolonizing community-based participatory research', *Qualitative Inquiry*, 20(5): 573–83.

Temple, N. and Steyn, N. (2011) 'The cost of a healthy diet: A South African perspective', *Nutrition*, 27: 505–8.

Wenhold, F., Annandale, J., Faber, M. and Hart, T. (2012) *Water Use and Nutrient Content of Crop and Animal Food Products for Improved Household Food Security: A Scoping Study*, Pretoria: Water Research Commission.

Wylie, D. (2001) *Starving on a Full Stomach: Hunger and the Triumph of Cultural Racism in Modern South Africa*, Charlottesville: University Press of Virginia.

10

Dilemmas and Issues Confronting Socially Engaged Research within Universities

Aninka Claassens and Nokwanda Sihlali

Introduction

The push back by universities against socially engaged work or activist researchers is well documented in many countries (Sherman and Torbert, 2000; Hurd et al, 2016; Oswald et al, 2016). A host of tensions and challenges arise at the interface between established modes of operation within universities and socially engaged or activist research. In the United States, formal associations of engaged scholars have been formed to share experiences and develop measures for assessing and recognizing the value of engaged scholarship.

These associations, many of which include international collaboration, focus on quality, relevance to societal problems and the measurable social outcomes of engaged scholarship. Engaged scholars operating in 'hard' sciences like medicine point to the effective outcomes of research programmes identified by the external constituencies with whom they partner, which may include patients, parents of patients and local community organizations.

Research produced in partnership with external constituencies facing specific challenges entails a significant amount of researcher time being invested in maintaining relationships of trust with such external partners. It also requires researchers to spend time on achieving the outputs that have been prioritized by the partners. The university default to peer-reviewed articles being the main measure of research output for young researchers thus penalizes activist researchers who prioritize investing time in complex relationships and achieving the priorities and outputs identified by their social justice partners, alongside writing articles.

This has various material outcomes. It rewards academics who avoid time-consuming engaged scholarship in favour of boosting their career prospects by churning out articles. Recent studies illustrate how it has encouraged academics at some universities to contribute numerous articles to low-quality or 'predatory' journals in order to obtain state subsidies (Mouton and Valentine, 2017). And it renders invisible the other high-quality outputs and societal impacts of engaged scholarship obtained from interacting with people facing societal problems.

At issue are different value systems and modes of academic capital. Rather than accommodating all of these, some (but not all) parts of the university community cling to the system of individualized incentives that reject measurements which encourage young researchers to invest in external partnerships, group products and socially relevant outcomes.

This chapter situates some of the dilemmas and challenges faced by the Land and Accountability Research Centre (LARC) at the University of Cape Town (UCT) in the context of this wider literature about attempts to 'open up' and 'close down' the space for engaged scholarship in universities. In doing this, we substantiate Arribas Lozano's argument that the co-production of knowledge together with communities is the basis for socially engaged research, and we join him in critiquing Burawoy's assertion that academic professionalism provides the best guarantee of rigour and standard of scholarly research (Lozano, 2018: 101). We argue that the knowledge produced through community engagement, and the publications produced for communities and to support parliamentary engagement as well as strategic litigation, are extremely rigorous and undergo tough processes of contestation and interrogation in all of these forums, constituting a process of 'peer review' that is more testing than most academic peer-review processes. Yet the university persists in maintaining narrow academic criteria that prevent it from recognizing or understanding the innovative production of socially relevant research. This threatens to marginalize the university from the most important social problems and controversies of the day. The time-consuming and complex process of building and sustaining community partnerships – which, as Arribas Lozano argues, is the foundation for such knowledge production – is ignored by academic criteria.

This introduction is foregrounded with two issues that may situate LARC somewhat differently from some other socially engaged university-based research centres. These are: its location in a law faculty and that its *explicit* purpose is to assist rural citizens in struggles to hold leaders to account and secure their rights to land and other natural resources. In relation to the former, semi-independent centres doing applied legal work or engaging in sociolegal studies are likely to be more common in law schools than in faculties of humanities. This may reflect the fact that disciplines such as sociology and politics are inherently self-reflective, whereas law tends to be taught as an applied skill or 'tool of the trade' with preordained rules and precedents. Alongside the mainstream teaching of law, semi-independent centres may specialize in specific aspects of 'law in practice', such as clinics for human rights litigation or refugee rights. They may also focus on the sociological impact of law in practice, as distinct from the ideal of law fulfilling a neutral, stabilizing role.

In relation to the latter – the explicit purpose of bringing about societal change – LARC sees research as but one of three interlocking activities necessary to do this. The others are litigation and mobilization (see Figure 10.1). The impetus for the existence of LARC and its modus operandi did not come from theories of socially responsive research. Instead, its methodology was developed in response to specific issues and challenges in South Africa today. These are shaped by local history and current circumstances rather than global debates about how to conduct research. The team is explicitly on the side of rural people in their struggles for change and transformation. This overt positionality has proved harder to accept for the academy than for the parties against whom LARC litigates and for parliament, to which submissions are made.

While the work LARC does is unusual compared to other research centres in the law faculty, LARC remains correctly situated there. The staff at the centre track and intervene in the legislative process; they engage in litigation as expert witnesses or 'friends of the court', write about the interface between law and society, and monitor how laws are enforced and implemented, or sometimes not enforced at all. A key focus of inquiry is the impact of law on power relations at the local level, in relation to both its coercive elements and the symbolic role that law plays in justifying and condoning patterns of conduct that are in breach of the Constitution and, in many instances, corrupt.

Scholars have long recognized that law plays a key role in normalizing inequality (E.P. Thompson and the critical legal studies movement in the United States, including Joseph Singer). It is also an important tool used by the vulnerable to assert and protect their rights (Abel, 1995). Therefore, compared to other disciplines, it is less easy to characterize the law's role as neutral, or apolitical. This is particularly the case in South Africa given the country's history of legislated racial discrimination.

The 1996 South African Constitution has been envisioned as an instrument for achieving radical change through law. The late Chief Justice Pius Langa wrote in a judgment:

> The Constitution is located in a history which involves a transition from a society based on division, injustice and exclusion from the democratic process to one which respects the dignity of all citizens and includes all in the process of governance. As such, the process of interpreting the Constitution must recognise the context in which

Figure 10.1: LARC's theory of change

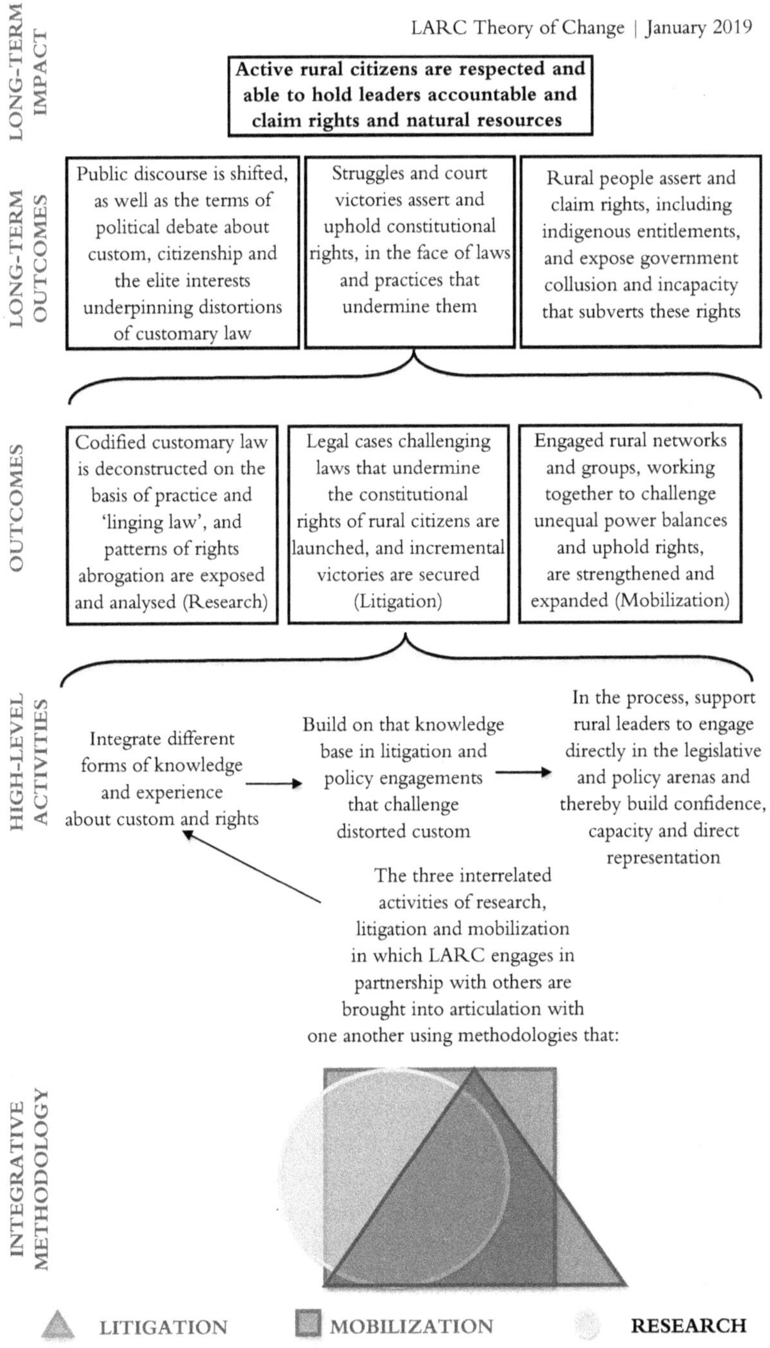

LARC Theory of Change | January 2019

LONG-TERM IMPACT

Active rural citizens are respected and able to hold leaders accountable and claim rights and natural resources

LONG-TERM OUTCOMES

| Public discourse is shifted, as well as the terms of political debate about custom, citizenship and the elite interests underpinning distortions of customary law | Struggles and court victories assert and uphold constitutional rights, in the face of laws and practices that undermine them | Rural people assert and claim rights, including indigenous entitlements, and expose government collusion and incapacity that subverts these rights |

OUTCOMES

| Codified customary law is deconstructed on the basis of practice and 'linging law', and patterns of rights abrogation are exposed and analysed (Research) | Legal cases challenging laws that undermine the constitutional rights of rural citizens are launched, and incremental victories are secured (Litigation) | Engaged rural networks and groups, working together to challenge unequal power balances and uphold rights, are strengthened and expanded (Mobilization) |

HIGH-LEVEL ACTIVITIES

Integrate different forms of knowledge and experience about custom and rights ⟶ Build on that knowledge base in litigation and policy engagements that challenge distorted custom ⟶ In the process, support rural leaders to engage directly in the legislative and policy arenas and thereby build confidence, capacity and direct representation

The three interrelated activities of research, litigation and mobilization in which LARC engages in partnership with others are brought into articulation with one another using methodologies that:

INTEGRATIVE METHODOLOGY

▲ LITIGATION   ◼ MOBILIZATION   ◉ **RESEARCH**

Source: Land and Accountability Research Centre at the University of Cape Town, used with permission

we find ourselves, and the Constitution's goal of a society based on democratic values, social justice and fundamental human rights. This spirit of transition and transformation characterises the constitutional enterprise as a whole.[1]

This is very different from the role that constitutions play in most other countries, where they seek to maintain a negotiated and agreed status quo rather than transform society. The Constitution's ambitious vision for law as a mechanism for transformation sets up a tension with the essentially 'backward-looking' precedent-based nature of law, and how it has been taught for generations. Law faculties in South Africa are faced with the challenge of breaking with their old precedent-based curricula sufficiently to produce lawyers who can rise to the challenge of using a backward-looking system to bring about forward-looking change (Davis and Klare, 2010). The Constitutional Court's vision and jurisprudence exists in tension with the highly formalist nature of South African law (Klare, 1998; Chanock, 2001). LARC works at the interface of this set of contradictions, which take a very particular form given South Africa's history and ambitious Constitution.

LARC also differs from many other research centres in that it did not emerge due to the research focus of a senior professor or develop from a teaching programme. Rather, it grew out of practical interventions to support litigation centred on land struggles and to document changing practices on the ground. In 2009, the Rural Women's Action Research (RWAR) programme joined the then Law, Race and Gender Research Unit at UCT. It had previously operated as part of the Legal Resources Centre in Cape Town. The research unit was subsequently renamed the Centre for Law and Society. The RWAR programme remained part of this centre until it established itself as a separate centre in 2016, named LARC and focusing exclusively on land issues and the former homelands. LARC is entirely donor funded with no university-funded posts. It receives funding support because of the applied nature of the work it undertakes and the impact of this work in relation to pressing societal problems in the former homelands. It is unusual in being entirely donor funded. Many research centres at universities receive some subsidy from the university, often in the form of salaries for the director and other key posts. The Society, Work and Politics Institute (SWOP), for example, is subsidized by the wider university, as is the Institute for Poverty Land and Agrarian Studies (PLAAS) at the University of the Western Cape. PLAAS is comparable to LARC in that it also specializes in rural land issues, but it is based in the Faculty of Economic and Management Sciences rather than a law faculty. In addition to their university subsidies, these centres also raise significant amounts of donor funding to employ researchers and undertake specific research projects. Unlike LARC, PLAAS and SWOP teach and supervize large numbers of students in the humanities and social sciences, thereby contributing to their universities' key mandate of educating students. While LARC has not focused on teaching students in the past, this is something that it looks to do in the future.

Much of LARC's research output tracks patterns of interaction between imposed state law and local struggles to defend rights. Similarly, LARC tracks how policy and bills are amended and changed in response to successful local struggles and court challenges. LARC has therefore been well positioned to engage with the Constitutional Court's jurisprudence of 'living' as opposed to 'official' customary law. The Court has rejected the official version of customary law inherited from apartheid as embodying distortions that were used for the purposes of racial subjugation (Claassens and Budlender, 2013). It has turned its focus to 'living' customary practices that change and adapt as society adjusts to changing circumstances.

LARC's methodology and experience at the interface between law and practice has enabled us to intervene both as a 'player' in supporting litigation about 'living customary law' and as an observer and commentator. The focus of our work has been on the conflicting discourses about history, tradition and custom that animate the traditional leader lobby and retrogressive bills about traditional leadership, on one hand, and the experiences of those who oppose the bills, and opposed their apartheid predecessor laws, on the other. Much of LARC's collaboration with historians and social scientists addresses the dual task of challenging the dominant narratives used to justify the laws and providing expert evidence in court about actual practice on the ground where necessary.

This chapter starts by discussing LARC's positionality in the law faculty and the challenges that have arisen for LARC researchers. It then describes how LARC works, focusing particularly on the partnerships that are intrinsic to LARC's methodology. Reference is made to international literature that considers partnerships with external actors to be the defining feature of engaged scholarship. In this section, we outline that partnerships are not seen primarily as a vehicle for disseminating knowledge generated within the university, but as a form of knowledge co-creation.

Finally, the argument is put forward that various outputs of LARC's work are no less scholarly for being produced from interactions with warm bodies and real-life challenges and contradictions. Various rigorous forms of societal and legal peer review that are currently not recognized by the Faculty of Law Performance Assessment Guidelines (UCT, 2016) will be referenced. This is followed by a discussion of some of the challenges and dilemmas arising from LARC's methodology.

None of this seeks to deny that a crucial component of the work of researchers is to read and write academic articles. It is only by doing so that they are able to grapple with, and master, the complex societal issues they are engaging with and ultimately become 'experts'. It is, rather, to caution against criteria that actively discourage time-consuming socially engaged research and, thus, insulate researchers and universities from engaging with pressing societal challenges. This is particularly pertinent in relation to questions about the role of universities within the changing social realities of neoliberalism and austerity in education.

Land and Accountability Research Centre at University of Cape Town and in the law faculty

UCT has engaged seriously with arguments in favour of socially engaged and transdisciplinary research and developed an evolving policy supporting such initiatives (UCT, 2012). It includes social responsibility as an output that must be measured alongside the two mainstays of teaching and research for ad hominem promotion from senior lecturer to associate professor or from senior researcher to chief researcher. It has also instituted a prize for social responsiveness alongside the pre-existing awards for teaching and research.

However, this does not mean that socially responsive research is placed on an equal footing with classical 'academic' research, because research scholarship continues to be measured primarily by publication in peer-reviewed academic journals, especially at the threshold levels for researcher and senior researcher. There are two academic tracks available. The first applies to academics whose salaries are paid by the university. The second applies mainly to people hired by soft-funded research institutions. The key difference between the two is that university-funded academics are expected to spend a significant amount of their time teaching students. They need to score their teaching output out of 100 points, their research output out of 100 points and their socially responsive activities out of 50 points.

Because soft-funded researchers generally do not have the same level of teaching responsibility, their socially responsive activities are scored out of 100 points, their research outputs out of 100 points and their teaching output out of 50 points. Academics in both categories must score their contribution to leadership, management and administration out of 100 points (UCT, 2016).

This chapter does not discuss the important measures for teaching and management, which are fully recognized as core components of the university's purpose. It confines itself to measures that assess research and social responsiveness. To qualify as a researcher or lecturer, a candidate must have produced two peer-reviewed articles over the previous four years, unless they can show their work was interrupted by significant progress towards a PhD or book. Similarly, the only measurement prescribed for progress to senior researcher or senior lecturer is 'regular peer-reviewed outputs', unless interrupted by the completion of a monograph or book.

At the higher levels of associate and full professor, criteria, including the impact and standing of the professor's work, become more flexible and inclusive. However, the main concern addressed here relates to the barriers confronting young academics making initial choices about the kind of research that is meaningful to them.

The Faculty of Law Performance Assessment Guidelines for socially responsive activities (as opposed to research) details more about roles than specific outputs. At all ranks, the requirement is that the candidate be an 'active participant in socially responsive activities' (UCT, 2016: 10). At the level of senior researcher, the requirement is that the individual '[p]lays an organizational role in: professional work; law reform; or policy formulation/ project work at local or national governmental levels, in civil society or NGOs [non-governmental organizations]' (UCT Law Faculty, 2016: 9).

In practice, it is often impossible to differentiate socially responsive outputs from research outputs, and the lack of specific outputs for socially responsive work means that the measure for both tends to default to the criteria set out for measuring research − publication in peer-reviewed journals. The ad hominem criteria thus require young researchers to be astute and individualistic about their self-advancement and to avoid tasks that do not result in published articles. To succeed, they must weigh up the 'opportunity costs' of engaging in complex partnerships and time-consuming joint endeavours that respond to threats and opportunities in the wider society.

This is not to say that the faculty fails to weigh up these criteria in a nuanced way in practice. The faculty often waives the requirement of two published articles at the level of lecturer where candidates are also faced with the daunting challenge of teaching and developing their first course outlines. But it means that those parts of the faculty that have reservations about socially engaged research can, and do, argue against the appointment and advancement of activist scholars on the basis that they do not meet the ad hominem requirements. Reinforcing standards that require researchers to be individualistic, ambitious and play within the system limits the calibre of scholars universities can hope to attract, the culture they recreate and, ultimately, the relevance of the research that is published.

The importance of partnerships

A small research unit based in Cape Town cannot aspire to bring about changes to power relations in the former homelands on its own. Thus, partnerships with others are an essential component of LARC's work. This is not only about issues of scale; a fundamental feature of LARC's modus operandi is that people in the rural spaces where the work is conducted extend an *invite* to the team. LARC does not choose specific research areas or topics remotely from Cape Town.

This framing is consistent with the understanding that activist researchers need to know how to build and maintain long-term relationships between university and community partners so that power imbalances are engaged with consistently (Oja, 1989). The literature emphasizes the active involvement of community partners during each phase of the planning process, from identifying the issues under study to collaborating on desired outcomes, and from the data collection and analyses phases of a project to the development of implementable proposals (Angotti et al, 2011).

Successful engagements hinge on establishing trust and transparency during all phases of a project. They also hinge on accountability. Specifically, university and community partners need to be accountable to each other (Checkoway, 1997). Partnerships need to be actively maintained if one is seeking real and meaningful impact in bringing about change. This can be overwhelming for researchers who are committed to the work and agreed purpose of the project, but who are sometimes expected, by desperate community partners, to have the power to solve intractable problems.

Over the years, LARC has developed a strong reputation for supporting rural citizens who face specific problems centred on the potential abrogation of their land rights in the former 'bantustans'. For the benefit of international readers, a brief sketch of how the bantustans came into existence will be detailed. The Natives Land Act of 1913 delineated separate territories for black and white ownership and occupation of land, setting aside 7 per cent of the land for the black majority – subsequently increased to 13 per cent by the Native Trust and Land Act 18 of 1936. After the Afrikaner National Party came to power in 1948, it used the rural reserves established by the Land Acts as the basis for establishing ten ethnically defined 'homelands' for speakers of different African languages. Some of the homelands, such as Bophuthatswana and Transkei, became 'independent states'. A feature of the anti-apartheid struggle of the 1980s was anti-bantustan uprisings in homelands such as Bophuthatswana, KwaNdebele, Lebowa and Ciskei. The bantustans were reincorporated into a unitary South Africa with the transition to democracy in 1994, and a system of elected local government was put in place throughout the country, replacing the system of chiefly rule over separate 'tribes' that had formed the bedrock of the bantustan system.

Despite the terms of the 1994 transition and the constitutional recognition of equality, property and citizenship rights, a series of laws enacted since 2003 reinscribe the boundaries of the former bantustans. These laws have attempted to empower traditional leaders to exercise control over the land and 18 million South Africans living within the boundaries of the former bantustans. Much of LARC's work has been, and is, engaged in processes of active opposition to these laws, including supporting submissions by rural groups to parliament. LARC has also participated in research projects that have fed into litigation. Partnerships with others about these issues have resulted in various laws being struck down by the Constitutional Court.

Community workshops are a key vehicle for LARC's partnership model. These meetings and workshops are jointly convened with local organizations, which identify strong leaders and emergent community-based organizations to invite along with village-based organizations. The agenda generally begins with several hours of input from community delegates around the agreed theme, during which they describe their experiences with the issue – whether it is the Traditional Courts Bill, land rights or the Ingonyama Trust Board leases, for instance.

Grounding the meetings in the concerns and experiences of the attendees in this way has proved crucial. It gives participants a platform where they can confidently assert their voices and feel a sense of ownership of the project from the beginning of the process. The external researchers can adapt their inputs to burning local concerns. The record of collected community 'testimonies' has (inadvertently) become one of our most important research 'products' – bringing to light issues, such as the resurgence of tribal levies and allocations of residential land to unmarried women, that we may not otherwise have realized were prevalent throughout the country.

After testimonies from the floor, the lawyers or researchers provide input on the law or policy under discussion, working slowly and stopping at regular intervals to elicit and answer questions. Thereafter, generally after supper on the first night, the delegates break into small groups to begin discussing the issue so that they can think about it overnight. They continue their discussions the following morning and then report to a plenary session.

The material distributed in the meetings is written in clear and simple language which the delegates can use to explain the issues in village-level meetings to report back. Holding regular community workshops has meant that when urgent issues or opportunities arise, it is relatively easy to contact key activists in each province. Thus, information is circulated, and different forms of follow-up action take place. These have included identifying problems that require legal intervention and support from lawyers as well as community leaders coming to parliament to make submissions concerning related laws and public hearings.

Submissions by rural delegates often carry more weight and legitimacy than those made by academics. It is, therefore, important that they can stand their ground when cross-questioned by officials or members of parliament. The best way to ensure that they have the self-confidence to do this – often under great pressure – is to ensure that they are speaking directly from their lived experience. Thus, a process was developed whereby the delegates from a particular area discuss how they plan to frame their issue and are supported by a skilled scribe from LARC or a partner organization. The researcher writes down the information as the delegate narrates it, and then they read it back, often leading to a process of adjustment and amendment.

Then, all the delegates stand up and present their submissions to the other delegates, who in turn cross-question them in a role-playing exercise. This process was found to be very successful in relation to the outcome of the delivery of submissions, and it was also very important in training both rural leaders and researchers to switch places with one another in relation to the different forms of 'expertise' they bring to the process (Law, Race and Gender Research Unit, 2011).

Another form of partnership in which LARC engages is with expert witnesses in litigation. As already highlighted, the historical context that created current conditions of inequality is often crucial in litigation. An example is that of the Lesethleng community's appeal against an eviction order in the Constitutional Court in 2018. An eviction order had been sought by a mining company headed by Kgosi Nyalala Pilane, and this was granted by the North West High Court. The community rejected the eviction on the basis that they were the rightful owners of the land and the mining company had failed to consult or compensate them. The High Court rejected this argument because no evidence of their landownership was put before the court. However, a research report by Professor Sonwabile Mnwana and Gavin Capps (SWOP researchers at the time) had been attached to their papers (Mnwana and Capps, 2015).

This research report detailed how syndicates of black purchasers were not allowed to register the land they bought because of the '6 native rule'. This rule held that any group of more than six black South Africans who wanted to purchase land had to form a tribe or affiliate with a tribe so that the land could be registered as held in trust on behalf of the tribe. Kgosi Pilane had argued that he, as the head of the tribe, and not the purchasers, had the right, through a tribal resolution signed by a handful of people, to consent to mining. This history was put before the Constitutional Court as well as the fact that the Lesethleng community had used the farms at issue on an exclusive basis for over 100 years. That historical context contributed to the court rejecting the eviction order[2] and ordering that the people whose land rights are directly affected must be consulted and their consent obtained in terms of the Interim Protection of Informal Land Rights Act 31 of 1996 (IPILRA).

Just as historical evidence can be crucial to the framing and outcome of litigation, so too can anthropological evidence, especially in relation to establishing the content of 'living' customary law. The courts have directed us to the 'actual practice on the ground' as a key element of living law. Ethnographic evidence of practices of land use, inheritance and decision-making can be crucial in proving the strength of family-held land rights and decentralized decision-making authority over land. Often the real experts are old people in the community who can point to examples and changes over time. But the courts continue to want academics to corroborate local evidence by reference to the body of work they have produced.

Approaching potential expert witnesses can be tricky, because it is not for LARC to suggest to experts what they should say. To be credible, expert witnesses must be true to their body of work. Therefore, sufficient consensus must be established between the objectives of a particular case and what experts in that field have written about in the past and are comfortable saying in affidavits. One of LARC's key roles has been to identify and engage with potential experts who consider the issues at stake to be important and their knowledge relevant. To this end, LARC has hosted several workshops and conferences with historians, social scientists and other academics about the intersections between litigation about customary law and social science disciplines.

Arenas in which Land and Accountability Research Centre is engaged and key outputs

LARC works in several different arenas: tracking how law operates in practice, engaging with parliament and the legislative process, analysing judgments and intervening in litigation. And they try to shape the public discourse by writing articles and engaging with, and on, various media platforms. To succeed in these arenas, the work has to be of a high enough standard to be taken seriously and to pass the various forms of rigorous internal review that are particular to each arena – for example, the scrutiny of expert affidavits in litigation.

Law in practice

Much of LARC's work tracks the impact of law on the ground. In some instances, protective laws, such as the IPILRA and the Land Reform (Labour Tenants) Act 1996, are simply ignored by government. They record the systematic refusal to enforce the law across provinces and the structural consequences for people's land rights, in this instance dispossession in relation to mining and investment deals on communal land throughout the former homelands (Booi, 2018).

Another example of examining law in practice is LARC's exposure of the patterns of abuse by traditional leaders that take place in the shadow of the Traditional Leadership and Governance Framework Act 41 of 2003 (the Framework Act). They have documented the systematic way in which traditional leaders are empowered by government to evade the accountability mechanisms in the Framework Act and to exercise powers that they do not have in law (Claassens, 2018). The Act plays a largely symbolic role in signalling government support for traditional leaders, while its protective provisions are routinely abrogated.

Similarly, LARC has documented how the terms of the Ingonyama Trust Act and IPILRA are systematically abrogated in KwaZulu-Natal (Sihlali, 2018a, 2018b). The Ingonyama Trust routinely enters into third-party leases with external investors without obtaining the consent of the people whose customary land rights are at issue or providing compensation for their losses. It has also initiated a process of downgrading customary ownership rights to leasehold, making customary rights dependent on the payment of annual rent to the trust. After unsuccessful attempts to resolve this issue politically via the High Level Panel recommendations (2017; Claassens, 2018) and the Portfolio Committee on Rural Development and Land Reform (Sihlali, 2018c), litigation was launched, and won,[3] in which LARC played a supporting role (Legal Resource Centre, 2018).

On a more hopeful note, LARC (then RWAR) played a key role in a survey by the Community Agency for Social Enquiry that documented patterns of single women demanding and being allocated residential sites across all former homeland areas after the transition to democracy in 1994 (Mnisi and Claassens, 2009; Budlender et al, 2011; Claassens, 2013). The survey was of 3,000 women in three different former homeland provinces. Of interest here is how women have managed to negotiate positive changes in the content of living customary law despite there being no statutory mechanism supporting this. Instead, the changes appear to reflect a different local balance of power derived from the Constitution's symbolic support for equality and the decreased legitimacy of patriarchal forms of traditional authority at the time of the transition to democracy. Accounts of brave women demanding and obtaining residential land had emerged 'spontaneously' at community workshops in different parts of the country. This amounted to 'anecdotal' evidence of changing customary law, and there was a need for quantitative evidence to support litigation about the changing nature of women's land rights. The literature review undertaken in preparation for the survey revealed a number of simultaneous (if rather fragmentary) accounts of single women claiming and obtaining land, which also helped to strengthen the legal argument about positive change. But the impetus for the research was not these references in the literature. It was the accounts arising from community meetings about other, related, topics.

Key to LARC's methodology and reach is observing patterns that emerge from multiple sites. A particularly fruitful way of identifying emerging patterns is through the rural workshops described in the previous section. The accounts arising from these workshops enabled the team to track the increasingly unlawful actions of government officials after the Communal Land Rights Act 11 of 2004 was found by the Constitutional Court to be unconstitutional in 2010 and the Traditional Courts Bill was rejected by Parliament in 2014. Officials began to treat traditional leaders as the de facto owners of communal land with the unilateral power to make decisions binding the land rights of their 'subjects' even though the laws had failed (de Souza Louw, 2018; Karimakwenda and Motala, 2018). This was possible only because government ignored and overrode the specific legal protections required by IPILRA and the few accountability mechanisms that had been included in the Framework Act.

Perhaps the most important learning arising from the community workshops and invited spaces pertains to the strength of opposition to this reversion to bantustan-era power dynamics. At stake are the land rights and livelihoods of rural people, particularly in mineral rich areas where the state has advised mining companies that they should deal with traditional leaders as opposed to the people directly affected (Chamber of Mines of South Africa, 2017). This has resulted in strong resistance in many areas and the deployment of pro-mining vigilantes to threaten and attack anti-mining activists.

Articles that track the process of how law is enforced, or not, and amended in response to court judgments and sustained opposition are recognized and rewarded by the university, provided they are published in peer-reviewed journals. But what of the other outcomes and outputs of LARC's work? What of the impact of legal victories in which LARC played a key role, sometimes not as a formal party to the litigation? Affidavits produced over months by LARC researchers do not qualify as research outputs. Similarly, there is no mechanism to recognize or reward years of sustained engagement with a parliamentary committee or government department that results in a key policy shift – except at professorial level, and then only for the professor as opposed to the researchers who have written voluminous submissions to parliament and government over many years.

Outputs such as submissions and affidavits are, however, higher up the food chain than the detailed reports and fact sheets that LARC researchers produce to document the problems and power relations that exist at the local level. Without these detailed reports, which are completed place by place and issue by issue, it would be impossible to understand the linkages between different laws and to prove the scale of corruption and denigration of rights.

LARC produces regular fact sheets explaining bills and laws in relation to the problems explained to us by rural people. Fact sheets entail a highly skilled combining of legal analysis with intimate knowledge of the problems faced by rural people as well as the impetus behind changing government policy. While one researcher may do the initial draft, others will add sections, and the entire product may be reworked after community input. Fact sheets are a collaborative product.

They are written in simple English and translated into local languages for distribution and use in community workshops. Translation too is a complex task which cannot simply be outsourced to professional translators. It is difficult to accurately translate legal terms and to keep the connection with the lived experiences of the relevant communities. It is preferred that LARC researchers with strong content knowledge translate the fact sheets. In doing so, a LARC researcher/translator may raise issues with the original author, because the English text cannot translate well and therefore needs to be changed.

Fact sheets enable rural activists to grapple with complex bills and make their own oral submissions at public hearings, focusing on specific examples within their different experiences. They are used by rural activists, but other academic institutions and NGOs rely on them heavily too. They are available for free download on the LARC websites (https://www.customcontested. co.za/). There appear to be no measures within the university to assess the transdisciplinary scholarly content of outputs such as fact sheets or the impact that fact sheets have in struggles to reshape debates about bills before parliament.

Therefore, LARC uses other measures to assess the impact of its work and to report to its funders. One measure is the number of invitations received to provide support to rural groups or to provide them with fact sheets and other resources. Often, such requests tend to snowball as engagement on specific issues increases. For example, when corrupt mining deals on the platinum belt were exposed, groups with similar problems started to contact LARC by phone and email despite its location in Cape Town – 1,000 kilometres away from them. This enabled the research team to collect the scale of evidence that makes the patterns being exposed irrefutable. Such snowballing also means that a critical mass of evidence is reached to enable successful litigation. However, the drawback is that LARC researchers become overwhelmed with requests for assistance from desperate people who have already exhausted all other avenues to protect their land rights.

The parliamentary arena

As already discussed, LARC makes submissions to parliament about bills and policies. It also assists others, particularly rural groupings and people, to make submissions directly. In many instances, parliamentary committees were experienced as hostile to LARC and the rural people who have criticized bills such as the Traditional Courts Bill (overseen by the Portfolio Committee on Justice and Correctional Services) (Duda, 2018) and the Traditional and Khoi–San Leadership Bill (overseen by the Portfolio Committee on Cooperative Governance and Traditional Affairs) (Mzwakali, 2017). Both LARC researchers and rural activists have been subjected to intense questioning and criticism by members of parliament (Parliamentary Monitoring Group, 2018, 2019).

Over the years, LARC researchers have learned that the best way to deal with this is by being extremely factual and accurate so that neither the researchers nor the rural activists can be rattled during cross-examination, or their comments dismissed as unfounded.

At the same time as parts of parliament have been critical of LARC, the team has been invited to make presentations to training workshops for newly inducted members of parliament or to brief committees on particular issues. This has happened at regular intervals. Because the inputs warn of the danger of government policies and bills infringing on constitutional rights, the research team has had to be extremely accurate and astute in preparing such presentations.

In 2016, Aninka Claassens, then director of LARC, was invited by the speakers of parliament to sit on a High Level Panel chaired by former President Kgalema Motlanthe. The purpose of the panel was to review the impact of laws enacted after 1994 on poverty and inequality, land reform and social cohesion. After two years of commissioned research, public hearings and round-table deliberations, the panel produced a 600-page report (High Level Panel Report, 2017).

Many South Africans contributed to the report, including many of LARC's researchers and community-based partner organizations that came together to work on alternatives to current failed land reform policies and laws. In the process, indicative draft bills were developed to replace existing problematic laws. There appears to be no way in which the university can recognize LARC's two years of input into the report produced by the panel, not least because this was not the output of a single individual, but rather of collaborative endeavours by collectives, including LARC researchers and partner organizations and universities. The report could never have been as comprehensive as it is were it not for these forms of transdisciplinary and trans-institutional cooperation. The point at issue is that engaging effectively with parliament requires LARC to abide by rigorous standards that fall outside the scope of what the university is currently able to recognize. Furthermore, such products necessarily require collaborative information-sharing and strategizing rather than the pursuit of individual expertise.

Courts and jurisprudence

A similar point is made in relation to our interventions in litigation. Affidavits by LARC researchers are subject to intrinsically onerous forms of challenge by other parties, whether lawyers or other expert witnesses. We must prove our expertise in the face of challenges from others who dispute it. And we must ensure that the content of our affidavits cannot be repudiated and discounted by other parties in the litigation. LARC suggests that this form of 'peer review' is often more thorough than that provided by the two anonymous reviewers required for academic articles. And yet affidavits that are accepted by the courts as measures of our scholarship and expertise in the field are not counted as research outputs for ad hominem promotion by the university.

Public discourse

An important part of LARC's work is to alert the public to the problems facing rural people and how bills before parliament would exacerbate pressing issues of structural inequality and rampant corruption. The public discourse about land rights and tradition plays a key role in influencing policymakers to weigh up the costs of pushing through legislation that will benefit the few at the expense of the many. LARC has been successful in placing opinion pieces in major newspapers such as *Business Day*, *City Press*, *Daily Maverick* and *Sunday Times*. LARC researchers are also regularly invited to appear on television discussion shows and to engage in radio and podcast interviews (for example, Gasa and Luwaya, 2016; Melane and Sihlali, 2018; Rapetti et al, 2019; Luwaya and Tumisang, 2020). This role has been dismissed by some in the faculty as having nothing to do with scholarly output, although it falls squarely within Lozano's (2018) vision of 'public sociology' in the sense of not merely disseminating knowledge, but also influencing public opinion that contributes to effecting social changes on the ground. Such opinion pieces and editorials and media interviews are also closely monitored by the university and used as a measure of the university's standing and contribution to university-wide societal debate. Those in the faculty who dismiss opinion pieces and editorials as irrelevant outputs for academics disregard the forms of peer review entailed in editors accepting pieces for publication and radio and television shows inviting LARC researchers to address topics. These opinion pieces are accepted, and LARC researchers are invited, partly because of the consistent standard of their work, but mainly because the research impacts on important societal issues of the day.

Conclusion

In this chapter, we demonstrate that social partnerships with communities and the co-creation of knowledge that is built on this foundation are crucial to the production of new knowledge as well as disciplinary innovation, such as substantiating and deepening the concept of 'living customary law' and analysing the significance of emergent practices such as the allocation of land rights to unmarried women. At the same time, these contribute to empowering communities, shaping constitutional law and strongly influencing the work of parliament. However, we push beyond both

Burawoy's concept of public sociology and SWOP's conception of 'critical engagement' to argue that the professionally established criteria for rigorous and autonomous social science are too narrow to recognize the innovation or value of this kind of knowledge; instead they threaten to render the university irrelevant to the solution of urgent and controversial social problems. Socially engaged research, in other words, presents a challenge to academic conceptions of knowledge. It is the latter that need to change rather than the former.

At a central level, the university acknowledges the need to look beyond peer-reviewed articles as the best measure of research excellence, and it sees the need to find measures to assess the social impact of research. The vice chancellor, Professor Mamokgethi Phakeng, announced on 6 May 2019 that 'UCT's position is that publishing papers simply for the sake of publishing does not advance research excellence, and incentivizing publication alone – irrespective of journal or research quality – can detract from the quality of the research itself and from goals such as positive societal impact.'

Speaking about the publication-based subsidies that South African universities receive from the Department of Higher Education and Training (DHET), she explained that DHET inadvertently penalizes collaboration by decreasing the subsidy when other institutions have contributed to the publication. She reiterated that the UCT is committed to focusing on research impact rather than high publication output. Such statements are encouraging, but more needs to be done to bring the performance assessment guidelines of the various faculties in line with this commitment.

Young activist researchers face a series of difficulties and dilemmas when choosing to work in centres like LARC. The process of trying, and failing, to make sense of complicated realities through the lens of their past university disciplines can be challenging and destabilizing to begin with. Moreover, the process of balancing responding to the needs of rural community partners with setting aside the time to produce scholarly articles is not easy. This is especially so during the early years when they may find themselves somewhat alienated from their previous discipline and operating at the boundary of several disciplines.

One of LARC's strengths is that it is invited into rural areas to address pressing social issues as they arise. This defines our 'research agenda' and ensures its relevance to emerging social issues. However, the responsive nature of LARC's work also means that the researchers may be overwhelmed by demands, especially in times of political crisis. Because of the time they spend in the field interacting with rural citizens, LARC researchers have ample empirical material at their disposal, but often fail to write it up due to time constraints. Moreover, LARC's hiring bias is to appoint people who can show their commitment to social change over those with long publication lists. People with long publication lists tend to be on the academic track and cannot afford to spend time doing social justice work. So, LARC seldom starts with researchers who are already skilled at writing articles, which means that many new LARC researchers have not yet crossed the daunting hurdle of producing their first peer-reviewed academic article.

A particular challenge facing young researchers is how to build up the body of work that enables them to become recognized 'experts' in litigation and in public engagements including parliamentary processes. If other products were recognized alongside academic articles, it would enable young activist scholars to focus on, and refine, the unique forms of knowledge that emerge from socially engaged research partnerships. Many older 'experts' come from trade union or NGO backgrounds, and the experience and outputs they built up over years took a variety of forms and was not confined to academic outputs. That environment enabled people to concentrate on working out their own analyses of complex problems through processes of trial and error, and to develop confidence and expertise without the constant pressure to translate the process of their growing mastery of the field into academic articles.

In retrospect, it is intriguing that LARC explicitly defined its key role as supporting struggles for change in all submissions to parliament and in all affidavits submitted to courts. This positionality does not contradict the high-value scholarly content and expertise that LARC contributes both to the courts and to an often-hostile parliament. The courts and parliament test, sometimes robustly, the accuracy of our facts and analysis. LARC has by and large passed those tests with flying colours. The researchers are regularly asked to make submissions to parliament and to address training workshops for members of parliament. They are asked to intervene in litigation, as expert and as amicus. Their work is cited in judgments by the Constitutional Court.

Ironically, it appears easier for parliament and the courts to accept that the explicitly political purpose of LARC does not undermine its scholarly integrity than it is for parts of the university community. There are very many types of socially engaged research units that operate differently from one another. The issue is not so much that universities be forced to adopt a particular new model, but that they encourage the work and forms of knowledge generated by these units, including when this throws up challenges to existing measures that maintain and reinforce deeply entrenched and individualist forms of academic capital.

Notes

[1] Paragraph 21 of the judgment in *Investigating Directorate: Serious Economic Offences and Others v Hyundai Motor Distributors (Pty) Ltd and Others*; in re *Hyundai Motor Distributors (Pty) Ltd and Others v Smit NO & Others* [2000] ZACC 12, 2001 (1) SA 545 (CC), 2000 (10) BCLR 1079 (CC).

[2]   *Maledu and Others v Itereleng Bakgatla Mineral Resources (Pty) Limited and Another* (CCT265/17) [2018] ZACC 41; 2019 (1) BCLR 53 (CC); 2019 (2) SA 1 (CC) (25 October 2018).
[3]   *Council for the Advancement of the South African Constitution and Others v The Ingonyama Trust and Others* (12745/2018P) [2021] ZAKZPHC 42; 2021 (8) BCLR 866 (KZP); [2021] 3 All SA 437 (KZP) (11 June 2021).

References

Abel, R. (1995) *Politics by Other Means: Law in the Struggle Against Apartheid, 1980–1994*, New York: Routledge.

Angotti, T., Doble, C. and Horrigan, P. (eds) (2011) *Service-learning in Design and Planning*, Oakland, CA: New Village Press.

Badat, S. (2013) 'Eleven theses on community engagement at universities: The social responsibility of universities: community and civic engagement – context and big picture', 4th International Exhibition and Conference on Higher Education, 16–19 April 2013 (4-IECHE), Riyadh, Saudi Arabia.

Booi, Z. (2018) 'Top court's ruling restores rights of landholders violated by mining giants', *Business Day*. https://businesslive.co.za/bd/opinion/2018-11-13-top-courts-ruling-restores-rights-of-landholders-violated-by-mining-giants/

Budlender, D., Mgweba, S., Motsepe, K. and Williams, L. (2011) *Women, Land and Customary Law*, Johannesburg: Community Agency for Social Enquiry.

Chamber of Mines of South Africa (2017) 'Letter to His Excellency Motlanthe', 28 July. https://www.parliament.gov.za/storage/app/media/Pages/2017/october/High_Level_Panel/Roundtable-Land_reform/CoM_Response_to_the_HLP-28_July_2017_FINAL.pdf

Chanock, M. (2001) *The Making of South African Legal Culture 1902–1936: Fear, Favour and Prejudice*, Melbourne: Cambridge University Press.

Checkoway, B. (1997) 'Reinventing the research university for public service', *Journal of Planning Literature*, 11(3): 307–19.

Checkoway, B. (2001) 'Renewing the civic mission of the American research university', *The Journal of Higher Education*, 72(2): 125–47.

Claassens, A. (2013) 'Recent changes in women's land rights and contested customary law in South Africa', *Journal of Agrarian Change*, 13(1): 71–92.

Claassens, A. (2018) 'The Ingonyama Trust land and power in the former homelands', Custom Contested. http://www.customcontested.co.za/the-ingonyama-trust-land-and-power-in-the-former-homelands/

Claassens, A. and Budlender, G. (2013) 'Transformative constitutionalism and customary law', *Constitutional Court Review*, 6: 75–105.

Claassens, A. and Matlala, B. (2014) 'Platinum, poverty and princes in post-apartheid South Africa: New laws, old repertoires', in G.M. Khadiagala, P. Naidoo, D. Pillay and R. Southall (eds) *New South African Review: A Fragile Democracy – Twenty Years On*, Johannesburg: Wits University Press, pp 113–35.

Custom Contested (nda) 'Laws and policies'. https://www.customcontested.co.za/laws-and-policies/

Custom Contested (ndb) 'Traditional Courts Bill (TCB)'. https://www.customcontested.co.za/laws-and-policies/traditional-courts-bill-tcb

Davis, D. and Klare, K. (2010) 'Transformative constitutionalism and the common and customary law', *South African Journal on Human Rights*, 26(3): 403–509.

de Souza Louw, M. (2018) 'Parliament's final push on dangerous traditional leadership bills'. https://www.customcontested.co.za/parliaments-final-push-on-dangerous-traditional-leadership-bills/

Duda, T. (2018) 'How MPs are pushing back against the Traditional Courts Bill'. https://www.customcontested.co.za/how-mps-are-pushing-back-against-the-traditional-courts-bill/

Favish, J. and McMillan J. (2009) 'The university and social responsiveness in the curriculum: A new form of scholarship', *London Review of Education*, 7(2): 169–79.

Hall, M. (2010) 'Community engagement in South African higher education', in Council on Higher Education (ed) *Community Engagement in South African Higher Education*, Kagisano 6, Pretoria: Council on Higher Education, pp 1–52.

High Level Panel on the Assessment of Key Legislation and the Acceleration of Fundamental Change (2017) *Report of the High Level Panel on the Assessment of Key Legislation and the Acceleration of Fundamental Change*. https://www.parliament.gov.za/high-level-panel

High Level Panel Report (2018) https://www.parliament.gov.za/storage/app/media/Pages/2017/october/High_Level_Panel/HLP_Report/HLP_report.pdf; http://www.customcontested.co.za/hlp-summaries-2018/

Hurd, C., Stanton, T., Connolly, B., Howard, J. and Litvak, L. (2016) *Research University Engaged Scholarship Toolkit* (5th edn), Boston: Campus Compact.

Karimakwenda, K. and Motala, A. (2018) 'Latest Traditional Courts Bill draft flouts constitutional rights even more disturbingly', *Daily Maverick*, 13 September. https://www.dailymaverick.co.za/article/2018-09-13-latest-traditional-courts-bill-draft-flouts-constitutional-rights-even-more-disturbingly/

Klare, K.E. (1998) 'Legal culture and transformative constitutionalism', *South African Journal on Human Rights*, 14(1): 146-88.

Law, Race and Gender Research Unit (2011) *Advancing the Human Rights of the Rural Poor: Building Resources for Local Activism, Strategic Litigation and Law Reform*, Expert opinion for the Atlantic Philanthropies.

Legal Resources Centre (2018) 'Legal challenge to Ingonyama Trust'. http://lrc.org.za/media-statement-legal-challenge-to-ingonyama-trust/

Lozano, A. (2018) 'Reframing the public sociology debate: Towards collaborative and decolonial praxis', *Current Sociology*, 66(1): 92–109.

Luwaya, N. and Tumisang (2020) 'Land reform and restitution amidst Covid-19', *POWER Business* [podcast], 6 May. https://omny.fm/shows/power-business/land-reform-and-restitution-amidst-covid-19#description

Melane, A. and Sihlal, N. (nd) 'Land hearings to come to Cape Town this week', *Weekend Breakfast with Africa Melane* [podcast]. http://www.capetalk.co.za/podcasts/121/weekend-breakfast-with-africa-melane/95996/land-hearings-to-come-to-cape-town-this-week

Mnisi, S. and Claassens, A. (2009) 'Rural women redefining land rights in the context of living customary law', *South African Journal on Human Rights*, 25(3): 491–516.

Mnwana, S. and Capps, G. (2015) *'No Chief Ever Bought a Piece of Land!' Struggles Over Property, Community and Mining in the Bakgatla-ba-Kgafela Traditional Authority Area, North West Province*, Working Paper 3, Johannesburg: Society, Work and Development Institute, University of the Witwatersrand.

Mouton, J. and Valentine, A. (2017) 'The extent of South African authored articles in predatory journals', *South African Journal of Science*, 113(7–8): 1–9.

Mzwakali, S. (2017) 'Traditional Khoi-San Leadership Bill'. https://www.customcontested.co.za/traditional-khoi-san-leadership-bill-mps-failed-dismally-consult-public/

Nomboniso and Luwaya, N. (nd) 'Traditional Khoi San Leadership Bill', *The Best of Redi Tlhabi* [podcast]. http://www.702.co.za/podcasts/252/the-best-of-redi-tlhabi/155481/traditional-khoi-san-leadership-bill

Oja, S.N. (1989) *Collaborative Action Research: A Developmental Process* (vol 7), London: Falmer Press.

Oswald, K., Gaventa, J. and Leach, M. (2016) 'Introduction: Interrogating engaged excellence in research', *IDS Bulletin*, 47(9): 1–18.

Parliamentary Monitoring Group (2018) 'Ingonyama Trust Board on land conversion to leases'. https://pmg.org.za/committee-meeting/25943/

Parliamentary Monitoring Group (2019) 'Land Dialogue Workshop: Ad hoc committee to initiate and introduce legislation amending Section 25 of Constitution'. https://pmg.org.za/committee-meeting/29283/

Phakeng, M. (2019) 'DHET publication count: Research excellence is more than a numbers game', University of Cape Town. https://www.news.uct.ac.za/article/-2019-05-06-dhet-publication-count-research-excellence-is-more-than-a-numbers-game

Rappetti, I., Duda, T., Maledu, G. and Nopote, N. (2019) 'The impact of traditional-leader rule on communities', *POWER Talk* [podcast], 27 March. https://omny.fm/shows/powertalk-archive/the-impact-of-traditional-leader-rule-on-communiti?in_playlist=powertalk-archive

Sherman, F. and Torbert, W.R. (eds) (2000) *Transforming Social Inquiry, Transforming Social Action: New Paradigms for Crossing the Theory/Practice Divide in Universities and Communities*, Boston, MA: Springer.

Sihlali, N. (2018a) 'Ingonyama Trust wants people to pay rent on land they already own', *Independent Online*. https://www.iol.co.za/news/opinion/ingonyama-trust-wants-people-to-pay-rent-on-land-they-already-own-13545713

Sihlali, N. (2018b) 'Mixing expropriation with Ingonyama is mischievous', *Sowetan*. https://www.sowetanlive.co.za/opinion/columnists/2018-07-26-mixing-expropriation-with-ingonyama-is-mischievous/

Sihlali, N. (2018c) 'Rural women fight for the right to own their land', *The Mercury*, 9 November. https://www.iol.co.za/mercury/opinion/rural-women-fight-for-the-right-to-own-their-land-17837520

UCT (University of Cape Town) (2012) *Social Responsiveness Policy Framework*, 12 September. www.socialresponsiveness.uct.ac.za/usr/social_resp/about/SocialResponsivenessPolicyFramework.docx

UCT (University of Cape Town) (nd) *Faculty of Law Performance Assessment Guidelines: Academic Staff*. http://www.hr.uct.ac.za/sites/default/files/image_tool/images/236/performance/promotion/academic/law_adhom_2016.pdf

11

Experiences of Meetings and Cooperation between Academics and Unions: The Work Studies Group from the South (GETSUR)[1]

Dasten Julián Vejar

Introduction

During 2010–14, I worked under the supervision of Dr Klaus Dörre (2014) while undertaking doctoral studies in the Institute of Sociology at the Friedrich Schiller University Jena. As a result, I was able to observe the workings of an academic institution and a research group focused on a developing a scientific and political approach. This line of action, together with a strong sense of excellence, commitment, collaboration and friendship, stood out as the identity of the entire academic team.

This experience had a significant impact on my life. In addition to acquiring extensive knowledge regarding labour sociology, social theory and methodologies, the time spent at the Institute of Sociology allowed me to gain an understanding of the experiences, faces and voices of research teams from the four corners of the world. This was in effect a nourishing intellectual engagement emanating from the contributions of leading researchers covering contemporary and emerging themes of the world of work.

During those years, I participated in various conferences and seminars. In one of them, I met Michael Burawoy. I had 'the mission' of accompanying and guiding him in the city of Jena. Thanks to this work, and to Michael's great kindness and humility, I was able to learn about his motivations, ideas and projects in doing sociology. I immediately saw a connexion with the proposal of 'public sociology', which has its own roots in Latin America due to the political relevance of action research (Fals Borda and Rodríguez, 1987).

On another occasion, the Institute of Sociology organized a conference around the concept of precariousness, and members of various universities around the world participated. There, I was able to meet Edward (Eddie) Webster, who explained the work of the Society, Work and Politics Institute (SWOP) and its research programme. I was surprised that the themes addressed by SWOP showed great harmony with the social, historical, political and cultural problems in Latin America. At the same time, it seemed paradoxical that we should meet in Germany to catch up on these agendas. In any case, this event opened a window: the Global South was in front of me.

On my return to Chile in September 2014, I joined the Universidad Católica de Temuco. This was to foster an application of the knowledge and experiences learned at the Institute of Sociology, particularly the speciality of Arbeits-, Industrie- und Wirtschaftssoziologie, in a society where the world of employment was delimited by neoliberal policies, social inequality, deregulation and labour flexibility, and job insecurity (Blanco and Julián, 2019).

Bearing in mind the general panorama that shaped these phenomena, a scheme and plan of work was organized. One strategic objective identified in this planning process was the development of a working link between trade union organizations, local communities and the academic world to generate the construction of knowledge geared to the needs of the social actors that form part of the work environment. In this sense, it had reference to the work at the Institute of Sociology and to SWOP. Both experiences would be key to thinking and inspiring our proposal in southern Chile.

Our target was to set up a local territorial work platform, fostering connections in global research networks and enhancing the cohesion of the national scientific community in terms of labour studies. For this purpose, the idea was to build a scientific research group that would allow for such local–global–national articulation. Thus were forged the origins of the Work Studies Group from the South (GETSUR).

To promote this endeavour from within a regional university and in a country as centralized as Chile, which is already part of the periphery at the global level, brought, and continues to bring, a challenge, with various obstacles including:

- *the characteristics of the region*: the relevance and sustainability of the project was based on its location in the Araucanía region, and required an honest diagnosis of the conditions, capacities, particularities and possibilities inherent to this territory;
- *scientific and research policy in Chile*: the neoliberal orientation of this policy entailed hazards; and
- *the need to construct a suitable team*: this team would need to be trained and committed to the objectives of the project.

To overcome these obstacles, I deployed a strategy that would enable collaboration with a wealth of experiences of social, scientific and political engagement at a global level. This is related to the promotion of public sociology (Burawoy, 2004; Julián, 2016; 2017a) – in Burawoy's words, an 'organic public sociology, in which the sociologist works in close connection with a visible, thick, active, local and often counterpublic' through 'a dialogue, a process of mutual education' oriented 'to make visible the invisible, to make the private public, to validate these organic connections as part of our sociological life' (2005: 7–8).

However, at this time, our group was following with curiosity and interest the proposal of SWOP. This led us to cross the Atlantic in January 2019 for a short stay. I had the pleasure of meeting the two former SWOP directors, Eddie Webster and Karl van Holdt, the current director, Prishani Naidoo, and Professor Ben Scully. I learned about their history, perspectives and projects. A great team of people with a great tradition of articulation between knowledge and social and political mobilization. Their work is an example at the international level and allows us to build a bridge of cooperation in the Global South.

This chapter aims to contribute to a learning process that is surely being repeated in many places and locations around the world and, though facing difficult challenges and setbacks, should find paths of action, collaboration and hope.

Finding a home: the Araucanía region

The emergence of neoliberalism as a hegemonic construct in the formation of a flexible pattern of accumulation was deeply embedded in restoring the power of the capitalist class in the process of accumulating and circulating capital at the global level (Harvey, 2007). Micheal Burawoy (2005: 7) calls this process the 'despotism of markets', which is possible through the institution of a disciplinary model at the social level (Gill, 1995), focused on dispossession and social precariousness as practices of control, while the state assumes a subsidiary role and provides institutional support for privatization.

Referred to as 'neoliberalism' (Harvey, 2007; Gaudichaud, 2015) or the 'neoliberal model' (Garretón, 2014), it has reinforced the emergence of new transnational actors and economic financing within a new dynamic of interconnection and annexation of the geography of capitalism throughout the world (Sassen, 2003; Sader, 2008). Neoliberalism has had an expansive and instituting role in terms of social relations (Harvey, 2007). The commodification of social goods, the monetization of social welfare, the incursion of the market into healthcare, education, pensions and so on – these have shaped various areas of profitability and competitiveness, serving not only to 'rationalize' social relations, but also to configure subjects and subjectivities from a situation of dependence, insecurity, precarity and vulnerability.

In the case of Chile, the neoliberalization of society has reached a point of maturity in terms of exercising contradictions in social relations and in terms of the application of policies by state institutions. Its maturity can be observed in the level of impact on social ordering in the different dimensions of life. This process has included the commercialization of social rights through private capital as well as the definition and occupation of space, producing an unequal and segmented social structure that instigates a scenario of expulsions, impoverishment, marginalization and poverty (Ruiz and Boccardo, 2014). This context has created a special space for the project of public sociology, especially in the 2019 social mobilizations against the government, the neoliberal policies of adjustment and the rising cost of life.

Chile is divided politically and administratively into 15 regions. The Araucanía region is characterized by having: a high percentage of the country's indigenous Mapuche population (33 per cent); different material and symbolic expressions of the Mapuche culture; an economy without the significant presence of large industrial companies; a concentrated labour force, mainly employed in the services, retail and agricultural sectors; a process of land concentration that coexists with smallholdings owned by communities and individuals; and the highest poverty rate in the country (23 per cent).

The historical formation of the region was afflicted by a violent colonial relationship. Between 1853 and 1857, the Chilean state began an offensive campaign of invasion, occupation and annexation of the territories belonging to the Mapuche (Pinto, 2000), a process that culminated in the War of Pacification of Araucanía (1881–86), which formed part of an anti-indigenous and colonialist policy of the Chilean state. Ignoring previously signed treaties and even its own political constitution of 1833, the Chilean government launched a genocidal military campaign with the objective of exterminating the Mapuche population. Then, in 1905, following the Pacification of Araucanía, the government initiated its most active intervention by promoting an extensive model of deforestation and extraction. Law 1768 was passed, leading to 80,000 hectares of what are now state-owned forests being felled and used in the steel industry. The government recognizes a total land area of around 407,695 hectares as having been expropriated from the Mapuche in the invasion of 1881.

This process represents commodification of nature in colonial dispossession and is addressed in the historical promotion of 'development models in Latin America' (Gudynas, 2018). More recently, forestry plantations in the Araucanía region have expanded from 419,000 hectares in 2013 (about 4 per cent of the total region) to 483,482 hectares in December 2014. This increase is associated with the loss of native forest reserves, which in 2013

Figure 11.1: Map of the Araucanía region

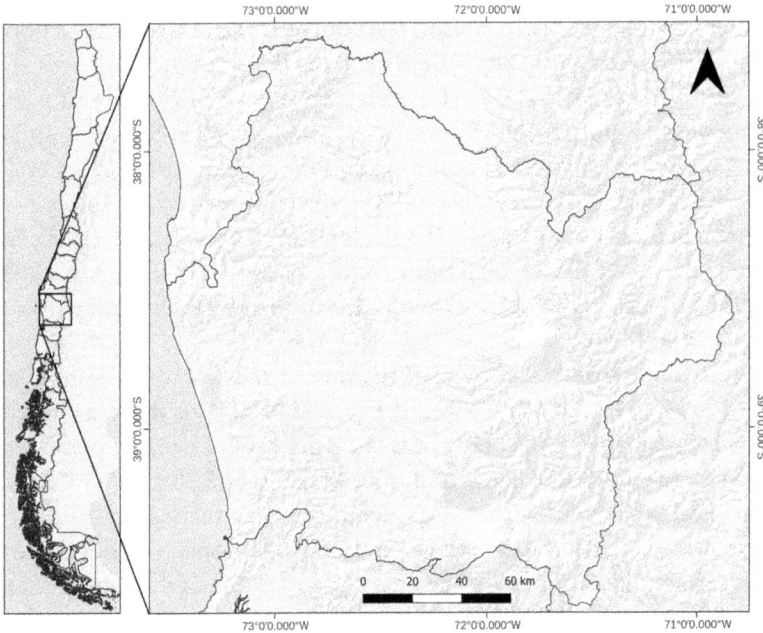

Source: Felipe Castro Gutiérrez

covered 296,732 hectares (2.1 per cent of the regional territory) but in 2014 made up 272,552 hectares.

The Araucanía region (Figure 11.1), located in southern Chile, has been shaped by processes of colonial occupation and capital investment by the extractive industries (Alister and Julián, 2018). However, the dynamics of appropriation and occupation of the territory have resulted in incessant conflict and tension over the last four centuries. It was only in the last 140 years that the Chilean state affirmed the incorporation of the territory into its national system by generating an offensive process of de-territorialization and re-territorialization.

This process has involved a series of conflicts which have had serious consequences for the local population (Antileo et al, 2015; Pinto, 2015). The Chilean army's occupation of the region meant a process of dispossession and genocide of the Mapuche people, who had inhabited the region for at least a thousand years. This intervention involved a transformation of property relations along with the building of forts, cities and other settlements. In that sense, this neocolonial framing provides a contrast to the discussion elaborated by the public sociology approach (Arribas Lozano, 2018).

In socio-demographic terms, according to the National Statistical Institute (INE), the population of the Araucanía region stood at 1,024,917 in 2018. This region had the highest multidimensional poverty rate in the country in 2017: 25.3 per cent according to the National Socioeconomic Characterization Survey (CASEN; CASEN, 2017) and the lowest schooling rate in 2015, with an average of ten years (INE, 2015).

In terms of labour statistics, according to the CASEN survey for 2017, among the total population of just over one million, 396,658 were employed in the agriculture, livestock, hunting and forestry industries (17.3 per cent) while wholesale and retail trade and construction employed 16.6 per cent and 10.7 per cent, respectively. Regarding forms of work, 19.2 per cent of workers are casual or seasonal workers and have the lowest percentages of signed contracts compared to other regions and a relatively high percentage of agricultural work.

In terms of income, the median income in the Araucanía region stood at CLP\$ 446,546 (US\$ 667) in 2017 (CASEN, 2017), the second-lowest among all regions in Chile. However, 44.8 per cent of workers in the region earned equal to or less than the minimum wage (CLP\$ 288,000 or US\$ 430).

However, even in this context, trade unionism in the region has not been characterized by use of strike action; rather, the region has one of the lowest trade union affiliation rates in the country and is one of the most limited in terms of union activity. In fact, the Araucanía region had the second-lowest union membership rate (8.9 per cent), after the Maule region (8.7 per cent) (INE, 2015). This is related to the structure of the labour force, as close to one third of the workforce are self-employed, thus weakening the initiatives and motivations of traditional trade union organizations. Nonetheless, union affiliation grew by 2.5 per cent between 2016 and 2020, to a rate of 20.2 per cent. If we look at the rate of collective bargaining, collective action in the region is also weak. At a national level, on average in the same period, collective bargaining has only taken place in 7.6 per cent of companies, but in the Araucanía region, collective bargaining had a coverage rate of just 4.5 per cent (author's elaboration based on data from the Labour Survey; ENCLA 2014).

Regarding the structure of trade unions and workers' organizations, the SIRELA Labour Relations Information System of the Chilean government's Labour Office indicates there is a total of 386 union organizations at a regional level (per data viewed on 11 October 2018). This total represents organizations for private sector workers, as it is only possible to distinguish trade union organizations and public sector workers associations in the data. While the former are found in the private sector and are independent, the public sector associations − which total 193 in the region − are linked to the public sector and state administration and adhere to a specific statute for the regulation of their work and forms of collective organization.

In Chile, trade union organizations can be classified into workers' centrals, confederations, federations and unions. In the case of the workers' centrals, there are four such national bodies located in the region. In relation to confederations, there are two: one is associated with the public sector through the National Association of State University Workers (ANTUE), and is currently active; the other is the Confederation of Multisectoral Trade Unions of Workers of the Araucanía region, which is currently in recess.

There are 29 trade union federations. However, only ten are active, the majority of which (60 per cent) are in the province of Cautín in the south of the Araucanía region. Of the ten active federations, six belong to the retail sector, two to industry, one to the agricultural sector and one to transport, specifically collective (shared) taxis. With respect to the size of the trade union federations, 37.8 per cent have between 26 and 50 workers. These unions are mostly present in large establishments or hypermarkets, the primary education sector and other personal service activities: 18.1 per cent of unions are concentrated in these sectors. In the public sector, active unions are mainly found in hospitals and clinics (30.1 per cent) and activities of other associations (17.1 per cent). It should be noted that the Araucanía region has one of the highest percentages of inactive unions in the country.

To sum up, trade union infrastructure in the Araucanía region is very weak and there is a significant deficit in terms of representation. Added to this, and one of the characteristic features of the region, union activity is concentrated in a particular province (Cautín) and one of its municipal districts (Temuco). Another significant aspect is the concentration of work in the agricultural sector, accompanied by the weak presence of trade union organizations for this sector. The number of workers who participate in or are represented by a trade union is also relatively low. This can be explained by various reasons and factors.

In this context, an active union organization is more the exception than the rule. The weakness and organizational difficulties faced by unions make inter-union articulation and links with social actors necessary. To this end, our objective has been to:

- understand the real and specific experiences, culture, practices and strategies of trade union organizations, and
- identify the possibilities of collaboration, engagement and dialogue between the academic sphere and active trade unions.

In this respect, since 2014, the possibility presented itself to work with important trade union organizations: the National Federation of Retail Workers; the Federation of Public Sector Fee-paid Workers; and the Federation of Industrial Workers and those employed in the Forestry Sector (Alister et al, 2020). These experiences have been documented and systematically analysed in relation to the interests of the union organizations, thus encouraging the formation, mobilization and revitalization of trade union practices. However, these actions have not been devoid of contradictions, obstacles and problems in terms of academic–union articulation.

Commitment and engagement practices

Trade unionism and trade unions are at a turning point globally. Although the structural weakening of trade unionism by economic liberalization is recognized in literature, including its crisis in terms of representation of (new) workers (Standing, 2011; Munck, 2018), in the case of Chile, the crisis was shaped by the former military dictatorship. The dictatorship continues to impact political-institutional and political-social spaces in the country. For jt is in these spaces that the connection and instrumentality of these same organizations are subject to, and encircled by, problems of distrust, precariousness and weakening that contribute to their fragmentation.

Distrust

Distrust, as an intersubjective relationship, intercedes in situations such as meetings, gatherings and alliance building, as well as being reflected in internal cohesion. This phenomenon contributes towards deepening the problems related to institutional structure, business strategies and working conditions. However, such distrust is not irrational, but rather a defence mechanism instituted and reinforced by collective experiences of betrayal and/or disappointment in collective practices undertaken by the trade union organizations.

Such distrust is reinforced by actors seeking institutional accommodation, especially in relation to political parties and their 'chain of transmission' of a policy of submission and union subordination. Although distrust produces a kind of defensive tactic in the form of suspecting instrumentalization and co-option, rather than expecting collaboration, it also creates difficulties when attempting to link unionism and unions with other social actors in their surroundings.

Precariousness

The precariousness of trade unionism comes from the fragility and helplessness produced and embedded by labour relations, the lack of a culture of rights and the deregulation of working conditions. The lack of protections and the limitation of collective rights reinforces a condition of vulnerability for workers and their organizations in the capital–work relationship, which is expressed in defencelessness and the normalization of (over-)exploitation (Julián, 2017b, 2017c).

The precarious nature of trade unionism is reflected in many areas and can even be part of conditions of reproducibility in the social matrix. Societal precariousness can be expressed in the different forms of work. Such precariousness demarcates the identities and spatio-temporal contours in which subjectivity is mobilized. Precariousness forges, in general, destabilization, uncertainty and lack of understanding of work, which means that trade unionism, as a stable and institutionalized form of organization, can be ruled out initially as a hub of coordination, organization and mobilization by workers (Standing, 2011; Atzeni and Ness, 2018).

Undermining

The undermining of unions reflects the role assigned to them in terms of labour relations. Trade unionism went from being a politically aware mass movement with significant political influence in the 1970s to having little capacity for political and social influence today (Gaudichaud, 2015). This process, which has different manifestations around the world (Silver, 2005), is, in the case of Chile, based on the weak composition and representation of trade unions.

This weakening represents a systematic government strategy that has sought to shape a working class that is mouldable to the diktats of capital. The weakness of the unions can be traced to:

- the forms of organization that are possible in the institutional framework;
- the model of privatization and commercialization of social rights; and
- the subjectivity of workers in relation to becoming part of a collective and identifying with a principle such as solidarity.

In the current nationwide crisis of trade unionism, the components of distrust, precariousness and weakening represent the key problems for involvement and participation. Within trade union organizations, there is a nurtured understanding of sociopolitical changes around the world and their impact on the organizational culture of trade unions.

Who we are?

At first, the team was made up of sociology students and social science researchers who were part of a process of training, preparation, learning and discussion in labour studies. This team was characterized by social and political commitment to an active practice of social militancy, as well as internal solidarity and collaborative operation. Over the years, the team has expanded with participation by students from other disciplines and the inclusion of thesis students and a group of young researchers, who have opened new lines of research and action.

Funds for the group's work came from the Ministry of Science Technology, Knowledge and Innovation, the Ministry of Labour and Social Security (trade union school programmes) and the German Academic Exchange Service (Deutscher Akademischer Austauschdienst) and as well as university funds for strengthening research within the institution. From this, we have produced: a collection of books edited by the group, entitled Estudios del Trabajo desde el Sur (Labour Studies from the South)[2]; three books authored/ joint authored by team members; more than 10 book chapters published in various countries (Argentina, Bolivia, Brazil, Chile, Colombia, Germany and Mexico); more than 15 scientific articles; and 22 undergraduate and postgraduate theses from academic programmes in Argentina, Brazil, Chile and Mexico.

The research has focused on responding to the need to strengthen the action and organization of trade unions in the face of symbolic, economic and political changes that have occurred within the context of neoliberal employment policies and labour relations in Chile. To this end, several collaborative initiatives have been promoted to shape an agenda that characterizes GETSUR today. This strategy of working with trade union organizations has enabled the researchers to shape and undertake the following research and union training projects:

- Research on trade unions, strikes and labour relations (2015–17): This research, carried out with support and funding from the Universidad Católica de Temuco, aimed at understanding of the difficulties encountered in exercising the right to strike and participate in labour movements in the Araucanía region.
- Mapping of labour precariousness and labour relations in the Central-Southern Zone of Chile (2016–19): This research project was funded by CONICYT-Chile. The objective was to investigate the relationship between precarious work and the collective action of workers in southern Chile.
- Internationalization and trans-nationalization of the agro-forestry economy of southern Chile, 1985–2010 (2016–20): This research project, funded by CONICYT-Chile, sought to identify precarious working conditions in the agricultural and agro-industrial sector in southern Chile.
- Patagonia Netzwerk (2016–21): Funded by the German Academic Exchange Service and supported by the Friedrich Schiller University Jena, this project aimed to strengthening a network of research on extractivism and precariousness in the forestry sector. This sector has impacted people's way of life and affected territories through a concentration of property, poverty, inequality and droughts.

- The Clotario Blest trade union training school (2018): This project was co-organized with the Federation of Industrial and Related Workers (FENASITRAIN) and the Federation of Retail Trade Unions (FESIR), and 30 union leaders from various sectors in the Araucanía region participated. The project ran over five months in 2018, and there was some controversy, as funding was provided by the Ministry of Labour and Social Security, and we were in competition with various institutions and groups funded by the ministry in previous years.
- Precariousness of work in the southern Macrozone of Chile: Intersections, territories and resistance in the Maule, Ñuble, Biobío and Araucanía regions (2020–23). Our main goal in this project is to identify and analyze the precariousness of work in terms of its extension to social and daily relationships, emphasizing the interrelation between subjectivity, precarious work and social hierarchies. Our research involves commitment from trade union organizations in the study areas.

This series of projects provided synergy pertaining to the needs of trade union organizations. The university contributed in terms of infrastructure and logistics as well as knowledge and research skills. These practices led to the formulation of an identity as a group and collective, which served to form a bond in academic-institutional and sociopolitical contexts. For example, in the case of the trade union training school, unions in the Araucanía region were very accustomed to the process of training established by the state, based on a top-down logic. This was normalized by the union leaders in different training sessions, seminars and conferences. The content, the 'teachers', the timing, the funding and the methodology of this training was always defined by the government in power, either by a bureaucratic staff of experts in the Ministry of Labour and Social Security or by outsourced public policy actors, without any input from the trade unions.

The interest in public sociology (Burawoy, 2005) and the use of action research (Fals Borda, 1999) meant that there was a focus on ideas and requirements expressed by the trade unions. The process of designing the school involved a series of meetings to identify the main goals of the trade unions and shape the school accordingly. The following questions were put to the unions: What do trade unions in the Araucania region need? Why do you need a training school? What topics must be covered at the school? How will other trade unions be invited to participate? How are we going to choose the contents and the lectures? Can workers be teachers in the school? This innovation provided a new way of working for the unions and a new way of understanding their role in the design of policies. They made a promise to make the school a strategic space for engagement between unions, union leaders in the region and GETSUR.

This practice of cooperation between trade unions in the Araucanía region and GETSUR simultaneously allowed the research team to:

- *generate new ties with organizations in other regions of the country*: We work with different trade unions in the territory. The projects give us the possibility to meet with organizations from all over the country to form new agendas and design research and collaborative activities.
- *join national action research networks in the union sphere*: There is a need, due to the weakness of the union movement in Chile, for better coordination in the form of networks. While the relationship between universities, non-governmental organizations (NGOs) and workers' organizations has great strategic importance, GETSUR also generates possibilities for workers from different enterprises, sectors and territories to meet.
- *participate in other existing networks*: Chile has a network of informal and popular spaces for debate, education and solidarity, founded by organizations across the country and with a political framework based on the interest of workers. Our group collaborates in these activities and projects through seminars, presentations and workshops.
- *generate a set of activities aimed at strengthening trade union organizations*: We are focused on creating knowledge and activities oriented by the needs and demands of workers' organizations. Our activities are a combination of solidarity, campaigns, organizing and organizational networking.

These experiences have been complemented by:

- Our collaboration in the NO+AFP (No to the Pension Fund Associations) social movement: This movement aims to end the pension fund model in Chile, which was established in 1981 during the military dictatorship. It is based on individual capital and private sector administration of pension funds (Julián, 2017c). We have collaborated in different activities at local, regional and national levels to promote a solidarity pension system elaborated by the workers' movement.
- Our participation in initiatives that bring together different social movements (for example, those relating to education, the indigenous community and the environment) has allowed us to achieve greater insertion in the region (Julián, 2017a). We have participated in working groups and meetings to discuss and coordinate activities relating to struggles for water, militarization of the region, public sector education and so on. These experiences have helped the team to understand the reality of work in terms of its interrelation with other social dimensions.

To a certain extent, the research work can be considered as a task focused on union regeneration. The experience of union regeneration demarcates the creation of a new scenario for the analysis and characterization of trade unionism by the social sciences, especially considering the crisis scenario experienced by workers' organizations the world over. For this reason, it generates a counterpoint that requires consideration of two epistemological elements of the 'undertakings' of the researcher:

- *the interrelation of the researcher with a social problem of a particular and specific group (such as a trade union)*: This interrelation implies a choice and a practical interest on the part of the researcher to contribute to the improvement/resolution of the organizational and institutional problems of unions;
- *research into the issues of regeneration as an articulating element of subjectivities and a trigger of collective coordination in the labour and union spheres*: This is part of a search for possibilities for resolving the conflicts and obstacles that affect the development and strengthening of trade union organizations.

For the reasons presented, union regeneration cannot be conceived from a segmented perspective of reality, but must be understood in relation to the political and historical processes developing at global and regional levels. Given these circumstances, there is a need to once again incorporate within social research meanings and narratives that accompany 'equity', 'equality' and 'democracy' as sociopolitical discourses and practices that seek to redefine the relationship between the state, society and capital.

Research practice

As indicated, the team's interest has been to generate research focused on the public sphere – work that links with social actors and promotes a horizontal exchange of knowledge about the field of labour relations and work. This line of research should be viewed not only as a public sociology experience (Burawoy, 2004, 2005; Braga et al, 2008; Julián, 2016), but also as continuation of the line of research action in Latin America and the Caribbean (Fals Borda and Rodríguez, 1987; Fals Borda and Anisur, 1991; Ortiz and Borjas, 2008).

Furthermore, it should be noted that, to date, development of a research activity such as the articulation proposed here (between public sociology and *regeneration*) has encountered serious complications and obstacles at the institutional, social and economic levels. Our perspective tries to conduct public sociology with a public that doesn't always know all the elements of the context – a context that always creates problems for sociological practice.

Institutional obstacles

Although universities undertake evaluations that incorporate production and sharing of findings as criteria, there are few institutions at national level that disseminate information in an accessible way to unions.

In our case, the support of the Universidad Católica de Temuco served to strengthen connections with the trade union movement, especially through the Clotario Blest trade union school and the diploma in trade union organization. Furthermore, opportunities were provided for activities such as the Workers' Congress of Southern Chile, and a series of seminars was held on topics such as migration, labour reform and the pension system.

However, the institutional standing of GETSUR was never formalized by the university, which hinders the team's work and the sustainability of the research team. It might be assumed that these obstacles have been created by the institution due to the group's non-compliance with the standards required for publications and research projects, which represent standardization in the neoliberal scientific field; however, this is not the case.

In January 2021 I was fired by the university. This happened amidst a demand for democratization and following a rebellion based on popular protest in 2019. In this context, our methodology of establishing links and networks among the community, workers' organizations and the academy was blocked at the institutional level. Now we are working in a new university (Universidad Austral de Chile) but we are organized formally, similar to an NGO, in a way that protects autonomy and a space for more activities such as action research.

Social obstacles

In the last few decades, social and trade union organizations have not had a highly developed process for finding channels of cooperation in the academic world. More than three decades after the end of the military dictatorship in Chile (1973–90), the rebuilding of the country's social fabric faces serious difficulties, particularly those to do the lack of association and support required for collaboration.

This fragility of the social fabric has been accompanied by a weak relationship between the academic world and trade union organizations, and with the latter not having a clear strategy to plan cooperative practices or even to set their own objectives and actions as organizations (Julián, 2017b). This circumstance has become a constant and persistent obstacle for the development of sustainable strategies for the improvement and modernization of the trade unions, and it contributes to the obstacles for engagement based on public sociology (Burawoy, 2005: 10) and for communication with 'precarious publics' (Bucklaschuk, 2014).

The lack of a culture of improvement, management, transparency and organizational capacity within union organizations has created an important barrier to the consolidation of working linkages. This has been accompanied by a lack of knowledge of sociology and the social sciences as providing possibilities to promote and build alternatives for and with the unions, representing a rift in terms of cooperation between the academic field and the unions.

It should be noted that there exists a fundamental element in the creation of this obstacle: the precariousness of work and life, and the persistence of consequences of Pinochet's dictatorship for the organization of civil society and the working class (Julián, 2017c). Although this issue has been mentioned before, the precariousness of life and the high intensity of work seldom permit opportunities for participation and organization in unions, which makes it even more difficult to strengthen relationships between actors while at the same time creating new forms of workers' organizations.

Economic obstacles

Finally, one of the most important obstacles encountered in this work is funding: to carry out its activities, the research group sought various sources of funding, which were usually subject to uncertainty, competitive processes and assessments that did not necessarily value the direction outlined in the research proposals. This is one of the most significant obstacles for public sociology (Burawoy, 2005), the thinking within the practices and habitus of the scientific field around problems and risks of institutionalizing the practice of cooperation between trade unions and sociologists (Burawoy, 2007).

In Chile, scientific policy promotes the funding of research initiatives that align with the institutionalization of scientific productivity indicators and standardization of scientific knowledge. As previously indicated, the search for funding has been based on diversification of donors, which has been successful as the team has understood the neoliberal reasoning associated with knowledge production. Moreover, as a group, we spread applications out through international networks, providing clear presentations of the research proposals.

However, this funding uncertainty, accompanied by institutional obstacles, has prevented the team from forging a fixed, permanent and stable working space. The research group has been constantly subjected to the pressures of temporary funding that has denied the ability to consolidate the work team and provide a permanent residence. Even so, while funds were not intended to provide continuity of research teams, they have allowed us to develop a series of research activities.

Increasing this complexity, the geographical location of the team in southern Chile brought a new problem in terms of funding – that of political centralism. The country's major universities are concentrated in the city of Santiago (the Chilean capital), and it is there that most of the research funded by national science and technology institutions is carried out. From the outset, this has implied both a recognition of the difficulties that would be encountered when applying for research funds in the resource allocation matrix, and the position that research practices external to the priorities of these funding bodies should be taken forward.

In summary, the public sociology research practices nurtured by the team to date have allowed for a particular way of generating knowledge – a knowledge that challenges government strategies in the scientific field by introducing a specific approach to knowledge creation: a social process of collective and cooperative learning about society. It is here that a set of conclusions can be identified. However, these are still under construction and reflect a set of political hurdles.

Conclusion

In the course of the research, it was found that the meaning of work conveys, in an evolving way, categories (or symbolic goods) such as 'dignity' and 'justice', underlining the regeneration of a trade union culture associated with a reassessment of the idea of work. This fact has been verified in the discourse of different union leaders in the country, based on conflicts and tensions such as those generated by the pension system and labour reform projects as well as various projects aimed at the precariousness of work and life.

The emergence of these discourses constitutes an important part of the process of reconstruction of a sociopolitical mindset that has begun to consolidate itself in social movements regarding neoliberalism and its consequences (Dörre, 2014; Harris and Scully, 2015). This process of reconstitution shows that precariousness, as a political assertion, takes on an importance in trade union and other social movements, and is being inserted into the public agenda in discussions regarding employment, protection and social welfare policies.

Dignity and justice involve collective re-elaborations of critical understanding of social inequality and the relationship between social classes. In this sense, it is easy to identify a certain social resonance of precariousness, as a focus for justification and politicization of the interventions of trade union and social actors, in the formation of resistance, protests, petitions and proposals.

For its part, union regeneration today represents a challenge for researchers and the social sciences in terms of the problems currently faced in Latin America and Chile, which can be characterized by three main points:

- *the need to overcome neoliberalism*: The various policies that have been implemented to deregulate work and dismantle welfare, security and social protection mechanisms, along with the commodification of social rights, represents a scenario that challenges trade union organizations and social movements to think strategically about their struggles as being for well-being and better living standards. This is the lesson of the riots in Chile in 2019, where the people are challenging the hegemony of neoliberal policies and the commodification of life.
- *the transformations of the modern world with respect to new productive models, the primary export model and this form of neo-dependence*: It is in the extractive sectors of the Latin American economy where the main groups of the organized working class are present. The emergence of new jobs, virtualization, automation and robotization have led to a process of redefinition of trade unionism. The articulation between union cultures and changes in working practices makes it necessary to elaborate new strategies and repertoires of action in the collective and unitary struggle for the trade union movement.
- *the demands of a praxis focused on political ecology and a systemic approach to human rights*: Regardless of the relationship with social science fields, the extinction threat hanging over humans, as well as the offensive against social rights and common goods, requires an ecological and systemic approach that integrates precariousness as a political exercise. The depredation, enclosure and expulsion that shapes the capitalist system today requires that scientific knowledge elaborates a research agenda focused on good living and the defence of society.

In the case of GETSUR, dealing with these three focal points has been made possible not only because of the technical capacity of the team and its knowledge of industrial relations and the sociology of work, but also because of the subjective peculiarities of GETSUR. These particularities are related to the backgrounds and personal, political and emotional motivations of team members, qualities that stem from an approach focused on respect and cooperation with the subjects of work and their experiences in terms of social change.

The hegemony and standardization of indicators and productivist rationales in the scientific field represent the consequences of neoliberal reification and neopositivism in scientific practice (Burawoy, 2004). In contrast to these tendencies, science needs to be constituted as a space of solidarity, and of forms of solidarity that are fraternally directed towards the unveiling and transformation of power relationships and society's knowledge about itself, with the objective of achieving social welfare for the majority of citizens and a more harmonious life with and within the ecosystem.

This statement about the role of science reflects a way to construct knowledge and share and apply it to specific situations. At the same time, it involves considering the state's scientific policy, with the aim of offering an intersection between the diagnoses, the collective participation of those who are to be investigated and the practice of visibilization/divulgation of knowledge. This issue represents a huge challenge, which organizations such as GETSUR will continue to confront decisively from the limits of the capitalist periphery.

Notes

[1] This chapter was funded by CONICYT-Chile (National Commission for Scientific and Technological Research) through FONDECYT (National Fund for Scientific and Technological Development) Regular Project No 1160321: Internacionalización y transnacionalización de la economía silvoagropecuaria del sur de Chile, 1985–2010 (2016–20) and FONDECYT Regular Project No. 1200990: Precariedades del trabajo en la Macrozona sur de Chile: Intersecciones, territorios y resistencias en las regiones del Maule, Ñuble, Biobío y La Araucanía (2020–2023). Tipología del Trabajo Precario y su incidencia en la práctica sindical en las regiones del Maule, Biobío y La Araucanía.

[2] These books are available via an open access platform: https://books.openedition.org/author?name=julian+vejar+dasten

References

Alister, C. and Julián, D. (2018) 'Precariedad(es) laboral(es) en territorios extractivos de la Araucanía', in M. Ramírez and S. Schmalz (eds) *¿Fin de la bonanza?: entradas, salidas y encrucijadas del extractivismo*. Buenos Aires: Biblos, pp 175–94.

Alister, C., Bravo, L., Galliorio, A., Julián, D. and Marchant, F. (2020) '¿Hay sindicatos en La Araucanía? Problemas organizacionales en experiencias de investigación y acción', *Revista Izquierdas*, 49: 3649–75.

Antileo, E., Huinca, H., Calfío, M. and Cárcamo, L. (2015) *Awükan Ka Kuxankan Zugu Wajmapu Mew. Violencias coloniales en Wajmapu*. Temuco: Comunidad Historia Mapuche.

Arribas Lozano, A. (2018) 'Reframing the public sociology debate: Towards collaborative and decolonial praxis', *Current Sociology*, 66(1): 92–109.

Atzeni, M. and Ness, I. (eds) (2018) *Global Perspectives on Workers and Labour Organizations*, London: Springer.

Blanco, O. and Julián, D. (2019) 'Una tipología de precariedad laboral para Chile', *Revista CEPAL*, 129: 99–137.

Braga, R., Gemignani, S. and Mello, L. (2008) 'Public sociology and social engagement: Considerations on Brazil', *Current Sociology*, 56(3): 415–24.

Bucklaschuk, J. (2014) 'Precarious publics: Interrogating a public sociology for migrant workers in Canada', in A. Hanemaayer and C. Schneider (eds) *The Public Sociology Debate: Ethics and Engagement*, Vancouver: UBC Press, pp 108–31.

Burawoy, M. (2004) 'Public sociologies: Contradictions, dilemmas and possibilities', *Social Forces*, 82(4): 1603–18.

Burawoy, M. (2005) 'For public sociology', *American Sociological Review*, 70: 4–28.

Burawoy, M. (2007) 'The field of sociology: Its power and its promise', in D. Clawson (ed) *Public Sociology: Fifteen Eminent Sociologists Debate Politics and the Profession in the Twenty-first Century*, Berkeley: University of California, pp 241–58.

CASEN (2017) Encuesta de Caracterización Socioeconómica. Ministerio de Desarrollo Social. Santiago, Chile.

Dörre, K. (2014) 'Precarity and social disintegration: A relational concept', *Journal für Entwicklungspolitik*, 30(4): 69–89.

ENCLA (2014) Encuesta Laboral. Ministerio del Trabajo y Seguridad Social. Santiago, Chile.

Fals Borda, O. (1999) 'Orígenes universales y retos actuales de la Investigación – Acción Participativa', *Análisis Político*, 38: 73–90.

Fals Borda, O. and Anisur, R. (eds) (1991) *Acción y Conocimiento: Cómo Romper el Monopolio con Investigación – Acción Participativa*. Bogotá: Centro de Investigación y Educación Popular, CINEP.

Fals Borda, O. and Rodríguez, C. (1987) *Investigación Participativa*, Montevideo: Instituto del Hombre y Ediciones de la Banda Oriental.

Garretón, M.A. (2014) *La sociedad en que vivi(re)mos: introducción sociológica al cambio de siglo*. Santiago de Chile: LOM ediciones.

Gaudichaud, F. (2015) *Las fisuras del Neoliberalismo chileno. Trabajo, crisis de la 'democracia tutelada' y conflicto de clases*. Santiago de Chile: Quimantú, Tiempo Robado Editoras.

Gill, S. (1995) 'Globalisation, market civilisation, and disciplinary neoliberalism', *Millennium*, 24(3): 399–423.

Gudynas, E. (2018) 'Disputas entre variedades de desarrollo y el cuadrilema de la globalización', in H. Cuevas, D. Julián Vejar and J. Rojas (eds) *América Latina: Expansión Capitalista, Conflictos Sociales y Ecológicos*, Santiago: RIL Editores, pp 173–91.

Harris, K. and Scully, B. (2015) 'A hidden counter-movement? Precarity, politics, and social protection before and beyond the neoliberal era', *Theory and Society*, 44(5): 415–44.

Harvey, D. (2007) *Brief History of Neoliberalism*, Cambridge: Oxford University Press.

INE (2015) Informe Socioeconómico. Instituto Nacional de Estadísticas. Santiago, Chile.

Julián, D. (2016) 'Una invitación a la sociología pública. La investigación social y la precariedad laboral en Chile', *Revista Austral de Ciencias Sociales*, 31: 75–90.

Julián, D. (2017a) 'La sociología pública en la nueva cuestión del trabajo: Sindicatos, conflicto laboral e investigación social', in N. Del Valle (ed) *Transformaciones de la Esfera Pública en Chile Reciente*, Santiago: RIL Editores, pp 69–97.

Julián, D. (2017b) 'Precariedad laboral en América Latina: Contribuciones a un modelo para armar', *Revista Colombiana de Sociología*, 40(2): 27–46.

Julián, D. (2017c) 'Unions opposing labour precarity in Chile: Union leaders' perceptions and representations of collective action', *Latin American Perspective*, 45(218): 63–76.

Munck, R. (2018) *Rethinking Global Labour: After Neoliberalism*, Newcastle: Agenda Publishing.

Ortiz, M. and Borjas, B. (2008) 'La Investigación Acción Participativa: aporte de Fals Borda a la educación popular', *Espacio Abierto*, 17(4): 615–27.

Pinto, J. (2000) *La formación del Estado y la nacion, y el pueblo mapuche. De la inclusion a la exclusión*. IDEA. Centro de Estudios Avanzados. Universidad de Santiago, Chile.

Pinto, J. (2015) 'La instalación del neoliberalismo y sus efectos en La Araucanía', in *Conflictos étnicos, sociales y económicos, Araucanía 1900–2014*, Santiago: Pehuén, pp 137–86.

Ruiz, C. and Boccardo, G. (2014) *Los chilenos bajo el neoliberalismo. Clases y conflicto social*. Santiago de Chile: Nodo XXI/El Desconcierto.

Sader, E. (2008) 'The weakest link? Neoliberalism in Latin America', *New Left Review*, 52: 5–31.

Sassen, S. (2003) *Los espectros de la globalización*. Mexico: Siglo XXI.

Silver, B. (2005) *Fuerzas de Trabajo. Los movimientos obreros y la globalización desde 1870*. Madrid: AKAL.

SIRELA (2018) Sistema Informático de Relaciones Laborales. Ministerio del Trabajo y Seguridad Social. Santiago, Chile.

Standing, G. (2011) *The Precariat: The New Dangerous Class*, London: Bloomsbury.

12

Critically Engaged Sociology in Turkey and 'Sociology across the South'

Ercüment Çelik

The rise of sociological knowledge production from the Global South has led some internationally influential scholars to call for a 'Southern sociology' perspective (Connell, 2007; Burawoy, 2010b; Comaroff and Comaroff, 2012; de Souza Santos, 2017). One of the central issues that these scholars have pointed out is the need to engage in 'learning from the periphery' or 'learning from the South' in order to break the unequal global division of labour that would then contribute to the development of global sociology and a non-hegemonic social science on a world scale (Connell, 2007; Burawoy, 2010a, 2010b; de Souza Santos, 2010, 2017). Burawoy's (2010b) typology, composed of 'sociology *in* the South', 'sociology *of* the South' and 'sociology *for* the South', which also included his concept of 'public sociology', has received great international attention and became a dominant approach in the understanding of Southern sociology. However, in these Southern sociology 'projects', the extent of the dialogue among sociologies in the South remained unexplained (Rosa, 2014: 863).

The rapid move from learning from the periphery or learning from the South towards a sociology *for* the South or a 'global sociology' undermined the necessary process of what I call 'learning across the South', which would, in turn, forge the establishment of a 'sociology *across* the South'. This sociology and sociological practice requires the interest of Southern scholars in knowing each other's society and sociology through direct contact and direct exchange of knowledge produced in the South before engaging in the Northern channels of knowledge that dominate and shape global sociology. In this way, counter-hegemonic sociology that communicates with Northern sociology on an equal basis can truly be upgraded to non-hegemonic global sociology.

The inclusion of an analysis of the 'critically engaged sociology' in Turkey in a volume covering topics from South African academic and political experience already exemplifies how sociology across the South should be understood and applied. What I attempt to do in this chapter is to add a new dimension to Burawoy's typology in order to explain the difference between the concepts 'critical engagement' and public sociology in accordance with the main objective of this volume. My argument is based, first, on my process of learning across the South, across Turkey and South Africa, and, second, on my analysis of knowledge production at the intersection of the academic and political practices in Turkey since the 1950s.

During my master's and doctoral studies (2003–09), I researched informal economy and labour organizations in South Africa and had the opportunity to work with critically engaged scholars such as Ari Sitas and Edward (Eddie) Webster. I recognized that there was a very valuable production of knowledge in the social sciences in South Africa, which, as a sociologist trained in Turkey, I had not been aware of. I also noticed that the critical structure and studies at universities in South Africa were very similar to the critical tradition in Turkey.

During my postdoctoral research project on the global production and circulation of knowledge in the social sciences (2010–14), I focused on the rising perspectives on Southern sociology in my analysis of the circulation of knowledge between scholars and the labour movement in South Africa in the 1970s and 1980s. I had the opportunity to establish a deeper intellectual relationship with many South African sociologists, such as Sakhela Buhlungu and Karl von Holdt, who have engaged in and contributed to Southern sociology, as well as Michael Burawoy, a central scholar of this globally developing field.

In an article based on this research, I identified critical engagement, political choice, ethical choice and commitment as some of the key characteristics of the engagement of these intellectuals (Çelik, 2013). The Institute for Industrial Education and the *South African Labour Bulletin* played prominent roles in the development of independent trade unions in the 1970s, and based on data collected in November 2011 through in-depth interviews with intellectuals such as Eddie Webster, Johann Maree, John Mawbey and Alec Erwin, I identified critical engagement as the most important characteristic of this intellectual engagement in South Africa. Moreover, with reference to Fischman and McLaren's (2005) concept of the 'committed intellectual', based on the Freireian foundations, I concluded that:

> a (shared) commitment is one of the core dimensions that trivialises the divisions between the traditional and organic intellectuals, in other

words, the university-based intellectuals and activists, and renders possible linking between these two different groups of intellectuals. Hence, the engagement of intellectuals in South Africa and their role in the labour movement can be characterised by their commitment to equality, economic and social justice, by their commitment to emancipation from both class and race oppression and by their ethical and political choice of identifying themselves with the working class. (Çelik 2013: 22; see also Çelik, 2012)

I first presented these ideas in a session of the International Sociological Association (ISA) Research Committee on Labour Movements (RC44) at the second ISA Forum of Sociology, 'Social Justice and Democratization', held in Buenos Aires on 1–4 August 2012, where Michael Burawoy further shared his concept of public sociology with the international sociological community and where Karl von Holdt engaged critically with this concept from a South African perspective.

In the last ten years, I have been committed to developing a sociology across the South by introducing South African sociology to the academic community in Turkey. I have regularly presented papers and organized sessions at social science national congresses as well as giving guest lectures at major universities. My research project titled 'The Development of Turkish Sociology through a Southern Sociology Perspective' enabled me to bring my intention of developing a sociology across the South to the ground through organization of an international workshop with the participation of South African scholars (one of whom was Andries Bezuidenhout, co-editor of this volume). The workshop titled 'Learning Across the South: The Past and Future of Sociology in Turkey and South Africa' was held in 2016 at Mülkiye (the Faculty of Political Sciences) at Ankara University. This enabled the two scholarly communities to take the first step of learning about each other's societies, social sciences, academic and university structures, major publications, research agendas and methodologies.

The culmination of this research was a book titled *Southern Sociology and Sociology in Turkey* (Çelik, 2018). Eddie Webster's (1982) view of social science for liberation and Burawoy's (2010b) Southern sociology perspective in his tribute to Webster were the two particular sources guiding my research. With the backdrop in 2015 of the last phase of peace negotiations between the Turkish state and the Kurdistan Workers' Party (PKK), I introduced readers in Turkey to Ari Sitas' *Ethic of Reconciliation* (2007). This together with Webster's (1982) assessment of contradictory positioning of academics in establishing practical links with organizations outside the university became a central perspective in both my sociological analysis and my own critical engagement in Turkey over the last decade. However, the current political regime in Turkey has curtailed my efforts to build a sociology across the South and has been a hindrance to my academic freedom and career.

Based on this background, I aim to contribute to the perspective of critically engaged sociology derived from the historical and contemporary scholarly and political practices in Turkey. First, I reflect on the critical engagement and positioning of academics in a response to the permanent condition of radical social change in Turkey since the 1950s. Here I argue how this condition differentiates the critical engagement of academics in Turkey from the public sociology perspective. The second aspect underlines the co-production of knowledge by intellectuals inside and outside the university around the debate on the Asiatic mode of production (AMP) and agricultural production that began in the 1960s in Turkey that, on the one hand, uniquely contributed to the development of Southern sociology and, on the other hand, corresponded to political visions divided into camps for a socialist revolution or a national democratic revolution.

Permanent condition of radical social change and positioning of academics

Michael Burawoy's concept of public sociology and his call for 'South Africanizing US Sociology' (Burawoy, 2003) should be appreciated in the sense that it has been an act in good faith to encourage sociologists in the United States to free themselves from their professional cage and engage more with civil society and community movements. In his analyses, while honouring the work of Eddie Webster and his colleagues, he also helped South African sociologists become known globally. However, the limitations of his perspective need to be addressed with regard to both the South African ongoing debate and different aspects and conditions of critical engagement in other parts of the world. Exploring the critical engagement of sociologists and other scholars in Turkey with a focus on the permanent condition of radical social change enables us to present a Southern critique that, as this volume underlines, interrogates the universalization of the notion of public sociology and its prominence as a global campaign.

Alberto Arribas Lozano (2018: 102) points out how Burawoy privileges professional sociology in his plausible try for 'smoother acceptance of the institutionalization of public sociology' in the US and argues that 'he theorizes and promotes public sociology but he does not practise public sociology'. Referring to Lozano (2018), Karl von Holdt (in Chapter 5 of this volume) underlines how Burawoy's perspective 'empties "public sociology" of the radical content that had been integral to critical engagement and liberation sociology'. Different from this view, I believe that Burawoy is well aware of the radical content of South African sociology and does not deliberately dismiss public sociology from this content. As will be shown in the case of Turkey, the main difference is that Burawoy and his colleagues have been conducting sociology in a society with a stable democracy, the rule of law, the autonomy of the university, job security and other civil and social security rights, and therefore, do not need to consider or call for a radical social change. Conversely, critically engaged scholars in Turkey have been doing sociology in a society going through radical social and political change since the 1950s, with an unstable democracy hit by military coups almost every ten years, heavy erosion of the rule of law and non-existent academic freedom. They have been paying high material and psychological costs for their engagement with political and social movements, losing jobs and all civil and social security rights, facing imprisonment and sometimes even losing their lives. Hence, the conditions in which Southern sociologists work and live can be read, understood, appreciated, but definitely not lived by a Northern sociologist! Respectively, the positioning and political and ethical choice of a critically engaged Southern scholar with a commitment to social justice and democracy at large should be understood in relation to this permanent condition of radical social change. Accordingly, knowledge production occurs differently in countries like Turkey, South Africa, Chile and Brazil compared to North America and Europe. Therefore, there will always be a conditional difference between the concepts of critical engagement and public sociology. How this conditional difference of critical engagement with a Southern character reflects also into the theoretical and conceptual sphere will be discussed in the second part of this chapter.

Sari Hanafi argues that for 'many social research[ers] in the Arab World [it is] suffice to understand/describe simply a social phenomenon without connecting it to the political economy and the nature of political choice adopted by the state' (2016: 28). He further states that 'one cannot understand the knowledge production or its current situation by simply delving into a remote past and forgetting how local political subjectivities shaped as well this very production' (Hanafi, 2016: 29). Similar to his analysis, starting with the early historical periods, the permanent radical social and political change, and the political choice of ruling party – the Republican People's Party (CHP) – directly influenced the professional work and positioning of sociologists in Turkey in the late 1940s. The Kemalist doctrine of *halkçılık* (populism – mainly meaning national unity without class conflict) led, on one hand, to the suppression of worker organizations and, on the other hand, to widespread dissatisfaction with the Republican People's Party. This enabled the growth of the opposition party supported by big landowners, conservatives and Islamists. At the same time, the anti-communist policy of the state was becoming more consolidated, probably even earlier than in countries like South Africa. Under these conditions, two prominent sociologists, Behice Boran and Niyazi Berkes, received their PhDs at universities in the United States and in 1939 were appointed to positions in the newly established Department of Sociology at Ankara University. 'They ran a sociology programme that was very new for Turkey. They were not teachers who describe theory, but teachers who focused on social structure analysis' (Çelebi, 2008: 684). (Hereafter, Turkish quotations are translated by the author.)

These two sociologists carried out extensive empirical research on rural social structure in the 1940s, and this disturbed the political power of the period; as a result, both sociologists were expelled from the university in 1948 on the grounds that they were communists. 'Cutting off the developing sociology programme at Ankara University in this way is one of the examples that shows how much the institutionalization of sociology departments at universities in Turkey is influenced by the dominant political structure' (Kasapoğlu, 2005: 546). Berkes went into exile and took a position at McGill University in Canada.

It was true that Behice Boran was a member of the Turkish Communist Party (TKP) and the editor of its journal, *Yurt ve Dünya* (Motherland and World). Losing her academic job, she became an organic intellectual and continued to produce knowledge at the interface of radical sociology and popular movements in Turkey. Boran came to be president of the Barışseverler Cemiyeti (Society for Peace) in 1950. In the same year, the Democrat Party (DP) won the elections under the leadership of Adnan Menderes, who, in contradiction to his liberal ideas, established a more authoritarian and religious regime, similar to that of President Erdoğan in today's Turkey (Karaveli, 2016). When the newly elected government sent troops to fight against the Korean people in the ranks of American imperialism, the Society for Peace protested this decision with a statement that ended up with Boran being imprisoned for 15 months. She was a member of parliament representing the Workers' Party of Turkey in 1965, and she came to be the party's president in 1970. With the military coup of 12 March 1971, the Workers' Party of Turkey disbanded, and Boran was sentenced to 15 years imprisonment. When the Workers' Party of Turkey was banned again by the 1980 military coup, Boran went into exile and was stripped of citizenship.

The growing anti-imperialist student movement ignited the fuse of the military coup on 27 May 1960. Although students and university professors supported the coup and called it a revolution against the authoritarian regime of the Democrat Party, 147 academics were expelled from universities by the (military) National Unity Committee. Nevertheless, this did not sway the commitment of students and intellectuals to the democratization of Turkish society. As Zürcher states, 'the universities had played an important role in toppling Menderes and in formulating the constitution of the second republic. It was only logical therefore that students and teachers began to see themselves as the moving force of the society' (2017: 257–8).

The growth of the left in the 1960s, thanks to a new and more democratic constitution, created a lively debate about emergent social and political issues in the country. On the one hand, leftist journals such as *Yön* (Direction), edited by Doğan Avcıoğlu, formed a rich and broad platform for these intellectual discussions. On the other hand, the launch of *Fikir Kulüpleri* (Idea Clubs, or Debating Societies) by student activists at all major universities – with the support of university professors – acted in a federation to protect the ideals of the unfinished Kemalist Revolution (particularly secularism and anti-imperialism) and to engage with revolutionary projects of that time. Two main projects created their own camps, which later split and multiplied. The Workers' Party of Turkey, led by Mehmet Ali Aybar, maintained the idea of a socialist revolution, as the successful period of import-substituting industrialization in the 1960s enabled the growth of class consciousness and worker organization. The other project, *Milli Demokratik Devrim* (national democratic revolution), led by Mihri Belli and Doğan Avcıoğlu, prioritized the dominance of feudal structures in an Asiatic society that could have only been beaten by state bureaucrats and intellectuals. The latter found a greater voice among the Debating Societies, which became Dev-Genç (Revolutionary Youth) in 1968. These political projects developed parallel to the more academic debates on the historical phase of Turkish society and the analysis of capitalism, feudalism and Asiatic mode of production, which will be elaborated in the second part of this chapter.

The emerging workers protest boycotts at the universities and the escalating clashes between rightist and the leftist students gave rise to the coup of 12 March 1971. Mülkiye (where historically the state bureaucracy and civil servants were educated) and the Middle East Technical University were targeted. The coup dissolved the university senates and expelled tens of academics. The next coup, on 12 September 1980, introduced Martial Law No. 1402 and removed 73 left-wing university faculty members from their posts. Among these were Korkut Boratav from Ankara University and Sencer Divitçioğlu and İdris Küçükömer from Istanbul University. These individuals were well versed in the AMP and produced valuable academic knowledge.

Divitçioğlu was a Marxist economist and historian known for his studies on the Asiatic mode of production. When this critically engaged scholar became a member of the Workers' Party of Turkey, which supported a socialist revolution perspective, he was harshly criticized and excommunicated by the other socialists, the national democratic revolution camp. When he submitted his book *Asya Üretim Tarzı ve Osmanlı Toplumu* (Asiatic Mode of Production and Ottoman Society) (Divitçioğlu, 1971) to the university for promotion to full professorship, he was excluded by his senior colleagues, who rejected his use of Marxist methodology in the historical analysis of the Ottoman society (Koçak, 2014). The decision of the faculty committee to decline his professorship was clearly influenced by the ruling party and its anti-communist policy. He then had to approach the court to receive his professorship and continued his work on Asiatic mode of production.

Küçükömer, a fellow member of the Workers' Party of Turkey and colleague in the same faculty as Divitçioğlu waited ten years to receive his professorship, for the same reasons. In his groundbreaking book *Batılılaşma ve Düzenin Yabancılaşması* (Westernization and the Alienation of Order) (Küçükömer, 2007), he argued that the despotic nature of the state in Turkey was one of the biggest obstacles to the development of civil society. His book engaged in a critique of the dominant political paradigm of the Kemalist state and its centre-left party, the Republican People's Party, as well as of the same tendencies in the national democratic revolution camp. Calling the Turkish left 'reactionary' and therefore 'right' (Küçükömer, 2007) resulted in him being silenced and excluded from the dominant faction of the socialist movement. Hence, both Divitçioğlu's and Küçükömer's standpoints present good examples of critical engagement in the sense that they were committed to the value of their scientific work while distancing themselves from the discipline of the political movement. In other words, they challenged the dominant paradigm in both the political movement and the university.

Military coups and coup attempts continue today. An unsuccessful coup attempt on 15 July 2016 was taken as 'a gift from God' by President Erdoğan to ground his own coup-like action to crack down on all the oppositional forces in the country (Ferhan, 2017). As Miyase İlknur from the newspaper *Cumhuriyet* (Republic) reported:

> after the July 15 coup attempt, the number of faculty members expelled from universities with KHK [emergency decree adopted within the framework of the state of emergency] exceeds 20 times the number of academics eliminated during all periods of the coup. The number of academics disbanded after July 15 approaches five thousand, while the number of academics disbanded during all periods of the coup does not reach 250. (İlknur, 2017)

Korkut Boratav from Ankara University, one of the most influential scholars of Turkish economy and economic history, who I like to call 'the Eddie Webster of Turkey', went through many of these coups and dismissals in his life. After the coup on 12 September 1980, he found refuge in Zimbabwe and taught at the University of Zimbabwe in Harare from 1984 to 1986. Boratav suffered from the anti-communist policy of the state even as a child, when his father, folklorist Pertev Naili Boratav, was expelled from Ankara University together with Behice Boran and Niyazi Berkes. He explained this in an interview after the dismissal of 330 academics by a decree-law in February 2017: 'In 1948 my father was expelled from the University, in 1980 myself, and now my assistants' (cited in Birgün, 2017). In the same interview,

Boratav emphasized the importance of the positioning of academics, similar to what Webster (1982 and in this volume) underlined in the case of South Africa in the 1980s:

> It gets more brutal every period. What's being done now is worse than the coup on September 12, 1980. A lot of my colleagues have problems with their pension rights, these people can't go abroad. Their passports are being taken away. ... What's worse is active collaborators. Active collaborators are more conspicuous. Active collaborating elements of academic circles are more disgraceful during this period. (Cited in Birgün, 2017)

Reminding us of the 'servants of apartheid', in Webster's categorization, Boratav approached the vice chancellor of Ankara University, who had blacklisted the signatories to the petition of the Academics for Peace (stating 'We will not be a party to this crime!'), all of whom were then dismissed by the decree-law. While, at the age of 82, to protect academic freedom and the honour of the university, Boratav was subjected to gas and plastic bullets from police in front of Mülkiye, 'the pragmatic realists' and 'privatists' remained in their offices, avoiding their listed colleagues.

It should be mentioned here that in the case of the Academics for Peace, we can see the importance of the ethical choice of the critically engaged scholar. The petition signed by these scholars – many of whom are internationally known in their academic fields – was directed against the military operation and human rights violations in cities in south-eastern Turkey (with a dense Kurdish population) and demanded the reactivation of the peace process, which started with negotiations between the Turkish state and the Kurdistan Workers' Party in 2013. The Turkish government began a campaign against Academics for Peace, with Erdoğan accusing them of being terrorists. These critically engaged scholars met an 'ethic of reconciliation' (Sitas, 2007) as well as producing excellent academic work. For example, Barış Ünlü (2016, 2018), who was a visiting scholar at the Centre for Diversity Studies at the University of Witwatersrand, produced unique knowledge on the crises of Turkishness concerning the Kurdish struggle. An article by Serdal Bahçe and distinguished economist Ahmet Haşim Köse, 'Social classes and the neo-liberal poverty regime in Turkey, 2002–2011', published in the *Journal of Contemporary Asia* in 2017, was named the best article of the year by the journal.

Making the ever-burning Kurdish question a topic of academic research has always been a challenge for scholars in Turkey. For example, İsmail Beşikçi (1969) showed empirically that Kurds are an ethnic group with their own language, in opposition to the official state ideology calling Kurds '"mountain Turks" who have forgotten their Turkishness' and their mother tongue (Aslan, 2011: 81). For his book *Doğu Anadolu'nun Düzeni – Sosyo/Ekonomik ve Etnik Temeller* (*The Order of East Anatolia – Socio/Economic and Ethnic Foundations*), first published in 1969, he was sentenced to 13 years imprisonment for violating the indivisibility of the Turkish nation after the 1971 coup. Beşikçi, a non-Kurdish critically engaged sociologist, is recognized as one of the founders of Kurdish studies. He defended the rights of the Kurds with his sociological studies and was sentenced to over a hundred years in total. Similarly, Yalçın Küçük – a non-Kurdish political economist, former president of the Debating Societies and an initiator of the Aydınlar Dilekçesi (Intellectuals' Petition) in 1984 – was sentenced overall to two centuries for his criticism of the 1980 coup and his commitment to social justice and the rights of Kurds over four decades. The lively academic and political debate on 'hierarchical imperialism', initiated by Küçük (1992) to explain Turkey's relationship with the Kurdish geography in the Middle East, was expanded by both himself and other writers to the Central Asian discussions between 1992 and 1998.

Before moving to the next part of the chapter, it should be remembered that increased threat of repression in Turkey has current parallels in contested societies like Afghanistan, Brazil, Colombia, Hungary, India, Myanmar and Nicaragua. The Academic Freedom Index, newly established by the Scholars At Risk network and the Global Public Policy Institute, reveals that there has been a remarkable decline in global levels of academic freedom in the last decade (Kinzelbach et al, 2021). This trend raises further questions in our understanding of the dilemmas scholars face and the tendency towards radical sociology that emerges in unstable societies, and probably soon in stable democracies.

Asiatic mode of production debate in Turkey

As the editors underline in this volume, 'critical engagement is conceived as a complete sociological practice involving distinctive processes of knowledge production in partnership with popular movements as well as the development of theory through the interaction between scholarly and political practices' (Chapter 1). Furthermore, the distinction between an academic audience and an external audience, which underlies the concept of public sociology, does not always hold from in the Global South.

An encounter of this kind of critical engagement, and a unique contribution to Southern sociology based on the social analysis of Turkish society (with a historical background of Ottoman social structure), can be demonstrated around the lively debate on the AMP. The agricultural production debate surrounding the AMP has been an example of distinctive co-production of knowledge in scholarly and political circles in Turkey for nearly three decades, starting in the 1960s.

Karl Marx's historical materialism thesis and his Eurocentric approach to transformation in societies such as China and India, through the model of transition from feudalism to capitalism in Europe, was the source of discussions in Turkey, as in many academic circles around the world. The idea of linear social revolution, the model based on European social experience, has been questioned in the analysis of societies outside Europe since the 1960s. The integration of these discussions with the problem of bourgeois and socialist revolutions, on the other hand, has brought academic social thought and political visions into a lively relationship in Turkey.

This historical phase was marked with major debates in both academic and political circles in the 1960s. Along with claims that the bourgeois democratic revolution identified with the Kemalist revolution of 1923 was unfinished by the 1950s, debate intensified about why the transition to a capitalist society, such as in Europe, had not taken place in Turkey and why capitalism had not transformed rural structures in Turkey. The quest to explain the 'difference of Turkey' was the motivating background to these discussions. In a political quest that extends from debates about the class structure of Turkey to the determination of models of social revolution in this period, the number of academic researchers in the field of history has substantially increased, with many academics, intellectuals and politicians to re-examining the Ottoman social structure. Though it was expected that these discussions would focus on sociological class analysis, political and economic analysis has come to the fore.

The different groups of intellectuals taking part in the debate on the AMP are primarily divided on whether Ottoman society was feudal or in line with the AMP. It is crucial to emphasize here that around this debate, knowledge was co-produced at the interface of academic and political practices. Both perspectives were discussed and presented by not only academic intellectuals but also non-academic intellectuals and leaders of political movements. All these different perspectives were published in both academic journals and periodical publications of political parties and movements. Whether Turkey was a feudal society or in line with the AMP had political relevance, especially for the national democratic tevolution. Divisions occurred within this camp notwithstanding whether or not the state (including the army) should be seen as 'a potential ally in a progressive coalition'. The supporters of the AMP thesis argued for a struggle against 'an oppressive state including the armed forces' (Zürcher, 2017: 258–9). When the debate shifted towards a deeper analysis of agricultural production, a division occurred between those advocating a socialist revolution and those in favour of a national democratic revolution.

The Turkish translation of the collective studies on the AMP at the Center for Marxist Studies (CERM) in France by Maurice Godelier in 1969 was followed by Sencer Divitçioğlu's book *Asya Üretim Tarzı ve Osmanlı*

Toplumu (see Divitçioğlu, 1971) in the same year, which can be considered the first milestone in this discussion series. According to Divitçioğlu, the Ottoman social structure fits the Asiatic type. One of the main reasons is that landownership belongs to the state. In feudalism, the main means of production was land. In this context, two classes are mentioned: feudal lords (or seigneurs, the aristocratic class) as the class that holds ownership of the land; and serfs as the class that processes the land and expends labour that reveals the product. In the AMP, as Marx noted, landownership was in the hands of the state. In Ottoman society, likewise, the sultan has absolute control over the land, and since ownership of the land belongs to the state, the fief-fee (*tımar*) owner does not have the freedom to rent out the land to the peasant (Divitçioğlu, 1971). According to Barkan, who was involved in this discussion against Divitçioğlu from the same faculty, the fief-fee owner did not own a property, mainly in relation to the tax taken from the land and what the peasants produced. The right to benefit, on the other hand, is a salary given only in exchange for duties (Barkan, 1980: 805). This coincides with Divitçioğlu's definition of the fief-fee owner as 'an officer of the state' (1971: 54). It was evident to him that the fief-fee owner does not refer to a lord or a land aristocracy based on nobility. Therefore, the economic and legal relations that the peasant was subject to in the Ottoman Empire differed from the conditions that the serf was subject to in European feudalism.

Divitçioğlu's perspective was shared earlier by the critically engaged sociologist Niyazi Berkes (1964), who pointed out the centrality of the Ottoman system ruled by a Sultan and its social structure, which differed from decentralized European feudalism. Taner Timur, a leading political scientist, similarly argued that the Ottoman order had an 'anti-feudal' nature with Eastern despotism (2010: 287–90). Küçükömer (2007) supported the pro–AMP approach with his focus on trade relations, which were not fully integrated into the Ottoman economy.

The AMP was also supported by influential intellectuals outside academia, such as Kemal Tahir, an intellectual novelist who argued in *Devlet Ana* (The Mother State) in 1967 that the *kerim devlet* (generous state) understanding in the Ottoman Empire was a model of the state that was free from class exploitation, merciful, protective and equal, and stressed that feudalism, an exploitative order, cannot be compared to the Ottoman order. Moreover, Mehmet Ali Aybar (1988), founder and first president of the Workers' Party of Turkey, initiated discussions inside and outside the party on the class structure of Turkey and argued that the central Ottoman state cannot be compared to the Western/European feudal state.

In contrast to the AMP, supporters of the feudalism perspective, such as well-known historian Halil Berktay, argued that the character of the Ottoman *reaya* (peasant, subject to the state) coincides strongly with that of the serf in feudalism. He described serfdom as a 'sea of simple production' with its own economic autonomy, but under the rent-collecting aristocracy (Berktay, 1983: 348, 349). The radical sociologist and organic intellectual Behice Boran (1962) focused on the labourer's serf-like dependence on land in the Ottoman system and, for this reason, viewed the Ottoman social structure as a variant of the feudal social order despite its unique characteristics. Doğan Avcıoğlu, a non-academic intellectual and political project leader, suggested that the Ottoman order was similar to feudalism and different from the AMP, as there was a transition towards private ownership over time in the Ottoman Empire, and despite all the legal regulations, there were serious similarities between lord-serf and fief-fee owner (1971: 20). Furthermore, he argued that it was not a question of the mode of production that prevented the transition to capitalism, but the colonization of the Ottoman Empire under Western rule. Avcıoğlu, with his unique approach, created a project of national democratic revolution from all these discussions and considered the cooperation of the national classes necessary.

From 1969 onwards, we can say that the axis of the AMP debate has shifted to agricultural production, with the dominance of debates on unequal development and underdevelopment in Africa and Latin America. Korkut Boratav's two-page article titled 'Tarımda Feodal Üretim İlişkileri, Feodal Kalıntılar ve Basit Meta Üretimi' (Feudal relations of production in agriculture, feudal remnants and petty commodity production) (Boratav, 1969b), in *Emek*, the publication of the Workers' Party of Turkey, triggered two years of heavy discussion on the problem of agriculture in Turkey, which continued to diversify with new works up to the end of the 1980s. Outlining his views in his book on income distribution, published in the same year (Boratov, 1969a), Boratav defined three different relations of production in Turkish agriculture: petty (or simple) commodity production, capitalist production and feudal (or semi-feudal) production. He suggested that the most common of these was petty commodity production. At the same time, he emphasized that petty producers who, aside from production for their own consumption and produce for the market, no longer lose their products to feudal elements; rather, they now lose their products to merchant and usurper capital. This means that petty producers are subject to primitive mechanisms of capitalist exploitation, and it is proof that capitalism in Turkey is 'backwards'. Simple commodity production is basically part of the capitalist distribution relations that operate through the market (Boratav, 1969a). Boratav's article provoked a very rapid reaction and brought on fierce criticism, especially by Muzaffer Erdost in *Aydınlık,* the journal of the national democratic revolution camp. Erdost – a non-academic intellectual and owner of Sol (Left) Publishers, which translated all Marxist classics into Turkish – claimed that the dominant form of production in agriculture in Turkey is still feudal, or semi-feudal, and he repeated this in the same year with a series of articles and books (Erdost, 1969a, 1969b, 1969c, 1969d).

Erdost argued that large landownership, especially in eastern and south-eastern Anatolia, was the dominant element of agricultural production, suggesting that exploitation occurs due to repression and dependency relations provided through the traditional *ağalık* (landownership district) institution. These discussions prevailed until the 1980s and were collected in valuable books by the two authors (Boratav, 1980; Erdost, 1984).

Another important name involved in these discussions is Çağlar Keyder, who takes his point of view from the world-system school of thought. Keyder criticized the application of a unilinear development perspective in the studies on landownership and small peasantry in the Ottoman Empire. He suggested investigating the small peasantry in light of changes led by the growing integration of the world market (Keyder, 1983: 130, 131). In a similar way to Boratav, Keyder argued that a small landownership structure is historically the dominant element in Anatolia, from the past to the present, due to the lack of labour to process the land and the abundance of land that can be processed. When developments of the 1950s spilt over into the 1960s, Keyder asserted that 'the reclaiming of land and its distribution; political favouring of the agricultural sector; the spread of mercantile and communications networks and of new technology contributed to the consolidation of peasant ownership' (1983: 144). Mehmet C. Ecevit (1999) contributed to this debate by examining the importance of household labour capacity in petty commodity production and how it was a critical element of competition in livelihood and market relations for these households.

Boratav and Keyder determined that merchants and usurers contributed to the exploitation of rural producers and argued that the dynamics of confiscation of surplus value occurs in the processes of commodity change. In contrast, Erdost and those who claim that exploitation relations are formed within relationships of commitment imposed by large landownership show that the confiscation process occurs in the relationship of production itself. Consideration of how to combat these relations, which resulted in further impoverishment of people in rural areas, also led to different analyses and revolutionary strategies in the Turkish left movement in the 1960s.

David Seddon and Ronnie Margulies (1984) and Zülküf Aydın (1987), who were instrumental in bringing these discussions to international academic circles, noted that the debate was conducted on two levels: academic and political. Different interpretations of the nature of Turkish agriculture and production and existing class relations in the countryside are closely related to the discussions of the Turkish left about the political strategy that is appropriate to the period and conditions. Boratav's analysis is said to support the thesis that the Socialist Revolution strategy of the Workers' Party of Turkey is possible, while Erdost's approach that feudalism is the dominant form of production drives those who advocate the national democratic revolution thesis. 'The debate on the agricultural problem ultimately – at least in most of the interventions of the parties to the debate – reflects a political commitment as well as a scientific interest in the forms of production and ongoing class relations in the countryside' (Seddon and Margulies, 1984: 3). Aydın noted that 'both Boratav and Erdost established a very clear interest between scientific analysis and political practice in their publications in the first two years of the debate, and in their later writings they did not mention political practice' (1987: 82).

Interestingly, Aydın claimed that neither Boratav nor Erdost say anything new (1987: 83) while also stating, based on the collected works of Boratav in 1980 and Erdost in 1984, that these studies provide a respectful contribution to both the analysis of agricultural structures in the third world and the research on rural Turkey (1987: 82). He specifically continued his criticism of Boratav in the journal *11. Tez* (Thesis 11), which marked the 20th-century Turkish intellectual life. He concluded that 'the views in the discussions on the agricultural problem in Turkey are theoretically weak and empirically unfounded' (Aydın, 1986: 182). According to Aydın, in Boratav's book of 1980, 'the dynamics of the peasant family are concepts taken from Chayanov, the creation of cheap labour of the peasant family from Meillasoux, the residual transfer of the industrial segment from the agricultural segment is also taken from Vergopoulos' (1986: 182).

Boratav's response to Aydın in *11. Tez* excellently summarized what we try to underline in this chapter by connecting critically engaged sociology and Southern sociology. Boratav first highlighted 'the built-in attitude of the international scientific division of labour', by which theory is produced in the West and empirical material is produced in what was referred to as the Third World at the time. Accordingly, 'theoretical contributions that will arise from [researcher's] own country [in the Third World] are not expected and are not taken seriously'. He criticized Aydın's approach as 'a reflection of this general attitude' that wrongly treats Boratav's work as a transfer from the West rather than an original theoretical contribution from the Third World (Boratav, 1987b: 184–5). He then explained further why Aydın's search for the original theoretical knowledge in the work of a Western writer was wrong: 'As can be determined from my references and bibliographies, I have never read Meillasoux. If there are similar results in Meillasoux and Boratav, isn't the search for the source of these common views in the Western writer another reflection of Aydin's attitude, which I have previously criticized?' (Boratav, 1987a: 202).

Boratav's standpoint can be seen as a call for the self-confidence of the Southern scholar, who too is capable of producing theoretical knowledge and who rightfully expects recognition for his/her work from an international community of scholars, but particularly from the local community of scholars, who need to highlight and respect their own country's intellectual heritage.

The lively discussions and exchanges we summarize in this chapter on the problem of agriculture and petty commodity production in Turkey within the framework of underdevelopment or late capitalism give us an idea of what place Turkey takes in Southern sociology in an academic and intellectual sense. Along with the discussion of the AMP, the social structure of Turkey has been covered in depth by many academics, activists, politicians and novelists with a clear focus on their society.

The editors argue in this volume that the fact that the discipline is less institutionalized, or perhaps institutionalized differently, makes our lived experience of the relationship between sociology and other disciplines more fluid than in the US and Europe. In these discussions on the AMP and agricultural production, we can similarly say that the typical disciplinary borders in the social sciences were expanded and that the analyses from sociology, political science and political economy were combined. Although it aimed to analyze the social structure of the 1960s in particular, this analysis turned towards the past: the Ottoman order and social structure were revisited through property and class relations. The diversification of history and the convergence of the fields of sociology and history, in particular, was an important gain of this period. In the practice of sociology, the dominant and established attempts to directly transfer theories and models from Europe and North America to Turkish society were replaced by prioritizing their social analysis. It has been insisted by many authors that the social structure of Turkey (as well as that of the Ottoman Empire) has its own characteristics. One of the original aspects of the discussions in this period was the realization of a serious analysis of state and landownership, which had been done only sparsely before then. In this analysis, the differences of the state structure in the Ottoman Empire from both European feudal structures and those in the East or Asia could be revealed. In this sense, a 'sociology *of* the South', as Burawoy (2010b) calls it, can be seen in the discussions of this period.

Moreover, the exchange of knowledge between academic and non-academic intellectuals has increased markedly. On one hand, academic social knowledge has been produced, and on the other, political and social transformation projects have been discussed. This exchange of knowledge has also been directed inwards to the academic community in Turkey. As can be seen from Boratav's thoughts, for scientific practice in Turkey, there is, at least as much as the interest in theoretical discussions in the North, interest in internal theoretical discussions to follow up different views and offer self-criticism.

One of the reasons for addressing this period here is to go further than the sociology *of* the South and connect this kind of engagement with a sociology *across* the South, which in turn contributes to global sociology. Discussions on agricultural production relations in Turkey and especially petty commodity production have crossed the borders of Turkish academia and politics, and have been translated and conveyed by foreign authors in leading international publications of their era, such as *The Journal of Peasant Studies*. Boratav's work examining the socio-economic structure of his society has contributed simultaneously and directly to the work carried out internationally, not only in an empirical sense but also in relation to theory. It is important to note that Boratav's contribution to the petty commodity production and unequal or underdevelopment analysis were driven by prominent scholars such as Andre Gunder Frank, Samir Amin, Henry Bernstein, R.L. Harris and John Harris. The ensuing analysis of Turkish society was increasingly connected to rising research on Africa and Latin America. In the same way, Keyder argued that in contrast to the Latin American experience, the lack of a dominant landlord class and the continued existence of an independent peasantry had a formative influence on Turkey's political and economic development. Keyder's (1987) work on state and class in Turkey not only contributed to the analysis of peripheral development but also has become a significant part of the world-system school analysis, which has persisted.

Last but not least, as I explained in the first part of the chapter, the conditional difference of critical engagement with a Southern character is reflected also in the theoretical and conceptual sphere. A commitment in society to social justice and democracy finds a place also in the democratizing structures of sociological knowledge production and circulation worldwide. Positioning of academics takes place also within the structures of global sociology. In other words, while these scholars are critically engaged with the hegemonic power structures in their societies, they are also critically engaged with the hegemonic power structures in their scientific fields. Although a more detailed analysis is needed beyond this chapter, it can also be argued that critically engaged sociologists might be more likely than mainstream sociologists to move beyond the theoretical concepts developed by sociologists of the Global North.

Conclusion

In this chapter, I have presented the specific form of sociology that is being discussed in this volume in accordance with the historical, contemporary, scholarly and political practices in Turkey. First, I examined the critical engagement and positioning of academics in response to a permanent condition of radical social change in Turkey since the 1950s. Through discussing historical and contemporary sociologists, such as Behice Boran and Niyazi Berkes in the mid-20th century and the case of Academics for Peace in the 21st century, I explained how scholars have constantly endured hardships, which, I argued, in the final analysis, is what differentiates critical engagement from public sociology. Second, focusing on the debate around the AMP and agricultural production concurrent with revolutionary projects in the 1960s,

I demonstrated that this sociology occurred at an intersection between the sociological and political field in Turkey. These academics not only engaged with social and political issues, but also focused on co-producing high-quality knowledge with other intellectuals outside the university, both in academic and political publications. Their collective knowledge production could not be separated from their shared commitment to social justice and academic freedom. As I showed in the cases of Divitçioğlu, Küçükömer and Boratav, the critically engaged scholars faced contradictions in universities, in their professional activities and the publication landscape, as well in their political activities and the publication spaces therein. Therefore, I argued that this critical engagement and the knowledge produced through it bears, without a doubt, a Southern character. Finally, as I argued elsewhere (Çelik, 2018), this chapter on Turkey informed by the South African experience shows that de-hegemonizing the conceptual battlefield requires not only counter-hegemonic or decolonial sociology, but learning and doing sociology across the South in a more conscious and programmatic way that would give a stronger meaning to the efforts of the authors in this volume.

References

Arribas Lozano, A. (2018) 'Reframing the public sociology debate: Towards a collaborative and decolonial praxis', *Current Sociology*, 66(1): 92–109.

Aslan, S. (2011) 'Everday forms of state power and the Kurds in the early Turkish Republic', *International Journal of Middle East Studies*, 43(1): 75–93.

Avcıoğlu, D. (1971) *Türkiye'nin Düzeni Cilt: 1*, Ankara: Bilgi.

Aybar, M.A. (1988) *Türkiye İşçi Partisi Tarihi I*, İstanbul: BDS Yayınları.

Aydın, Z. (1986) 'Kapitalizm, Tarım Sorunu ve ve Azgelişmiş Ülkeler', *11 Tez*, 3: 171–211.

Aydın, Z. (1987) 'Turkish agrarian debate: New arguments old scores', *New Perspectives on Turkey*, 1: 81–108.

Bahçe, S. and Köse, A.H. (2017) 'Social classes and the neo-liberal poverty regime in Turkey, 2002–2011', *Journal of Contemporary Asia*, 47(4): 575–95.

Barkan, Ö.L. (1980) *Türkiye'de Toprak Meselesi, Toplu Eserler 1*, İstanbul: Gözlem.

Berkes, N. (1964) *The Development of Secularism in Turkey*, Montreal: McGill University.

Berktay, H. (1983) *Kabileden Feodalizme*, İstanbul: Kaynak.

Beşikçi, İ. (1969) *Doğu Anadolu'nun Düzeni – Sosyo/Ekonomik Ve Etnik Temeller*, İstanbul: E Yayınları.

Birgün (2017) 'Korkut Boratav: 1948'de babamı, 1980'de beni, bugün de asistanımı üniversiteden attılar', 8 February. https://www.birgun.net/haber/korkut-boratav-1948-de-babami-1980-de-beni-bugun-de-asistanimi-universiteden-attilar-146210

Boran, B. (1962) 'Metod Açısından Feodalite ve Mülkiyet İlişkileri II: Osmanlılarda Mülkiyet Meselesi', *Yön*, 5: 13.

Boratav, K. (1969a) *Gelir Dağılımı*, İstanbul: Gerçek Yayınevi.

Boratav, K. (1969b) 'Tarımda Feodal Üretim İlişkileri, Feodal Kalıntılar ve Basit Meta Üretimi', *Emek*, 6.

Boratav, K. (1980) *Tarımsal Yapılar ve Kapitalizm*, Ankara: Ankara Üniversitesi SBF Yayınları.

Boratav, K. (1987a) 'Birkaç Son Saptama', *11 Tez*, 5: s-200–s-202.

Boratav, K. (1987b) 'Eski Bir Tartışmanın Yansımaları Üzerine', *11. Tez*, 5: s-182–s-192. İstanbul: Uluslararası Yayıncılık.

Burawoy, M. (2003) 'South Africanizing US sociology', From the Left. http://burawoy.berkeley.edu/PS/Marxist%20Newsletter.pdf

Burawoy, M. (2010a) 'Forging global sociology from below', in S. Patel (ed) *The ISA Handbook of Diverse Sociological Traditions*, London: Sage.

Burawoy, M. (2010b) 'Southern windmill: The life and work of Edward Webster', *Transformation*, 72/73: 1–25.

Çelebi, N. (2008) 'Türkiye'de Sosyoloji Dernekleri: Süreksizliklerin Ardındaki Süreklilik', *Türkiye Araştırmaları Literatür Dergisi*, 6(11): 677–90.

Çelik, E. (2012) *The Role of Intellectuals in the Circulation of Knowledge in the South African Labour Movement, 1970s–1980s*, Second ISA Forum of Sociology, 'Social Justice and Democratization', 1–4 August, Buenos Aires, Argentina.

Çelik, E. (2013) 'The academy and the rest? Intellectual engagements, circulation of knowledge and the labour movement in South Africa, 1970s–1980s', *Transcience, a Journal of Global Studies*, 4(2): 19–35.

Çelik, E. (2018) *Güney Sosyolojisi ve Türkiye'de Sosyoloji*, İstanbul: Notabene.

Comaroff, J. and Comaroff, J.L. (2012) *Theory from the South: Or How Euro-America is Evolving toward Africa*, Boulder, CO: Paradigm Publishers.

Connell, R. (2007) *Southern Theory: The Global Dynamics of Knowledge in Social Science*, Sydney: Allen & Unwin.

de Sousa Santos, B. (2010) 'From the postmodern to the postcolonial – and beyond both', in E.G. Rodríguez, M. Boatca and S. Costa (eds) *Decolonizing European Sociology. Transdisciplinary Approaches*, Farnham: Ashgate, pp 225–42.

de Sousa Santos, B. (2017) 'A new vision of Europe: Learning from the South', in G.K. Bhambra and J. Narayan (eds) *European Cosmopolitanism: Colonial Histories and Postcolonial Societies*, London: Routledge, pp 172–84.

Divitçioğlu, S. (1971) *Asya Üretim Tarzı ve Osmanlı Toplumu* (first published in 1967), İstanbul: Köz.

Ecevit, M.C. (1999) *Kırsal Türkiye'nin Değişim Dinamikleri: Gökçeağaç Köyü Monografisi*, Ankara: T.C. Kültür Bakanlığı Yayınları.

Erdost, M. (1969a) 'Doğu Anadolu'da Hayvancılığın Feodal Niteliği', *Aydınlık Sosyalist Dergi*, 8.

Erdost, M. (1969b) 'Türkiye'de Feodalizm Var Mı?', *Türk Solu*, 80.

Erdost, M. (1969c) *Türkiye Sosyalizmi ve Sosyalizm*, Ankara: Sol Yayınları.

Erdost, M. (1969d) 'Türkiye Tarımında Hâkim Üretim İlişkisi Üzerine', *Aydınlık Sosyalist Dergi*, 8.

Erdost, M. (1984) *Kapitalizm ve Tarım*, Ankara: Onur Yayınları.

Ferhan, M. (2017) 'Gift from God: How Erdogan turned July 15 into windfall'. https://theglobepost.com/2016/12/05/gift-from-god-how-erdogan-turned-july-15-into-windfall/

Fischman, G.E. and McLaren, P. (2005) 'Rethinking critical pedagogy and the Gramscian and Freirean legacies: From organic to committed intellectuals or critical pedagogy, commitment, and praxis', *Cultural Studies/Critical Methodologies*, 5(4): 425–47.

Hanafi, S. (2016) 'Global knowledge production in the social sciences: A critical assessment', *Sociologies in Dialogue*, 2(1): 16–30.

Godelier, M. (1969) *Asya Tipi Üretim Tarzı* (çev. İrvem Keskinoğlu), İstanbul: Ant Yayınları.

İlknur, M. (2017) 'Askeri darbeden beter tablo', Cumhuriyet, 9 February. https://www.cumhuriyet.com.tr/haber/askeri-darbeden-beter-tablo-6735031

Karaveli, H. (2016) 'Erdogan's journey: Conservatism and authoritarianism in Turkey', *Foreign Affairs*, 95(6): 121–30.

Kasapoğlu, A. (2005) 'The study of sociology in Turkish higher education', *International Education Journal*, 6(4): 537–46.

Keyder, Ç. (1983) 'The cycle of sharecropping and the consolidation of small peasant ownership in Turkey', *The Journal of Peasant Studies*, 10(2–3): 130–45.

Keyder, Ç. (1987) *State and Class in Turkey: A Study in Capitalist Development*, London: Verso.

Kinzelbach, K., Saliba, I., Spannagel, J. and Quinn, R. (2021) *Free Universities: Putting the Academic Freedom Index into Action*, Berlin: Global Public Policy Institute.

Koçak, C. (2014) 'Prof. Sencer Divitçioğlu'nun başına gelenler'. https://t24.com.tr/haber/prof-sencer-divitcioglunun-basina-gelenler,271382

Küçük, Y. (1992) *Emperyalist Türkiye*, İstanbul: Başak Yayıncılık.

Küçükömer, İ. (2007) *Batılılaşma ve Düzenin Yabancılaşması* (5th edn), İstanbul: Bağlam Yayıncılık.

Rosa, M.C. (2014) 'Theories of the South: Limits and perspectives of an emergent movement in social sciences', *Current Sociology*, 62(6): 851–67.

Seddon, D. and Margulies, R. (1984) 'The politics of the agrarian question in Turkey: Review of a debate', *The Journal of Peasant Studies*, 11(3): 1–41.

Sitas, A. (2007) *Ethic of Reconciliation*, Durban: Madiba Press.

Tahir, K. (1967) *Devlet Ana*, Ankara: Bilgi Yayınavı.

Timur, T. (2010) Osmanlı Toplumsal Düzeni, Ankara: İmge.

Ünlü, B. (2016) 'The Kurdish struggle and the crisis of the Turkishness contract', *Philosophy and Social Criticism*, 42(4–5): 397–405.

Ünlü, B. (2018) *The Turkishness Contract: Its Formation, Functioning, and Crisis* (in Turkish), Ankara: Dipnot Press.

Webster, E. (1982) 'The state, crisis and the university: The social scientist's dilemma', *Perspectives in Education*, 6(1): 1–14.

Zürcher, E.J. (2017) *Turkey: A Modern History* (4th edn), London: I.B. Tauris.

13

Reflections on Critical Engagement

Michael Burawoy

In 1990 I returned to South Africa for the first time in 22 years. It was the beginning of the end of apartheid; it was the year Mandela walked to freedom. It was also the year Jack Simons, my teacher in Zambia, and Harold Wolpe, my friend from London – both freedom fighters and members of the South African Communist Party, both sociologists of distinction – returned from over 20 years of exile. It was the year I recharged my relations with Edward (Eddie) Webster and met Karl von Holdt for the first time. It was the year Blade Nzimande, later Minister of Higher Education, Science and Technology, and general secretary of the South African Communist Party, invited me to address the Association for Sociology in Southern Africa. The topic was the collapse of communism in Eastern Europe, based on my decade-long research in Hungary.

That year, I came away from South Africa inspired by the engaged research being conducted by sociologists, joined to the struggles against apartheid. It led me to rethink the meaning and potential of sociology. By the end of the 1990s, I was visiting the Society, Work and Politics Institute (SWOP) regularly, working with students, listening to colleagues, trying to understand the fast-moving changes in South Africa. At the same time, I was advancing the idea of 'public sociology' within my own department in the University of California, Berkeley – a challenge to the 'professional sociology' that dominated the discipline in the United States and so different from the 'policy sociology' driven by what had been the party state in the Soviet Union and Eastern Europe, but also from the 'critical sociology' with its origins in Europe, especially in France and Germany. I would take this fourfold scheme back to South Africa, highlighting the changing combination of these four knowledge practices that defined the history of sociology in South Africa.

At first there was interest in being brought within the scope of a scheme that was designed to classify different national sociologies. After all, engagement with 'Northern' knowledge had been the hallmark of Eddie Webster's contributions from *Cast in a Racial Mould* (Webster, 1985) to *Grounding Globalization* (Webster and Bezuidenhout, 2011), as it had been of Karl von Holdt's research on South Africa's triple transition (2003) and his application of Pierre Bourdieu to South Africa (2018). From the beginning, however, there was rising resentment towards my conceptualizing South African sociology from the outside, made all the more infuriating by the South African inspiration behind public sociology. There was mounting resistance to fitting South African sociology into a scheme elaborated in the North. It was made in the United States for the United States, so what was I doing imposing it on South Africa? I was forcing a false universal onto the particularity of South African sociology – another case of the symbolic violence of the global division of knowledge production, backed up by the material and ideological resources of US universities and its 'high-ranking' journals.

If SWOP's first step had been to adapt Northern concepts to the local context, the second step was to challenge Northern hegemony with an alternative 'Southern' hegemony – to regard 'critical engagement' not as a species of public sociology, what I had called organic public sociology, but as an alternative to public sociology tout court. Rather than repeat my effort to represent different national sociologies as different articulations of the four sociologies, I will examine the concept of critical engagement, starting with Eddie Webster's formulation:

> Pressure exists on scholars to make a clear declaration that their research and teaching should be constructed as support for, and on behalf of, particular organizations. To prevent this subordination of intellectual work to the immediate interests of these organization, I prefer the stance of critical engagement. Squaring the circle is never easy, as it involves a difficult combination of commitment to the goals of these movements while being faithful to the evidence, data and your own judgement and conscience. (Webster, 1995: 18)

Critical engagement refers to the contradictory interdependence of social movement actors driven by movement goals and the sympathetic social scientist subscribing to the logic of social science and their own moral judgement, between, as Alain Touraine (1981) once put it, the voice and the eye.

Webster's examples (Chapter 3) are well chosen to illustrate the practice and challenges of critical engagement. In the first case, SWOP collaborated with its sponsor, the National Union of Mineworkers (NUM), conducting research that showed how the mining companies turned a blind eye to the safety of their African miners and how miners collectively developed protective countermeasures. This research was pronounced a success, enthusiastically endorsed by the NUM, contributing to better working conditions for miners and, thereby, increasing support for the union. Science, moral commitment and the interests of the NUM coincided. In the second case, sponsored by an international non-governmental organization concerned with HIV/AIDS[1] prevention, SWOP research angered the NUM for reproducing racist stereotypes of the sexual mores of African miners. The research explained the spread of HIV/AIDS through the proliferation of sexual partners, itself the product of the system of migrant labour, but the research was conducted without consultation with the mining unions. If in the first case, critique was married to engagement, in the second case, critique was divorced from engagement. There is a broader issue here: when sociologists place their cases in a broader context, they often clash with participants or clients, who are focused on immediate interests.

In the HIV/AIDS project, the *research protocols* of the professional sociologist clashed with the interests of the union, whereas in Crispen Chinguno's research, as presented by Karl von Holdt (Chapter 5), it was his *moral judgement* that clashed with the NUM. Chinguno, a graduate student and committed trade unionist, collaborated with the NUM leadership to discover the causes of strike violence on South Africa's platinum belt – violence that would eventually explode in the 2012 Marikana uprising in which 34 workers were killed by the South African police. As his research developed, Chinguno became increasingly sympathetic to the rank and file's charge that the union stifled worker demands and acted as an agent of management. His moral compass turned Chinguno's research against the sponsors of his research; he shifted his engagement from one side to the other. The NUM returned the compliment by labelling him a 'traitor' and blamed him for inciting opposition to the union from its members.

Continuing with platinum mining, Sonwabile Mnwana (Chapter 6) takes us into rural areas to study the struggle over land rights and compensation. He shows how interconnected moral and scientific commitments pose a challenge to engagement. To gain admission to the fieldsite, he had to gain support from the local chief, but to accept the chief's conditions would have meant the end of critique – the chief would have controlled the research. Mnwana's patience and manoeuvring paid off, and the chief and his entourage finally gave him the scientific autonomy he requested. Once immersed in the field, however, he discovered chiefs and mining companies colluding in dispossessing villagers of their land rights – rights that had been bought over a century before. His moral compass turned his sympathy towards the villagers, but the fieldwork disclosed a further complication: some villagers were able to establish their lineage to the original land purchase, while others were not. The result was clashing interests among the villagers. For both moral and scientific reasons, Mnwana refused to take sides or be an expert witness in the legal adjudication, even if this risked alienating one or other or both the village factions. It was a risk he was prepared to take, rather than compromising his moral and scientific stance. Torn between the horns of critical engagement, with some trepidation, he negotiated his way through this minefield.

As sociologists, we tend to engage those communities with whom we have the greatest sympathy, those whose values are likely to be most consonant with our own, but it can still happen that the values of the sociologist and the interests of the community diverge so that no reconciliation is possible. Jacklyn Cock (Chapter 7) describes her research for a just transition to an ecologically sound future. She engaged coal communities only to discover their immediate interests in economic survival make them uninterested in the restriction of fossil fuel consumption. Once again, the broader concerns of the sociologist are at odds with the community. There appeared to be no space for a negotiated rapprochement. Where Cock hangs on to her ecological critique, the participatory action research adopted by Ntokozo Yingwana (Chapter 8) and Brittany Kesselman (Chapter 9) started out by adopting the standpoint of the communities they study; critique was suspended in favour of engagement. Aninka Claassens and Nokwanda Sihlali (Chapter 10) describe how difficult it can be to work back from community engagement to the research community within the university.

These studies, and so many of the studies undertaken by SWOP (see Chapter 2), underline the dilemmas and tensions of critical engagement, but the dilemmas are not confined to SWOP. In a parallel formulation to Webster, Harold Wolpe (1985) argues that committed research takes the goals of the liberation struggle as a point of departure, but then follows its own logic, often coming to conclusions that put him at odds with the movement. He writes: 'In this sense, the priorities defined at the political level became also the priorities of social research. But, and this is the fundamental point which cannot be overemphasized, not as conclusions but as starting points for investigation' (Wolpe, 1985: 75). This got Wolpe into hot water, from those who criticized him for his commitment to the South African Communist Party as well as from those who criticized him for defending his autonomy from the party (Burawoy, 2004).

Critical engagement is not confined to South Africa. Ercüment Çelik (Chapter 12) suggests that critical engagement is a feature of research in countries of the Global South. Beset with unstable democracies and authoritarian regimes, there is a fluidity between academic and public issues and discourses. Political and academic fields are often barely distinguishable and theoretical debates flow through into and around the public arena. Critical engagement is part and parcel of everyday life. Still, we can say that critical engagement is hardly confined to the South. For example, it is central to the sociology of Alain Touraine (1988) and his French colleagues, who engage the leaders of social movements in the co-production of knowledge with a view to raising their consciousness through the infusion of sociological insights. We can see a similar critical engagement defining the public sociology of the Community of Research on Excellence for All in Barcelona (Soler-Gallart, 2017), led by Ramón Flecha and Marta Soler. In the United States, there are institutions similar to SWOP, such as the Labor Studies Department at CUNY (the City University of New York), chaired by Ruth Milkman, or the Center for Urban Research and Learning at Loyola University Chicago, led for many years by Phil Nyden (Nyden et al, 2012).

An acute tension between autonomy and engagement runs through the case studies brought together under the title of *Precarious Engagements* (Burawoy, 2014). It is present in César Rodriguez-Garavito's defence of the rights of indigenous peoples in the face of paramilitary and guerrilla violence in Colombia; in Nandini Sundar's defence of indigenous groups in India, caught between state-sponsored vigilante groups and left-wing Maoist guerrillas; in Karl von Holdt's recounting of research into the struggle between a new black administrative elite and largely white professionals in the reconstruction of a major hospital in post-apartheid South Africa; in Sari Hanafi's defence of Palestinian refugees' right to work against the interests of both the Lebanese governing authorities and the Palestinian leaders for whom integration threatened the 'right of return'; in Pun Ngai et al's exposure of the conditions of work at the huge Chinese factories of the Taiwanese corporation FoxConn, which manufactured Apple's iPhone; in Fran Piven's strategic analysis of the Occupy movement in New York, based on her idea of 'interdependent power'; in Ramon Flecha and Marta Soler's use of 'communicative methodology' to develop new forms of democracy within Romani barrios in Barcelona; in Michel Wieviorka's sociological intervention, attempting to unseat or weaken deeply held prejudices of racism and anti-Semitism in France through the engagement of militants of right-wing social movements; in Anna Temkina and Elena Zdravomyslova's troubled account of the trajectory of gender studies in the face of patriarchal authoritarianism, led by the Russian Orthodox Church; and in Walden Bello's breaking into the World Bank for confidential documents detailing the collaboration between the Marcos dictatorship and the World Bank – documents that became the basis of a book that contributed to the downfall of the regime.

These are dramatic cases of sociological intervention at the intersection of *two or more fields* – the intersection of the academic field with the political, the economic, the media and so on. But critical engagement also operates at a more mundane level, most obviously in the practice of ethnography, where the scientist enters the world of the subject(s) and is, therefore, accountable to those subjects while trying to remain morally and scientifically erect. As the literature on participant observation demonstrates, there is a range of responses to the dilemma. From the side of 'engagement' one can choose between overt and covert participation, between being a fly on the wall and 'going native'. From the side of 'critique', there are variations too: some assume theory springs spontaneously from the data, while others pursue the reconstruction of pre-existing theory. In the ethnographic vision, then, critical engagement lies at the intersection of *two dialogues* – between theory and data on the one hand and between participant and observer on the other.

We can go further to say that critical engagement increasingly captures the more general dilemma of all social science, that of participating in the world we study. We can pretend to hide behind the walls of academia, placing ourselves on a pedestal of objectivity, but social forces swarm around and overflow its ramparts, making it ever more difficult to defend autonomy and to deny that one has a position, even if it is a position 'on our own side'. Alternatively, we can accept our fate and directly engage the very world we study. In so many countries of the South, including South Africa, the university has not the symbolic, political or material resources to withstand insurgencies from within as well as without. In these circumstances, it is difficult to maintain any autonomous research, as Julián (Chapter 11) describes for his institute in Chile. Even in the richest countries with established traditions of academic freedom and autonomy, the illusion of objectivity, of some sort of outsider, non-engaged position, is ever more difficult to sustain as the storm of capitalism commodifies the production and dissemination of knowledge. In short, critical engagement becomes the defining and underlying posture of all social science – it is necessarily 'engaged', and so it has also to be 'critical'; the researcher is at once insider and outsider, both outsider within and insider without. We can distinguish, therefore, two stances in the production of knowledge: critical engagement founded on the postulate that we are part of the world we study and positivist objectivity founded on the assumption we are outside the world we study. Each has its own challenges and paradoxes (Burawoy, 1998).

So what then can we make of the idea of Southern sociology? Is there a Southern sociology, demarcated from a Northern sociology – two sciences, one based on critical engagement and the other based on positivist objectivity. Let us think in terms of fields, as von Holdt suggests. If sociology is a field of domination, is that field national, regional or global? Historically, South African sociology operated within a national container, very much a product of the enclosed and opposed political fields of apartheid. There was a relatively clear demarcation between apartheid and anti-apartheid sociologies. The question of whose side we are on was stark. Today, polarization within sociology is weaker, but at the same time, as Sakhela Buhlungu (Chapter 4) shows, the divide between sociologists and their erstwhile allies in civil society has widened. Trade union leaders have less use for and less trust in sociology, especially if they have their own research establishments. In this context, it is not surprising that sociologists might seek linkages with sociologists in other parts of the Global South, leading to the imagination of a Southern sociology. What is the common interest – moral or scientific – that brings together sociologists from Brazil, China, Russia, South Africa? How homogeneous is this emergent Southern field – what role do smaller nations, satellites of these great nations, play in this Southern field? Are we witnessing a collaboration among leading cosmopolitan sociologists, conversant in English, coalescing into a Southern bloc?

What is the nature of the collaboration across national boundaries? Webster et al (2011) offer a rare instance of collaboration around strategies to contest international capital in the white goods industry involving Australia, South Africa and South Korea. That is indeed stretching critical engagement across national boundaries. Alternatively, as von Holdt suggests in his conclusion, one can seek to develop a 'whole' sociology, including theoretical perspectives that will substantiate a *Southern* perspective. Does this whole sociology involve more than critical engagement? Is there more to sociology than critical engagement? Does not the idea of 'critique' in critical engagement imply some sort of autonomous 'theoretical practice', as Louis Althusser once called it? When members of SWOP package their research for academic journals, as they do with increasing frequency, is this work still *part of* critical engagement or is it scientific work *based on* critical engagement? Is knowledge only produced in projects of critical engagement? Is the work of constructing this book and its critique of public sociology reducible to critical engagement? Can any version of Southern sociology leave the development of abstract theory – starting with succinct formulation of the results of research, leading to generalizations – to academics in the North? Or does 'theory' spontaneously arise from critical engagement? Can we stretch the meaning of engagement to the criticism of existing bodies of social thought, especially dominant bodies of social thought? What, then, does engagement mean?

If we talk of Southern sociology, then we must also talk of Northern sociology. What is the basis of demarcation? Are there two sociologies: Southern and Northern? Or is there a single global sociological field bound together by the hegemony of the North? Is it not the case that many of the criticisms of Northern sociology originate in and develop in the North – whether they be feminist, critical race theory, decolonial, postcolonial. Are they different from the criticisms developed in the South? If there is a distinctive Southern sociology, what are its theoretical and conceptual underpinnings? Reading the contributions to this volume, I am struck how the framing of the projects share so many concepts and concerns of US sociology.

In his conclusion, von Holdt claims that there is a Southern sociology that is 'counter-hegemonic' to the dominant sociology of the Global North. What should we mean by 'counter-hegemonic'? Antonio Gramsci, the originator of the theory of hegemony, never used the term 'counter-hegemonic', arguing that most struggles are on the terrain of hegemony as defined by a dominant group – that the dominant group sets the terms of struggle. The concept of field captures the same idea – that conflicts are played out in terms of the underlying values and principles that define the field. To speak of counter-hegemony is to speak of an alternative hegemony, an alternative field that offers a set of assumptions and defining values fundamentally different from the dominant hegemony. In the field of sociology, that claim is usually made on behalf of an 'indigenous' sociology that springs not from the academy but from the people themselves and which rejects the conventions of science and modernity. Can there be an alternative hegemony that revolves around the idea of critical engagement?

The criticisms levelled against my notion of public sociology in this volume have been frequently voiced in the United States, but I don't believe the latter have been as successful as sociologists of the South, SWOP in particular, in developing the alternative practice of critical engagement. Whether the distinctiveness of Southern sociology be due to unstable democracies, authoritarian regimes, overlapping political and academic fields, I believe that the North is following the South. As North and South face common problems of increasing inequality, pandemics, global warming, precarious migration and refugees, finance capital, so critical engagement has to become the defining trope of sociology globally – that is, if sociology wants to maintain its relevance. This applies not just to sociology, but all the social sciences. Even economics is developing a new consciousness of the threats to planetary existence, sceptical that markets are a universal panacea. Under the rubric of critical engagement, founded on the awareness that we are part of the world we study, social science not only shifts its priorities towards communities of suffering, but also traces the source of that suffering to the global forces of capitalism. As Wiebke Keim (2011) puts it, SWOP has advanced an engaged sociology that the world badly needs and which has to spread to other countries in the North as well as the South. That was what I meant when I spoke of the South Africanization of US sociology!

Note
[1]   Human immunodeficiency virus/acquired immune deficiency syndrome.

References

Burawoy, M. (1998) 'The Extended Case Method', *Sociological Theory*, 16(1): 4–33.

Burawoy, M. (2004) 'From liberation to reconstruction: Theory & practice in the life of Harold Wolpe', *Review of African Political Economy*, 31(102): 657–675.

Burawoy, M. (ed) (2014) *Precarious Engagements: Combat in the Realm of Public Sociology*, Current Sociology, 62(2), Monograph 1.

Keim, W. (2011) 'Counterhegemonic currents and internationalization of sociology: Theoretical reflections and an empirical example', *International Sociology*, 26(1): 123–45.

Nyden, P., Hossfeld, L. and Nyden, G. (2012) *Public Sociology: Research, Action and Change*, Thousand Oakes, CA: Sage Publications.

Soler-Gallart, M. (2017) *Achieving Social Impact: Sociology in the Public Sphere*, Cham, Switzerland: Springer Press.

Touraine, A. (1981) *The Voice and the Eye: An Analysis of Social Movements*, Cambridge: Cambridge University Press.

Touraine, A. (1988) *Return of the Actor: Social Theory in Postindustrial Society*, Minneapolis: University of Minnesota Press.

von Holdt, K. (2003) *Transition from Below: Forging Trade Unionism and Workplace Change in South Africa*, Durban: University of KwaZulu Natal Press.

von Holdt, K. (2018) 'Reading Bourdieu in South Africa: Order Meets Disorder', in J. Sallaz and T. Medvetz (eds) *The Oxford Handbook of Pierre Bourdieu*, New York: Oxford University Press, pp 105–28.

Webster, E. (1985) *Cast in a Racial Mould: Labour Process and Trade Unionism in the Foundries*, Randburg, South Africa: Raven Press.

Webster, E. (1995) 'Taking labour seriously: Sociology and labour in South Africa', in A. Van der Merwe (ed) *Industrial Sociology: A South African Perspective*, Johannesburg: Lexicon Publishers, pp 1–27.

Webster, E., Lambert, R. and Bezuidenhout, A. (2011) *Grounding Globalization: Labour in the Age of Insecurity*, London: John Wiley and Sons.

Wolpe, H. (1985) 'The liberation struggle and research', *Review of African Political Economy*, 32: 72–8.

14

Conclusion: Towards a Southern Sociology

Karl von Holdt

This book is animated by three big questions. First, in what way does critical engagement represent a *Southern* sociology that is both scholarly and politically engaged, as we claim? Second, does critical engagement constitute a *whole* sociology, in that it engages in knowledge production and theoretical innovation, not only the dissemination of academic knowledge to non-academic publics? Third, does it constitute a *counter-hegemonic* sociology in relation to the dominant sociology of the Global North? In order to illuminate these questions, we asked each of our contributors to concentrate their attention on the processes of knowledge production in their chapters, and in particular on the interplay between the production of political knowledge and the production of scholarly knowledge. In the conclusion, I discuss each of our three questions in turn.

Southern sociology

In considering this question, I concentrate on the chapters that reflect on the Society, Work and Politics Institute (SWOP) experience together with the chapters on the Chilean project and Turkish sociology. These chapters present three case studies: a young research entity engaged with precarious labour and indigenous communities in southern Chile; radical sociology in Turkey from the 1950s to the 1990s; and the four-decades-old SWOP in South Africa.

From these cases, we can draw out certain key features which distinguish critical engagement. In all three, the political environment is defined by an oppressive and repressive regime (even if a democracy), by political instability and violence, and by resistance by significant social forces – what Çelik (in this volume) describes as 'a permanent condition of radical social change' characterized by regular military coups and a variety of popular resistance movements. Chilean social reality in the region where Julián is based has been shaped by more than a century and a half of wars and policies of dispossession, and civil society has been deeply scarred by the Pinochet coup and counter-revolution against the socialist revolution which brought Allende to power 50 years ago, and by the precarious work and life of savage neoliberalism. Resurgent mass protests over the last few years suggest ongoing instability and struggle for radical social change. In South Africa, critical engagement arose in the struggle against apartheid – in the case of SWOP, the struggles of the labour movement – and it re-emerges in the struggles of the marginalized and dispossessed communities in a democracy characterized by vast inequalities and exclusion. In these conditions, unlike 'public sociology', critical engagement seeks radical social change, allies itself with the social forces for change and engages in a critique of the official or licenced sociology that supports the regime.

Çelik, Julián, Webster and Buhlungu all agree that this context requires of those scholars who practise critical engagement strong value commitment to social justice, equality and democracy, and it brings the necessity to choose sides, as Webster puts it, in the struggle for social change against an unjust regime. One might add that personal courage is also a requirement in the face of political hostility and, at best, an unsympathetic university. While these sociologists choose sides, they are working in a highly charged and conflictual environment, and they are well aware of the intellectual costs of subordinating themselves to the factional demands of the subaltern organizations with which and for which they conduct research; hence the concept of critical engagement, which stresses the critical independence and scholarly ethics of the university-based researcher.

Working with oppositional forces, including militant trade unions or social movements, and radical political parties and liberation movements, generates tensions and contradictions for the university-based intellectual who 'chooses sides' for emancipation or liberation. From the popular movements, there may be incomprehension about academics and what they may be able to offer, as Julián points out, or even positive distrust or hostility. On the other hand, the critically engaged academic may experience prejudice or hostility in the university – for example, Çelik shows how providing intellectual support for a radical minority may attract academic victimization. Indeed, both Çelik and Julián pay a high personal price for their political engagement – Çelik was forced to flee Turkey and return to Germany in the face of the systematic academic repression of the Erdoğan regime, while Julián was fired and his unit was closed down, and he had to seek refuge in another university.

The South African chapters provide the most sustained examination of such contradictions. Webster explores the tension produced by the racial identity of white academics in the context of apartheid, where they are researching highly sensitive sexual practices among the members of a trade union organizing black workers and led by black officials. Buhlungu, a black trade unionist for most of the 1980s before he returned to his studies, joining SWOP and pursuing a PhD, presents a more critical account of the limitations and contradictory positions of the white intellectuals who forged the practice of critical engagement and, he argues, tended to have a two-dimensional view of black workers, towards whom they displayed a patronizing and didactic attitude. The strength of his chapter rests on his account of the growing power and assertiveness of the labour movement and its increasing capacity to develop its own voice rather than rely on white academics or activists, which substantially transformed the relationships entailed in critical engagement.

Thus Buhlungu argues that trade union members often appropriated what they were taught by white academics and activists, giving terms or ideas new meanings that were more appropriate to their lives and histories, and forcing the former to revise their strategies and thinking. By the late 1980s, the general secretary of the Congress of South African Trade Unions (COSATU) was welcoming support from university intellectuals, but warned that 'we have generated a working class leadership that is competent enough to debate its position and to direct the movement itself' (Naidoo, cited in the chapter by Buhlungu). With the transition to democracy, COSATU turned to its political allies, the African National Congress and the South African Communist Party, as well as to its own research institute, the National Labour and Economic Development Institute, rather than to academics, for theory, strategies and research. Thus Buhlungu predicts the end of critical engagement as well as the broader field of labour studies, as academics retreated from labour and turned to new questions regarding the state, democracy and development and, at the same time, it became increasingly difficult to recruit new students, particularly the growing cohort of black students, to the study of labour.

While the critical engagement with labour, and the discipline of labour studies, did decline for a few years, SWOP continued conducting research for some of the trade unions in the COSATU fold, and by the 2010s a new generation of black students was conducting innovative and searching studies of the labour movement and workplace change. However, as Bezuidenhout and von Holdt (Chapter 2) and von Holdt (Chapter 5) show, the symbiotic and mutually rewarding research characteristic of critical engagement reached an impasse with the Marikana strikes and massacre, which highlighted the institutionalization and decay of the labour movement in democratic conditions. Labour studies has continued to develop, but minus the critical engagement that used to underpin it; indeed, critical engagement has moved on to different struggles, as several chapters show.

But to reiterate: Buhlungu's article reveals an important truth, one too often elided in the sometimes inflated accounts by academics of their own impact on the world – that is, the agency and autonomy of the movements concerned, which are increasingly able (as Arribas Lozano, 2018, points out) to speak back to the would-be academic researcher and insist on a more equal partnership defined by both parties.

As pointed out by Çelik here, to speak of Southern sociology requires that we think about 'South' – which is to say, about the relationship between countries and scholars in the Global South, and their relations to scholars in the Global North. In all three of our case studies, the relationship between North and South has been important in the evolution of a Southern critical engagement. Çelik shows how Turkish sociologists studied in the North before returning home and forging an indigenous sociology there, mostly through challenging the Eurocentrism of the prevailing versions of Marxism; however, they are sometimes forced to return to the North when exiled by repression. Çelik himself exemplifies a rare process in that he undertakes his postgraduate research in South Africa, where he encounters critical engagement as idea and practice, continues his studies in Germany and then returns to Turkey committed to forging closer understanding between Turkish and South African radical sociology. Nonetheless, he too falls victim to the repressive turn and has to return to Germany.

Julián's path to South Africa takes a more complicated route. He undertakes his PhD at a research institute in Germany (with which SWOP also has ties), where he meets Michael Burawoy and is inspired by the idea of public sociology. He then meets Edward (Eddie) Webster, from whom he learns about SWOP in South Africa. On his return to Chile, he sets up a project which resembles the origins of SWOP, and then he travels across the Atlantic to Johannesburg to learn more about SWOP's work.

In the case of SWOP, this entire volume provides a critical reflection on four decades of concept formation in the intellectual exchanges between Michael Burawoy and Eddie Webster, and then with new generations of SWOP scholars. Von Holdt tracks the origins of a reflexive practice of critical engagement in South Africa, which inspires the development of new theory in the United States (public sociology), and the way this displaces South African theorization of its own practices. Ultimately this is placed back on the agenda by Alberto Arribas Lozano, a Spanish postdoctoral fellow with extensive experience of Latin America, who presents a decolonial critique of public sociology while based at SWOP (Arribas Lozano, 2018), which is widely read globally and stimulates new theoretical work in SWOP – of which this book is the fruit. This case presents a complex set of exchanges along both North–South and South–South axes.

Thus, in all three cases, we see the varied paths through which ideas circulate in the Global South, involving a process of dialogue and dependence on the Northern centres of sociological production as well as a mix of both deliberate and contingent encounters across the South, in some cases brokered through the North and in other cases independent. These pathways suggest both the productiveness of South–South encounters and the continuing power of the Global North as a sociological resource and as a broker for the formation of scholars in the Global South, and the way this inevitably shapes the formation of sociology in the South, making it a complex task to forge and even define a genuinely Southern sociology.[1] As a corrective to this, Çelik proposes a conscious attempt to forge sociology across the South, learning from each other's innovations and impasses.

The whole sociology of critical engagement

This brings us to the second of our three questions – concerning *a whole sociology*. In this section, we consider again the chapters on SWOP and Chile and Turkey. Bezuidenhout and von Holdt present a narrative of the development and changing focus of SWOP's research and engagement with theory, thus illustrating the way knowledge production entailed complex interactions between researchers and movements, as well as engagements with social theory, and the generation of both political and scholarly knowledge.

Webster demonstrates how the sociological practice of critical engagement developed in the 1980s, showing clearly how sociological knowledge is translated into political knowledge in the field of labour struggles in the case of SWOP's research into mining health and safety, empowering the union to strengthen its struggles for a greater voice in the workplace. In his second case, where sociological research revealed fertile conditions for the spread of HIV/AIDS[2] in migrant worker hostels, there is a failure to translate this into political knowledge that has symbolic power in the political field – largely because of the failure to involve the union in any kind of co-production of knowledge. The union leadership rejected the research as racist, reinforcing Buhlungu's point about the agency of working-class movements. This in turn made it easier for management to dismiss the findings out of hand.

Von Holdt argues that the practice of critical engagement in SWOP constituted a whole sociology, involving the production of both sociological knowledge and political knowledge – that is, knowledge that has meaning in a political field constituted by the struggle between dominant forces in society and the forces of resistance. It is therefore a sociology which produces complex knowledge, including conceptual innovation and the making of theory that tends to involve critique not only of systems of domination in society but also of the dominant sociology in the scholarly field. In this, it is profoundly different from public sociology, conceived of as the engagement with publics beyond the university while the production of knowledge occurs elsewhere, in professional and critical sociology.

In the case of Turkey, Çelik also argues that the practice of critical engagement constitutes a whole sociology, engaging politically, producing innovative theory and conducting research. In contrast to SWOP's granular ethnographic research into workplace relations and practices, Çelik describes scholarly research and engagement with very large questions regarding the historical mode of production in Turkey and the social structures of contemporary agricultural production – all of which had acute implications for political orientation and strategy on the left and emerged in the context of a continuing process of exchange between scholars and activists. This research was theoretically innovative and sophisticated, constituting Turkey as a site of theoretical production which was influential in both Latin America and Africa. Here too we see critical engagement operating as a whole sociology – producing new knowledge through research that is theoretically powerful and politically engaged, constituting an impressive Southern sociology.

Julián describes both the struggles to establish a project based in the contemporary Chilean university and working with the unions weakened by the coup in 1970 and the subsequent neoliberal onslaught. He also describes a whole sociology emerging at the interface between the political and scholarly fields and concerned with research, teaching and developing an analysis and the attendant concepts adequate for the entirely new reality of precarious work and precarious life. While the theoretical work is in its infancy, his chapter is rich with observations that point in the direction of conceptual innovation; one of the most interesting of these is the discovery that the aspiration for security and dignity still animates the precarious workers and their equally tenuous organization, pointing towards the basis for wider alliances with social movements. However, the very tenuousness of the organizations and the immense pressures confronting workers make it extremely difficult to sustain the relationship between the academic and the political field. It is clear that this project is at the beginning of a long struggle, like that of the left-wing academics who began working with the trade unions in South Africa in the 1970s – although, if anything, they face even more daunting circumstances.

Knowledge production and 'whole sociology'

Here we continue with our interrogation of the extent to which critical engagement constitutes a *whole sociology*, but focusing specifically on the question of *knowledge production*. This is done through reflecting on the accounts presented in a diverse range of South African case studies. We explore in each case the production of two quite distinct forms of knowledge – scholarly knowledge and political knowledge. It is necessary that each of these knowledges find recognition in its specific field.

Each of the chapters considered here takes up a somewhat different position on navigating the interface between academic and political fields, and on the production of knowledge specific to them. At the one end of the spectrum, Sonwabile Mnwana and Jacklyn Cock, in their chapters, explicitly approached their research as academics committed to the production of scholarly knowledge in their institution and, at the same time, committed to producing political knowledge that will empower subaltern groupings in contesting the various oppressive spaces in which they find themselves. At the other end of the spectrum are the chapters by Ntokozo Yingwana, Brittany Kesselman, and Aninka Claassens and Nokwanda Sihlali, where the emphasis is on the activist role of the researcher – perhaps it can be said that their primary identification is as activists in the political field concerned to support the struggle for social change, while their position in the academic field affords them a vantage point from which to produce particularly powerful political knowledge because of the degree of autonomy and scholarly rigour it imparts to their work. Each of the positions occupied by the authors of these chapters is, of course, a quite specific combination of the role of scholar and activist, and each exemplifies the tensions intrinsic to critical engagement in quite specific ways, with fascinating resonances across different experiences.

To start with Mnwana, the autonomy of the scholarly researcher is quite crucial, not only to his ability to achieve the necessary scholarly rigour, but also to his ability to navigate the political field – which is actually two distinct political fields, that of village and chiefly power, and the legal field. He faces numerous attempts to capture his allegiance, not only in relation to the dominant powers, but also in the process of contestation between local networks and powerholders among the subalterns. Each of the powerholders recognizes the power of the external academic researcher to amplify their own voice and lend authority to their particular narrative. Mnwana in turn engages in a long-term struggle to negotiate his autonomy and to demonstrate to his interlocutors that they all stand to benefit from this as it will provide them with the depth and nuance of knowledge that will ensure authority. Over the years of his research visits, many of them come to realize the force of his argument.

At the same time, he is able to demonstrate his commitment to engagement with the villagers so that they are able to trust in his integrity and his commitment to social justice. This integrity is also demonstrated in his refusal to provide an affidavit for a court strategy that will divide the villagers and favour some over others. Thus he remains true to his findings. The knowledge produced out of this process of interaction and autonomy is particularly rich and indeed unique, and as such it provides a crucial piece of evidence in the Constitutional Court case that ultimately decides in favour of the villagers (see also the chapter by von Holdt and the chapter by Claassens and Sihlali for a further description of this watershed case). The paradoxical nature of political knowledge in the legal field is demonstrated in this case study: not only does the knowledge produced by scholarship have to be interpreted and translated into the necessary form for a legal intervention, but it also gains its symbolic power in the legal field precisely from the fact that it is academically rigorous scholarship – that is, it is academic knowledge. Here we see the symbolic power of the academic field to provide influential evidence in the legal field. In other political fields, academic knowledge may have the opposite impact, conveying negative symbolic power as 'merely academic' and out of touch; this is not infrequently the case with academic knowledge in the trade union field, as the chapters by Buhlungu, Webster and von Holdt show.

If Mnwana's chapter demonstrates the necessity of the critical autonomy leg of critical engagement when conducting research in power-laden and highly conflictual social realities, Jacklyn Cock demonstrates the necessity for the social engagement leg of critical engagement in the production of new knowledge that explains the weakness of resistance to coal both among trade union members and in the communities affected by the dispossession and toxic pollution of coal mining. The co-production of knowledge with poor and dependent communities is essential in order to understand the deep ambivalence towards coal mining and the ambiguity of popular struggle against the coal mining companies. Thus, in the first of her studies, she undertakes a classical project of imparting sociological knowledge (understood as the translation of a Northern concept to a Southern context) to trade unionists; this knowledge is about the threat to humanity posed by climate change and the need to terminate coal mining. This project remained ineffective, as did Webster's similarly constituted project on HIV/AIDS. In contrast, Cock's second project involves a genuinely open mind to the experiences and dilemmas of mining communities in order to understand their choices. This process gives rise to new knowledge that deepens Cock's academic analysis; while it may prove to be empowering for these communities and their resistance, it is not yet political knowledge in that there is no actively constituted movement which can recognize it as such.

Yingwana approaches her research on sex workers and feminism from the point of view of an activist who has seen the academic appropriation and production of knowledge which ends up failing to assist sex workers in their struggle for change, and as someone who understands the necessity for the sex workers to define and own their research. She adopts a feminist participatory action research methodology in order to facilitate co-production of knowledge, and she manages the tension within the role of scholar activist by adopting the stance of 'conscious partiality' to ensure a critical and reflexive conceptual distance from her role as an activist. Creative techniques enable sex workers from different African countries and with different languages to communicate with each other as they explore complex issues regarding the relationship between feminism and sex work. Ultimately, this process produced a potent political knowledge through which participants were empowered to work out a collective definition of what it means to be an African feminist sex worker, and to develop the confidence to engage with mainstream feminists in activist, academic and media forums. Simultaneously, the process produced new scholarly knowledge which 'contributes to expanding sociological understandings of feminism and women's rights into challenging, uncomfortable and stigmatized domains of women's lives' (see Yingwana, this volume).

Kesselman also adopts a participatory action research methodology in order to understand the nature of food injustice in the city of Johannesburg and to assist in building and strengthening a food justice movement. However, she encounters a fundamental problem: there is no food justice movement with which to engage, and her research with urban food gardeners as well as with participants in an urban skills training project finds that while participants are interested in what she can teach them about nutrition and the availability of nutritious food, they are not particularly interested in participating in a movement. The problem Kesselman confronts here as a scholar activist resembles that confronting Cock in her attempts to work with a mass environmental movement against coal mining: such a movement does not exist. What becomes of critical engagement or participatory action research in this situation?

Kesselman and Cock adopt similar solutions: in line with their commitment to co-production of knowledge, they pursue a series of engagement workshops, an interaction which allows for mutual learning together with participants from marginalized communities. The scholar is able to present new information regarding a profound social problem while at the same time learning more about the nuances and complexities in the existential experience of community participants. The result is a recasting of sociological knowledge and the formation of new social knowledge in the community. Whether or not this becomes political knowledge depends on whether any of the participants gravitate towards non-government organizations or incipient movements that may be present in their neighbourhoods.

Like Yingwana and Kesselman, Claassens and Sihlali approach their research process as activist scholars, perhaps primarily as activists. Their research centre, the Land and Rural Accountability Centre (LARC), differs from SWOP, whose primary mandate as a research institute is to produce high-quality scholarly research; LARC's mandate is, rather, to 'assist rural citizens in struggles to hold leaders to account and secure their rights to land and other natural resources', and to use research, mobilization and litigation to this end. The co-production of knowledge with communities is intrinsic to their method, and the fundamental forum for this is the community workshop – again reminiscent of the methods used by Kesselman and Cock – where community members voice their experiences and struggles over the land and new laws that strengthen the control of the chiefs over land and life. New knowledge is continuously produced through these interactions and forms the basis of fact sheets and briefs used in the villages as well as submissions to parliament and affidavits used in litigation. All of these constitute diverse forms of political knowledge focused on different political arenas – communities, parliament and courts – and all of these are vigorously tested and contested in those arenas. This, they argue, amounts to a tougher process of assessment and verification than the typical academic peer review. But while such briefs, submissions and affidavits are accepted as publications demonstrating credible and rigorous expertise in these various forums, they are prevented from recognition as scholarly knowledge in the university system of accreditation, which is an issue that stunts the careers of young researchers in particular.

Unlike all our other researchers who stress the innovative nature of the scholarly knowledge produced alongside the political knowledge produced through critical engagement with social movements, Claassens and Sihlali argue that the particular nature of the political knowledge they produce – which generates new political and legal concepts and policies – means that it should be simultaneously regarded as scholarly knowledge, rupturing the self-referential nature of much that is written in the academy. Failure to do so, they argue, condemns the university to insulation from and irrelevance to the most pressing social problems stunting the lives of the marginalized. Just as academic knowledge has a privileged status in the legal system, as pointed out by Mnwana as well as Claassens and Sihlali, so the kind of legal knowledge produced in fields of lawmaking should be accorded a privileged status in the academic field.

In sum, these chapters reveal the wide range of critical engagement practices and the diversity of social sites and popular struggles in which critically engaged social scientists are conducting research. These encompass very different kinds of movements and very different conditions for knowledge production, but in each case the researcher is concerned to produce both scholarly knowledge and political knowledge. Some of the research sites are more power laden, contested and violent than others, but in all of them our research participants themselves are confronted by precarious and violent conditions that can impose on them a high cost to participating in research premised on the struggle for social change. All of these case studies demonstrate a whole social science in action – including research based on varying degrees of knowledge co-production, the generation of new critical knowledge and theoretical or conceptual innovation.

In these various cases, scholarly autonomy and political engagement – that mix which defines critical engagement – are combined differently, with different emphases depending on the nature of the political field and the academic location and personal judgement of the researcher. The nature of co-production of knowledge changes accordingly. Judging by these chapters, there is a degree of difference between the SWOP researchers engaged in a practice of critical engagement (Webster, Buhlungu, Cock, Mnwana and Chinguno) and those practising participatory action research (Yingwana, Kesselman, Julián and perhaps also Cock). SWOP researchers emphasize a certain degree of autonomy and the importance of scholarly knowledge, while Yingwana and Kesselman each stress that the co-production of knowledge in the research process itself is directly empowering for participants and, perhaps, articulate a primary commitment to the activist dimension of their work (probably shared by Claassens and Sihlali), in contrast to the scholarly commitment of the SWOP researchers. It is important to reflect carefully on these different methodologies and what exactly occurs during the research process – as we try to do in this volume. In fact, taken together, these chapters seem to present a continuum, rather than a sharp distinction, between critical engagement and participatory action research with, on one end, a greater emphasis on autonomy and scholarly knowledge and, on the other, a greater emphasis on activism and political knowledge.

These choices are strongly influenced by the nature of the research problem and the research field, particularly the power dynamics within the field. In power-laden fields characterized by acute contestation between different subaltern factions, a researcher such as Mnwana may choose to retain a greater degree of professional autonomy in an effort to avoid capture by one or other interest; in other circumstances, the researcher may identify much more fully with a subaltern collective, as is the case with Yingwana and Claassens and Sihlali. In the case of Kesselman and Cock the absence of a social justice movement compels the researcher to adopt a more pedagogical approach, facilitating knowledge about an unrecognized social problem – contrary, perhaps, to the principle that the subaltern decides on the purpose and meaning of the research. Even in cases of stronger autonomy, there is usually also a strong component of political identification and loyalties to research partners, which may blind the researcher to significant fractures and weaknesses – hence the accusation by some scholars that SWOP identified too closely with COSATU and its affiliates. This is doubtless an occupational hazard of critical engagement – though one which is offset by the satisfaction of contributing to social and political change. It is important to continue documenting and reflecting on the subtleties of these diverse experiences and the way our own intentions and goals are deflected, modified or appropriated in these research encounters.

With reference to SWOP itself, it is worth noting that the decline in the opportunity for genuine critical engagement with the institutionalized labour movement predicted by Buhlungu in 2009 has indeed come to pass, as suggested in the chapters by von Holdt and Cock. But this has not meant the end of critical engagement for SWOP – on the contrary, it has found fertile new fields for the development of critical engagement in the struggles of rural villagers against oppressive chiefly rule and dispossession by mining corporations. This field is, however, very different from the labour field, and it has required significant innovation in the practices of critical engagement, as the chapters by Mnwana and Cock make clear. Claassens and Sihlali work in the same field, while Kesselman and Yingwana explore the challenges and opportunities presented by critical engagement in the very different fields of food justice and sex work. This is a whole sociology, or a whole social science, in motion, replete with theoretical insights and the possibility for a counter-hegemonic social science.

A counter-hegemonic social science?

This brings us to the third question posed at the beginning of the conclusion – to what extent does critically engaged social science contribute to a counter-hegemonic sociology capable of challenging the hegemony of Northern sociological paradigms?

What does counter-hegemonic mean in the scholarly field? It is not enough that it produces better and more sophisticated knowledge of Southern reality than the prevailing paradigms in the North, nor that it operates at the frontiers of disciplinary development, as Keim (2017) would have it. As Burawoy (2010) argues, it must go beyond a sociology *of* the South and become a sociology *for* the South – one that constitutes a critique of the North and its sociology. Northern sociology, and social science in general, tends to place the history of Europe at the centre of world history, as the paradigmatic source for the forging of modernity, regarding capitalist development as endogenous and produced by uniquely European characteristics (Bhambra, 2007; Anievas and Nisancioglu, 2015). Counter perspectives such as subaltern studies tend to concentrate on reinterpreting the history of the South in an attempt to free it from the history of the North, but frequently they fail to rethink the North's history of itself, as Anievas and Nisancioglu argue. In their exemplary attempt to rectify this, they argue that Europe was produced by the world and that, specifically through its interaction with the more advanced civilizations of the Mongol and Ottoman empires, north-western Europe was enabled to take advantage of new world markets and assimilate some of the knowledge and technologies from those empires to leapfrog into a position where it became the centre of world trade and accumulation. This is an example of a counter-hegemonic sociology and history that attempts to fundamentally displace the domination of social science by paradigms which contribute to the legitimation of Northern domination in the real world.

This is ultimately the kind of task that faces a Southern sociology that aspires to counter-hegemony. It is our argument in this book that critical engagement, as a sociology grounded in forging a new knowledge of local reality while supporting popular struggles with political knowledge, has the potential to make a strong contribution to counter-hegemonic Southern sociology. To what extent is this potential realized by the work collected in this book?

For the most part, SWOP has operated as a sociological mediator, as argued by Bezuidenhout and von Holdt (Chapter 2), introducing Northern sociological concepts into South African debates while at the same time adding to them or extending them in new directions. One reason for this may be the settlor-colonial origins of South Africa's radical white intelligentsia, which may have produced an unconscious orientation towards the radical sociology of the Northern countries of settlor origin rather than towards the South. As a consequence, there was ignorance of the critical perspectives of the small number of black social scientists who managed to carve out a space for radical rethinking.

The work produced within SWOP was often conceptually innovative, as is demonstrated in Webster's invention of the concept of critical engagement or the invention of the concept of 'social movement unionism' by a network of Southern scholars including Webster; however, insufficient intellectual energy was devoted to elaborating these innovations and projecting them into the global sociological field. Thus when the practice of critical engagement was recast as public sociology in the context of Northern paradigms, SWOP abandoned its own conception and deployed the new term. Likewise, the concept of social movement unionism was appropriated by US scholars as they attempted to define an emerging challenge to the established models of trade unionism in that country – though they were able to do this blithely unaware of its genealogy in the South and, in the process, recast it to fit their own conditions. This hegemonic sociology from the North tended to absorb and recast our innovations, rather than SWOP's innovations challenging their hegemony.

There are exceptions. Keim argues that von Holdt (2003) and Ari Sitas (2004) – who practised a very similar cultural sociology with trade unions in the city of Durban – are counter-hegemonic texts because they forge a sociological perspective with little or no reference to Northern sociology, but grounded solely in local practice. But this assessment depends on a more constrained notion of counter-hegemonic sociology than ours, as noted above. More recently, however, as documented in the chapter by Bezuidenhout and von Holdt, there has been a more explicit attempt to develop a counter-hegemonic sociological perspective which entails a critique of prevailing Northern paradigms. This may represent an incipient counter-hegemonic sociology based in the practices of critical engagement.

Turning to the cases of Chile and Turkey, these present an interesting contrast. Julián's account describes a young project that is still engaged in the struggle for its place in the neoliberal university system, in the context of a vastly weakened labour movement. Embedded in his account are rich new understandings that are beginning to generate conceptual innovations, but it is too early yet to identify counter-hegemonic aspirations; for now, rather, the project depends on Northern linkages for its survival.

In contrast, the history of radical Turkish sociology presented by Çelik demonstrates a conscious critique of the Northern theoretical universe as well as the creative fashioning of alternative Turkish and Southern perspectives that resonate with other radical sociologies in Latin America and Africa. This, much more clearly than either the Chilean or the South African cases, illustrates the elements of a counter-hegemonic sociology, though this potential is regularly cut short by political coups and academic repression. Nonetheless, Çelik is able to draw from this experience the prescription that to forge a genuine Southern sociology with counter-hegemonic potential requires a more conscious project of engagement across the Global South and, specifically, a collective project to learn from each other and forge a more robust theoretical basis. Since both SWOP and Julián and his colleagues are committed to building South–South relations, there appears to be scope for this kind of development, though recent repression of both Julián and Çelik is a reminder of how fraught the project of Southern sociology remains.

Here we may turn to Michael Burawoy's wide-ranging chapter on critical engagement. He puts aside the framework of public sociology in order to examine the practices of critical engagement discussed in this volume, using this to pose tough questions about the concept, its meaning and its scope. He pushes critical engagement beyond SWOP, South Africa and the Global South to argue that it characterizes all sociology – all social science – that acknowledges the dilemma of participating in the world we study, rather than removing ourselves. Burawoy uses this argument to raise the big questions about some of the arguments we make in this book: what is 'Southern sociology' and what distinguishes it from 'Northern sociology'? What could be meant by 'counter-hegemonic' sociology?

The answers to these questions are not of course definitively established by this volume; however, we believe it does offer significant pointers to how we may think about them and how we may pursue them more rigorously in future. Ultimately, we would like to present this volume as a contribution to the formation of a counter-hegemonic project from the Global South. It deliberately solicits analysis from two fellow countries of the Global South, from colleagues who have visited SWOP and know its work, in an attempt to explore patterns of similarity and difference. It entails a critique of Northern conceptions of public sociology and presents a rich interrogation of an alternative Southern conception of critical engagement. Claiming this is a practice restricted to the Global South would make it less than counter-hegemonic. This volume is not just an invitation to other sociologists and social scientists from the Global South to deepen their reflection on their own practices and whether these resonate with ours; it is also an invitation to critical and radical sociologists of the North to consider the relevance of our critique to their own practice and indeed to learn from our practices, as Michael Burawoy did 30 years ago. This is the way of counter-hegemony – to build North–South solidarity and mutual learning in a challenge to the dominant paradigms that are located in the North.

Notes

[1] Keim (2017) argues that the isolation of South African scholars due to the academic boycott under apartheid provided the space for the development of a robust local sociology.

[2] Human immunodeficiency virus/acquired immune deficiency syndrome.

References

Anievas, A. and Nisancioglu, K. (2015) *How the West Came to Rule: The Geopolitical Origins of Capitalism*, London: Pluto Press.

Arribas Lozano, A. (2018) 'Reframing the public sociology debate: Towards a collaborative and decolonial praxis', *Current Sociology*, 66(1): 92–109.

Bhambra, G.K. (2007) *Rethinking Modernity: Postcolonialism and the Sociological Imagination*, London: Palgrave Macmillan.

Burawoy, M. (2010) 'Southern windmill: The life and work of Edward Webster', *Transformation*, 72/73, 1–25.

Keim, W. (2017) *Universally Comprehensible, Arrogantly Local: South African Labour Studies from the Apartheid Era into the New Millennium*, Paris: Editions des archives contemporaines.

Sitas, A. (2004) *Voices that Reason: Theoretical Parables*, Leiden: Brill.

von Holdt, K. (2003) *Transition from Below: Forging Trade Unionism and Workplace Change in South Africa*, Scottsville, South Africa: Natal University Press.

von Holdt, K. (2014) 'On violent democracy', in J. Kilby and L. Ray (eds), *Violence and Society: Towards a New Sociology*, Chichester: John Wiley, pp 129–51.

von Holdt, K. (2018) 'Reading Bourdieu in South Africa: Order meets disorder', in J. Sallaz and T. Medvetz (eds) *The Oxford Handbook of Pierre Bourdieu*, New York: Oxford University Press, pp 105–28.

Index

References to figures appear in *italic* type.